AF655008

Alibre Atom3D V28

Basics Tutorial

Tutorial Books

Send us an email to online.books999@gmail.com to get resource files

Contents

Scope of this book viii

Chapter 1: Getting Started with Alibre Atom3D 1

Starting Alibre Atom3D 3

User Interface 4

Ribbon 4

The Model ribbon tab 4

The View ribbon tab 5

The Inspect ribbon tab 5

Sketch ribbon tab 5

Assemble ribbon tab 5

Drawing Environment ribbon tabs 5

File Menu 6

Quick Access Toolbar 6

Design Explorer 6

Status bar 7

View Cube 7

Understanding the Origin 3D Indicator in Autodesk Inventor 7

Shortcut Menus 8

Dialogs 8

Chapter 2: Part Modeling Basics 10

TUTORIAL 1 10

Starting a New Part File 10

Starting a Sketch 10

Adding Constraints 13

Creating the Base Feature 14

Adding a Extruded Feature 16

Filleting the Corners 17

Shelling the model 18

Saving the Part 19

TUTORIAL 2 20

Starting a New File 20

Creating the Extruded Feature 20

Creating the Sweep Feature 22

Chapter 3: Assembly Basics **26**
TUTORIAL 1 26
Starting a New Assembly File 26
Inserting the Base Component 26
Adding the second component 27
Creating Constraints 27
Chapter 4: Sketching **32**
Creating Polygons 32
Constraints 32
Coincident Constraint 32
Horizontal Constraint 32
Vertical Constraint 33
Tangent Constraint 33
Parallel Constraint 33
Perpendicular Constraint 33
Midline Constraint 33
Concentric Constraint 33
Equal Constraint 34
Collinear Constraint 34
Make Symmetric 34
Fix Constraint 34
Coradial Constraint 35
Intersection Constraint 35
Automatic Constraints 35
Tutorial 1 37
Ellipses 39
Extend 41
Trim 42
Offset 42
Intersect 43
Circular Sketch Pattern 43
Linear Sketch Pattern 45
Text 46
Chapter 5: Additional Modeling Tools **48**

TUTORIAL 1 48
Creating the First Feature 48
Creating the Cut feature 49
Adding the Extruded Boss feature 52
Creating a Counterbore Hole 53
Creating a Threaded Hole 54
Creating a Circular Pattern 56
Creating Chamfers 56
TUTORIAL 2 56
Creating the First Section and Rails 56
Creating the second section 60
Creating the Loft feature 61
Creating the Extruded feature 61
Creating Fillets 62
Shelling the Model 62
Adding Threads 62
TUTORIAL 3 66
Creating the First feature 66
Creating the Extruded Cut Feature 67
TUTORIAL 4 70
Constructing a cylindrical shell 70
Adding a Slot 70
Constructing the Linear and Circular patterns 71
TUTORIAL 5 73
Constructing the Groove feature 74
TUTORIAL 6 75
Creating the Base Feature 75
Creating the Extruded Cut Features 76
Creating the Extruded Cut Feature on the left side 81
Creating the Angled Cut 82
Creating the Extruded Cut feature on the left 83
Creating the Extruded feature on the right 84
Adding the Extruded Boss Features 87

TUTORIAL 7......90
Creating the first feature......90
Creating the Flanges......92
TUTORIAL 8......97
Chapter 6: Creating Drawings......101
TUTORIAL 1......101
Modifying the Layer Properties......103
Creating the section view......104
Creating Centerlines and Centered Patterns......105
Applying Dimensions......108
Chapter 7: Top-Down Assembly and Joints......113
TUTORIAL 1......113
Creating a New Assembly File......113
Creating a part in the Assembly......113
Creating the Second Component of the Assembly......116
Creating the third Component of the Assembly......117
Adding Bolt Connections to the assembly......119
Inserting Duplicate components into an assembly......121
Applying the constraint to the components......121
Exploding the Assembly Parts......123

INTRODUCTION

Alibre Atom3D is a comprehensive and powerful 3D CAD software package that delivers exceptional value. It offers a suite of easy-to-use tools for designing and documenting 3D models, making it an ideal choice for everyone from hobbyists and makers to small business owners.

This book provides a step-by-step approach for users to learn Alibre Atom3D, and it is aimed specifically at those with no previous experience. You will be guided through the entire process, from starting your first session to creating complex parts, assemblies, and production-ready drawings. To ensure a practical learning experience, each chapter explains key concepts using real-world models.

Scope of this book

This book is written for students and engineers who are interested to learn Alibre Atom3D for designing mechanical components and assemblies, and then create drawings.

This book provides a step-by-step approach to learning Alibre Atom3D. The topics include Getting Started with Alibre Atom3D, Basic Part Modeling, Creating Assemblies, Additional Modeling Tools, Creating Drawings, and Top-down assembly design.

Chapter 1 introduces Alibre Atom3D. The user interface and terminology are discussed in this chapter.

Chapter 2 takes you through the creation of your first Alibre Atom3D model. You create simple parts.

Chapter 3 teaches you to create assemblies. It explains the Top-down and Bottom-up approaches for designing an assembly. You create an assembly using the Bottom-up approach.

Chapter 4: In this chapter, you learn the sketching tools.

Chapter 5: In this chapter, you learn additional modeling tools to create complex models.

Chapter 6 teaches you to create drawings of the models created in the earlier chapters.

Chapter 7 teaches you to create a top-down assembly

Chapter 1: Getting Started with Alibre Atom3D

This tutorial book brings in the most commonly used features of Alibre Atom3D.

In this chapter, you will:

- Understand the Alibre Atom3D terminology
- Start a new file
- Understand the User Interface

In Alibre Atom3D, you create 3D parts and use them to create 2D drawings and 3D assemblies.

Alibre Atom3D is Feature Based. Features are shapes that are combined to build a part. You can modify these shapes individually.

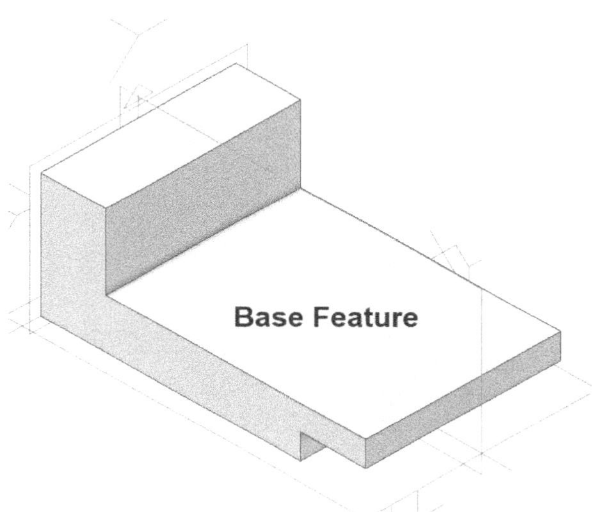

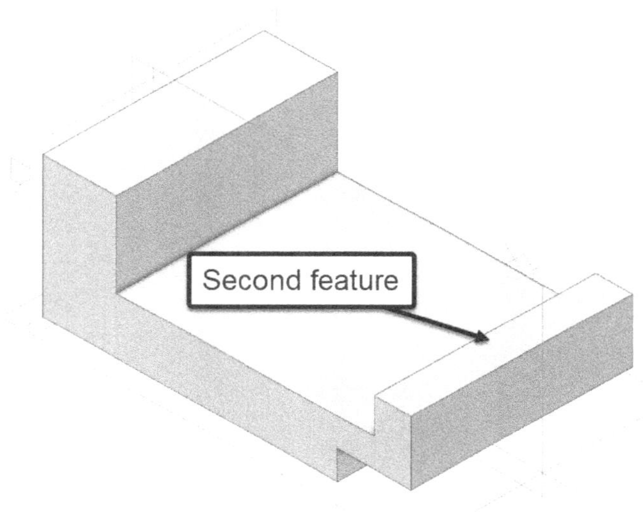

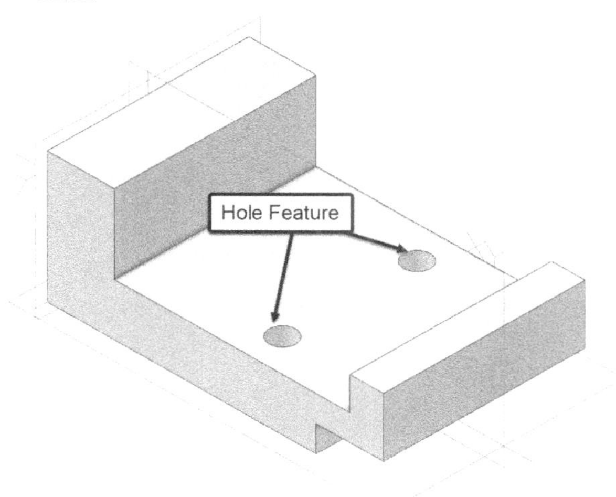

Most of the features are sketch-based. A sketch is a 2D profile and can be extruded, revolved, or swept along a path to create features.

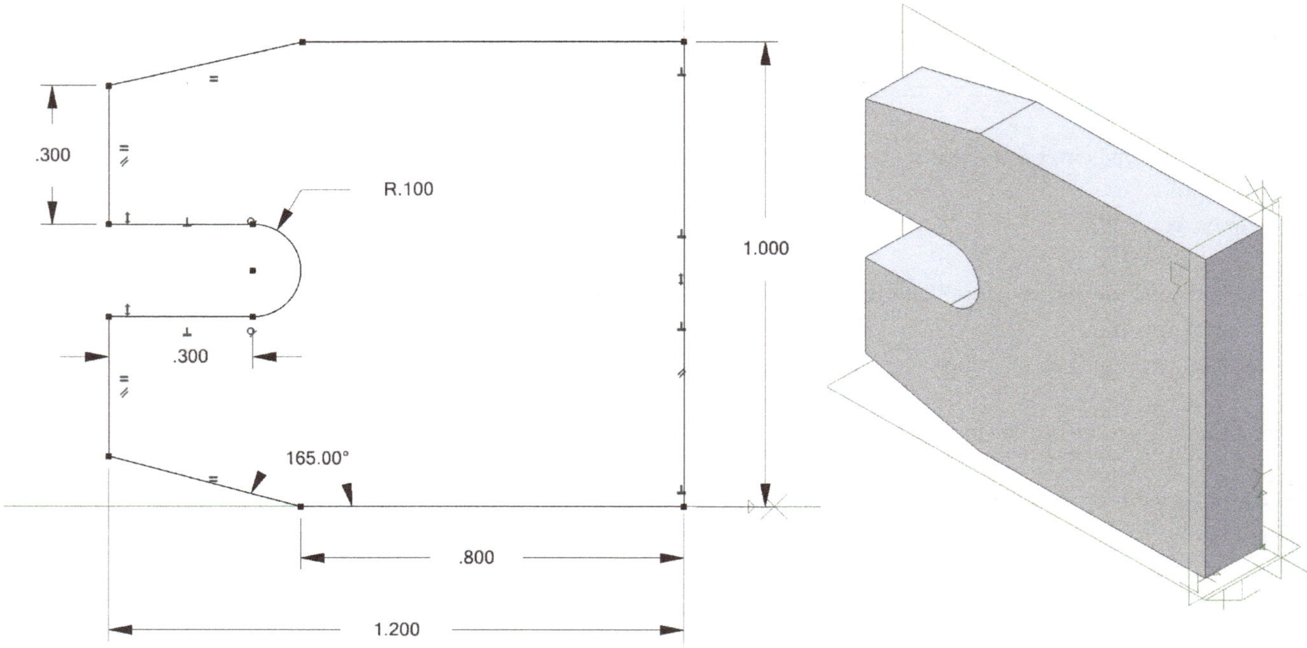

Alibre Atom3D is parametric. You can specify standard parameters between the elements. Changing these parameters changes the size and shape of the part. For example, see the design of the body of a flange before and after modifying the parameters of its features.

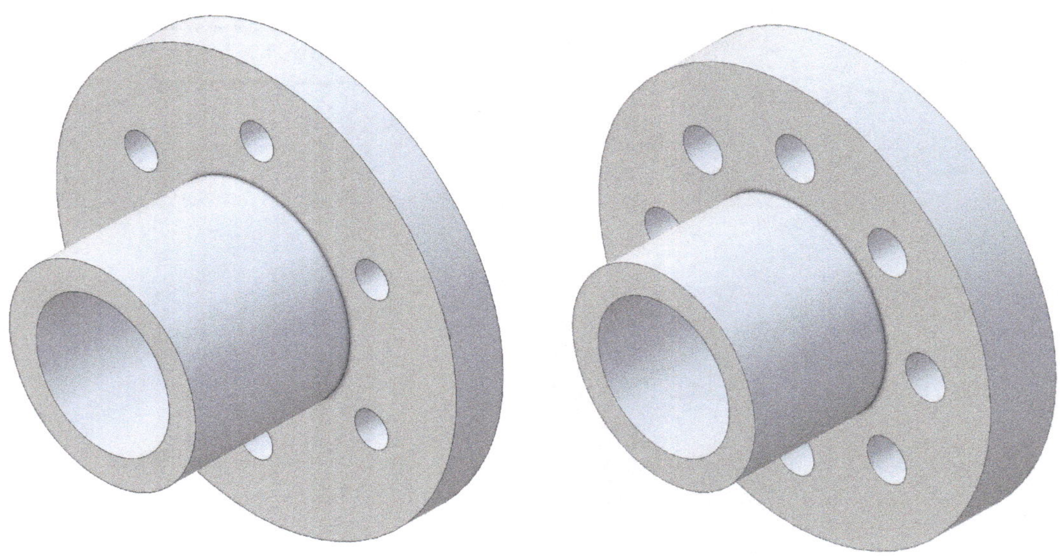

Starting Alibre Atom3D

- Click the Windows icon on the taskbar.
- Click **All apps > A** > **Alibre Atom3D 28.1.1.28227**.
- On the **Home** window, click **Home > Create New > Part** to start a new part file.

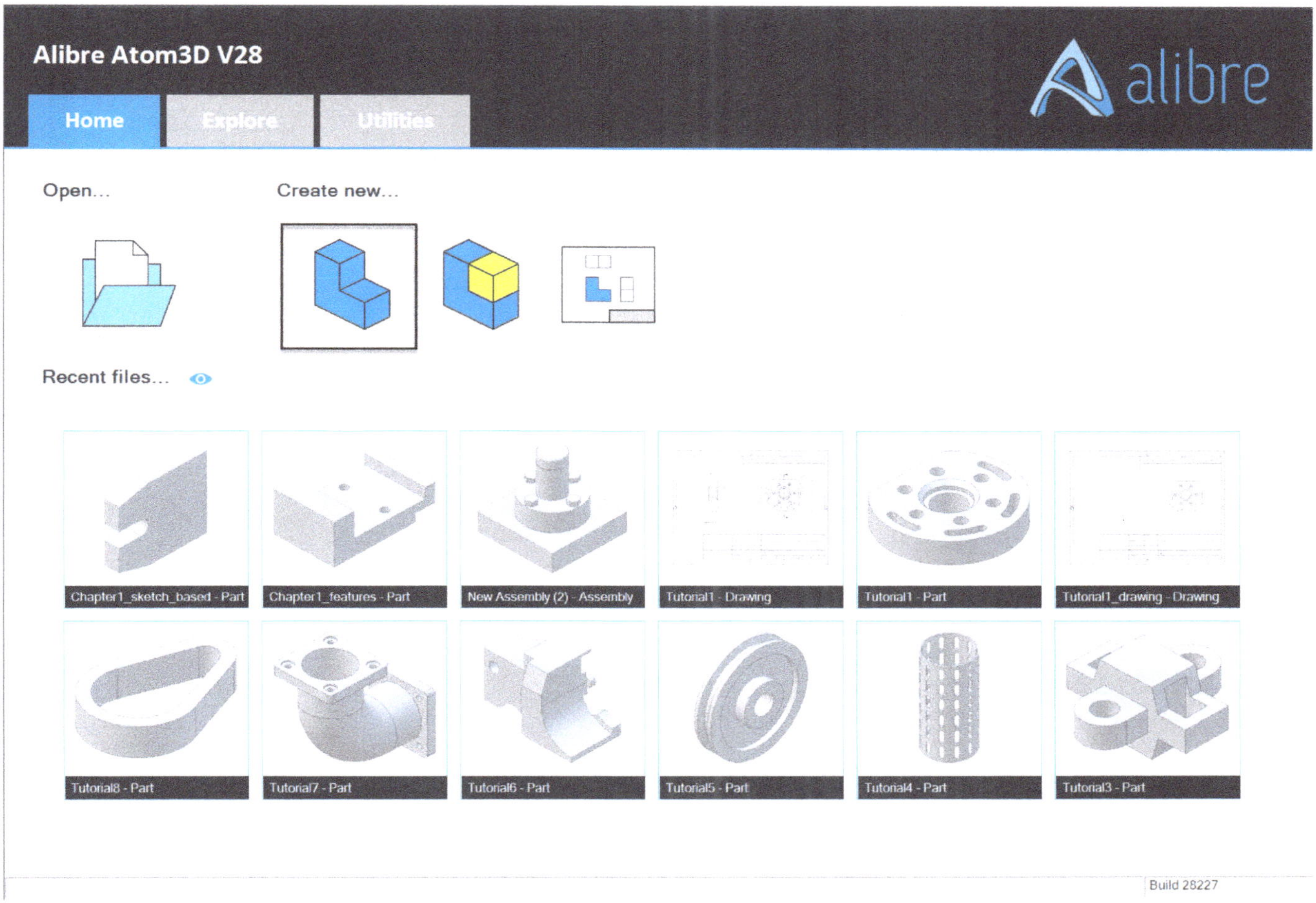

Notice these essential features of the Alibre Atom3D window.

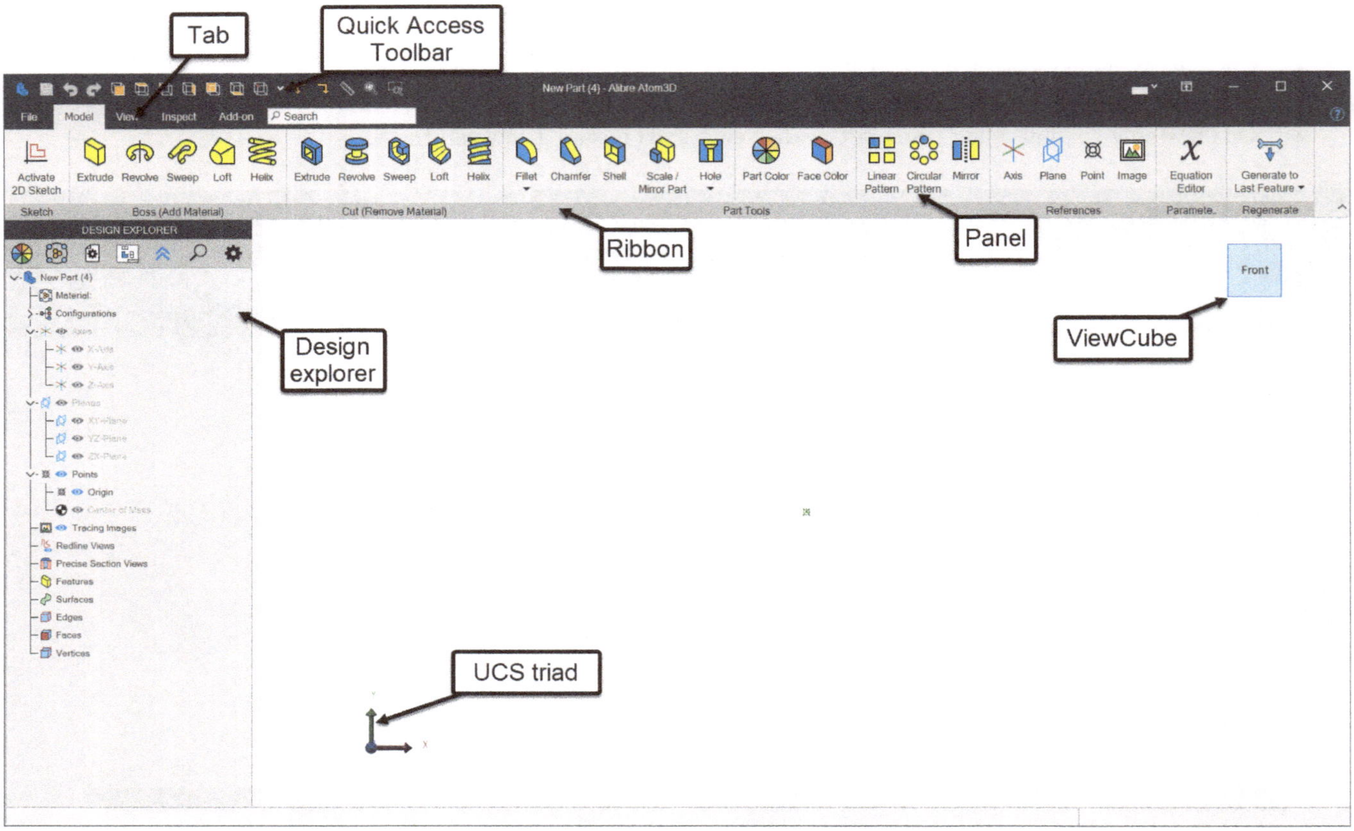

User Interface

Various components of the user interface are discussed next.

Ribbon

The ribbon at the top of the window contains multiple tabs. Clicking a tab reveals a set of tools organized in panels. The highlighted tab displays relevant commands, with frequently used ones represented by larger icons on the left and less common ones by smaller icons on the right. Some commands are accessible through drop-down lists or panel names.

The ribbon located at the top of the window has tabs. Click a tab to see tools grouped in panels. The active tab shows important commands with large icons on the left and less common commands with smaller icons on the right. Some commands can be accessed through drop-down lists or by clicking panel names.

You can also right-click on the ribbon and select **Minimize the Ribbon** to minimize the ribbon.

The following sections explain the various tabs of the ribbon available in Alibre Atom3D.

The Model ribbon tab

This ribbon tab contains the tools to create 3D features, planes, and surfaces.

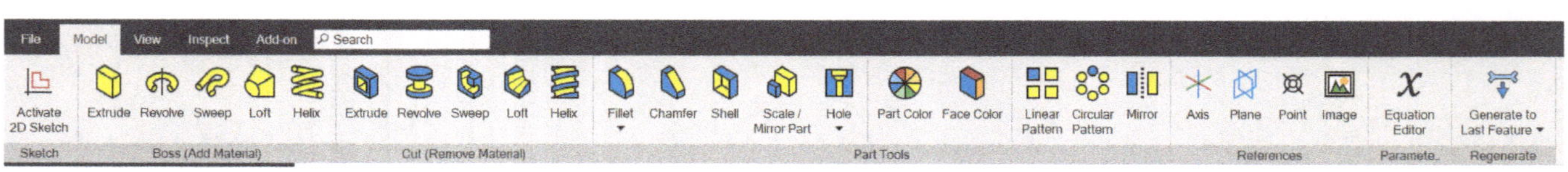

The View ribbon tab

This ribbon tab contains the tools to modify the display of the model and user interface.

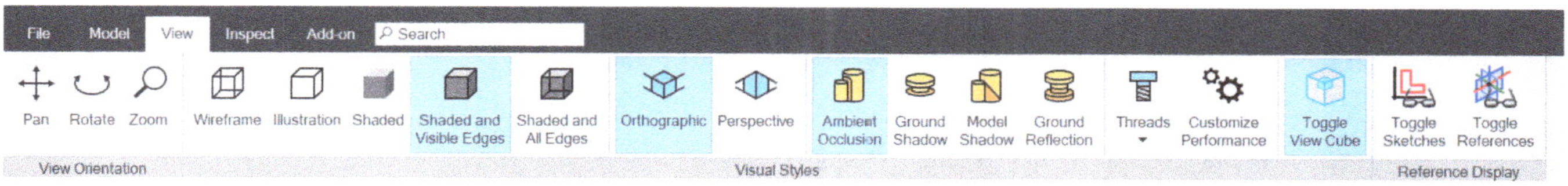

The Inspect ribbon tab

This ribbon tab has tools to measure the objects. It also has analysis tools to analyze the draft, curvature, and surface.

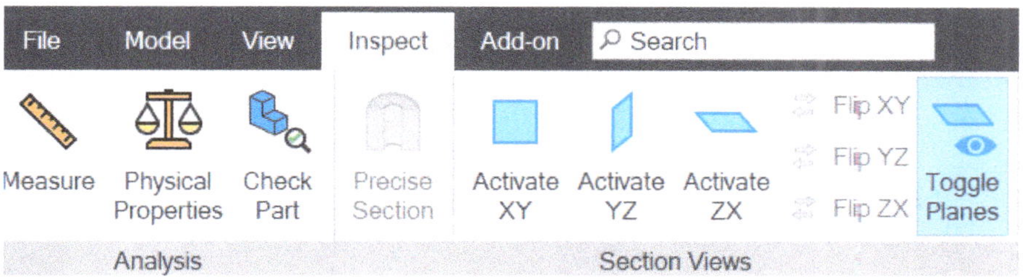

Sketch ribbon tab

This ribbon tab contains all the sketch tools.

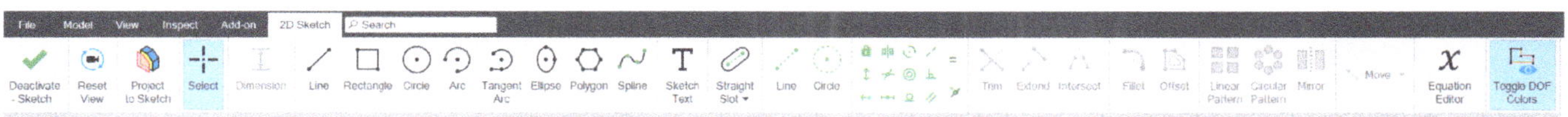

Assemble ribbon tab

This ribbon tab contains the tools to create an assembly. It is available in an assembly file.

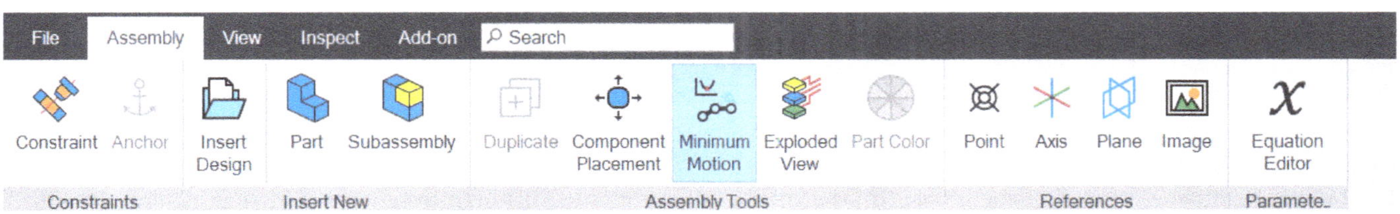

Drawing Environment ribbon tabs

In the Drawing Environment, you can create print-ready drawings of a 3D model. The Drawing Management ribbon tab in this environment contain tools to create 2D drawings.

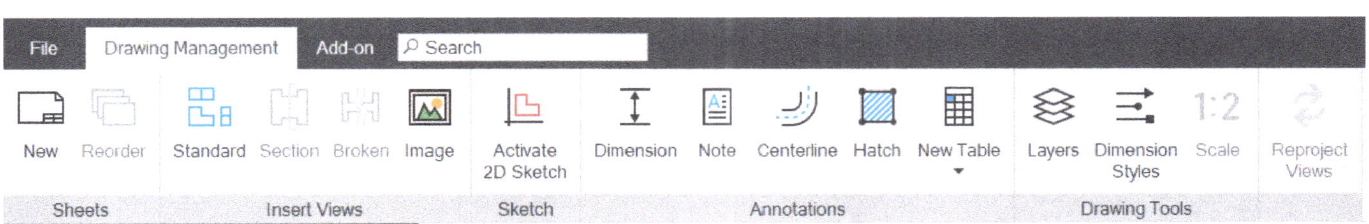

File Menu

The File Menu appears when you click on the File tab located at the top left corner. This menu contains the options to create, open, save, export, package, and print a file, as well as access properties and system options.

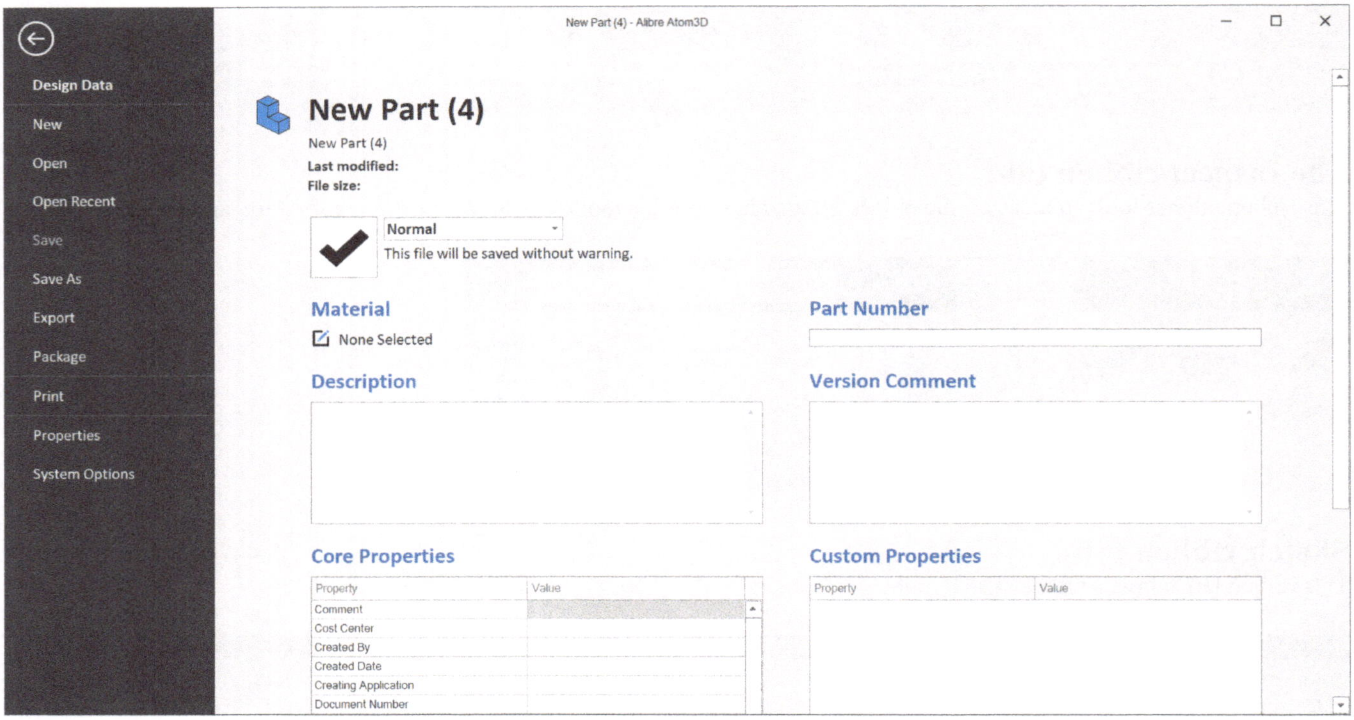

Quick Access Toolbar

The Quick Access Toolbar is available at the top left of the window. It contains tools such as Save, Undo, Redo, view orientations, rotate, measure, and zoom options.

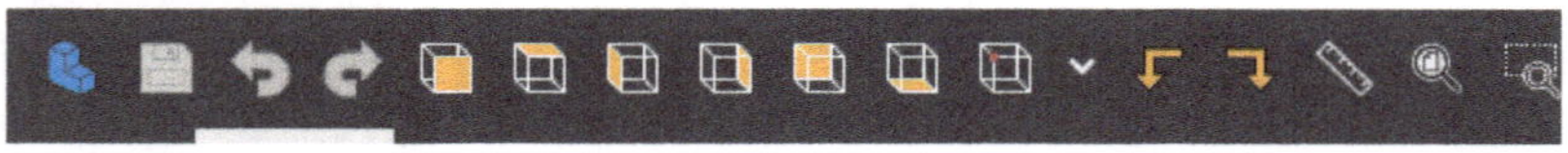

Design Explorer

The Design Explorer is located on the left side of the window. It contains the list of operations carried in an Alibre Atom3D file.

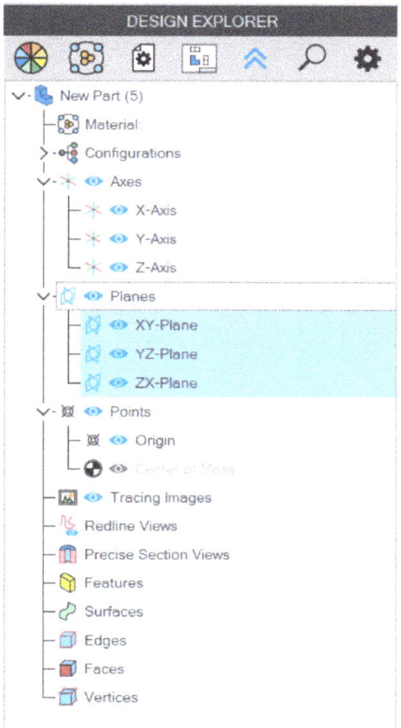

Status bar

The Status bar is available below the Design Explorer. It displays the prompts and the actions taken while using the tools.

View Cube

The **ViewCube** is a navigation tool permanently located in the top-right corner of the graphics window. Its primary function is to control the view orientation of the displayed model.

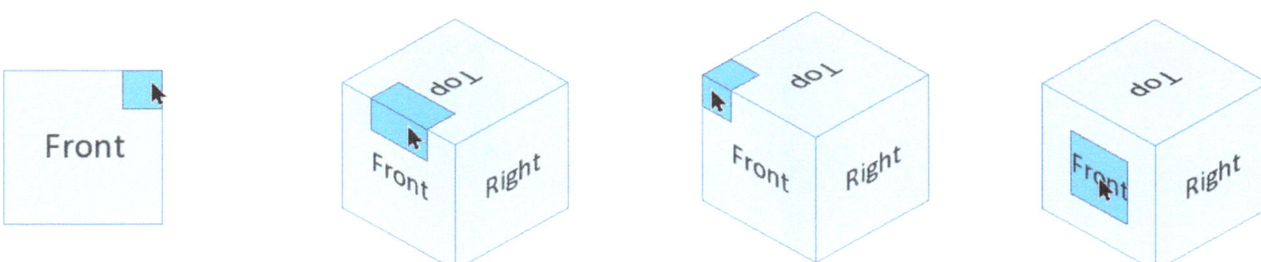

Understanding the Origin 3D Indicator in Autodesk Inventor

In the graphics window, you'll find an XYZ axis indicator in the lower left corner. This indicator represents the world coordinate system and helps you understand the orientation of your model. This helps you to know the orientation of the model.

Axis Colors:

- Red arrow: X-axis

- Green arrow: Y-axis
- Blue arrow: Z-axis

Shortcut Menus

When you click the right mouse button, a shortcut menu appears. A shortcut menu contains a list of some relevant options. It allows you to access the tools quickly.

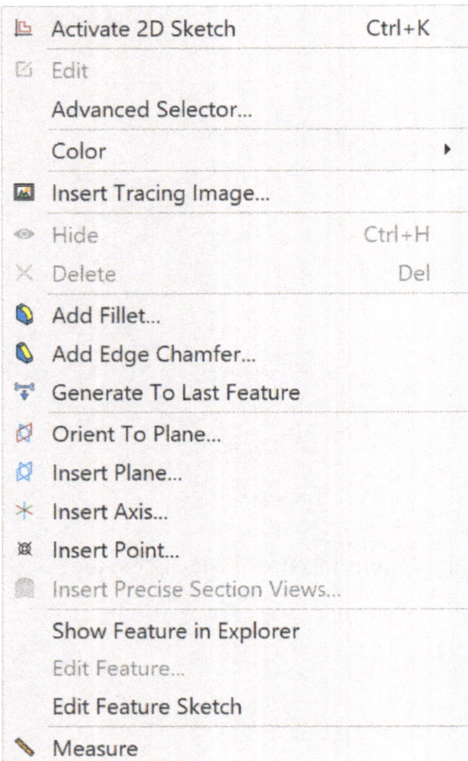

Dialogs

When you activate any tool in Alibre Atom3D, the dialog related to it appears. It consists of various options, which help you to complete the operation. The following figure shows the components of the dialog.

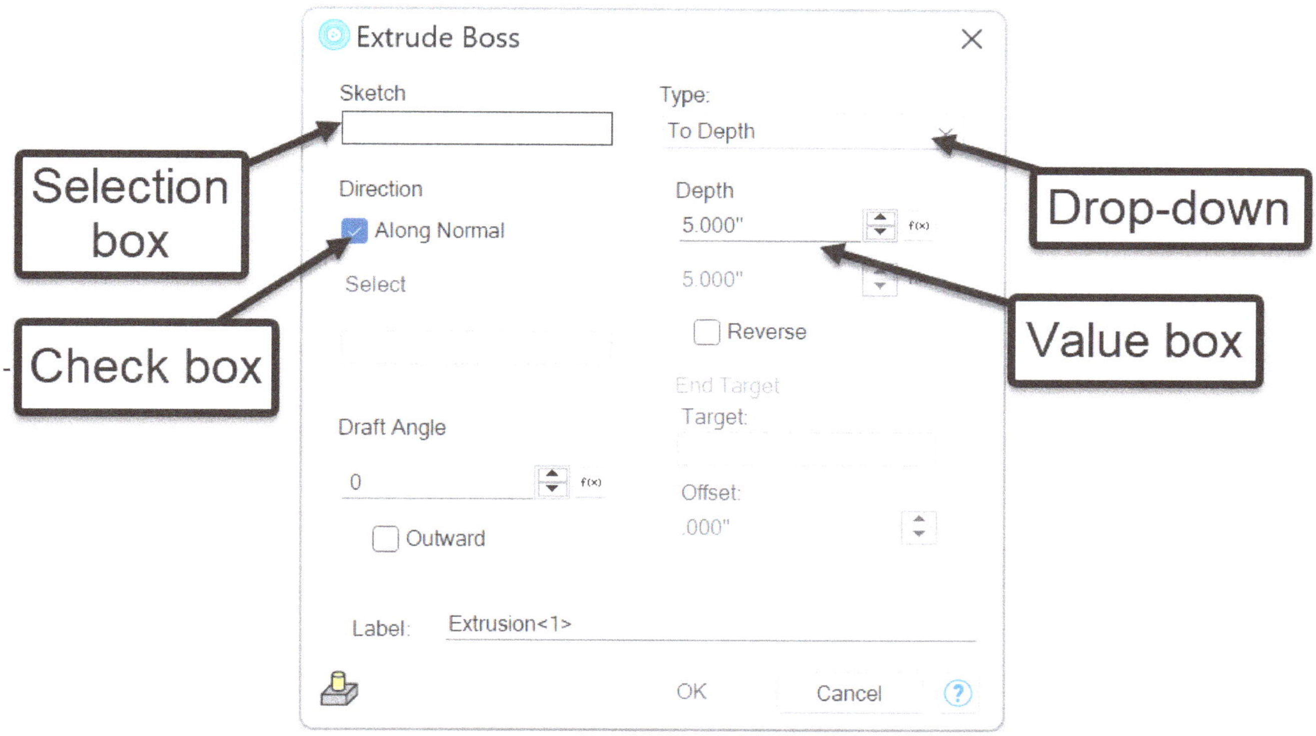
Extrude Boss
Sketch
Type:
To Depth
Direction
Along Normal
Select
Depth
5.000"
5.000"
Reverse
End Target
Target:
Draft Angle
0
Outward
Offset:
.000"
Label:
Extrusion<1>
OK
Cancel
Selection box
Check box
Drop-down
Value box

Chapter 2: Part Modeling Basics

This chapter takes you through the creation of your first Alibre Atom3D model. You create simple parts:

In this chapter, you will:

- Create Sketches
- Create a base feature
- Add another feature to it
- Add fillets
- Shell the model
- Create Cut features

TUTORIAL 1

This tutorial takes you through the creation of your first Alibre Atom3D model.

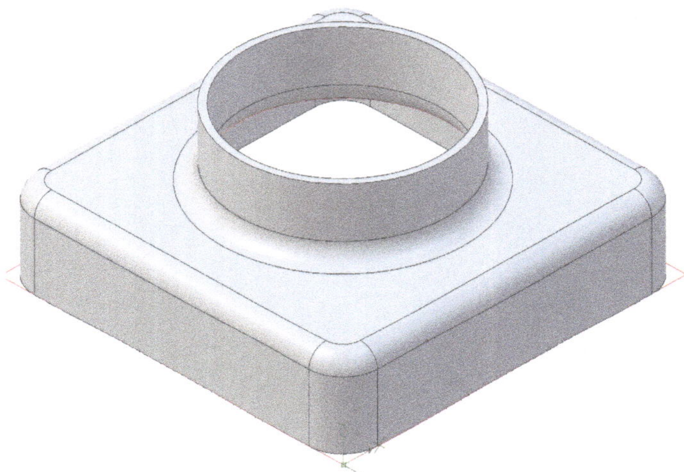

Starting a New Part File

1. Click the **Alibre Atom3D V28** icon on the Deskrop.
2. Click the **New Part** icon on the **Home** window.

A new model window appears.

Starting a Sketch

1. To start a new sketch, click **Model** tab > **Sketch > Activate 2D Sketch** on the ribbon. This step is done to initiate the sketching process.

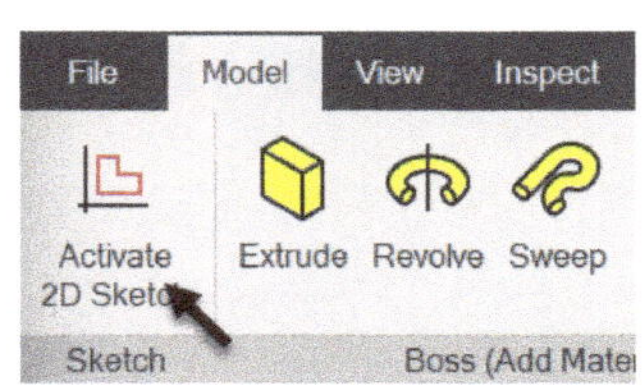

2. Select the **ZX-Plane** from the Design Explorer. The sketch starts. This step is necessary to define the plane on which you will be sketching your design.

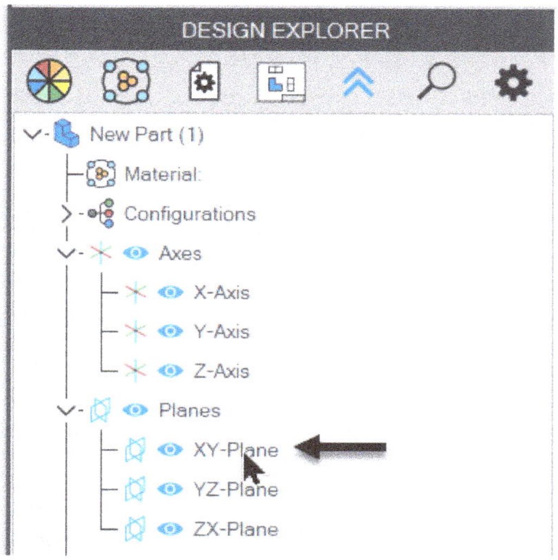

After completing these steps, you will notice the following:

- The sketch origin appears at the center. This indicates the reference point for your sketch and helps in positioning and aligning your design elements
- The **2D Sketch** ribbon tab is displayed. It provides you with various options and tools for creating and editing your sketch.

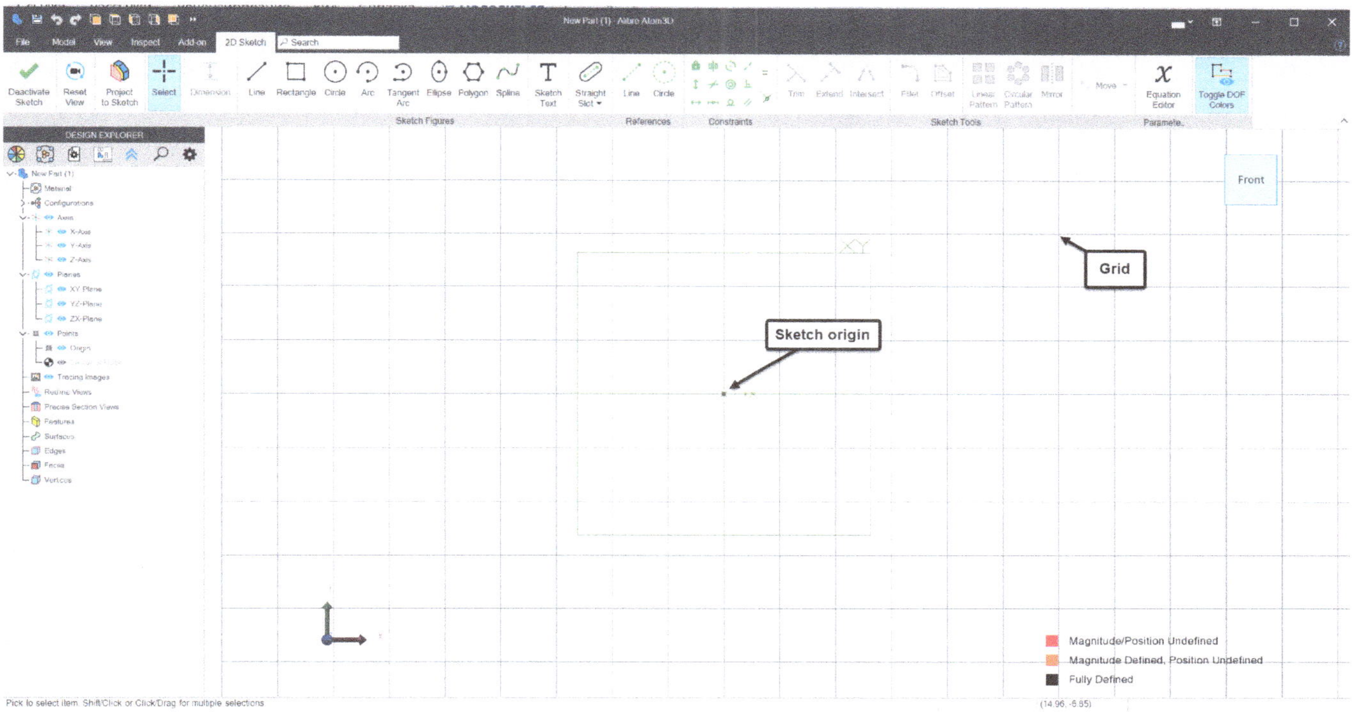

Before you begin sketching, it is recommended to ensure that your Alibre Atom3D settings match the settings used in this tutorial. Follow the next steps to adjust the settings.

3. Click **File > Properties**. This will open the **File Properties** dialog box, where you can customize various properties of the file.
4. On the **File Properties** dialog box, click the **Units > General** option at the left side.
5. Select **Unit > Millimeters**. This setting ensures that Alibre Atom3D uses millimeters.
6. Type **2** in the **Precision** box. This setting determines the number of decimal places displayed for measurements and dimensions.
7. Check the **Set current settings as the default setting for parts, sheet metal, and assemblies** option.
8. Click **Apply** and **Save** to save the changes and close the **File Properties** dialog box.

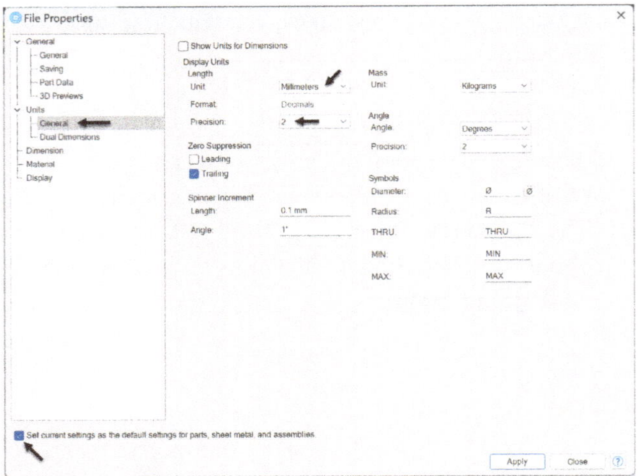

9. Click **File > System Options**; the **System Options** dialog appears.
10. Click **Parts/Assemblies > Sketching** from the left side the dialog.
11. Make sure that the **Display grid** option is checked in the **Grid** section. It enables the grid display in your sketch, which can help you align and position your sketch elements.

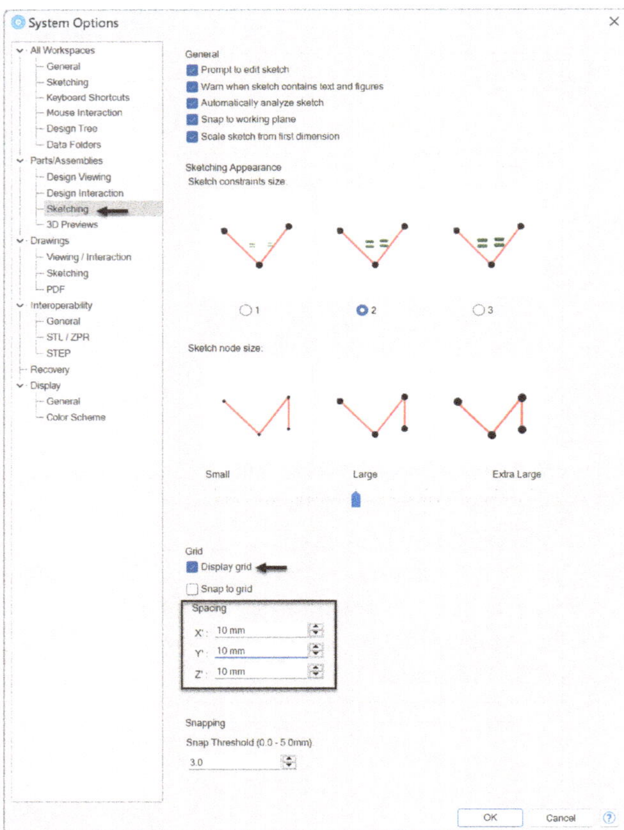

12. Type **10** in the **X**, **Y**, and **Z** boxes; it indicates the distance between two consecutive grid lines. It serves as the default value when the **Grid auto spacing** option is selected.
13. Click **OK**.

In this tutorial, the first feature is an extruded feature from a sketched rectangular profile. You begin by sketching the rectangle.

14. Click **2D Sketch > Sketch Figures > Rectangle** on the ribbon.

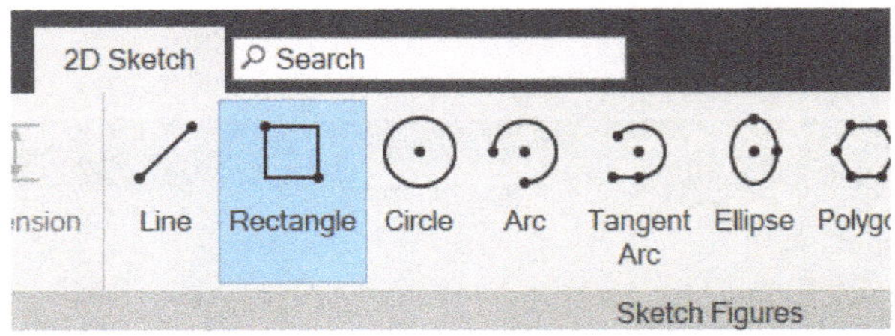

15. Move the cursor to the sketch origin located at the center of the graphics window, and then click on it.
16. Drag the cursor towards the top right corner, and then click to create a rectangle. This step creates a rectangle by dragging the cursor from the origin towards the top right corner and clicking to set the size of the rectangle.

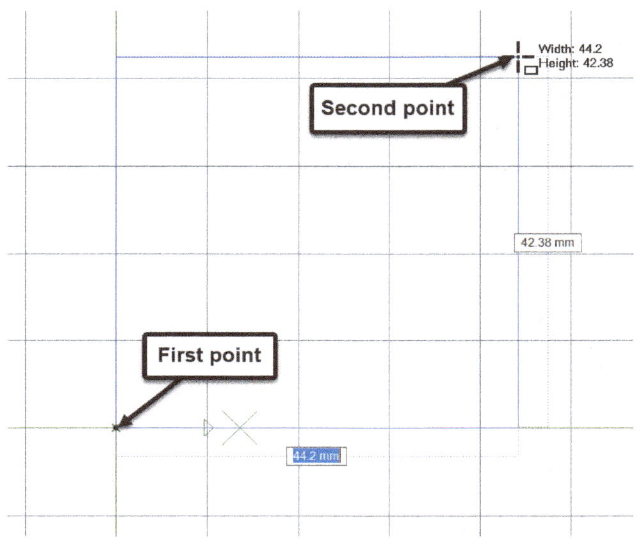

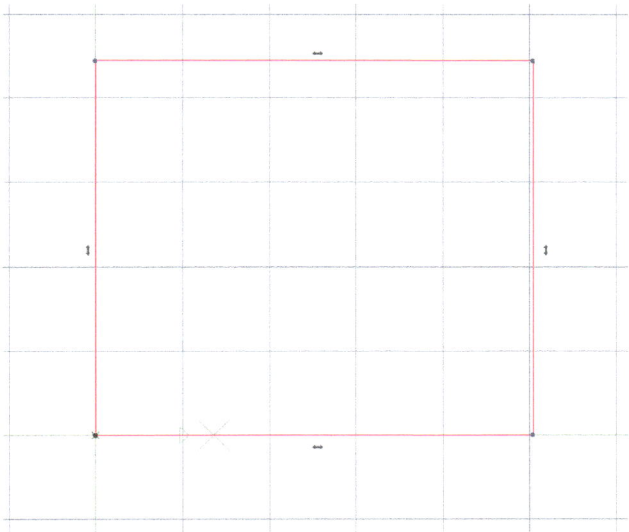

Adding Constraints

In this section, you specify the size of the sketched rectangle by adding constraints. As you add constraints, the sketch can attain any one of the following states:

Fully Defined Sketch:

- When you're working on a fully defined sketch, it means that every element within the sketch is precisely defined by constraints. These constraints can include dimensions, angles, distances, and relationships between sketch entities.
- In a fully defined sketch, you've applied enough rules and measurements to ensure that the sketch has no degrees of freedom left. This implies that the sketch is immovable and won't change its shape or size no matter what adjustments you make elsewhere in the design.
- Visually, all entities in a fully defined sketch are typically highlighted in black or some other distinct color, indicating that they are locked in place and will not change unless you modify the constraints themselves.

Achieving a fully defined sketch is a crucial goal in parametric modeling because it guarantees that your design is precise and won't result in unexpected changes during modifications.

Under Constrained Sketch:

An under-constrained sketch means there are still degrees of freedom—some sketch elements can be moved or adjusted because not all necessary constraints are applied.

Under-constrained sketch elements may appear in red (Magnitude/Position Undefined) or orange (Magnitude Defined, Position Undefined), indicating which specific constraints are missing.

Red: Neither the magnitude nor the position of the entity is specified, allowing free movement and resizing.

Orange: The magnitude (such as length) is defined, but the position is not, permitting the entity to move within the sketch.

These colors provide a quick visual cue that more constraints are needed for full definition.

While being under-constrained can allow flexibility for adjustments and experimentation, it can also lead to instability and unwanted changes if left unresolved.

1. Click **2D Sketch > Sketch Figures > Dimension** on the ribbon.

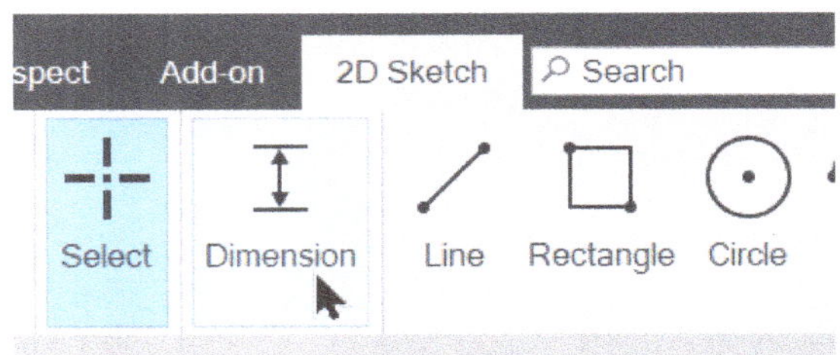

2. Select the right vertical line of the rectangle. Next, move the pointer toward right and click.
3. Enter **100** in the **Edit Dimension** dialog and click **OK**. This step sets the length of the selected line.

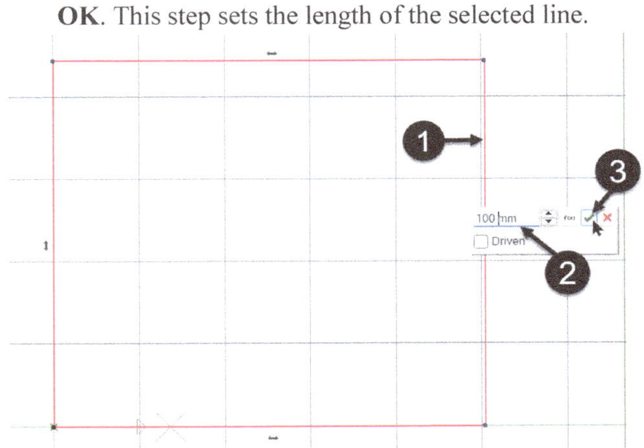

4. Select the bottom horizontal line of the rectangle.

5. Enter **100** in the **Edit Dimension** dialog and click **OK**.

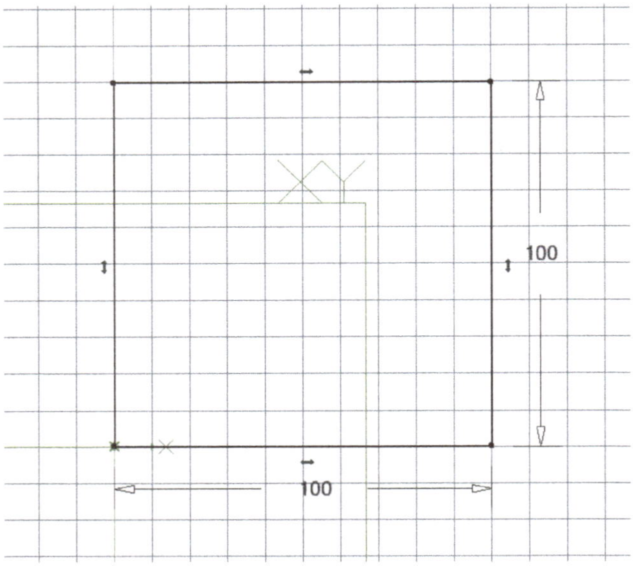

6. Press **Esc** to deactivate the **Dimension** tool.
7. Click **Deactivae Sketch** on the **2D Sketch** tab of the ribbon.

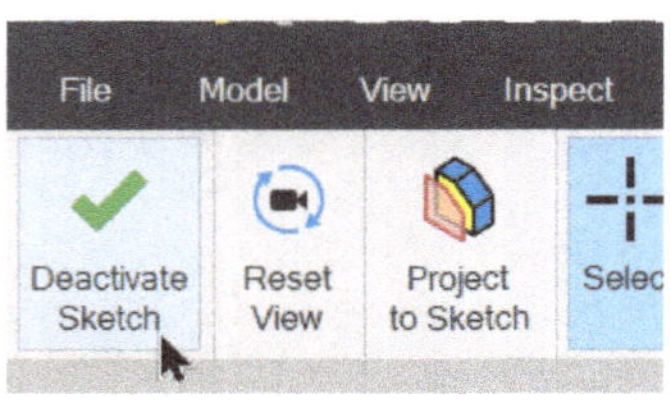

Creating the Base Feature

The first feature in any part is called a base feature. You now create this feature by extruding the sketched rectangle.

1. Click **Model > Boss(Add Material) > Extrude** on the ribbon.

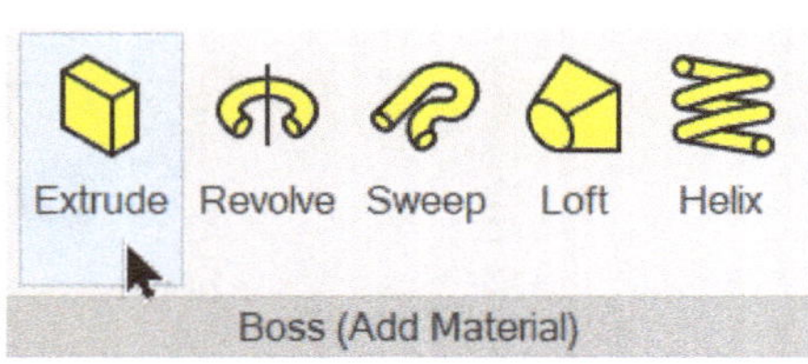

2. On the **Extrude Boss** dialog, select **Type > Depth**.
3. Type-in **25** in the **Depth** box available on the **Extrude Boss** dialog.

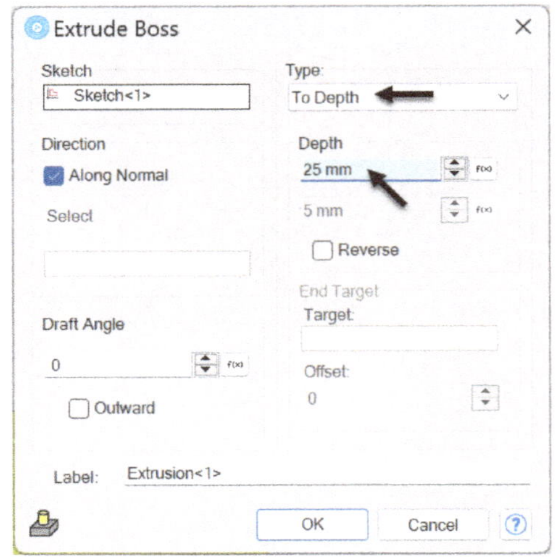

4. Click **OK** to create the extruded boss feature.

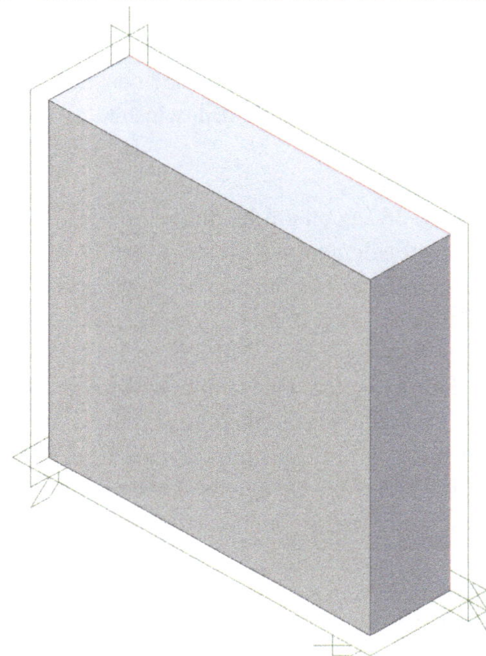

Notice the new feature, **Extrusion**, in the **Design Tree**.

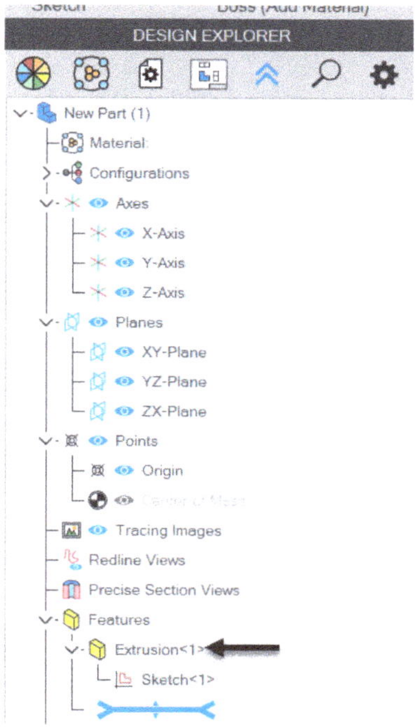

To magnify a model in the graphics area, you can use the **Zoom** tool available on the **View Orientation** panel of the **View** ribbon tab.

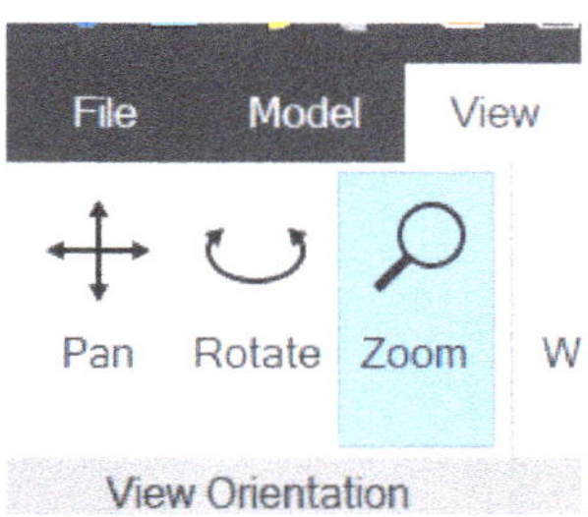

To display the part in different Visual styles, select the options in the **Visual Styles** panel on the **View** ribbon tab.

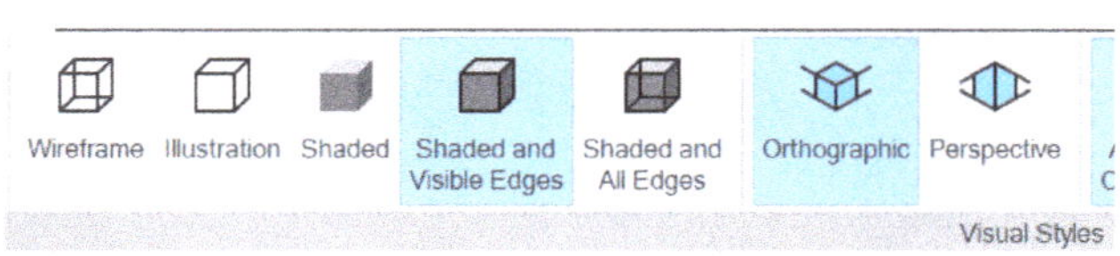

Shaded and Visible Edges

Shaded and All Edges

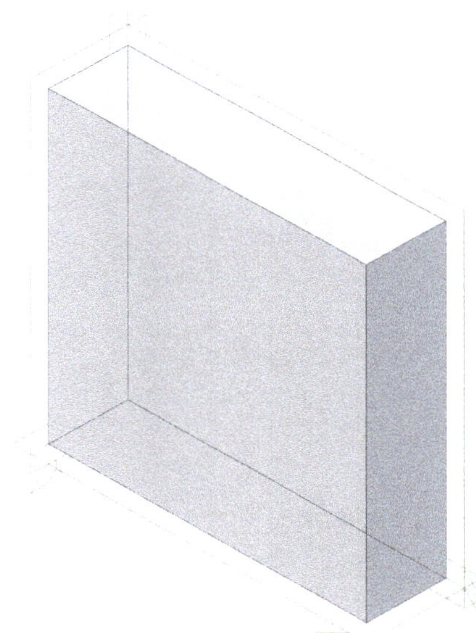

Shaded

Wireframe

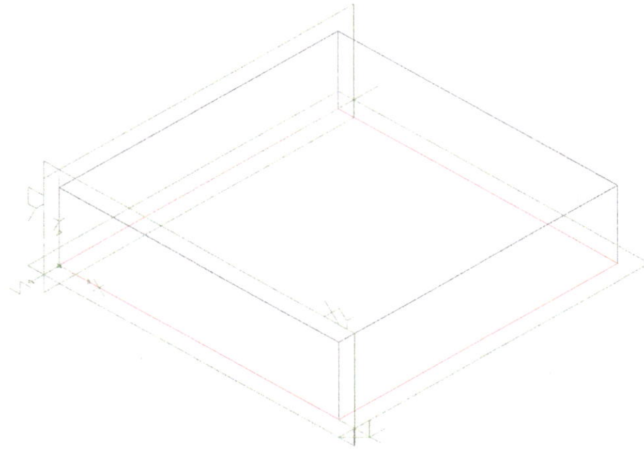

Illustration

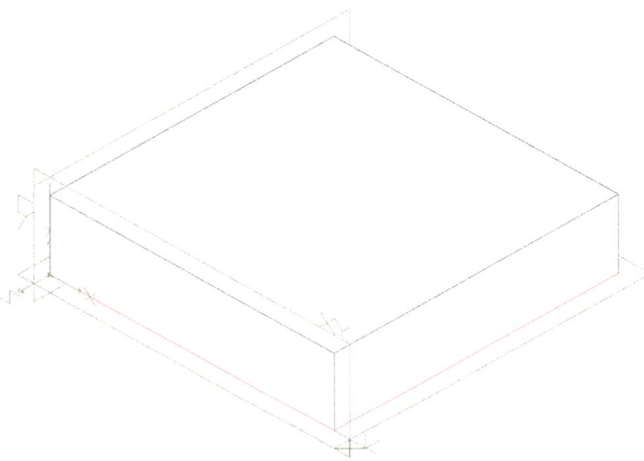

The default visual style for parts and assemblies is **Shaded and Visible Edges**. You may change the draw style whenever you want.

Adding a Extruded Feature

To create additional features on the part, you need to draw sketches on the model faces or planes, and then extrude them.

1. Click the Top face of the ViewCube; the top face of the model is oriented parallel to the screen.
2. Click **Model > Sketch > Activate 2D Sketch**.
3. Click on the top face of the first feature.

4. On the ribbon, click **2D Sketch** > **Sketch Figures** > **Circle.**

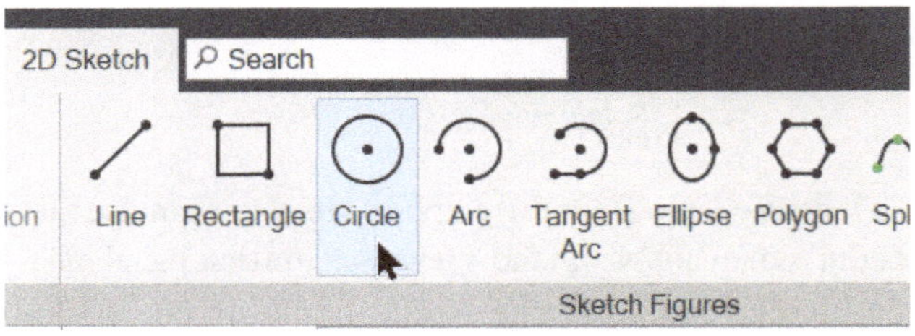

5. Click to specify the center point of the circle.
6. Move the pointer outward and click to create the circle.

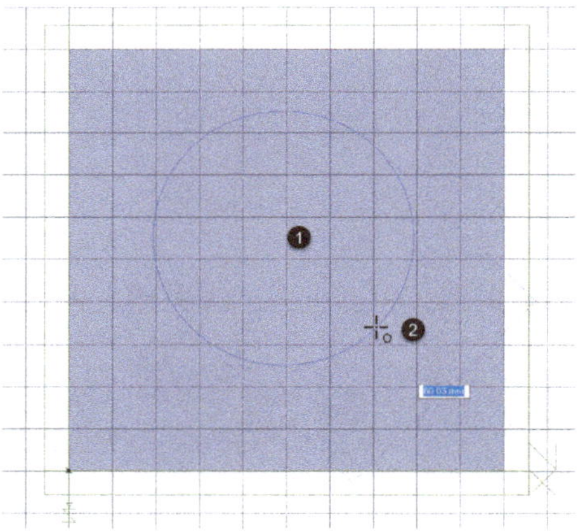

7. On the ribbon, click **2D Sketch** > **Sketch Figures** > **Dimension** .
8. Select the center point of the circle.
9. Select the origin of the sketch.
10. Move the pointer toward right and click.
11. Enter **50** in the **Edit Dimension** dialog and click **OK.**

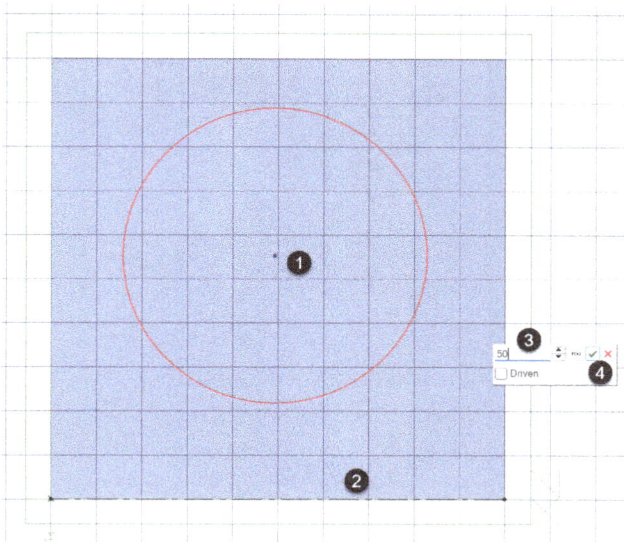

12. Select the center point of the circle and the origin of the sketch.
13. Move the pointer toward up and click.
14. Enter **50** in the **Edit Dimension** dialog and click **OK**.

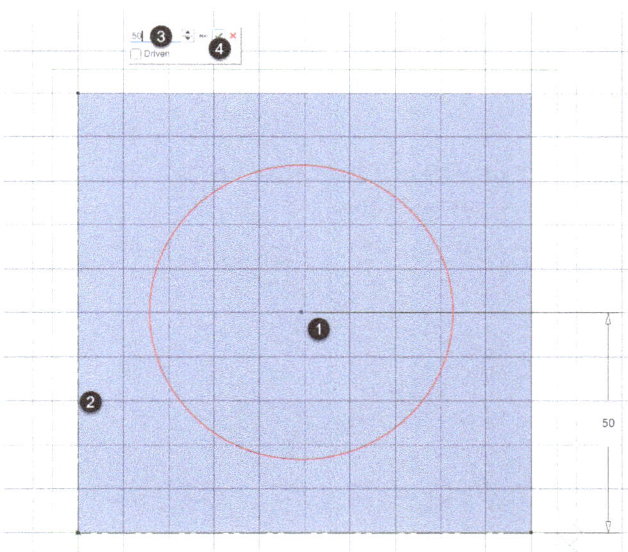

15. Enter **60** in the **Edit Dimension** dialog and click **OK**.

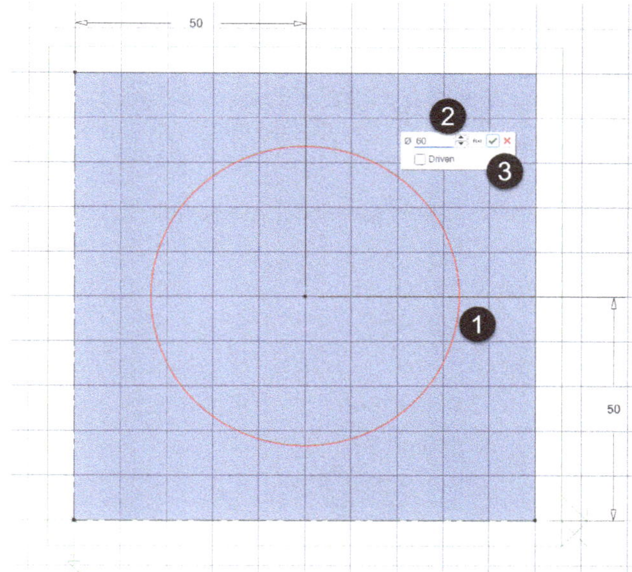

16. Click **Deactivae Sketch** on the **2D Sketch** tab of the ribbon.
17. Click **Model > Boss(Add Material) > Extrude** on the ribbon.
18. On the **Extrude Boss** dialog, select **Type > Depth**.
19. Type-in **20** in the **Depth** box available on the **Extrude Boss** dialog.
20. Click **OK**.

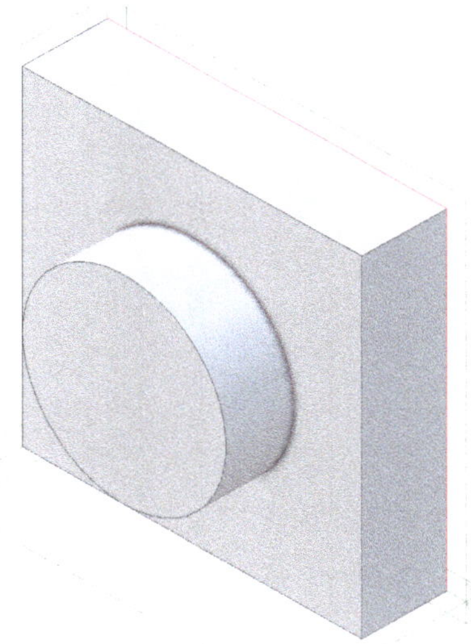

Filleting the Corners

The **Fillet** tool allows you to fillet the corners of the model.

1. Click **Model > Part Tools > Fillet** on the ribbon.

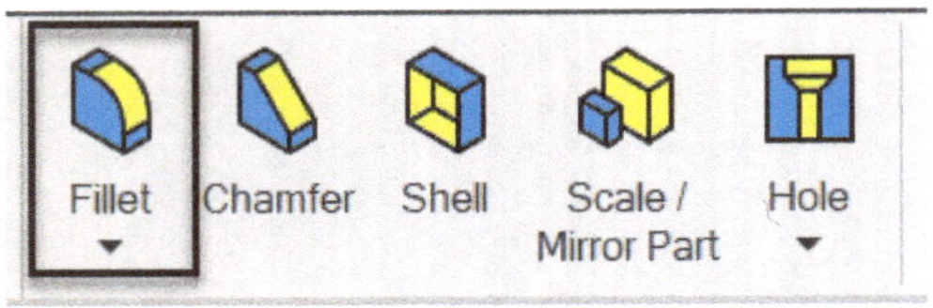

2. Select the edges of the model, as shown.

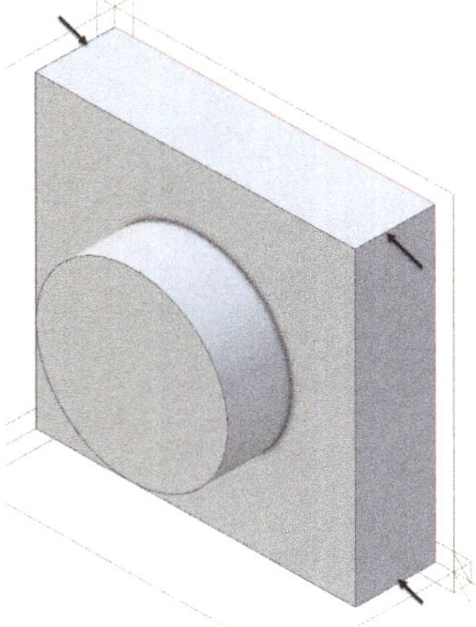

3. Click the lower-left corner of the ViewCube.

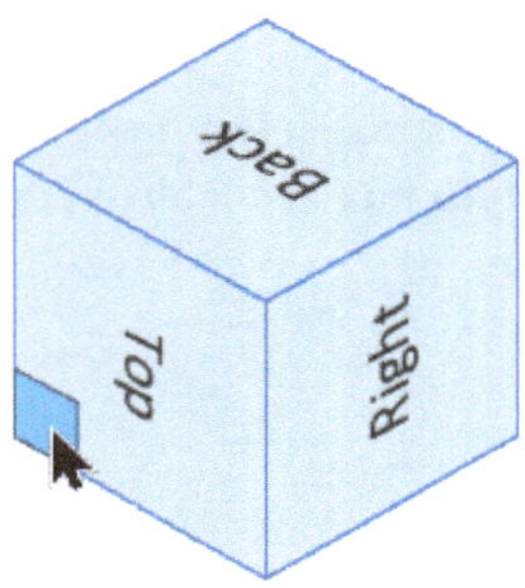

4. Select the remaining vertical edge of the model.

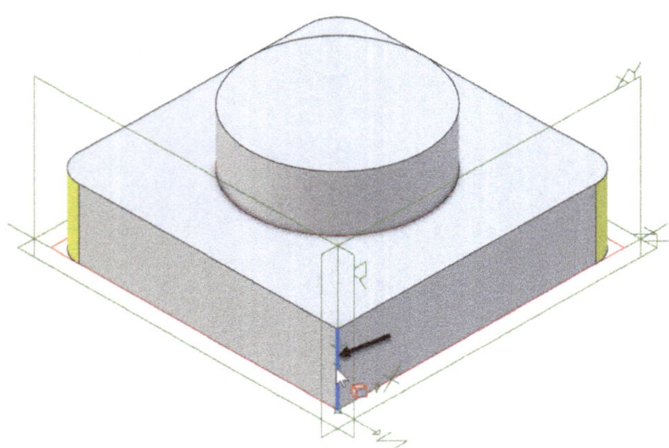

5. Type **10** in the **Radius/Chord Length** box.
6. Click **Apply**.

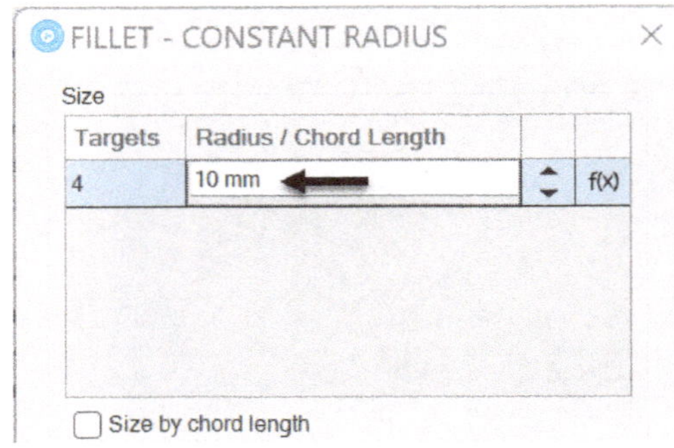

7. Type **5** in the **Radius/Chord Length** box.
8. Click on the horizontal face of the model, as shown.

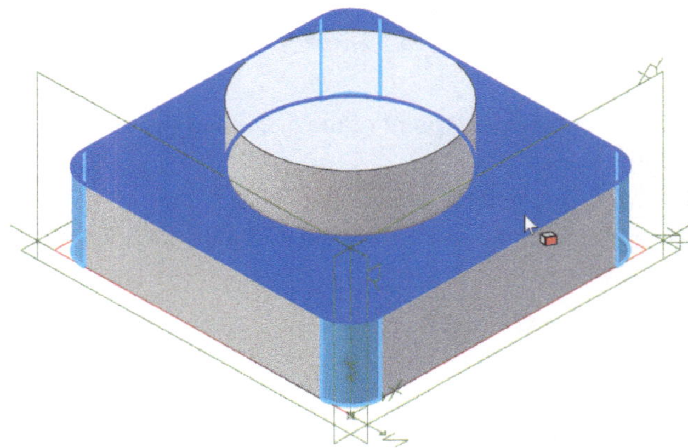

9. Check the **Tangent Propagate** option.
10. Click **Apply** and **Close**.

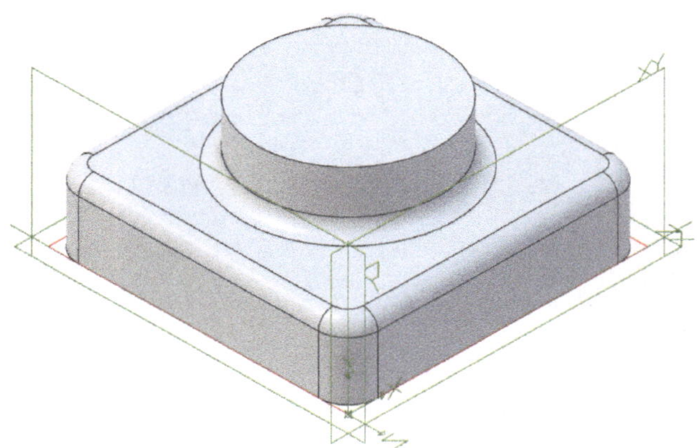

Shelling the model

The **Shell** tool allows you to shell the model.

1. Click **Model > Part Tools > Shell** on the ribbon.

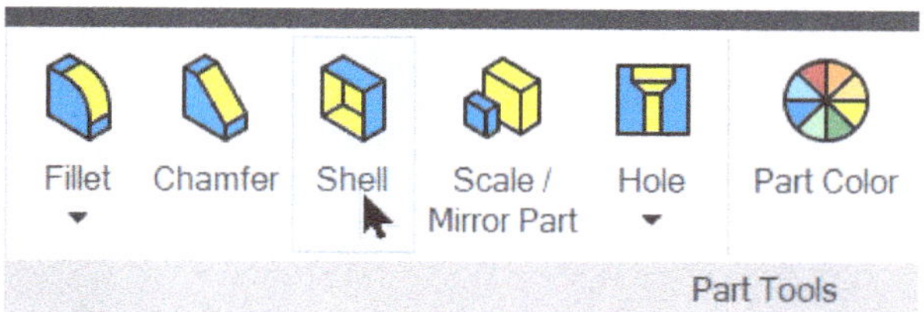

2. Click on the lower right corner of the ViewCube.

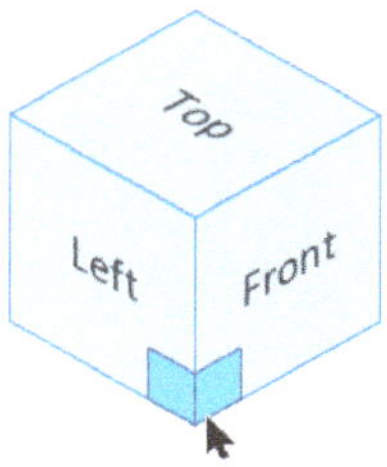

3. Click on the bottom face.

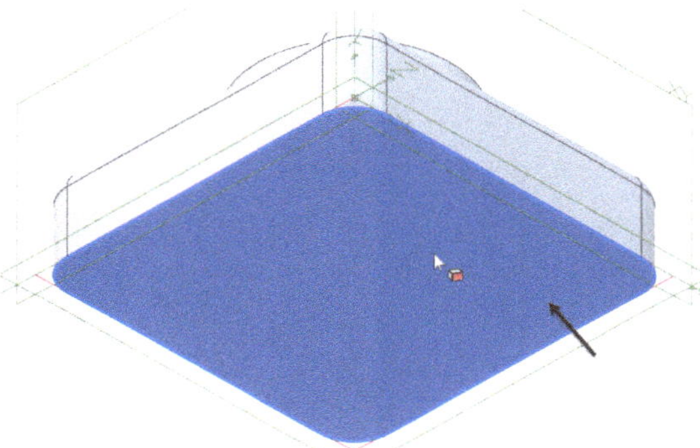

4. Type **2** in the **Standard Thickness** box.
5. Click on the top-right corner of the ViewCube.
6. Click in the **Faces to remove** selection box.
7. Select the top face of the second feature.

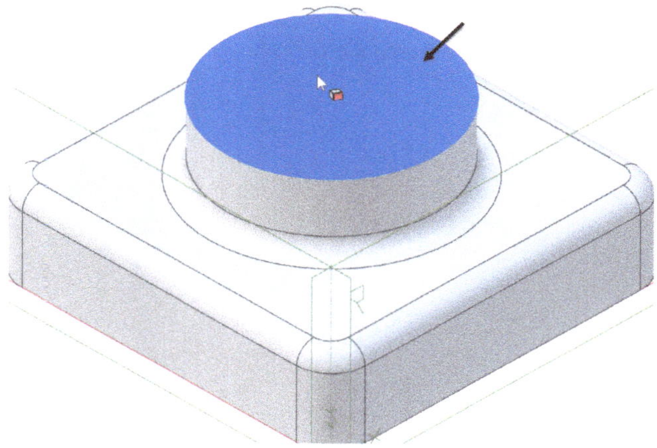

8. Click **OK**.

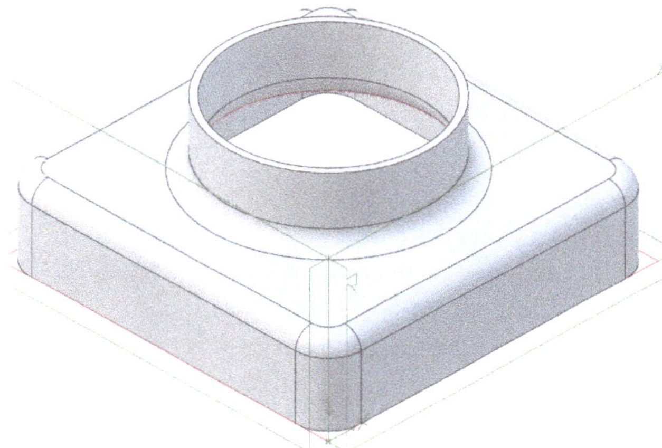

Saving the Part

1. Click **File > Save**.
2. On the **Save As** dialog, type-in **Tutorial1** in the **File name** box.
3. Click **Save** to save the file.
4. Click **Close** on the top right corner of the window.

Note:
*.AD_PRT is the file extension for the part files that you create in Alibre Atom3D.

TUTORIAL 2

In this tutorial, you create the part shown below.

Starting a New File

1. Click the **New Part** icon on the **Home** window.

Creating the Extruded Feature

1. To start a new sketch, click **Model** tab > **Sketch > Activate 2D Sketch** on the ribbon.
2. Select the **ZX-Plane** from the Design Explorer.
3. Click **File > System Options**; the **System Options** dialog appears.
4. Click **Parts/Assemblies > Sketching** from the left side the dialog.
5. Make sure that the **Display grid** option is checked in the **Grid** section.
6. Click **OK**.
7. Click **Rectangle** on the **Sketch Figures** panel of the **2D Sketch** ribbon tab.
8. Create a rectangle, shown in the figure.

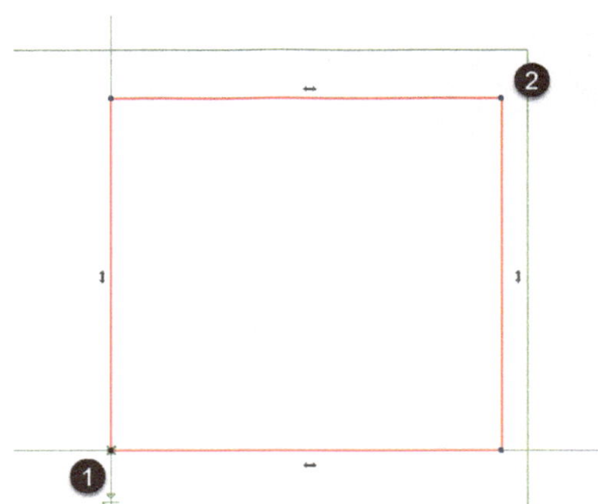

9. On the ribbon, click **2D Sketch** > **Sketch Figures** > **Dimension** 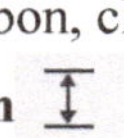 .
10. Add vertical and horizontal dimensions to the rectangle, as shown.

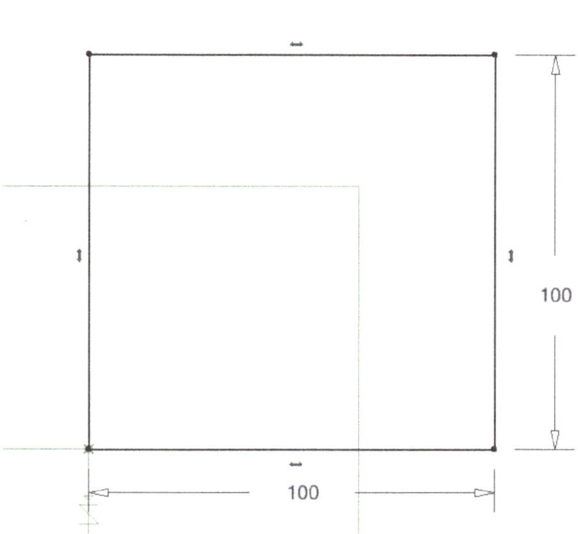

11. Click the **Deactivate Sketch** icon on the **2D Sketch** ribbon tab.
12. Click **Model > Boss(Add Material) > Extrude** on the ribbon.
13. Type **80** in the **Depth** box and click **OK**.

14. Click **Model > Part Tools > Fillet** on the ribbon.
15. Select the edges of the model, as shown.

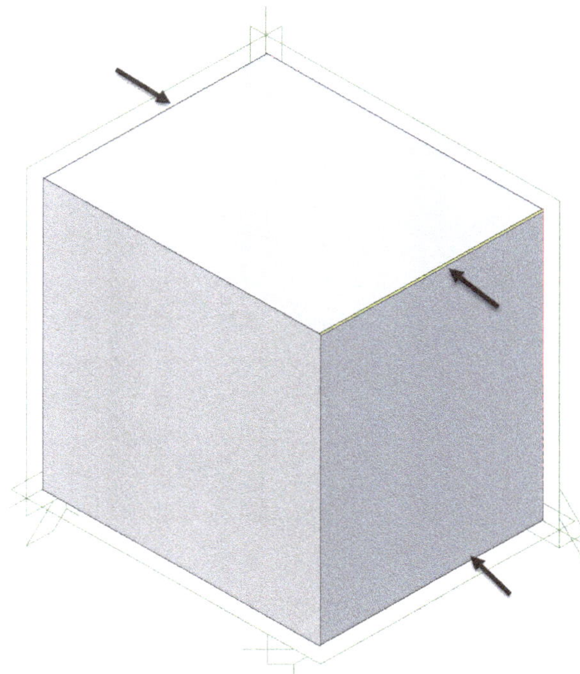

16. Click the lower-left corner of the ViewCube.

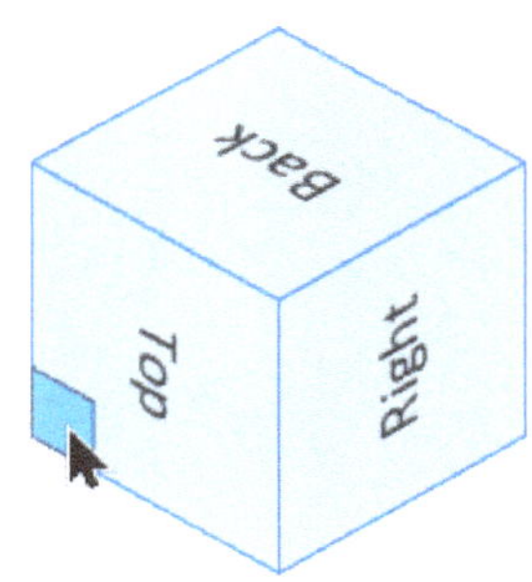

17. Select the remaining vertical edge of the model.

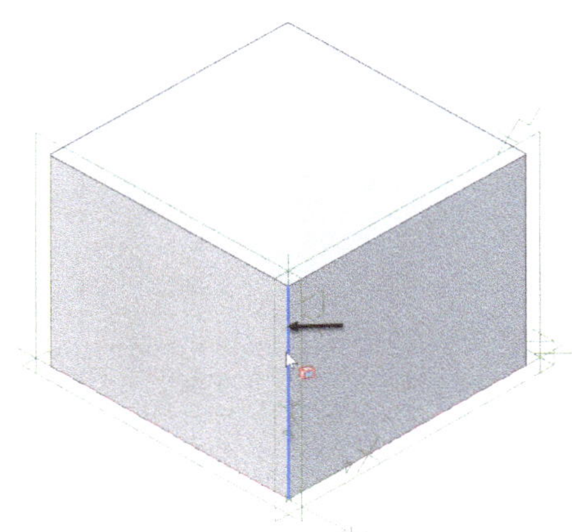

18. Type **10** in the **Radius/Chord Length** box.
19. Click **Apply** and **Close**.

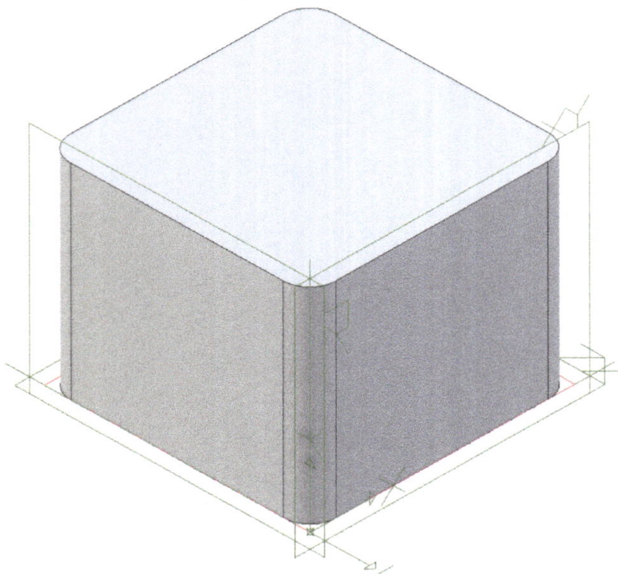

20. Click **Model > Part Tools > Shell** on the ribbon.
21. Click on the top face of the model.
22. Type **4** in the **Standard Thickness** box.
23. Click **OK**.

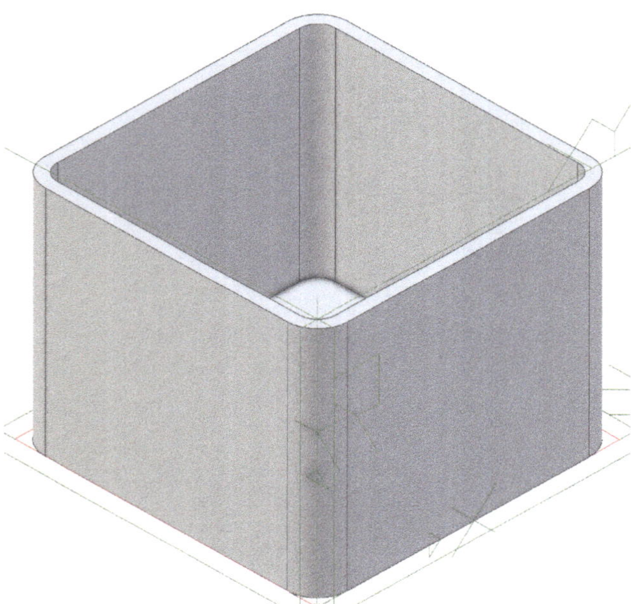

Creating the Sweep Feature

1. On the ribbon, click **Model > References > Plane**.

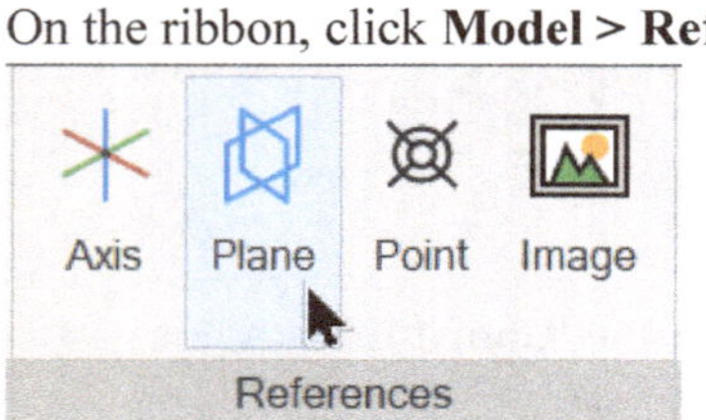

2. On the **Insert Plane** dialog, click **Creation Method > Offset Plane/Face**.
3. Select the **YZ-Plane** from the Design Explorer.

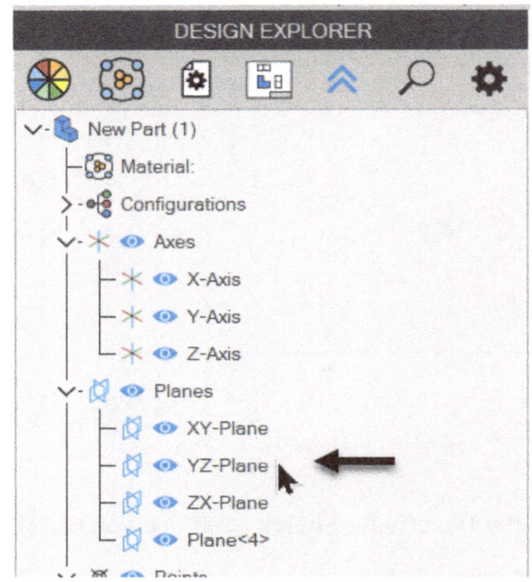

4. Type **50** in the **Distance** box and click **Apply**.

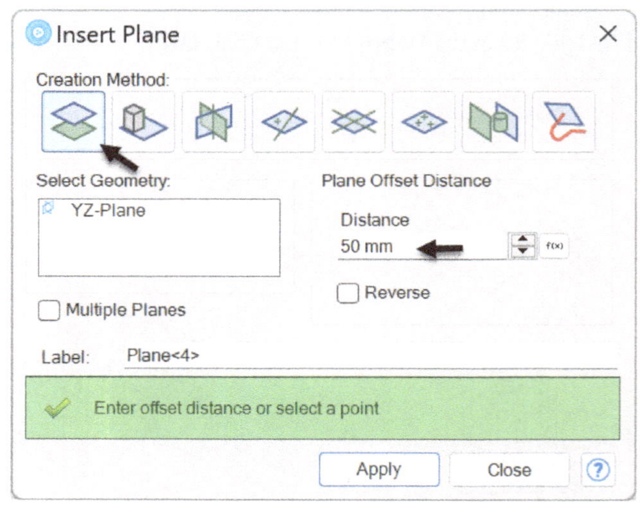

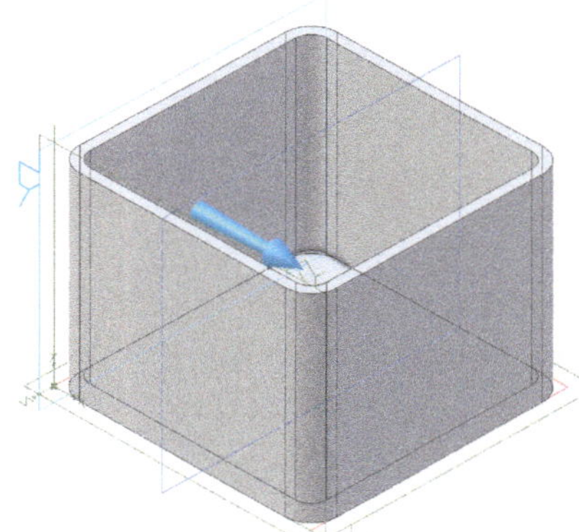

5. Click **Close**.
6. To start a new sketch, click **Model** tab > **Sketch > Activate 2D Sketch** on the ribbon.
7. On the ribbon, click **View > Visual Styles > Shaded and All Edges**.
8. Click the **Project to Sketch** icon on the **2D Sketch** tab of the ribbon.
9. Click on the inner edge of the model, as shown.

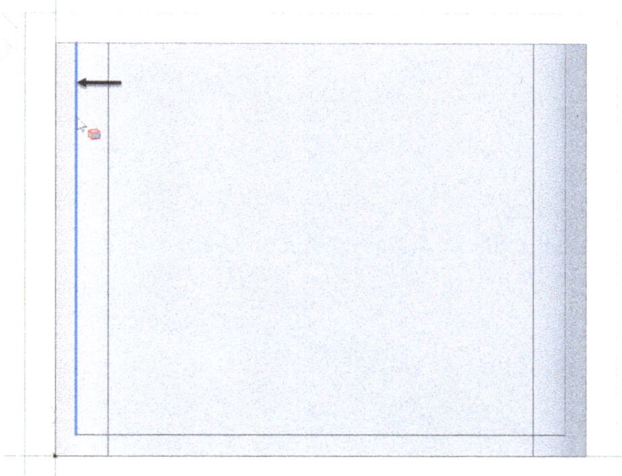

10. Select **Ouptut Options > Create reference figure** from the **Project To Sketch** dialog.
11. Check the **Maintain association to source entity** option.

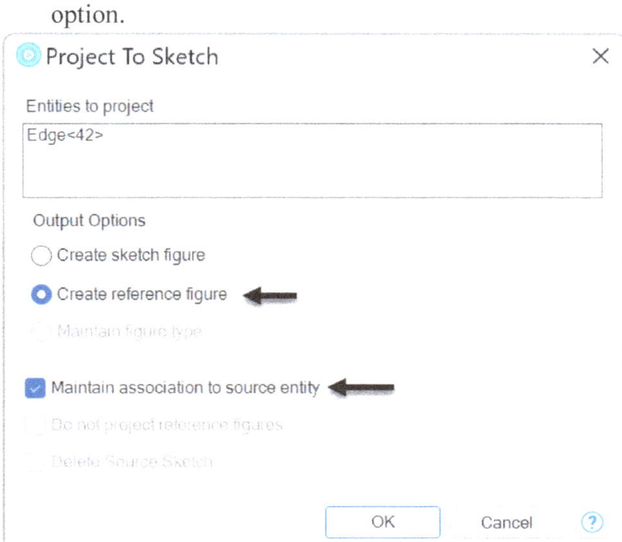

12. Click **OK**.
13. Click **Rectangle** on the **Sketch Figures** panel of the **2D Sketch** ribbon tab.
14. Select the top end point of the vertical reference line.
15. Move the pointer toward top-left corner and click.
16. On the ribbon, click **2D Sketch** > **Sketch Figures** > **Dimension** .
17. Add vertical and horizontal dimension to the rectangle, as shown.

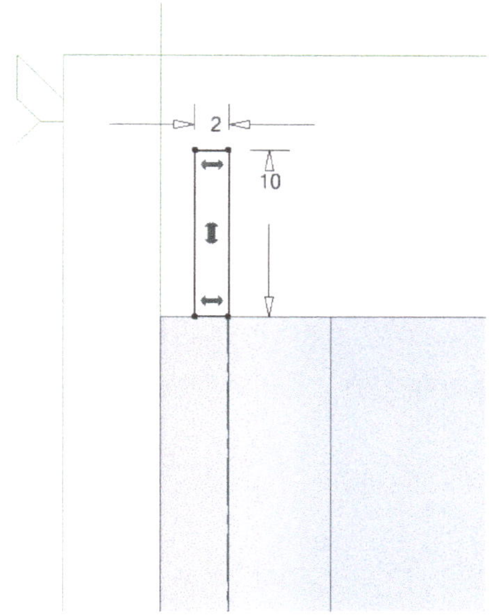

18. Click the **Deactivate Sketch** icon on the **2D Sketch** ribbon tab.
19. Click the top-right corner of the Right face of the ViewCube.

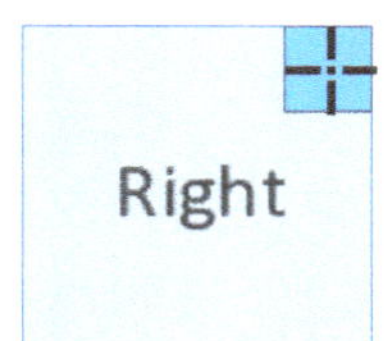

20. To start a new sketch, click **Model** tab > **Boss (Add Material) > Sweep** on the ribbon.

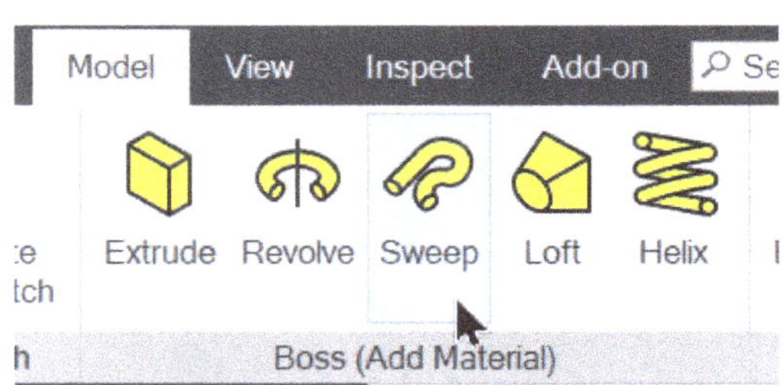

The rectangle is selected as the **Sketch to Sweep** and is displayed in the **Sketch to Sweep** selection box. Next, you need to select the path along which the sketch is to be swept.

21. Click in the **Path Objects** selection box.
22. Select the inner edges of the model, as shown.

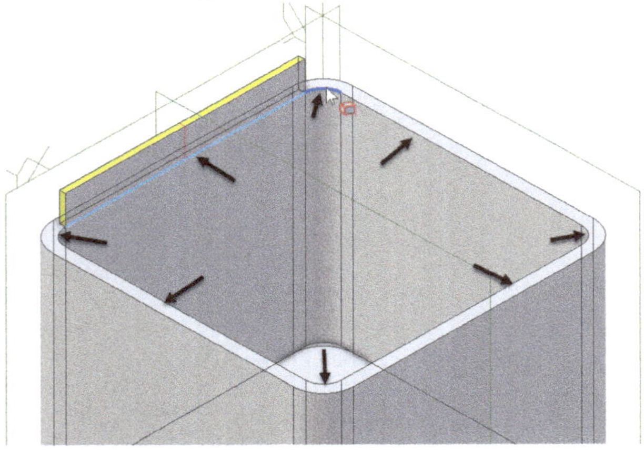

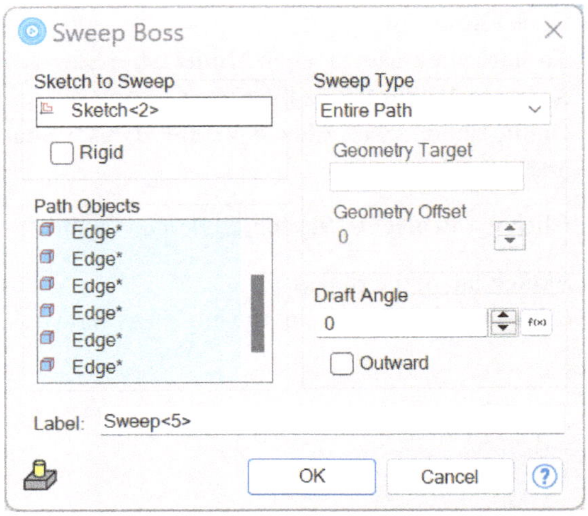

23. Select **Sweep Type > Entire Path**.
24. Click **OK**.
25. Save the file as Tutorial2 and close it.

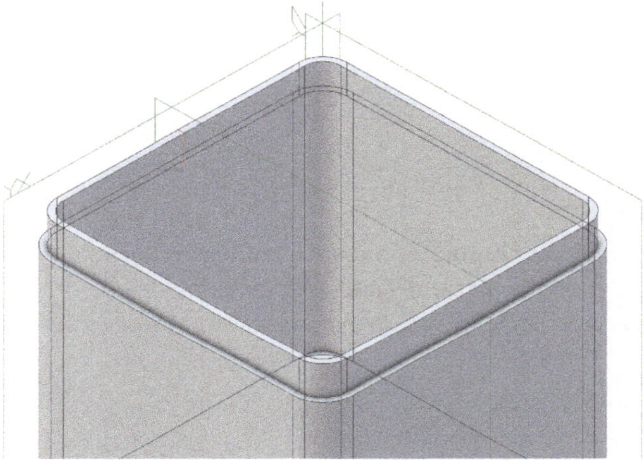

Chapter 3: Assembly Basics

In this chapter, you will:

- Add Components to assembly
- Apply constraints between components

TUTORIAL 1

This tutorial takes you through the creation of your first assembly.

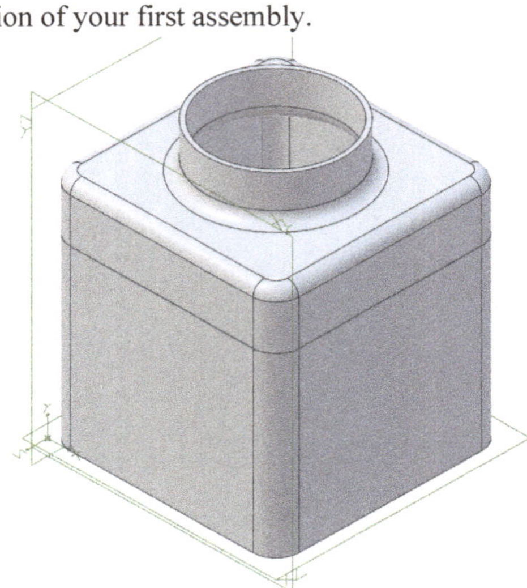

Starting a New Assembly File

1. Open the **Alibre Atom3D** application.
2. Click the **New Assembly** icon on the **Home** window.

The **Insert Part/Subassembly** dialog appears. .

Inserting the Base Component

1. Browse to the location of the **Tutorial 2** file of Chapter 1, and then double-click on it.
2. Select the origin point of the coordinate system, as shown.

3. Click the **Finish** button on the **Inserting** dialog.

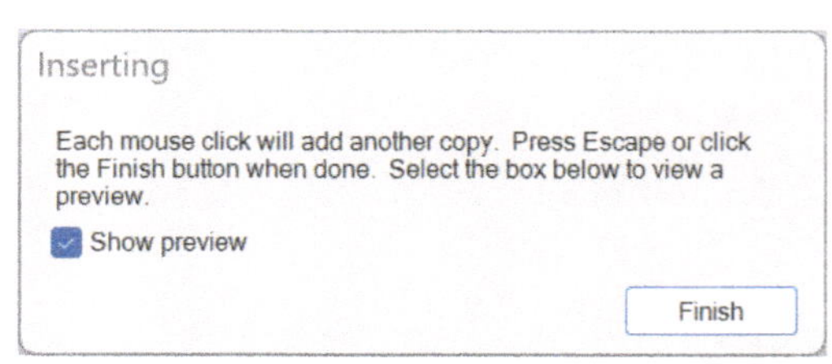

4. Click the top-right corner of the Front face of the ViewCube.

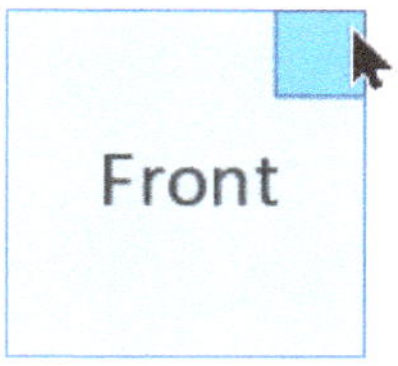

5. Select the **Tutorial2** part file from the **Design Explorer**.

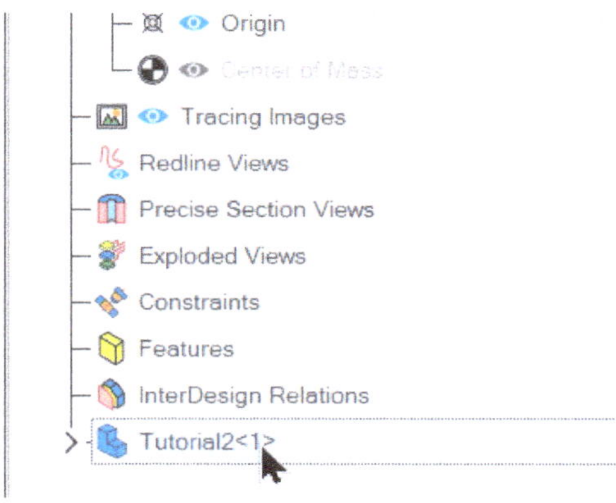

6. On the ribbon, click **Assembly > Constraints > Anchor**.

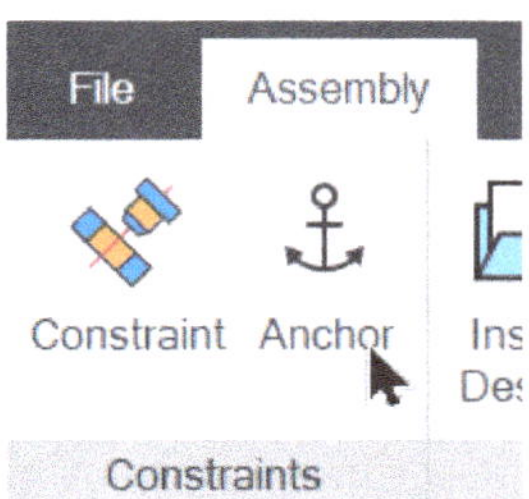

Adding the second component

1. On the ribbon, click **Assembly > Insert New > Insert Design**.

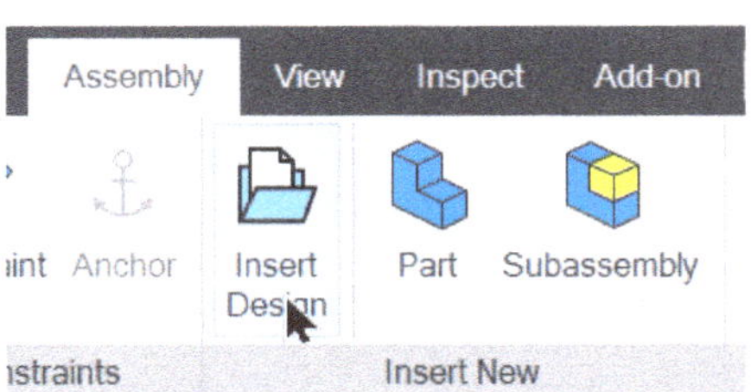

2. Browse to the location of the **Tutorial** 1 file of Chapter 1, and then double click on it.

3. Click in the graphics window; the selected part file is inserted into the assembly.

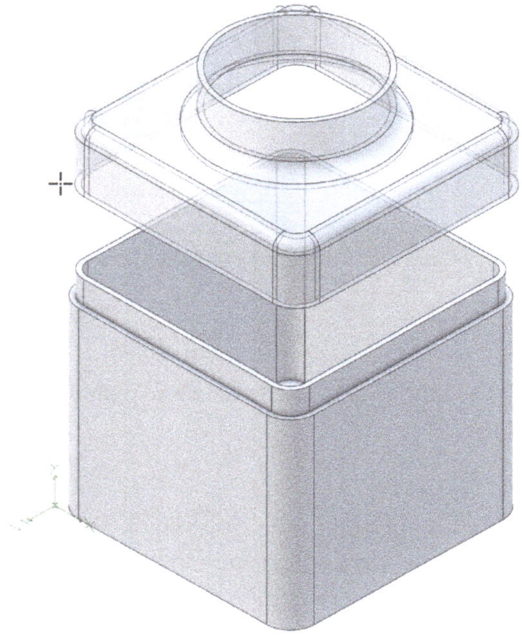

7. Click the **Finish** button on the **Inserting** dialog.

Creating Constraints

After adding the components to the assembly environment, you need to define constraints between them. By applying constraints, you establish precise geometric and positional relationships that control how components fit and move relative to each other.

To add constraints, click **Assembly > Constraints > Constraint** on the ribbon; the **Assembly Constraint** dialog appears..

The **Assembly Constraint** dialog has various options to apply constraints between the components.

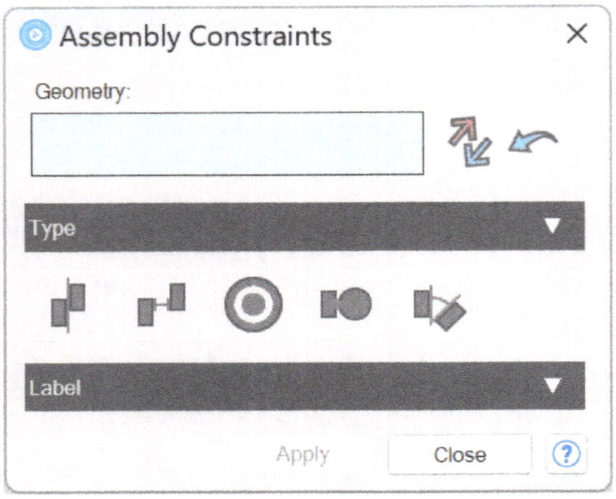

Different assembly constraints that can be applied are given next.

**Coaxial constraint:** This constraint aligns the axes of two cylindrical faces so that they are collinear. It is used to make sure one cylindrical feature, like a shaft, is perfectly aligned within another, such as a hole. To apply this constraint, select two cyndrical faces and click **Type > Coaxial** on the **Assembly Constraints** dialog.

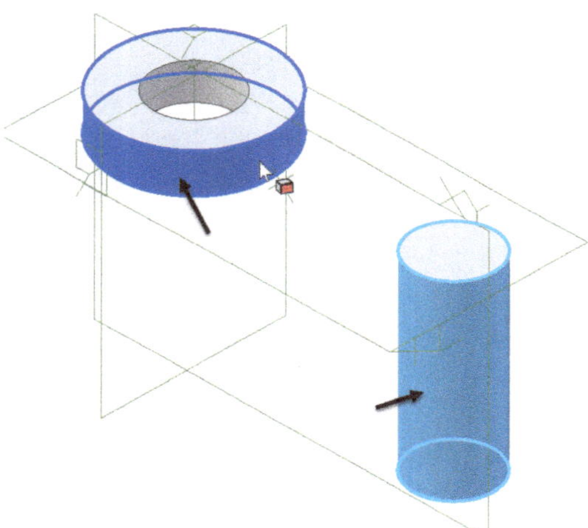

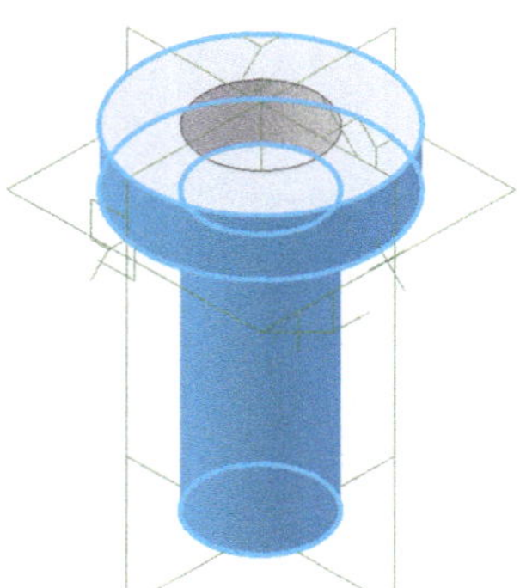

Click the **Flip**  button on the **Assembly Constraints** dialog to reverse the direction.

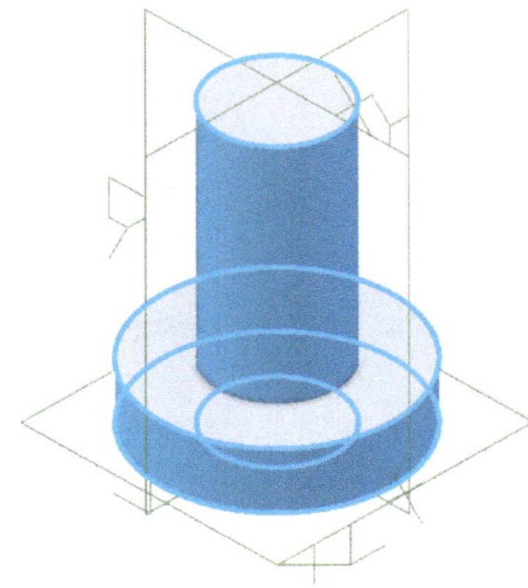

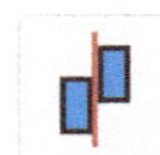**Coincident Constraint**: Using this constraint, you can make two planar faces coplanar to each other.

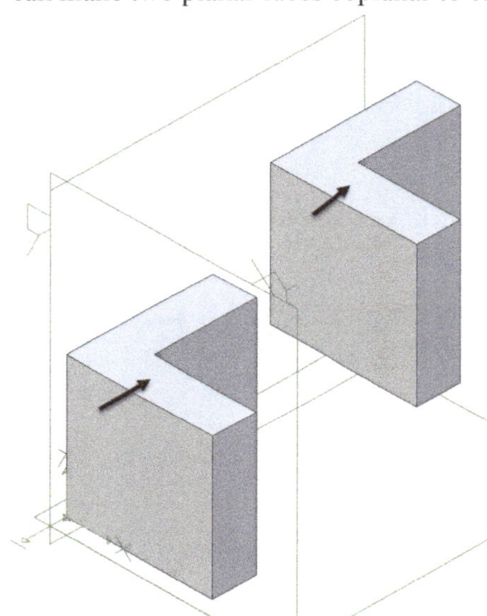

You can change the direction in which the planar faces touch each other. To do this, click the **Flip** 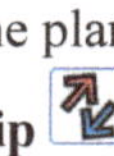 button on the **Assembly Constraints** dialog.

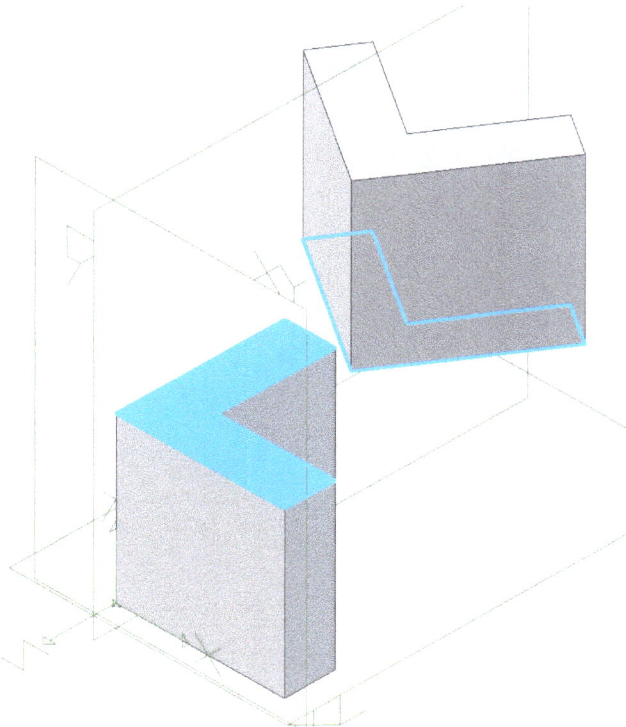

Offset Constraint: This constraint make the two planar faces parallel to each other. It allows you to specify a fixed distance between two selected faces or features. To do this, select two planar faces and click **Type > Offset** on the **Assembly Constraints** dialog. Next, specify a value in the **Offset** box available on the **Assembly Constraints** dialog.

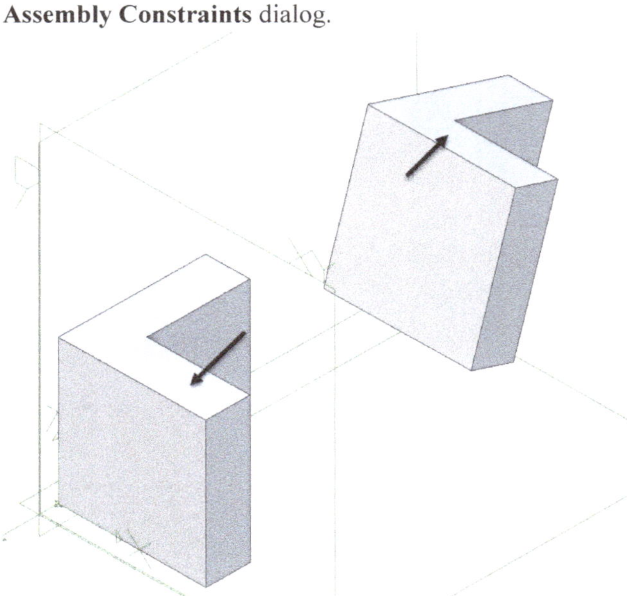

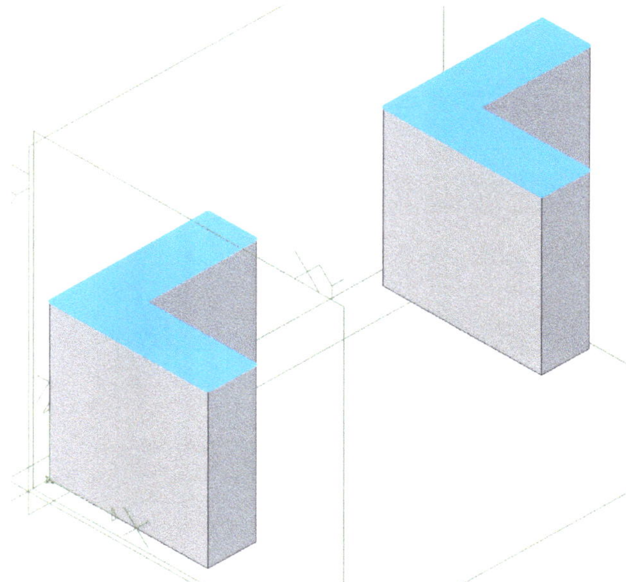

Angle constraint: Applies the angle constraint between two components. Activate the **Constraints** command select the faces to be constrained.

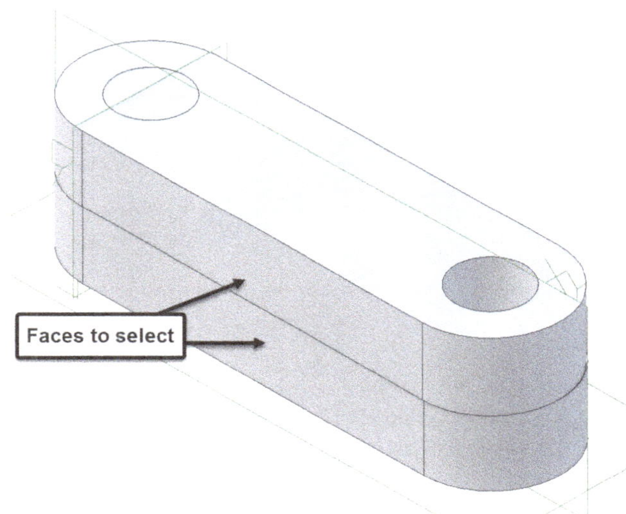

On the **Assembly Constraints** dialog, click the **Angle** icon. Next, type 45 in the **Angle** box. Click the **Accept** button.

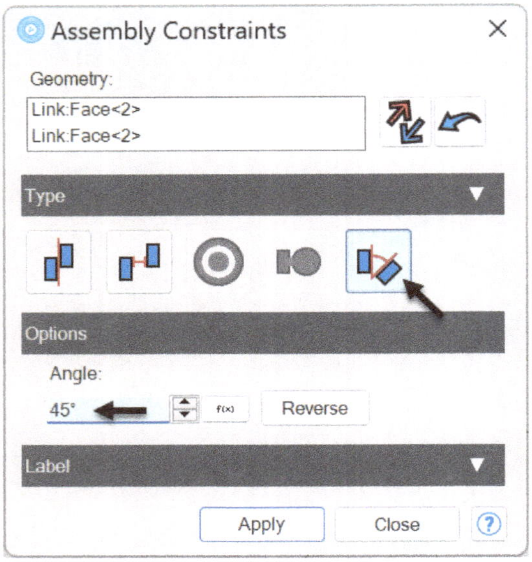

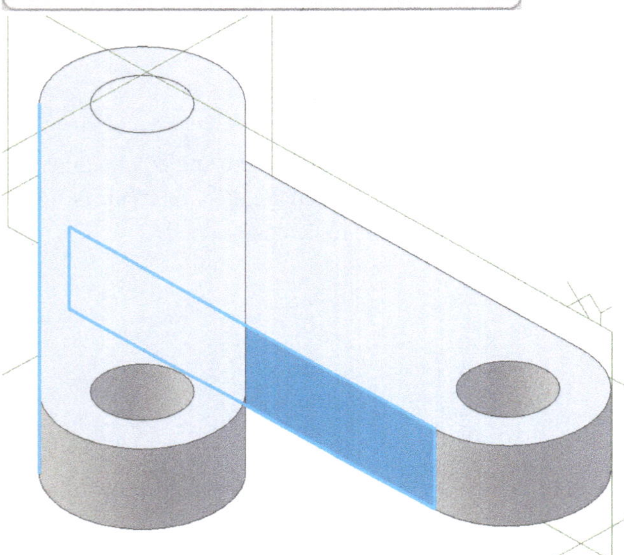

1. Click the **Constraint**  icon on the **Constraints** panel of the **Assembly** ribbon tab.
2. Click on the planar faces of the two parts, as shown.

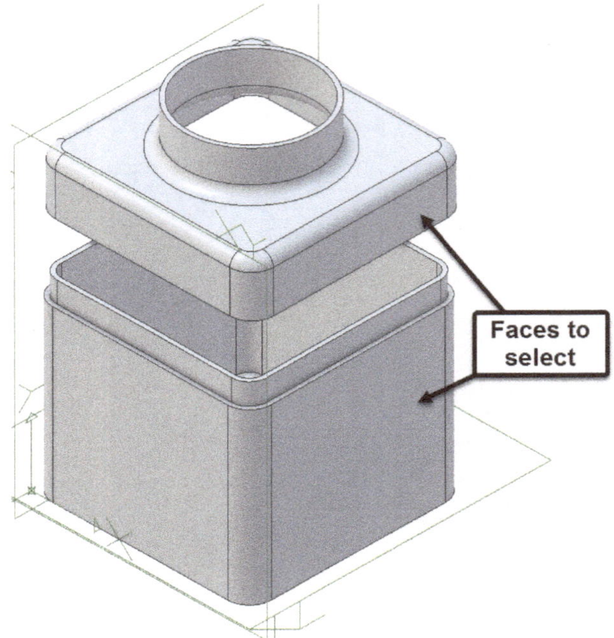

3. On the **Assembly Constraints** dialog, click the **Coincident** 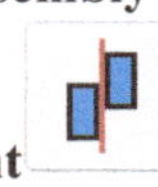 icon under the **Type** section.
4. Click the **Accept** button on the **Assembly Constraints** dialog.
5. Select the planar faces of the two parts, as shown.

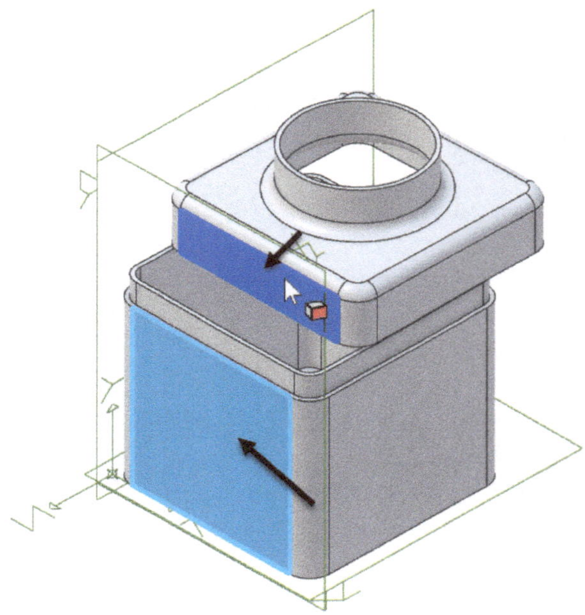

6. On the **Assembly Constraints** dialog, click the **Coincident** icon under the **Type** section.
7. Click the **Accept** button on the **Assembly Constraints** dialog.

8. Select the first face.

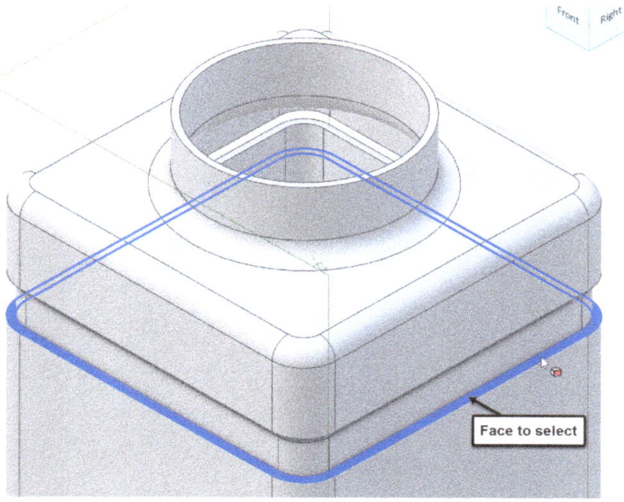

9. Select the lower right corner of the ViewCube.
10. Select the second face, as shown.

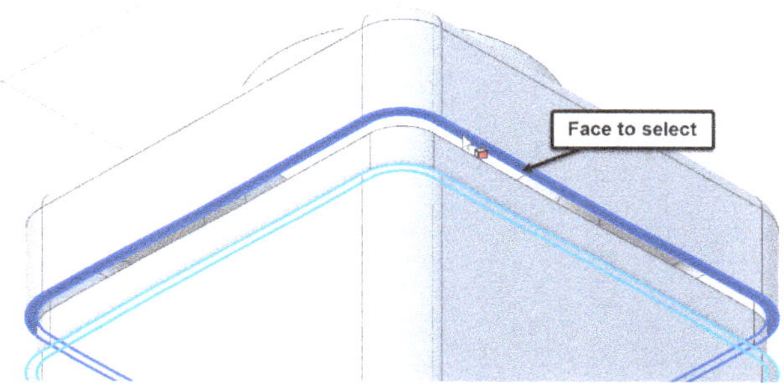

11. On the **Assembly Constraints** dialog, click the **Coincident** 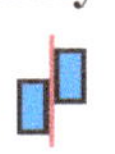 icon under the **Type** section.
12. Click the **Accept** button on the **Assembly Constraints** dialog.
13. Close the **Assembly Constraints** dialog.

The assembly is constrained fully.

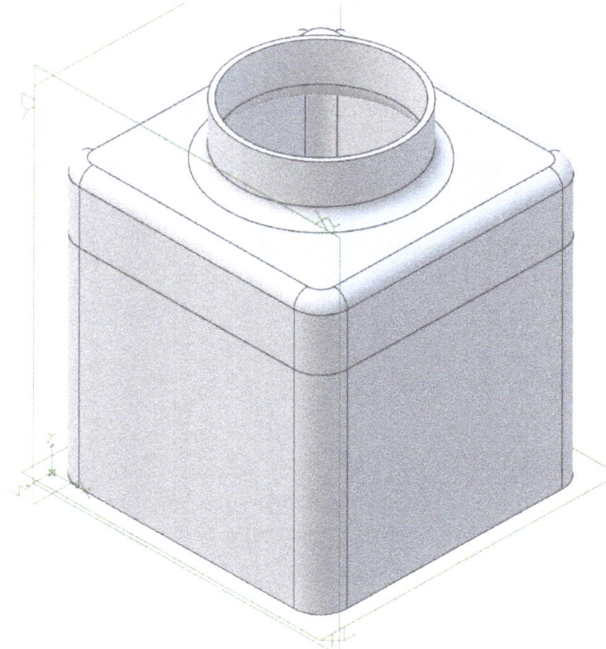

14. Click **File > Save**  on the Quick Access toolbar.
15. Type **Assembly_tutorial** in the **File name** box.
16. Click **Save**.
17. Click **Close** on the top right corner of the window.

Chapter 4: Sketching

In this chapter, you learn the sketching tools. You learn to create:

- Polygons
- Slots
- Constraints
- Ellipses
- Circles
- Trim
- Extend
- Text
- Construction geometry

Creating Polygons

A Polygon is a shape having many sides ranging from 3 to 1024. In Alibre Atom3D, you can create regular polygons having sides with equal length. Follow the steps given next to create a polygon.

1. Activate the **Sketch** mode.
2. On the ribbon, click **2D Sketch > Sketch Figures > Polygon** .
3. On the Regular Polygon dialog, type **8** in the **Sides** box.
4. Select **Inscribed circle** . This option creates a polygon with its sides touching a dotted circle. You can also select the **Circumscribed circle** option to create a polygon with its vertices touching a dotted circle.
5. Click to define the center of the polygon.
6. Move the pointer and click to define the size and angle of the polygon.

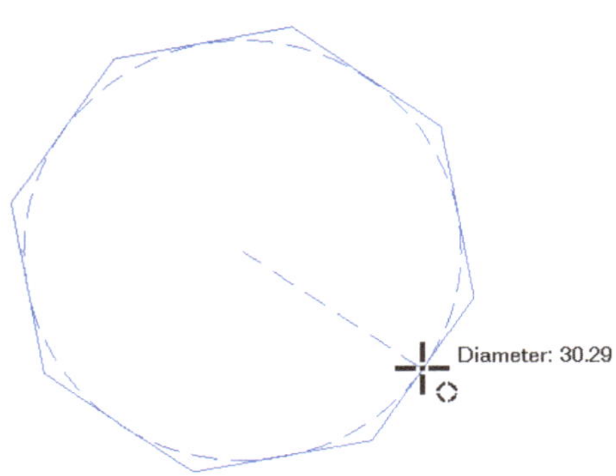

7. Press **Esc** to deactivate the tool.

Constraints

Constraints are used to control the shape of a sketch by establishing relationships between the sketch elements. You can add constrains using the tools available on the **Constraints** panel of the **Model** tab.

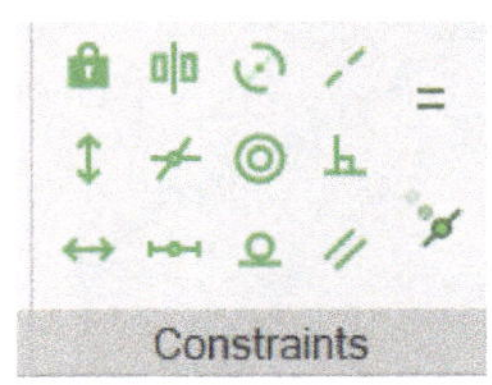

Coincident Constraint

This Coincident Constraint connects a point to another point.

1. On the ribbon, click **2D Sketch > Constraints > Coincident Constraint** .
2. Select two points. The selected points will be merged.

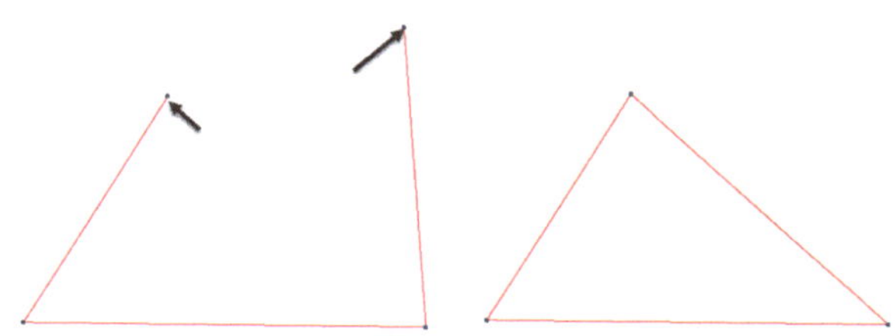

Horizontal Constraint

To apply the **Horizontal** Constraint , click on a line and click the **Horizontal Constraint** icon on the **Constraints** panel of the **2D Sketch** ribbon tab.

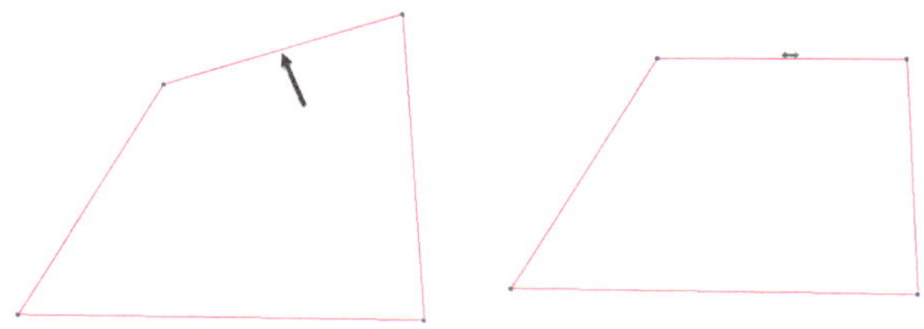

You can also align two points or vertices horizontally.

Click the **Horizontal Constraint** icon on the **Constraints** panel of the **2D Sketch** ribbon tab. Select the two points.

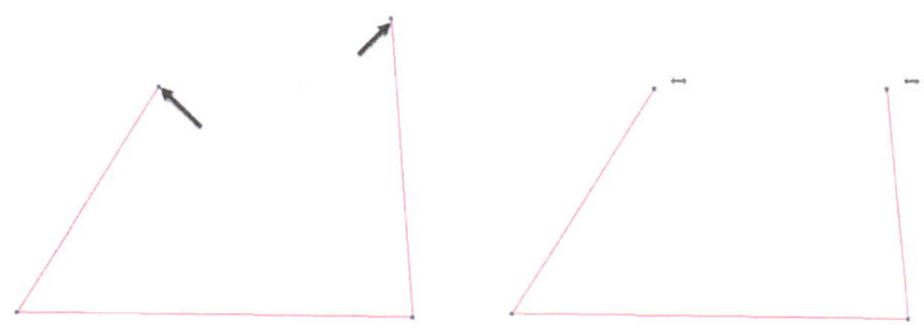

Vertical Constraint

Use the **Vertical Constraint** to make a line vertical. You can also use this constraint to align two points or vertices vertically.

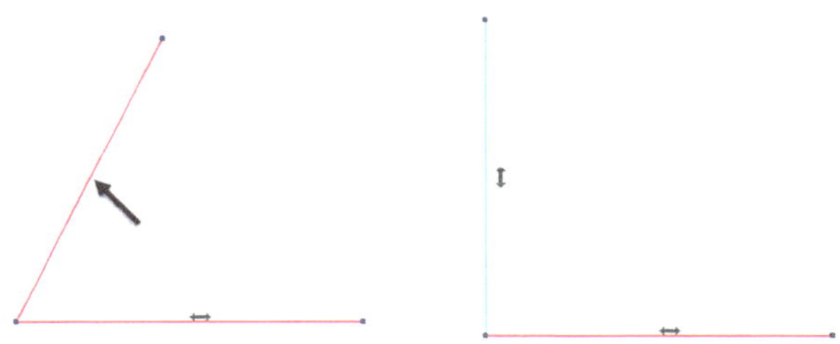

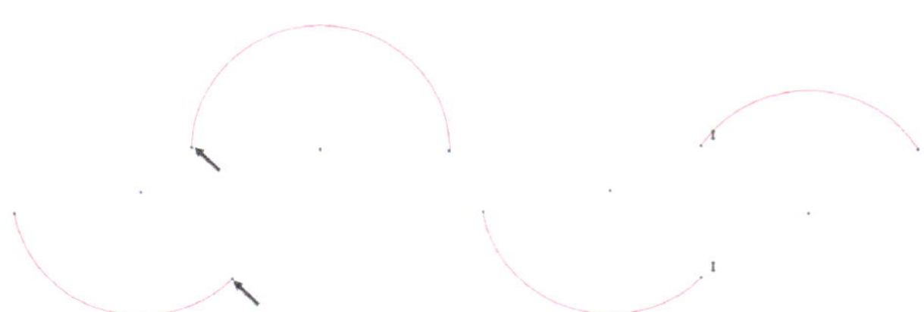

Tangent Constraint

This constraint makes an arc, circle, or line tangent to another arc or circle. On the ribbon, click **2D Sketch > Constraints > Tangent Constraint** . Next, select a circle, arc, or line. Select another circle or arc. The two elements will be tangent to each other.

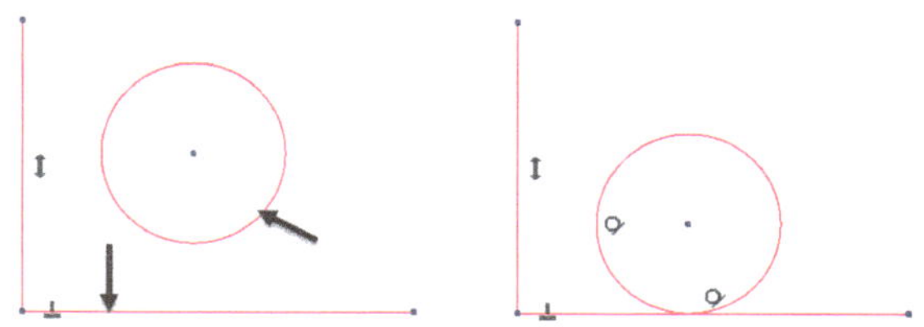

Parallel Constraint

Use the **Parallel Constraint** to make two lines parallel to each other. To do this, click **2D Sketch > Constraints > Parallel Constraint** on the ribbon. Next, select the two lines to be parallel.

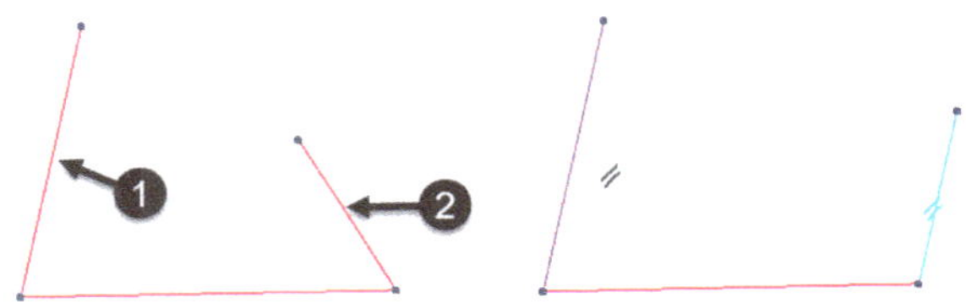

Perpendicular Constraint

Use the **Perpendicular Constraint** to make two entities perpendicular to each other.

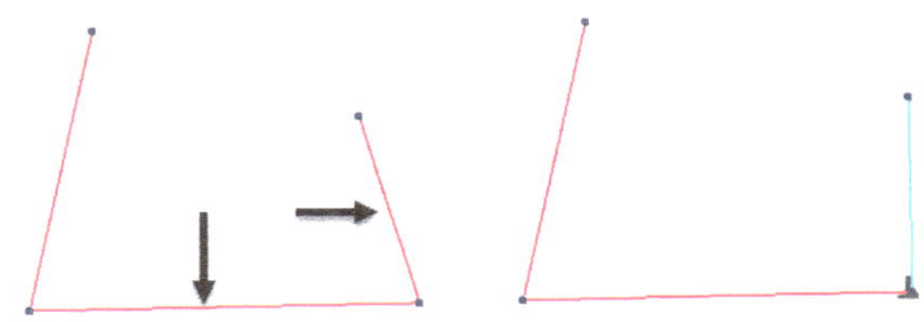

Midline Constraint

Use the **Midline Constraint** to make a point coincide with the midpoint of a line or arc.

1. Click **2D Sketch > Constraints > Midline Constraint** on the ribbon.
2. Select a line/arc and a point.

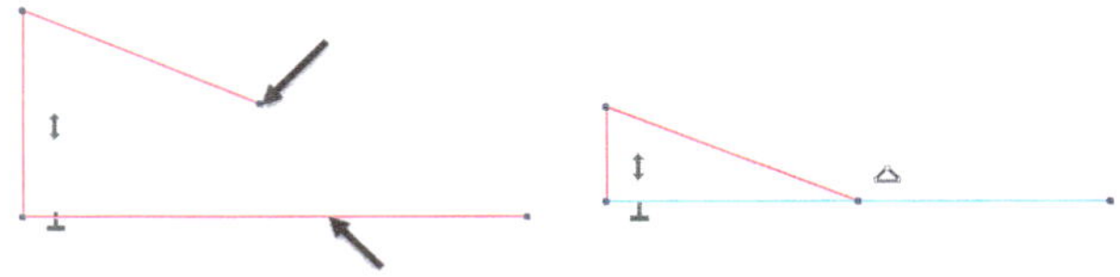

Concentric Constraint

This constraint makes the center points of arcs, circles or ellipses coincident.

1. Click **2D Sketch > Constraints > Concentric Constraint** on the ribbon.

2. select a circle or arc from the sketch. Next, select another circle or arc. The first circle/arc will be concentric with the second circle/arc.

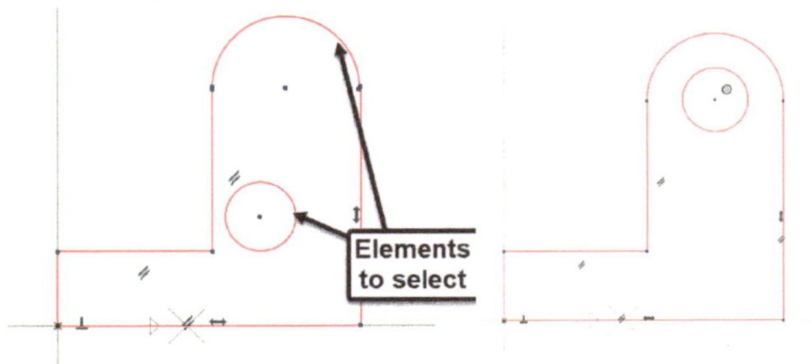

Equal Constraint

The **Equal Constraint** = makes two lines equal in length.

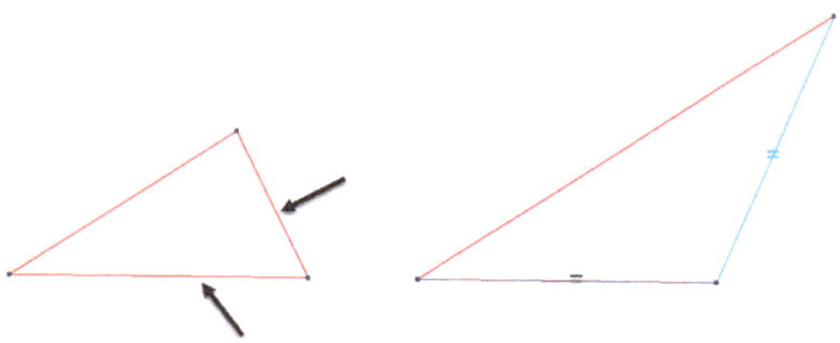

You can also make two circles or arcs equal in radius.

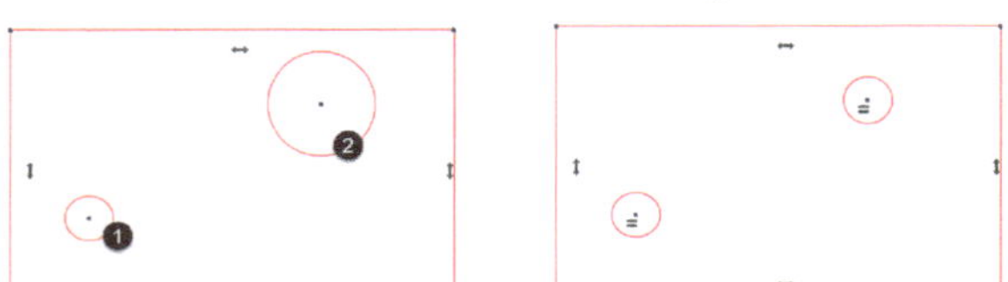

Collinear Constraint

The **Collinear Constraint** forces a line to be collinear to another line. The lines are not required to touch each other.

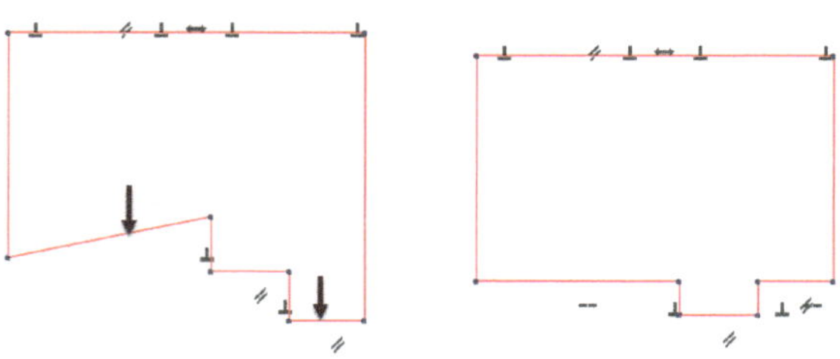

Make Symmetric

This command makes two objects symmetric about a line. The objects will have the same size, position, and orientation about a line.

1. Click **2D Sketch > Constraints > Symmetric Constraint** on the ribbon.
2. Select the axis of symmetry.
3. Click on the first and second figures. The two objects will be made symmetric about the line of symmetry.

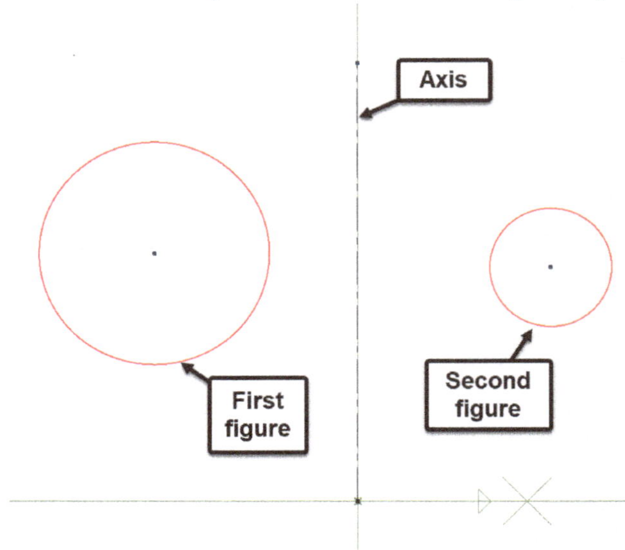

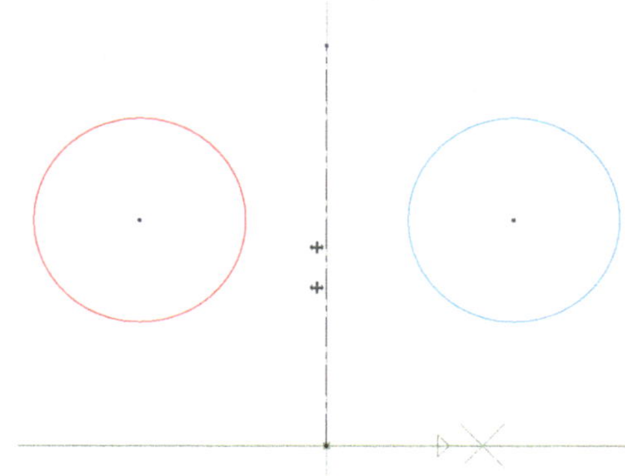

Fix Constraint

The **Fix Constraint** fixes a sketch element so that it cannot be moved.

1. Click **2D Sketch > Constraints > Fix Constraint** on the ribbon.
2. Select a sketch element; it will be fixed at its current position.

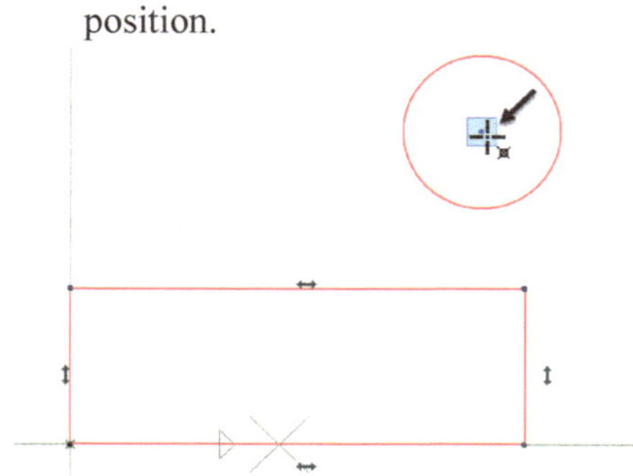

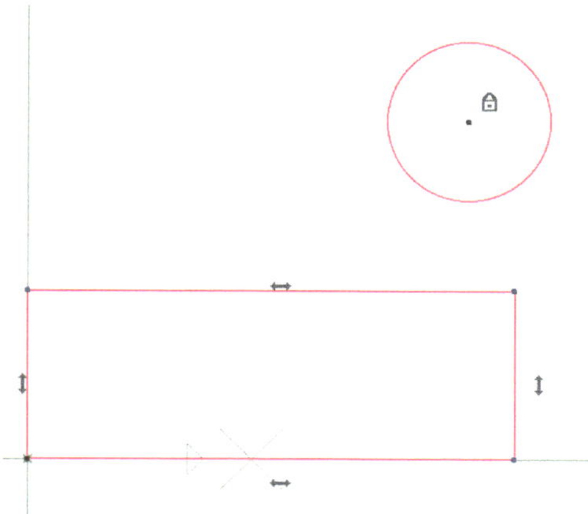

Coradial Constraint

Use the **Coradial Constraint** to make two arcs to share the same center point. Also, the radius of the arcs become equal.

1. Click **2D Sketch > Constraints > Coradial Constraint** on the ribbon.
2. Select two arcs.

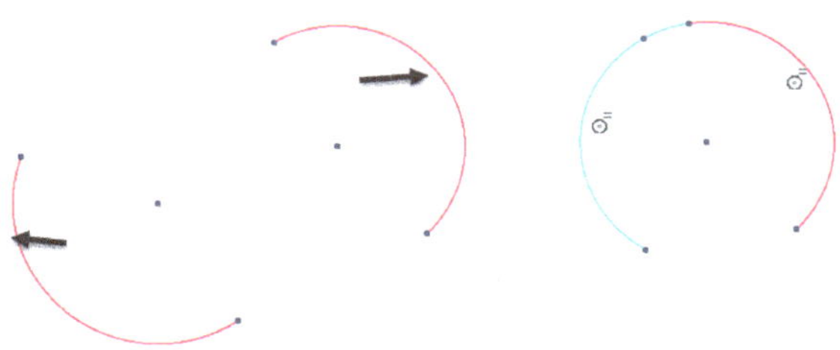

Intersection Constraint

Use the **Intersection Constraint** to make a point coincident with the intersection point of two sketch elements.

1. Click **2D Sketch > Constraints > Intersection Constraint** on the ribbon.
2. Select the First Element.
3. Select the Second Element.
4. Click on the **sketch point** you want to move. This is the entity that will be constrained.

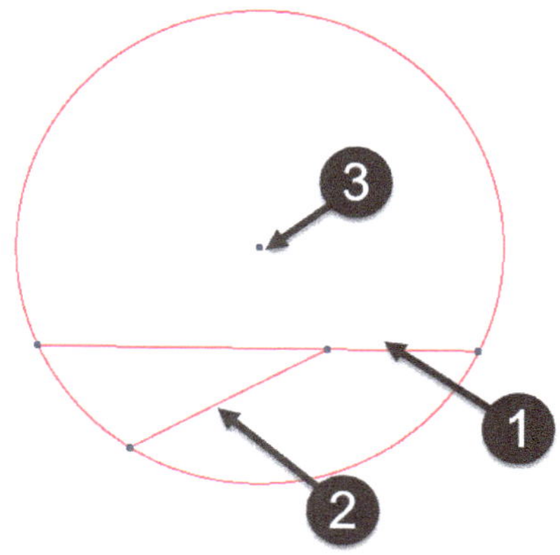

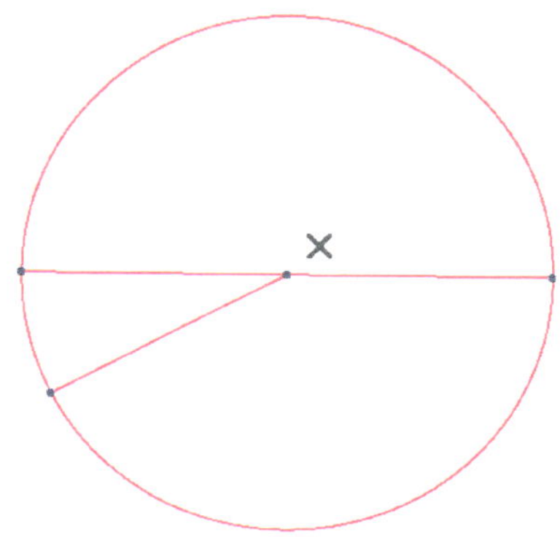

Automatic Constraints

Alibre Atom3D automatically adds constraints when you create sketch elements.

1. Start a new sketch and click the **Line** tool on the **Sketch Figures** panel.
2. Click to specify the start point of the line.
3. Move the pointer in the horizontal direction and notice the **Horizontal** constraint flag.
4. Click to create a line with the **Horizontal** constraint.

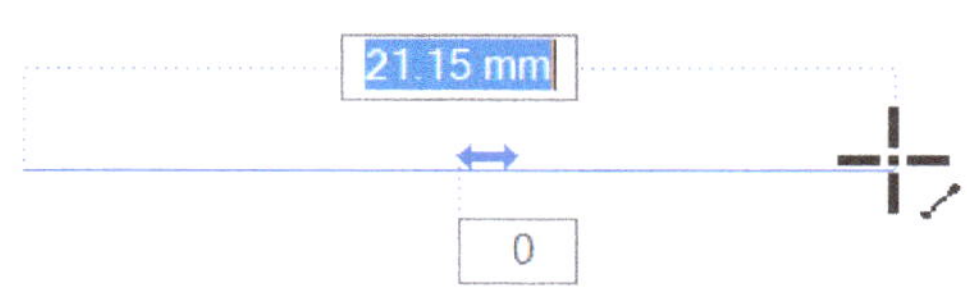

5. Move the pointer vertically and click when the **Perpendicular** constraint flag is displayed.

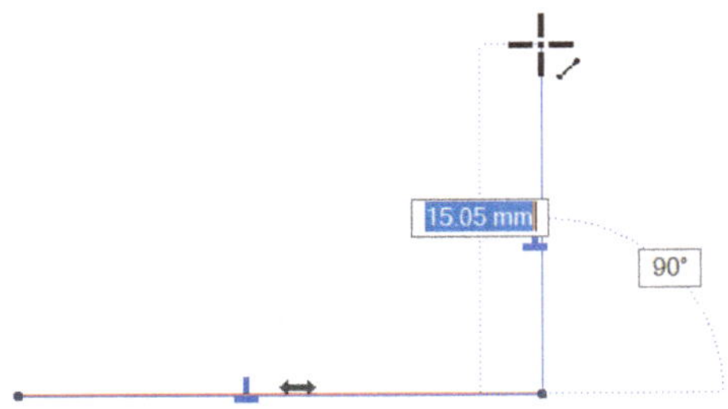

6. Create an inclined line, as shown.

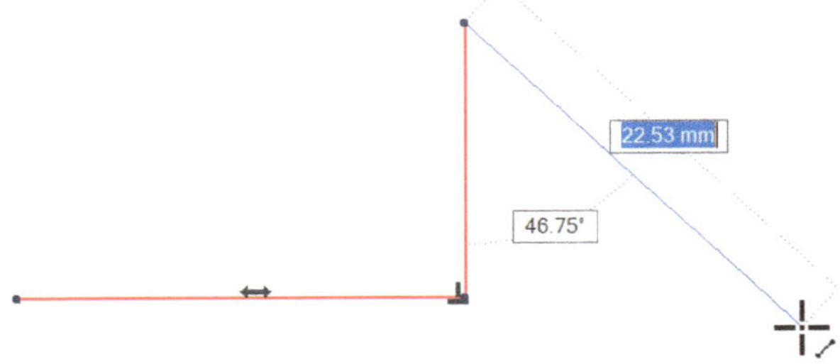

7. Move the pointer along the inclined line and notice the **Collinear** constraint flag.

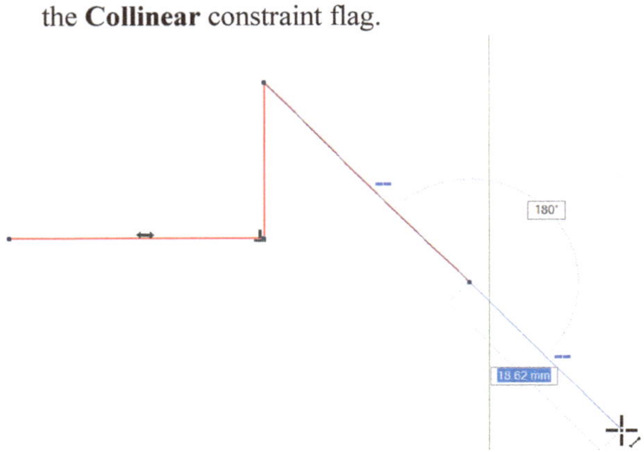

8. Press Esc to deactivate the **Line** tool.
9. Right click and select **Line**.
10. Click in the graphics window to specify the start point of the line.
11. Move the cursor in the direction parallel to the inclined line; the **Parallel** constraint flag is displayed.

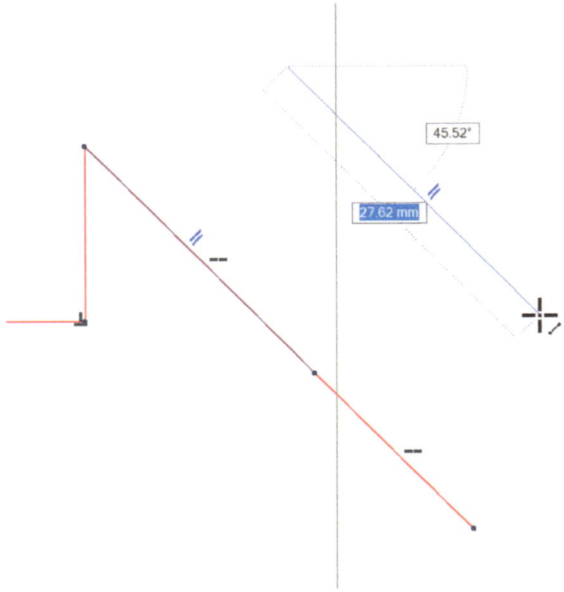

12. Click to create a line parallel to the selected line.
13. Press **Esc** to deactivate the **Line** tool.
14. On the ribbon, click **2D Sketch > Sketch Figures > Circle**.
15. Click in the graphics window.
16. Move the pointer outward and click to create a circle.
17. Activate the **Line** tool and click on the circle.

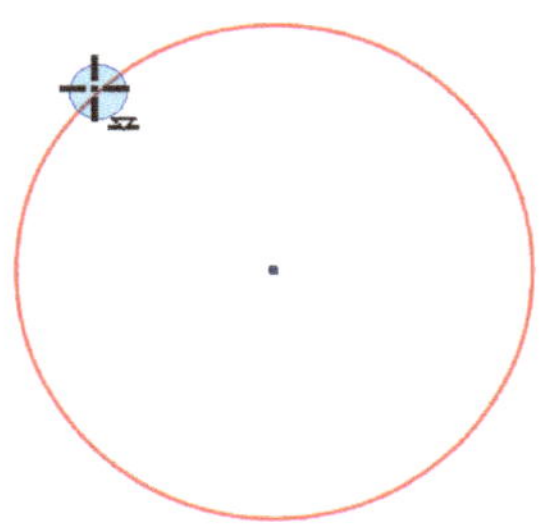

18. Move the pointer around the circle and notice that the line maintains the **Tangent** constraint with the circle.

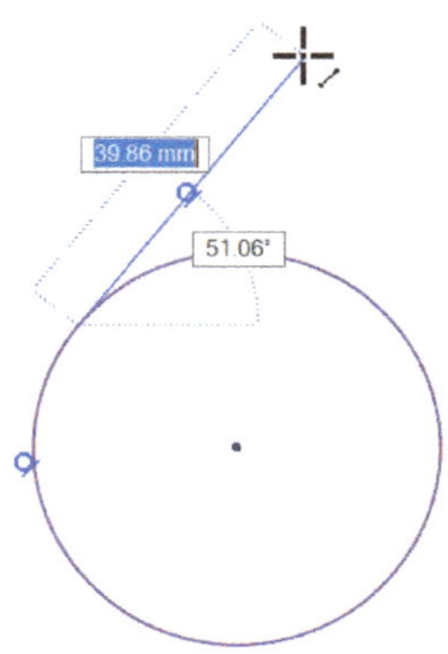

19. Click to create a line that is tangent and coincident to the circle. Right click and select **Select**.

Tutorial 1

In this tutorial, you will create a sketch using the **Line, Arc, Tangent Arc** and **Circle** tools.

1. Activate the **Sketch** mode.
2. On the CommandManager, click **Sketch > Line** drop-down > **Midpoint Line** .
3. Click on the origin point to define the midpoint of the line.
4. Move the pointer horizontally toward the right and click.

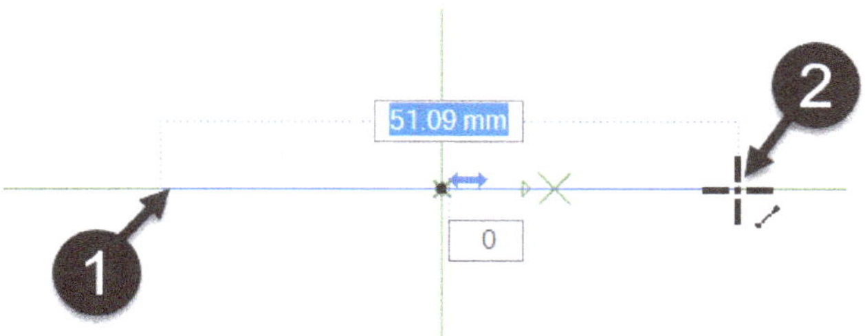

5. Move the pointer upward and click when the **Perpendicular** constraint flag appears.

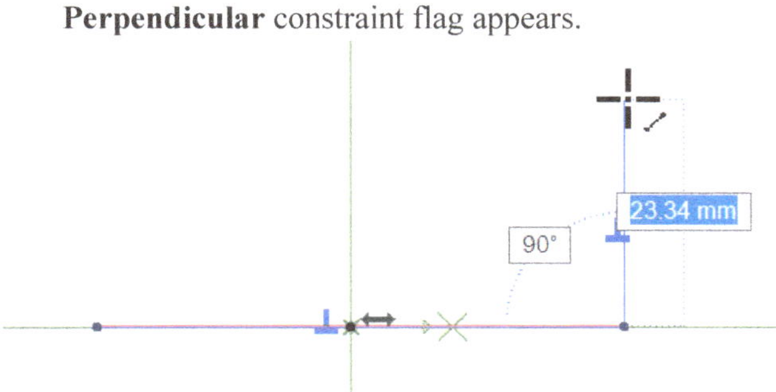

6. Right-click and select **Select**.
7. On the ribbon, click **2D Sketch** > **Sketch Figures** > **Arc**.
8. Place the pointer on the endpoint of the vertical line.
9. Move the pointer vertically up along the dotted line and click to specify the centerpoint of the arc.

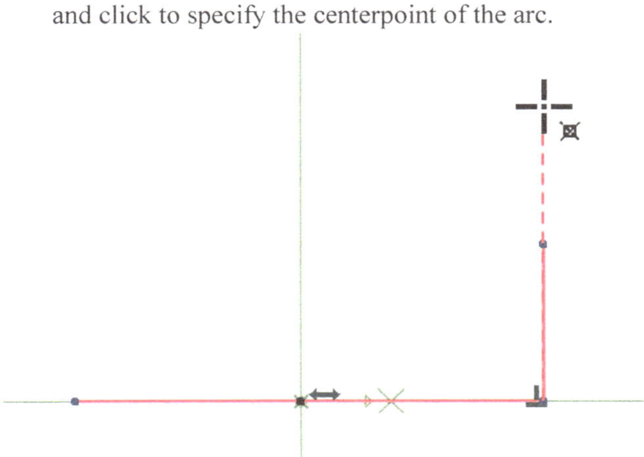

10. Select the endpoint of the vertical line.

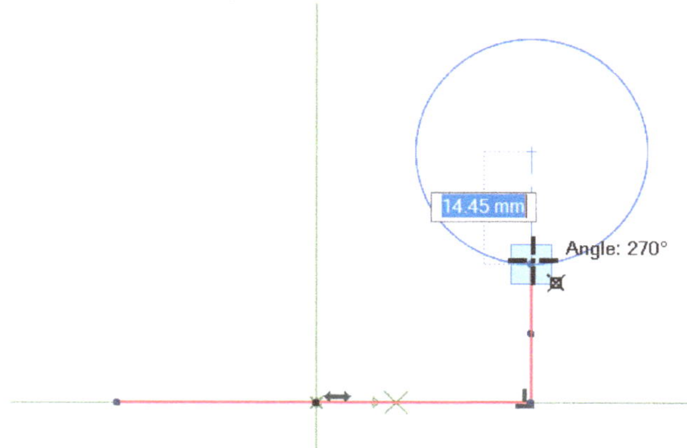

11. Move the pointer diagonally toward the top left corner and click. Next, right click and select **Select**.

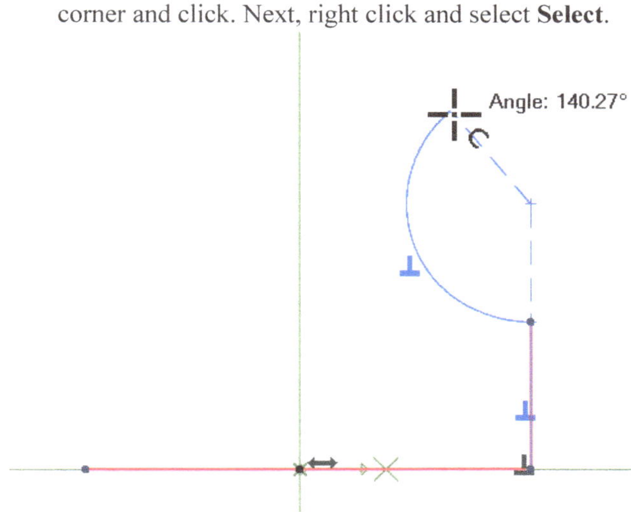

12. ON the ribbon, click 2D Sketch > Constraints > Midline Constraint.
13. Select the horizontal line.
14. Select the sketch origin; the midpoint of the horizontal line is made coincident to the sketch origin.

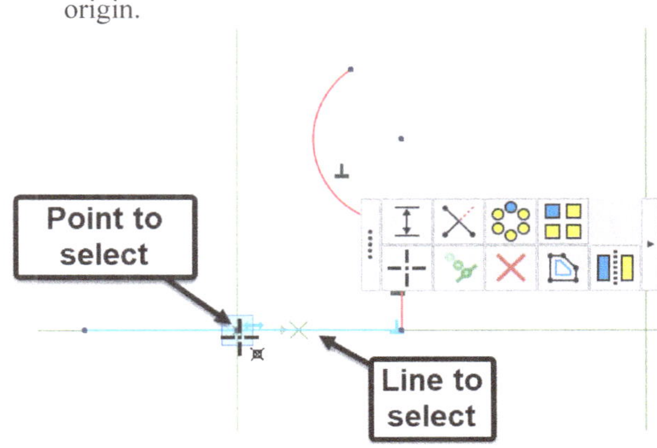

15. On the ribbon, click **References > Reference Line** .

16. Select the origin point of the sketch, move the pointer vertically upwards, and click. Press **Esc**.

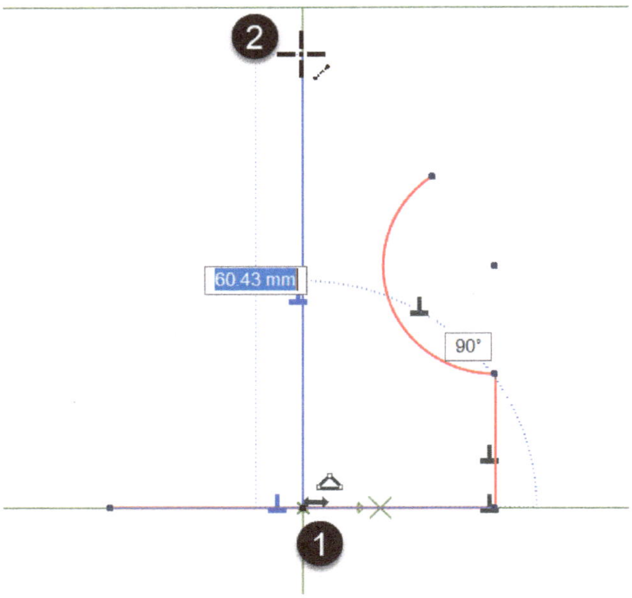

17. On the ribbon, click **2D Sketch > Sketch Tools > Mirror** .
18. Select the arc and the vertical line.
19. On the **Mirror Figure** dialog, click in the **Mirror axis** selection box and select the vertical reference line. Click **OK**.

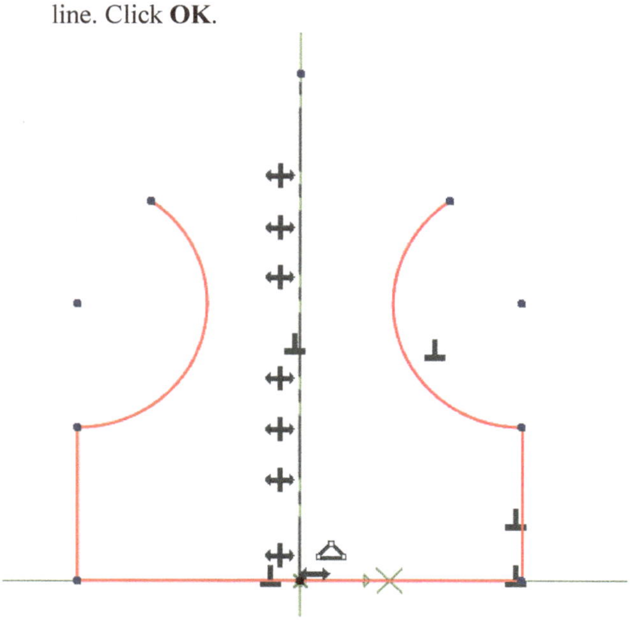

20. On the ribbon, click **2D Sketch** > **Sketch Figures > Tangent Arc** .

21. Select tthe right arc, and then move the pointer upward.

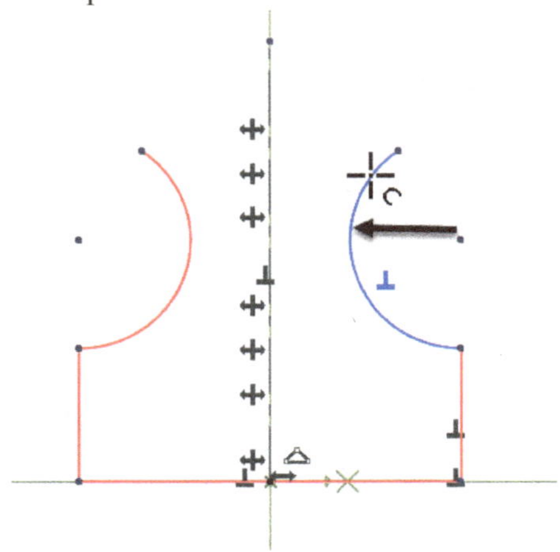

22. Select the endpoint of the left arc; an arc tangent to the both existing arcs is created.

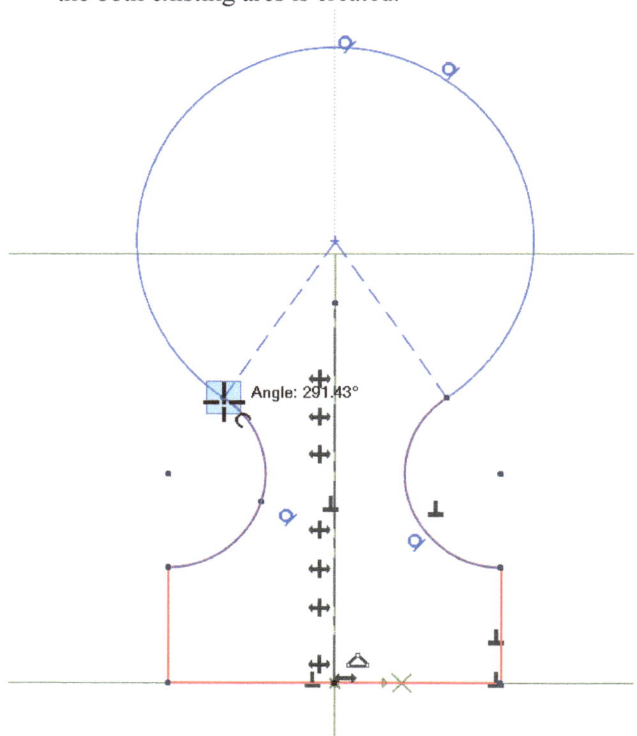

23. On the ribbon, click **2D Sketch > Sketch Figures > Circle**.
24. Select the centerpoint of the tangent arc, move the pointer outward, and click to create the circle.

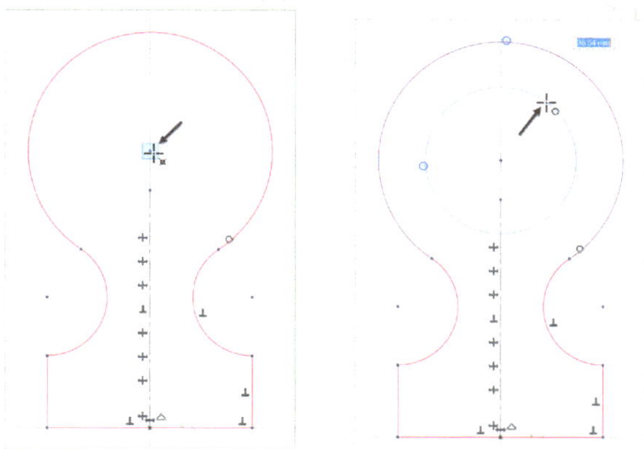

25. On the ribbon, click **2D Sketch > Sketch Figures > Dimension**  .
26. Select the horizontal line, move the pointer downward and click. Next, type 30 and press ENTER.

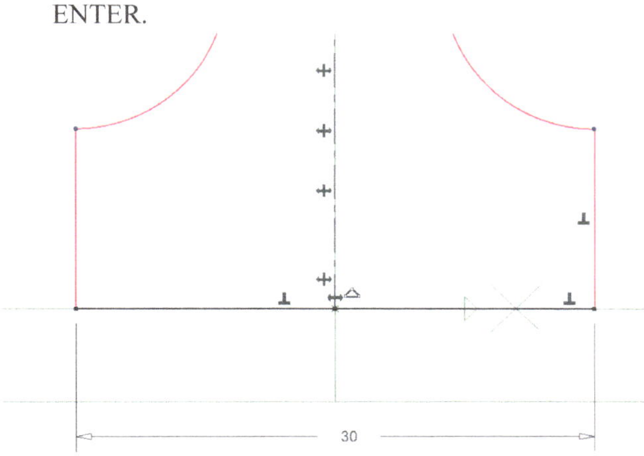

27. Select the right vertical line, move the pointer toward and click. Next, type 10 and press ENTER.

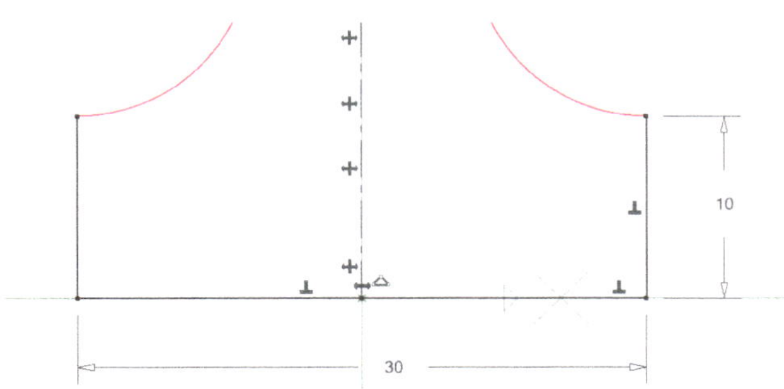

28. Select the small arc on the right side, move the pointer and click. Next, type 5 and press ENTER.
29. Likewise, add dimensions to the remaining arc and circle.
30. Add dimensions to the sketch, as shown. Press ESC to deactivate the **Smart Dimension** command.

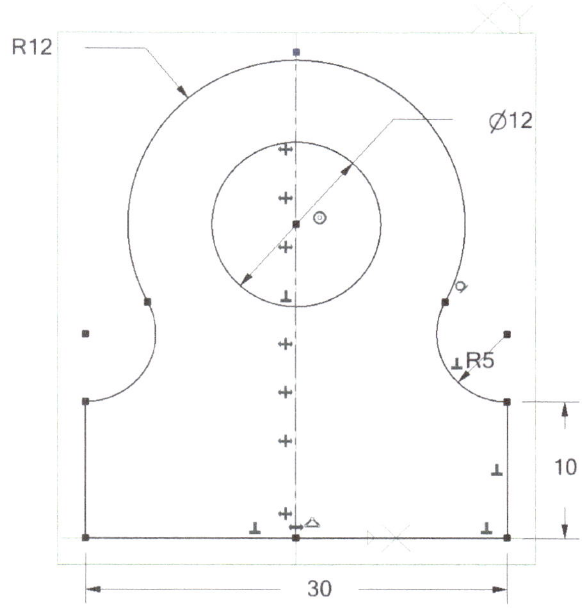

31. Click **Deactivate sketch** on the ribbon.

Ellipses

Ellipses are **uniform curves** with a regular, closed shape, defined by two axes: the **major axis** (longest diameter) and the **minor axis** (shortest diameter). Ellipses are used in designs requiring symmetrical curves, such as cam profiles, optical lenses, or aerodynamic shapes.

1. Activate the **Sketch** mode.
2. On the ribbon, click **2D Sketch > Sketch Figures > Ellipse**.
3. Pick a point in the graphics window to define the center of the ellipse.
4. Move the pointer and click to define the radius and orientation of the first axis.

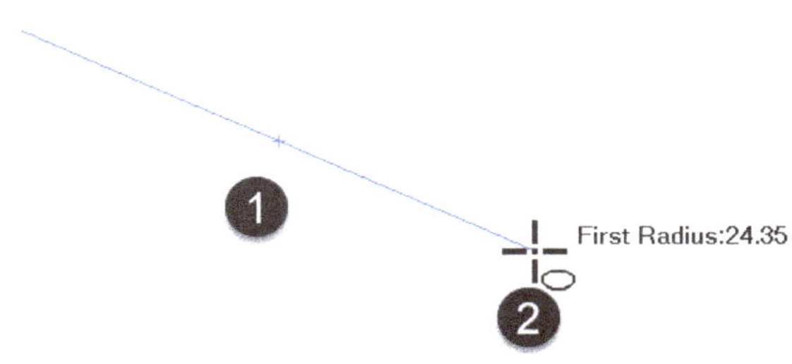

5. Move the pointer and click to define the radius of the second axis.

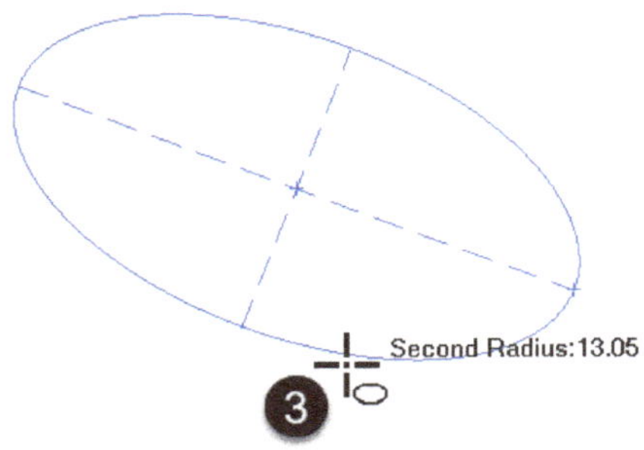

Click and drag the ellipse, notice that it is under-defined. You need to add dimensions and constraints to fully define the ellipse.

32. On the ribbon, click **2D Sketch > References > Reference Line.**

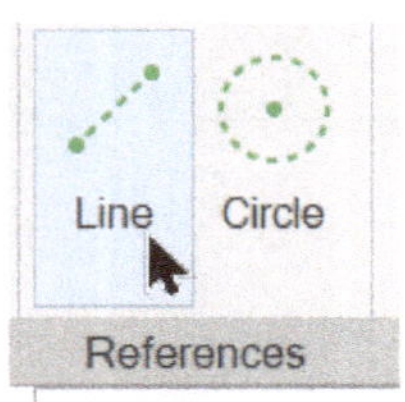

6. Select the center point of the ellipse, move the pointer horizontally toward right and click.

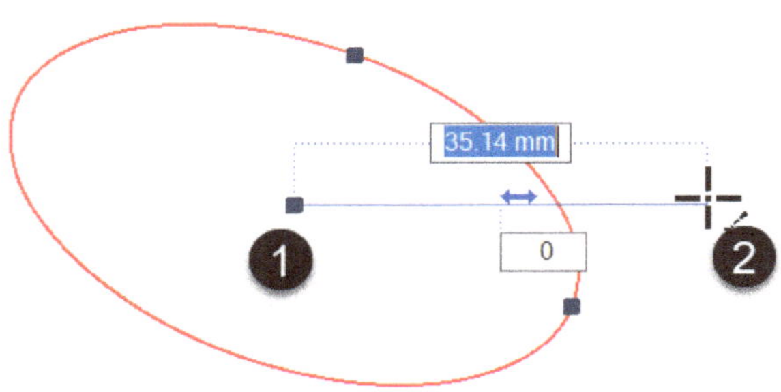

7. Right-click and select **Select**.
8. On the ribbon, click **2D Sketch > References > Reference Line.**
9. Select the minor axis point of the ellipse, as shown.
10. Select the centerpoint of the ellipse.

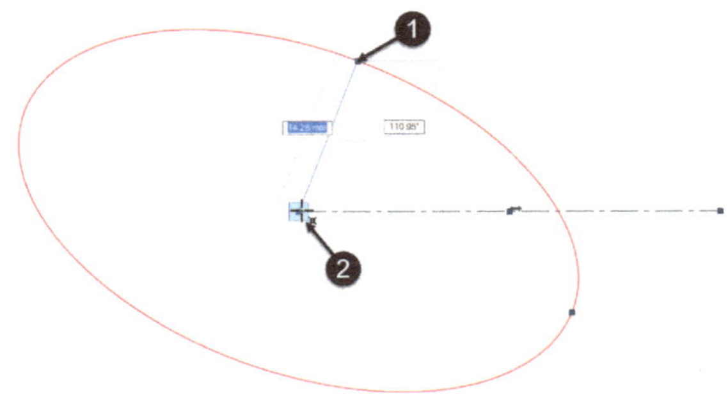

11. Select the major axis point of the ellipse, as shown.
12. Right-click and select **Select**.

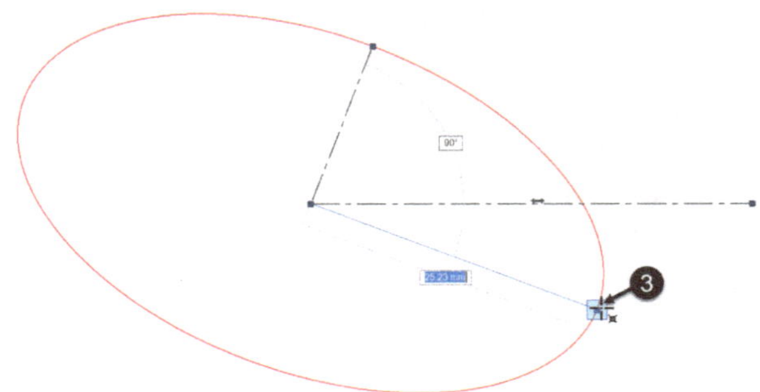

13. On the ribbon, click **2D Sketch > Sketch Figures > Dimension** .
14. Select the major axis line of the ellipse.
15. Select the horizontal reference line. The angled dimension is attached to the pointer.
16. Move the pointer and place the angled dimension.

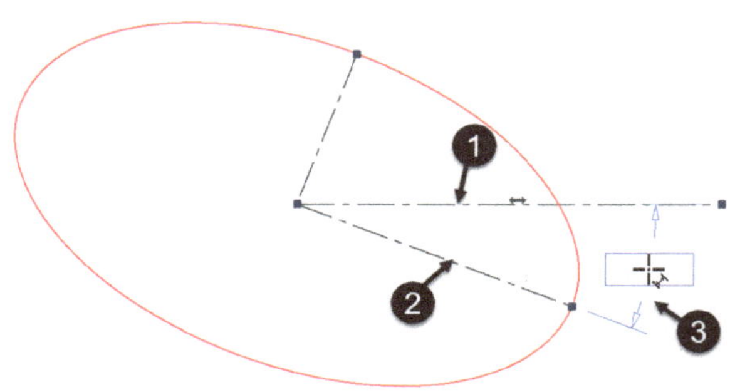

17. Type 15 and click **OK**.
18. Select the refeence line along the major axis.
19. Move the pointer in the direction perpendicular to the selected line.
20. Click when the dimension is aligned to the selected line is displayed.

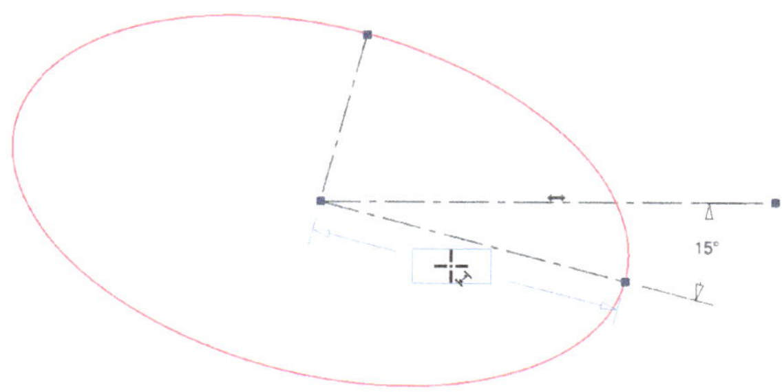

21. Type-in the dimension value and press ENTER.
22. Select the reference line along the minor axis.
23. Move the pointer and click when an aligned dimension is displayed.

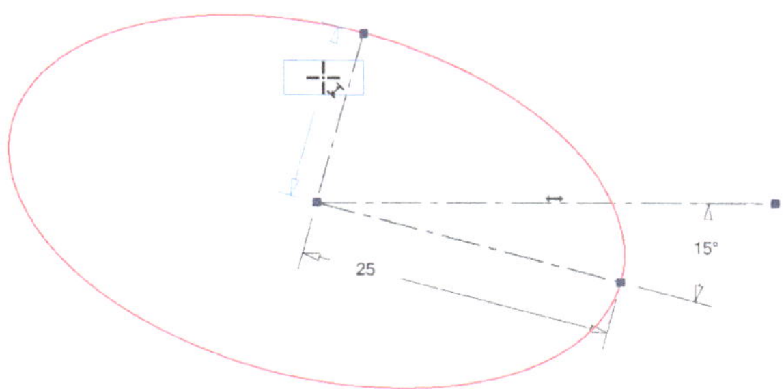

24. Type-ine the dimension value and press ENTER.

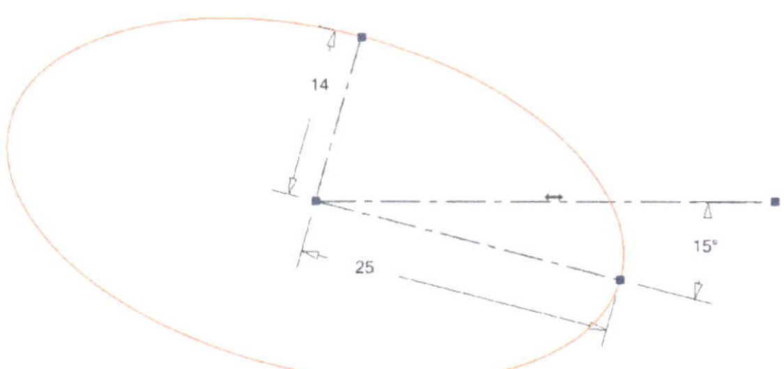

25. Add horizontal and vertical dimensions between the center point of the ellipse and the sketch origin. This fully-defines the sketch.

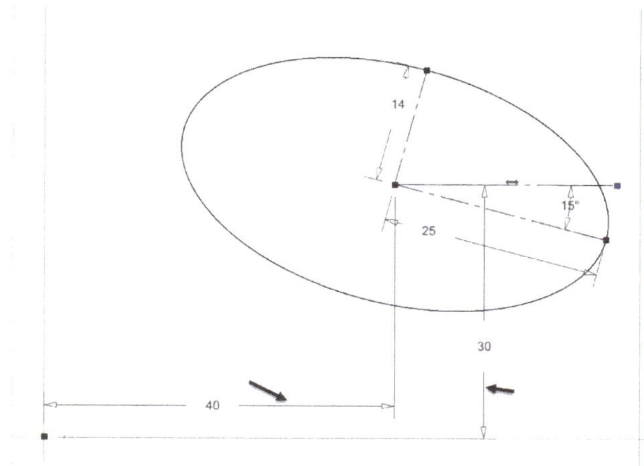

Extend

The **Extend** tool is used to extend lines, arcs, and other open entities to connect to other objects.

1. Create a sketch, as shown below.

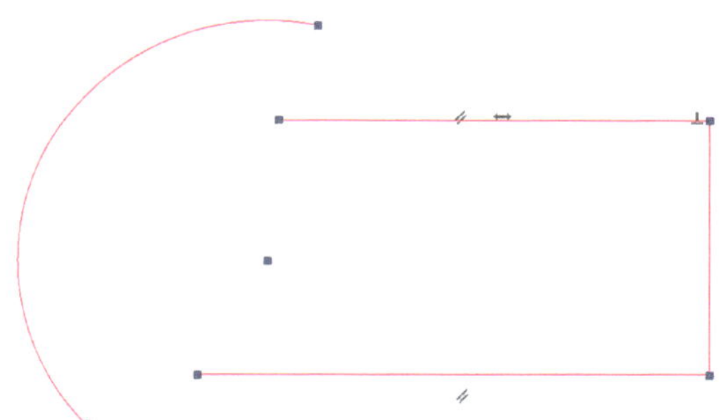

2. Click **2D Sketch > Sketch Tools > Extend** on the ribbon.

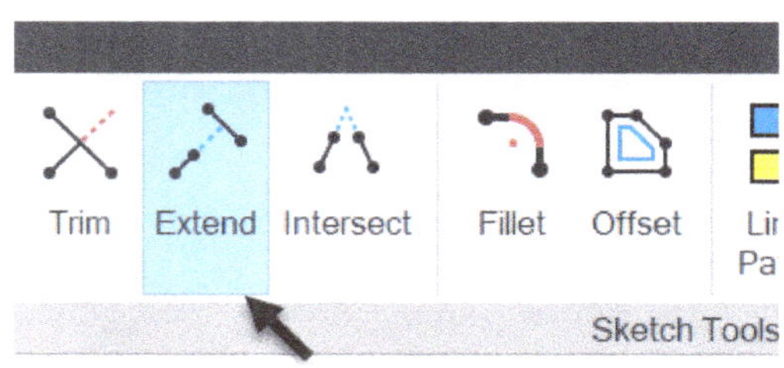

3. Select the horizontal open line. This will extend the line up to arc.

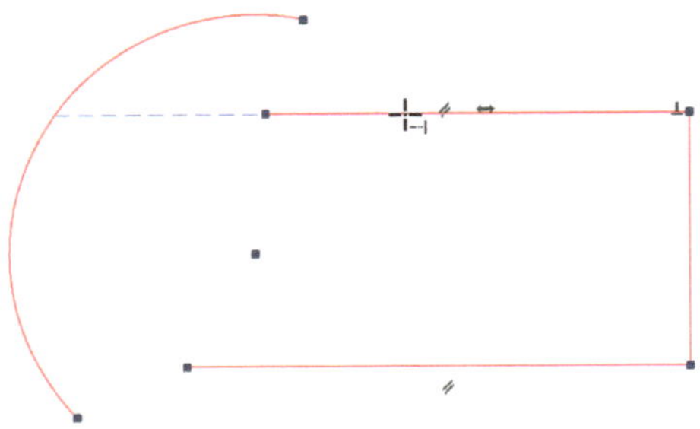

Likewise, extend the other elements, as shown.

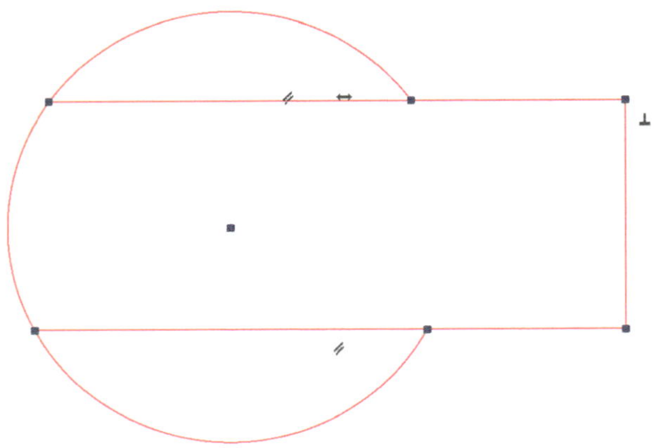

Trim

This tool trims the end of an element back to the intersection of another element.

1. Click **2D Sketch > Sketch Tools > Trim** on the ribbon.

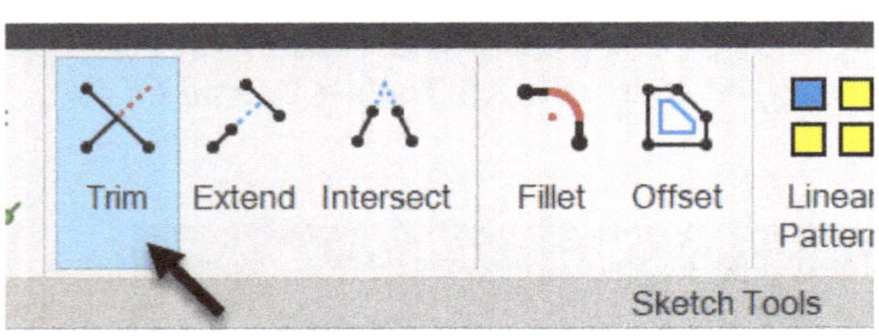

2. Select the element or elements to trim, as shown.

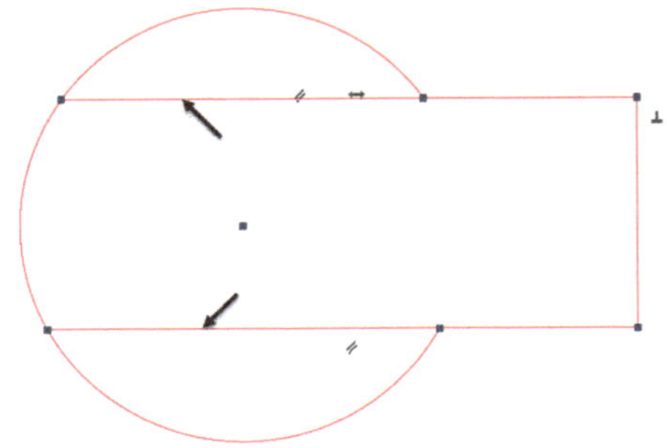

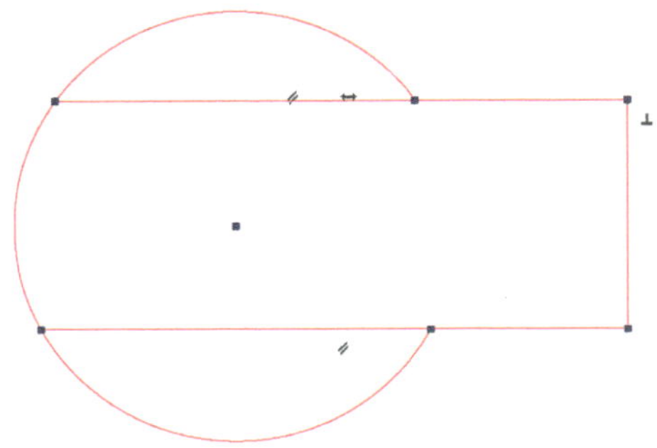

Offset

The **Offset Entities** tool creates parallel copies of lines, circles, and arcs.

1. Click **2D Sketch > Sketch Tools > Offset** on the ribbon.
2. Right-click on anyone of the connected entities, and then select **Chain Select**. Notice that all the connected entities are selected.

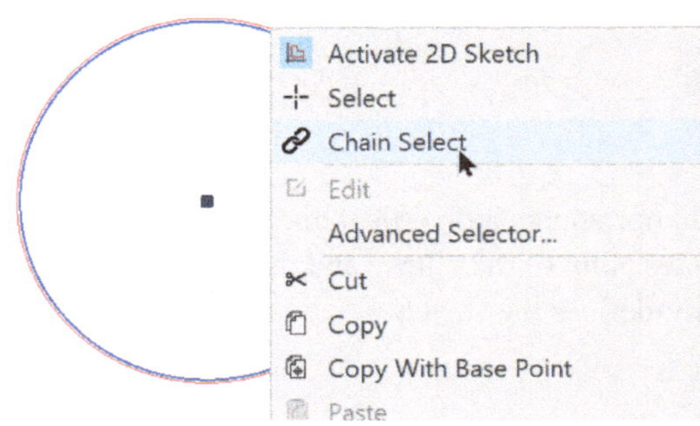

3. Type-in a value in the **Distance** box on the **Offset** dialog.
4. Check/uncheck the **Flip direction** option to define the offset side.

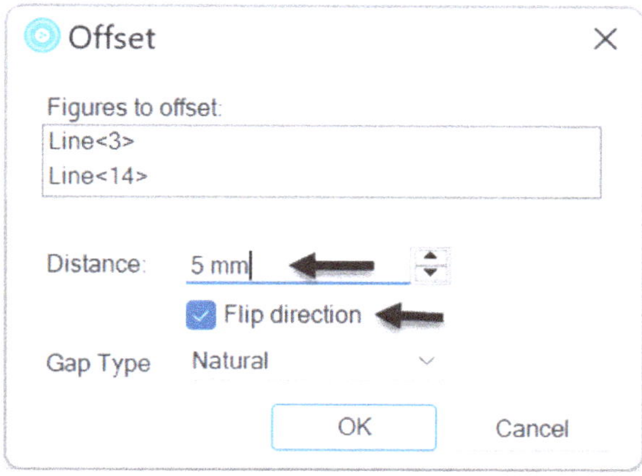

5. Select **Gap Type > Round** the corners of the offset figure are rounded.

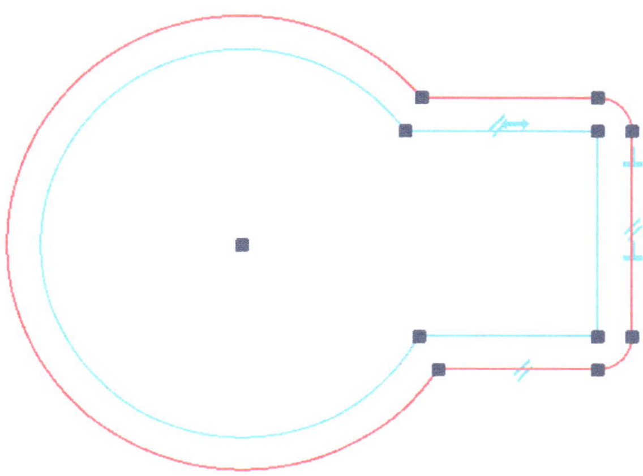

Intersect

This tool trims and extends elements to form a corner.

1. Click **2D Sketch > Sketch Tools > Intersect** on the ribbon.

2. Select two intersecting elements. The elements will be trimmed and extended to form a closed corner.

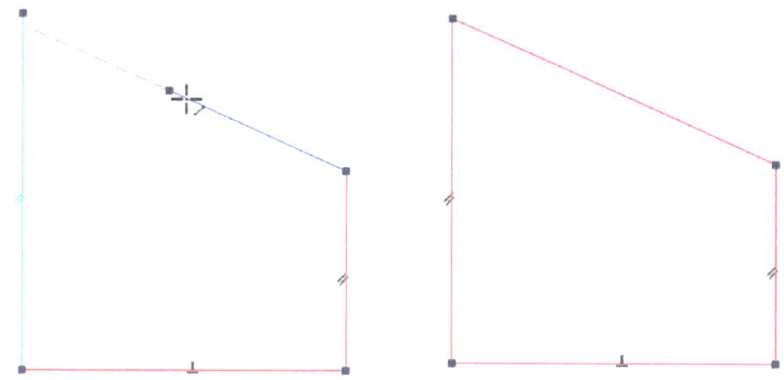

Circular Sketch Pattern

The **Circular Sketch Pattern** tool creates an arrangement of objects around a point in circular form.

1. Create two concentric circles of 140 and 50 diameters.

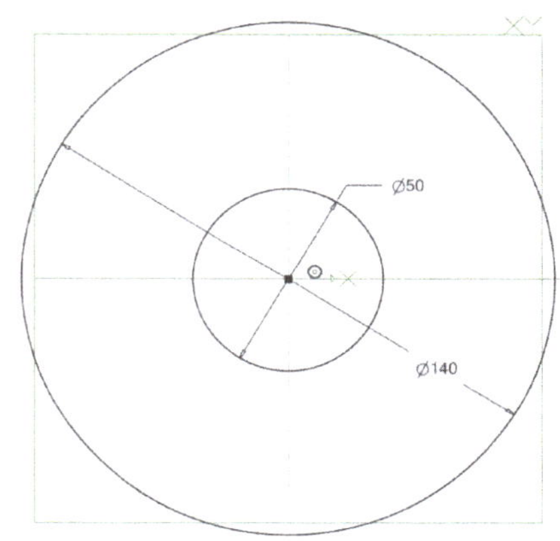

2. On the ribbon, click **2D Sketch > Sketch Figures > Arc**.
3. Move your pointer to the quadrant location on the circle. Click when you see a dotted line extending from the center of the circle.

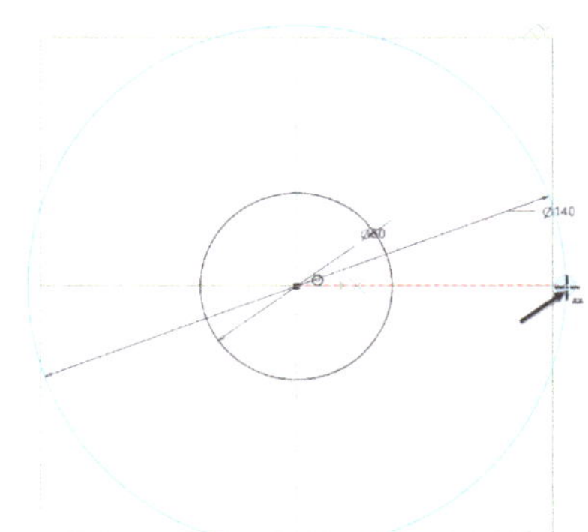

4. Move the pointer down and click on the circle.

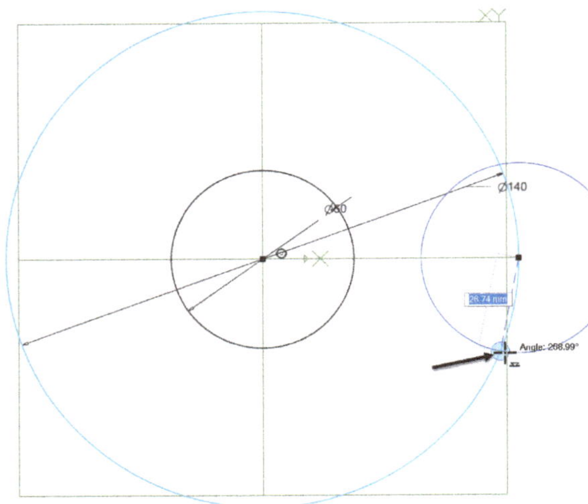

5. Move the pointer leftwards and up.
6. Click on the circle when the Coincident symbol appears.

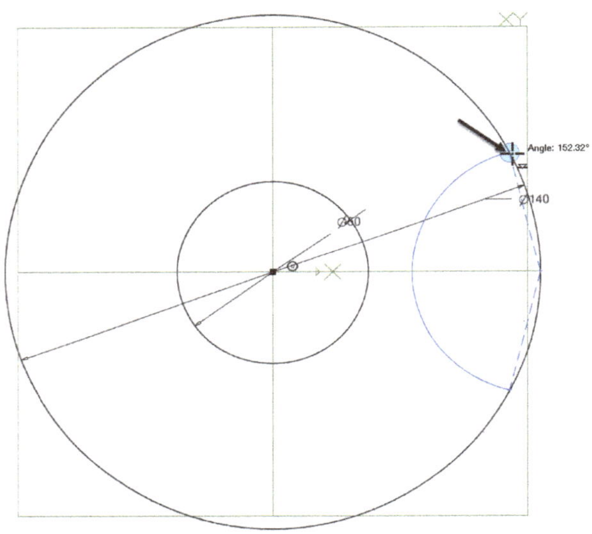

7. Dimension the arc with radius 30.

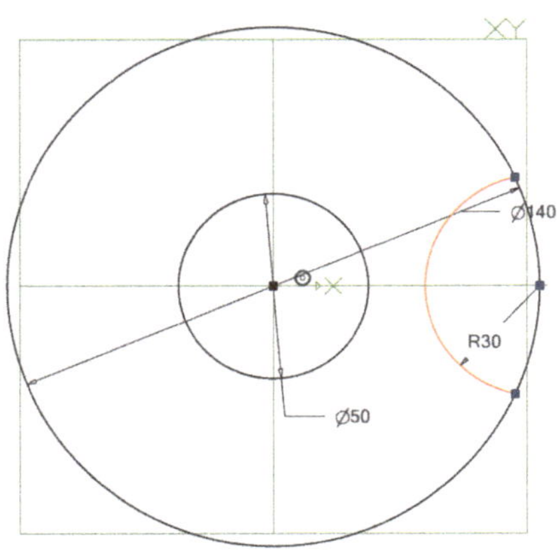

8. On the ribbon, click **2D Sketch > Sketch Tools > Circular Sketch Pattern**.
9. Select the arc.
10. Type **4** in the **Instances** box.
11. Select the **Complete Revolution**  option from the **Angle** section.
12. Click in the **Center** selection box, and select the center point of the circles.The preview of the circular pattern appears as the center of the pattern is selected automatically.

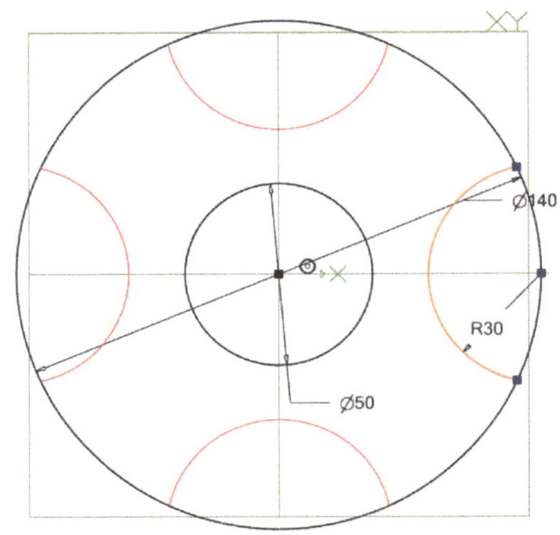

13. Click **OK**.
14. Trim the unwanted portions, as shown below.

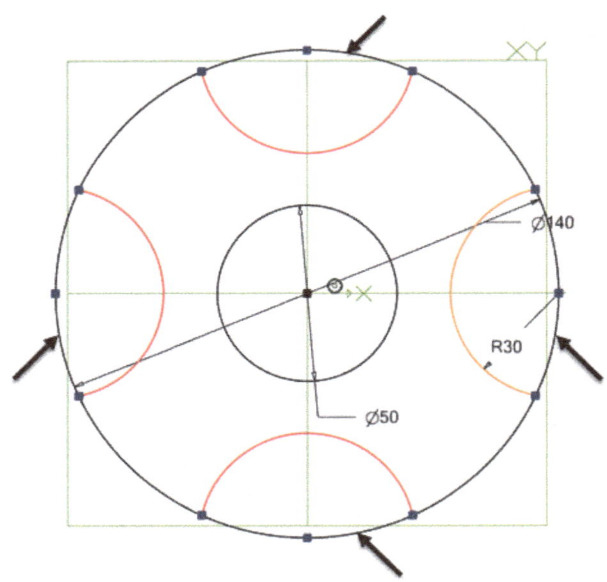

15. Click **2D Sketch > Sketch Constraints > Equal Constraint** on the ribbon.
16. Select the arcs of the circular pattern in the clockwise direction.

17. Select the last and first arc.

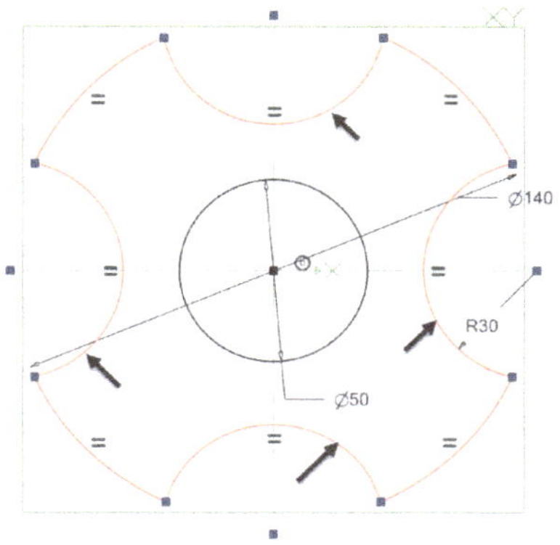

18. Make the center points of the arcs in the circular sketch pattern coincident with the corresponding peripheral arcs.

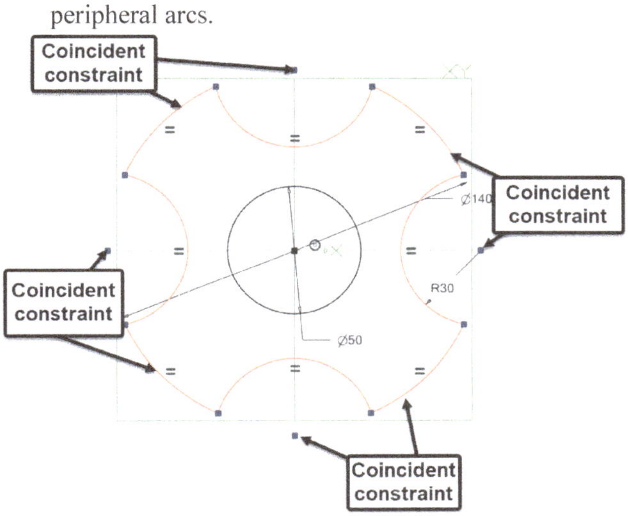

19. Click **2D Sketch > Sketch Constraints > Horizontal Constraint** on the ribbon.
20. Select the centerpoint of the right arc, centerpoint of the circle, and centerpoint of the left arc.

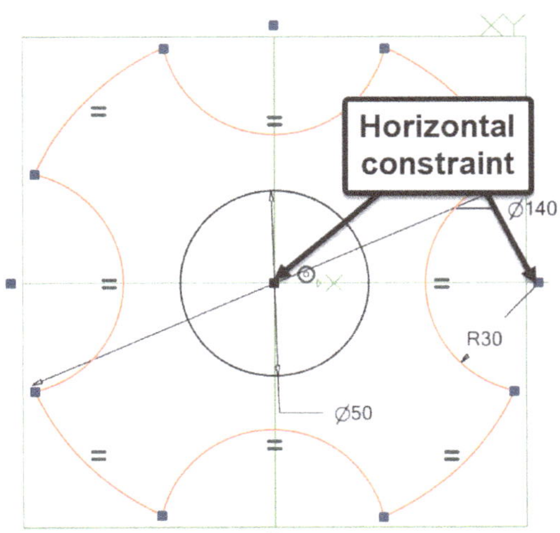

21. Click **2D Sketch > Sketch Constraints > Vertical Constraint** on the ribbon.
22. Select the centerpoint of the top arc, centerpoint of the circle, and centerpoint of the bottom arc.

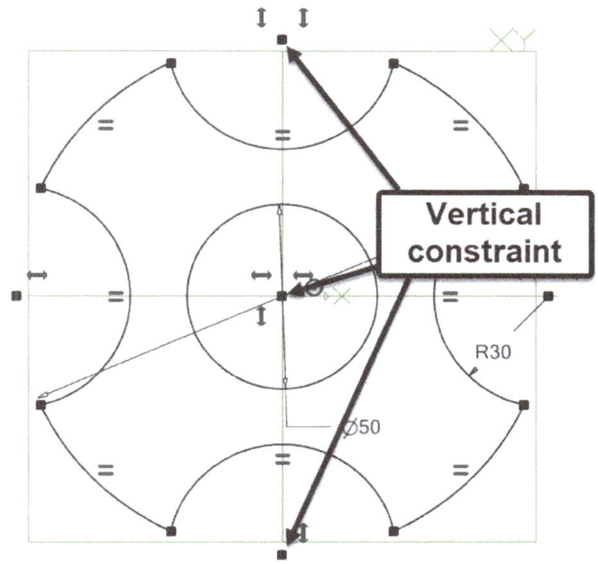

Linear Sketch Pattern

The **Linear Sketch Pattern** tool creates an arrangement of objects along a line.

1. Create two concentric circles of 80 and 50 diameters.
2. Create an inclined line, as shown.

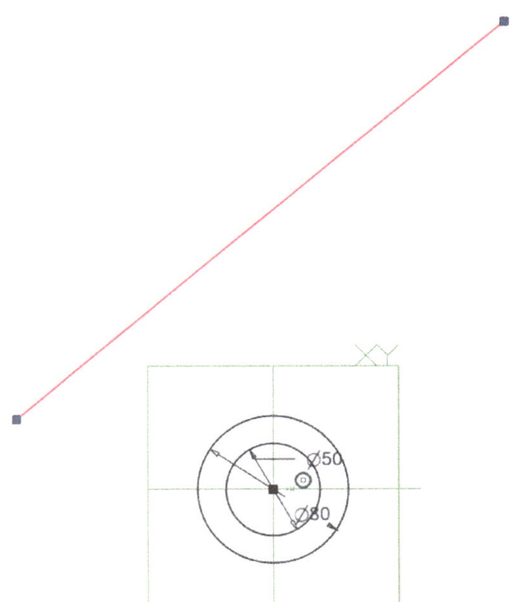

3. On the ribbon, click **2D Sketch > Sketch Tools > Linear Sketch Pattern**.

23. Select the two circles
24. On the **Linear Repeat** dialog, click in the **Linear Path** selection box and select the line.
25. Type **100** in the **Spacing** box.
26. Type **5** in the **Instances** box.
27. Click **OK** to create the linear pattern.

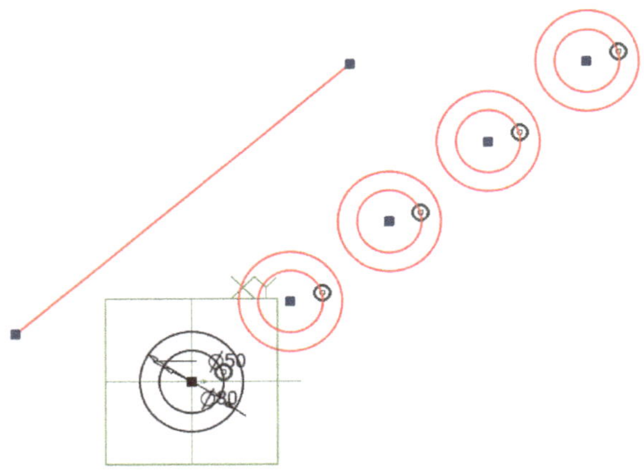

Text

Texts are used to provide information on the models, such as company name and model specifications.

1. Start a new sketch.
2. On the ribbon, click **2D Sketch > References > Reference Circle**.
3. Select the sketch origin. Next, move the pointer outward and click.
4. On the ribbon, click **2D Sketch > References > Reference Line**.
5. Select the sketch origin. Next, move the pointer vertically upward and click. Next, press ESC.
6. On the ribbon, click **2D Sketch > References > Reference Line**.
7. Select the sketch origin. Next, move the pointer toward right and click..
8. Add dimension to the reference circle, as shown.
9. Create the circle and two lines perpendicular to each other, as shown. Note that you need to check the **For Construction** option in the **Options** section of the PropertyManager while creating sketch elements.

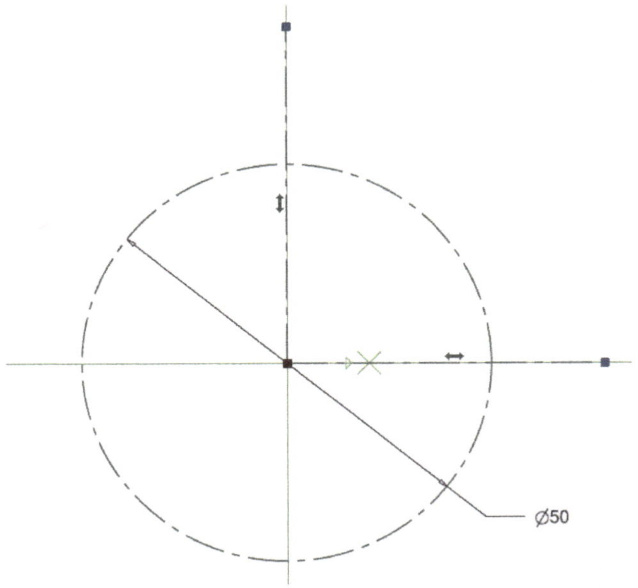

10. On the ribbon, click **2D Sketch > Sketch Figures > Sketch Text**.
11. On the **Text Figure** dialog, select **Along Path** option.
12. Select the horizontal line as the path figure.
13. Click in the Text box on the **Text Figure** dialog and type ALIBRE ATOM3D.

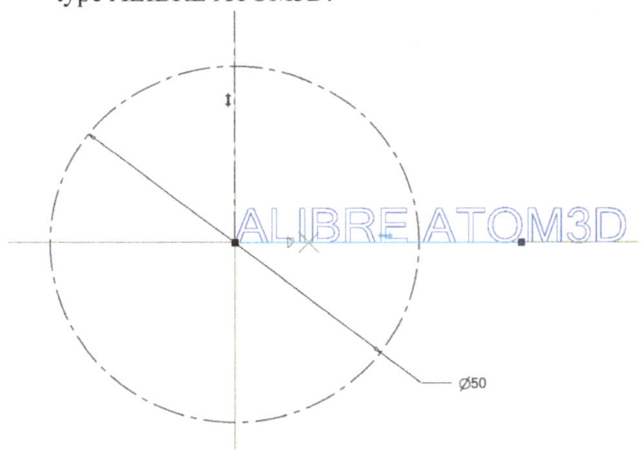

14. Click the **Font** dropdown to select and modify the typeface (such as Microsoft Sans Serif),
15. Use the Bold or Italic buttons to change the style of the font.
16. Set the **Size** to adjust font height and use **Line Spacing** for vertical spacing.
17. To adjust spacing along a path, use the **Spacing** slider and input values shown in the dialog.
18. Click the right mouse button in the **Path Figures** box and select the **Clear All** option. Next, click on the vertical reference line.

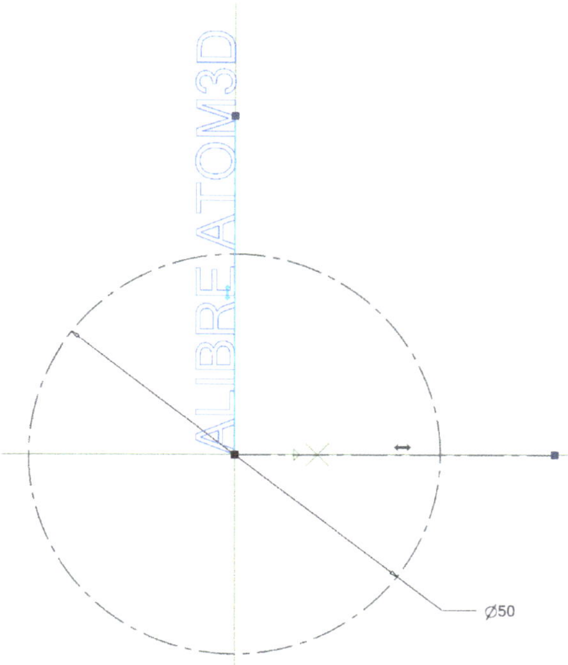

19. Right click in the **Path Figures** box and select **Clear All**.
20. Select the circle as the path figure. The text follows the circle.
21. Adjust the **Start At (percent)** slider to shift where the text starts along the path.
22. Adjust the **Spacing** slider to increase or decrease the distance between each character or segment of the text.
23. Adjust the the **Offset** slider to push the text away from or toward the reference path, changing its position.
24. Check the **Reverse Path** option to make the text flow in the opposite direction along the path.

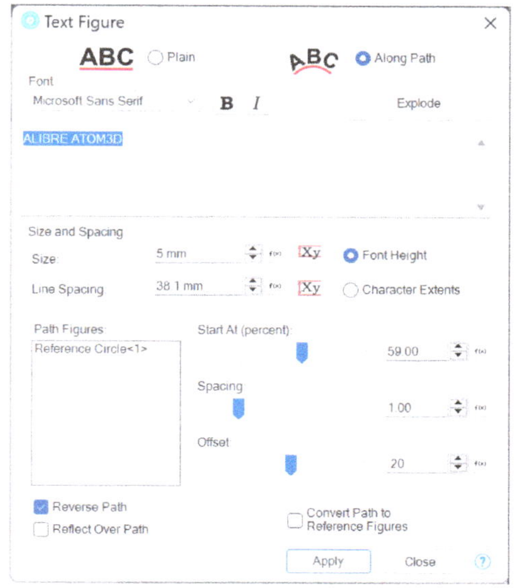

25. Click the **Apply** and **Close** on the **Text Figure** dialog.

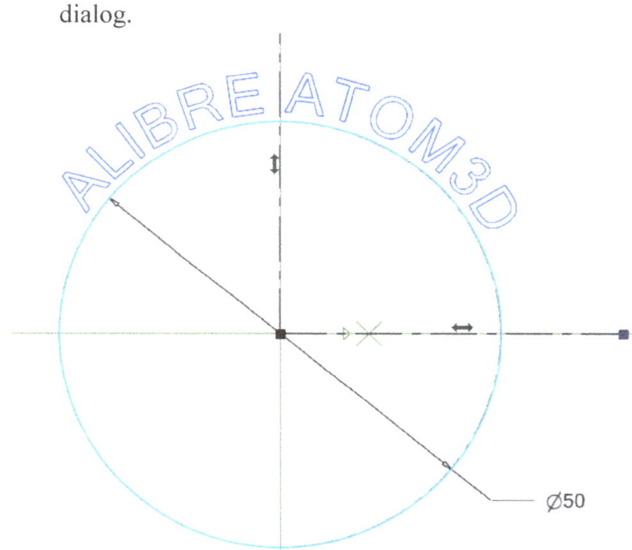

Chapter 5: Additional Modeling Tools

In this chapter, you create models using additional modeling tools. You learn to:

- Create slots
- Create circular patterns
- Create holes
- Create chamfers
- Create shells
- Create helix
- Create a loft feature
- Create a sweep feature

TUTORIAL 1

In this tutorial, you create the model shown in the figure:

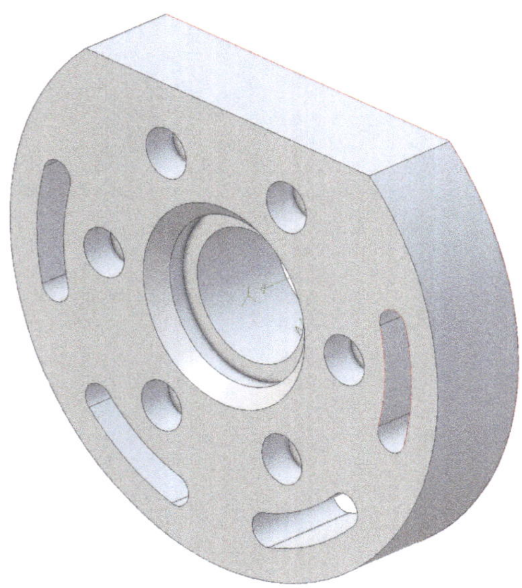

Creating the First Feature

1. Click the **Alibre Atom3D V28** icon on the Deskrop.
2. Click the **New Part** icon on the **Home** window.
3. Click **File > Properties**. This will open the **File Properties** dialog box, where you can customize various properties of the file.
4. On the **File Properties** dialog box, click the **Units > General** option at the left side.
5. Select **Unit > Inches**. This setting ensures that Alibre Atom3D uses inches.
6. Type **3** in the **Precision** box. This setting determines the number of decimal places displayed for measurements and dimensions.
7. Check the **Set current settings as default settings for parts, sheet metal, and assemblies** option.
8. Click **Apply** and **Save** to save the changes and close the **File Properties** dialog box.
9. To start a new sketch, click **Model** tab > **Sketch > Activate 2D Sketch** on the ribbon.

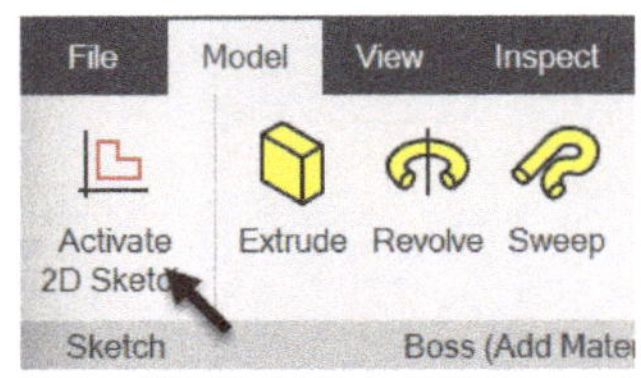

10. Select the **XY-Plane** from the Design Explorer.
11. On the ribbon, click **2D Sketch** > **Sketch Figures** > **Circle.**
12. Select the origin point of the sketch.
13. Move the pointer outward and click to create the circle.
14. On the ribbon, click **2D Sketch** > **Sketch Figures** > **Line.**
15. Specify a point at the location outside the circle, as shown.

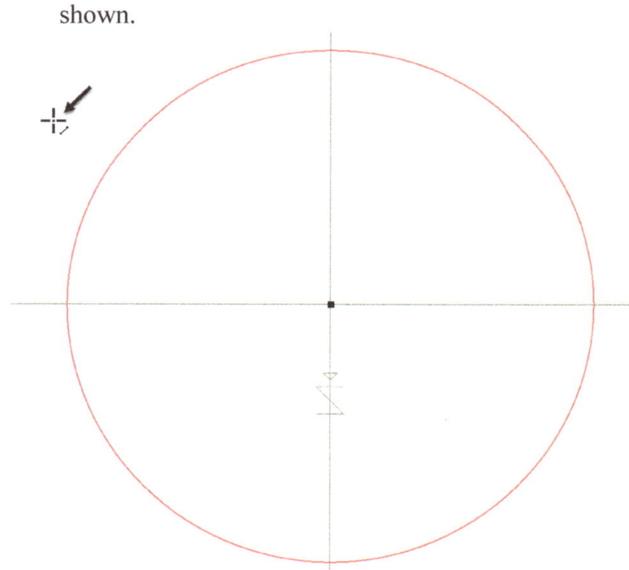

16. Move the pointer horizontally and notice the Horizontal constraint symbol.
17. Click outside the circle. Press Esc to deactivate the **Line** tool.

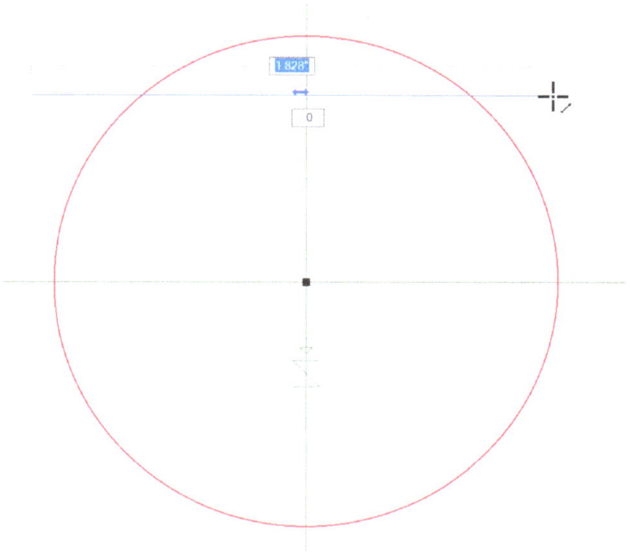

18. On the ribbon, click **2D Sketch** > **Sketch Tools** > **Trim.**
19. Click on the portions of the sketch to be trimmed, as shown below.

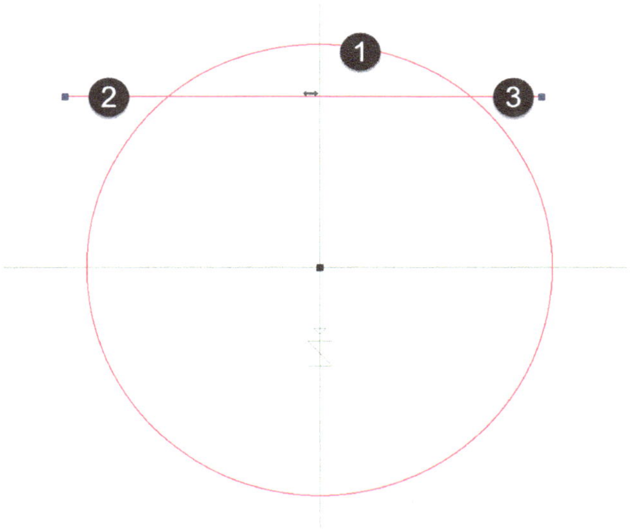

20. On the ribbon, click **2D Sketch** > **Sketch Figures** > **Dimension** .
21. Add the **Radius** and **Horizontal Distance** constraints to the sketch.

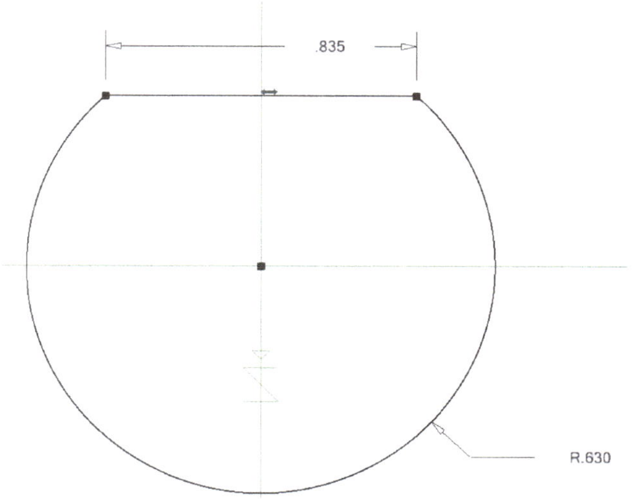

22. Click **Deactivae Sketch** on the **2D Sketch** tab of the ribbon.
23. Click **Model > Boss(Add Material) > Extrude** on the ribbon.
24. On the **Extrude Boss** dialog, select **Type > Depth**.
25. Type-in **0.236** in the **Depth** box available on the **Extrude Boss** dialog.
26. Click **OK** to create the extruded boss feature.

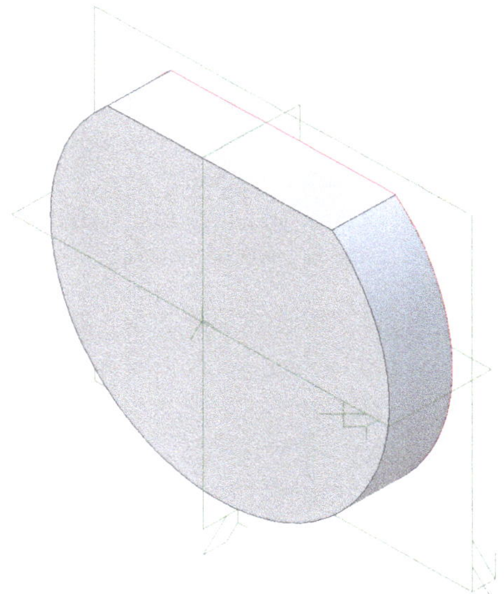

Creating the Cut feature

1. To start a new sketch, click **Model** tab > **Sketch > Activate 2D Sketch** on the ribbon.
2. Click on the front face of the model.

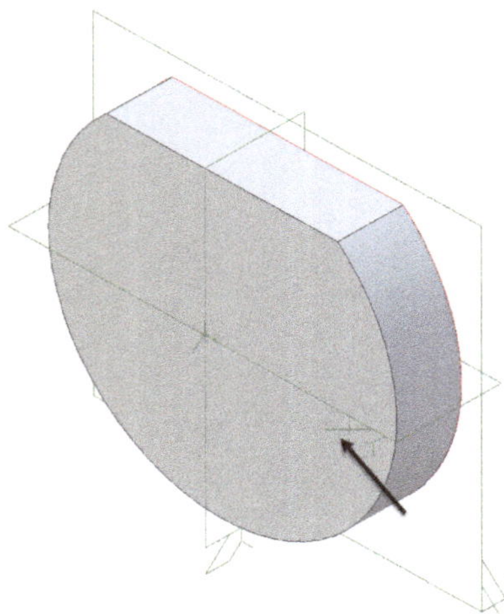

3. On the ribbon, click **2D Sketch** > **Sketch Figures** > **Slot** drop-down **> Circulat Slot – Center, Start, End Arc.**

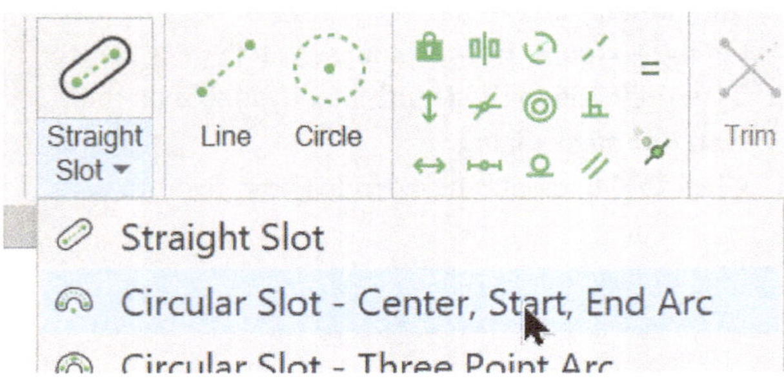

4. Select the origin as the center point.
5. Move the cursor outside and click in the first quadrant of the circle to specify the start point of the slot arc.
6. Move the cursor and click in the fourth quadrant of the circle to specify the endpoint of the slot arc.

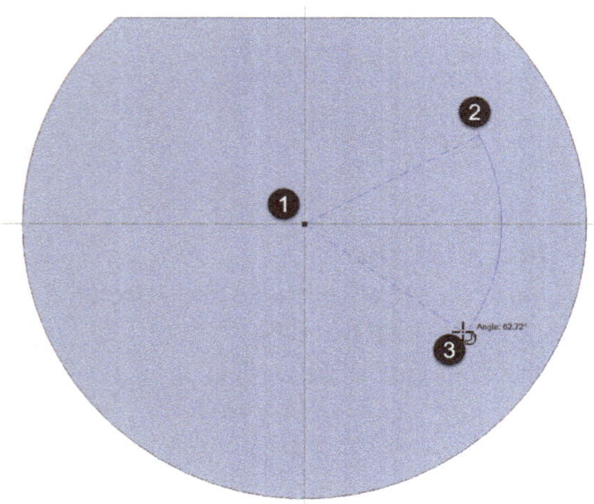

7. Move the cursor outward from the arc and click.

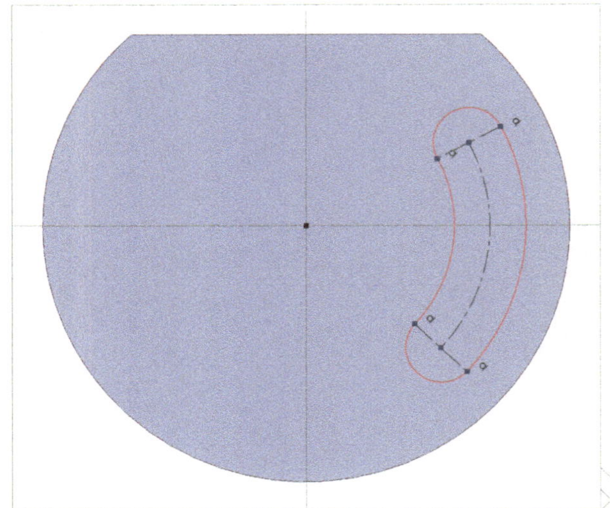

8. Click the **Dimension** button on the **Sketch Figures** panel.
9. Select the refrence line passing through the start point of the slot arc.
10. Select the refrence line passing through the endpoint of the slot arc.
11. Place the angular dimension of the slot.

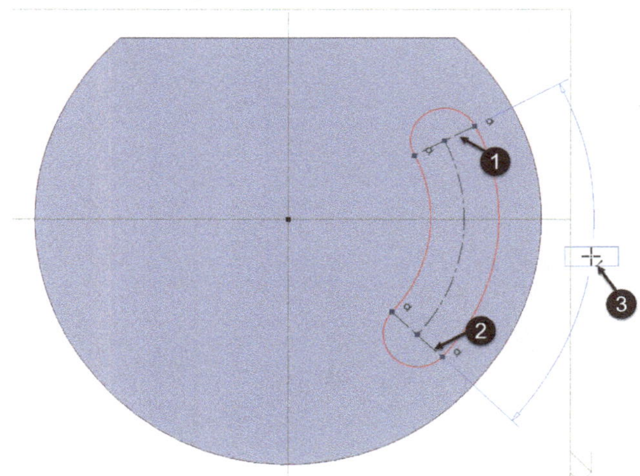

12. Enter **30** in the **Dimension** box and click the green check.

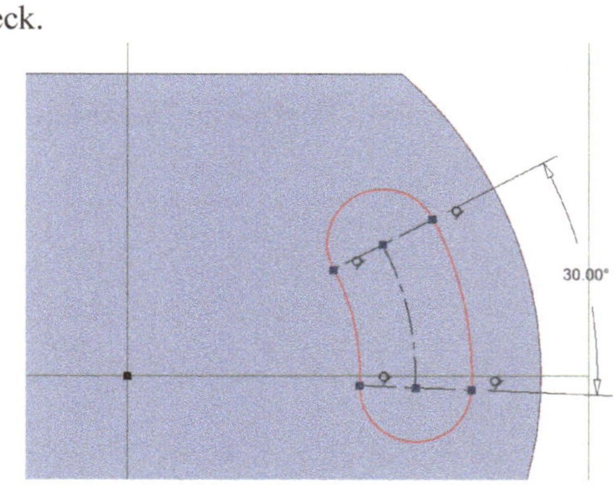

13. Click the **Line** button on the **References** panel.

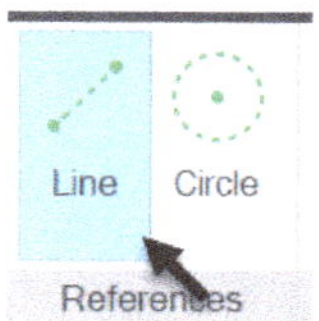

14. Draw a horizontal line passing through the origin. Press ESC.

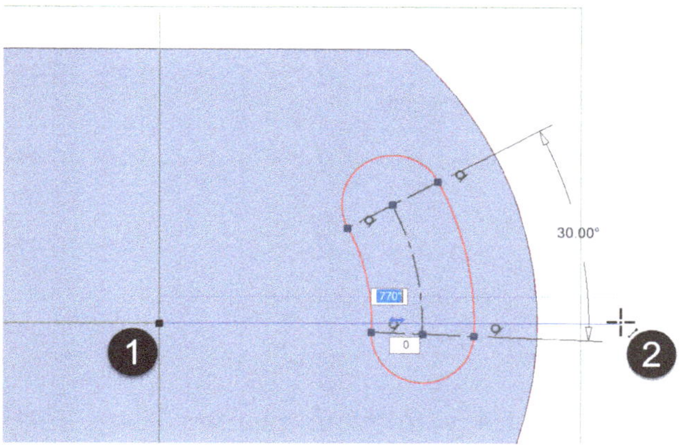

15. Click the **Symmetric Constraint** button on the **Constraints** panel.
16. Select the horizontal reference line.
17. Select the centerpoints of the end caps of the slot; the slot is made symmetric about the construction line.

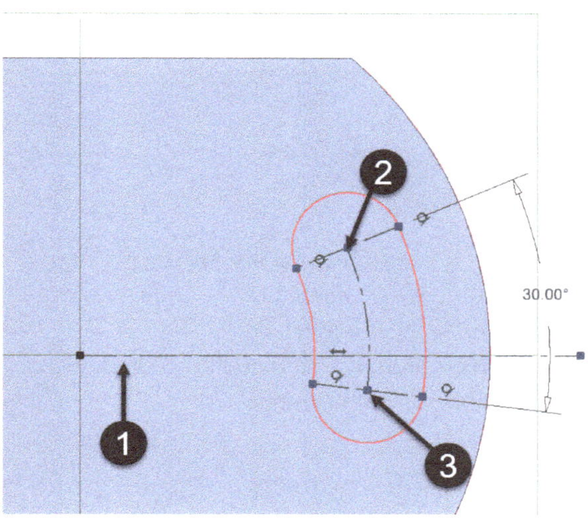

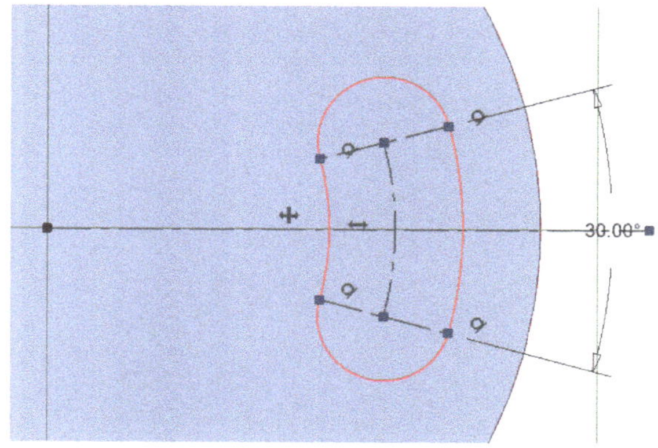

18. Apply other dimensions to the slot, as shown.

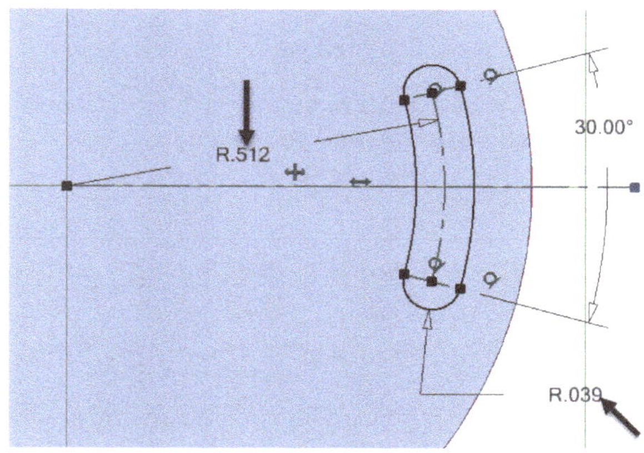

19. Click **Deactivae Sketch** on the **2D Sketch** tab of the ribbon.
20. Click **Model > Cut(Remove Material) > Extrude** on the ribbon.

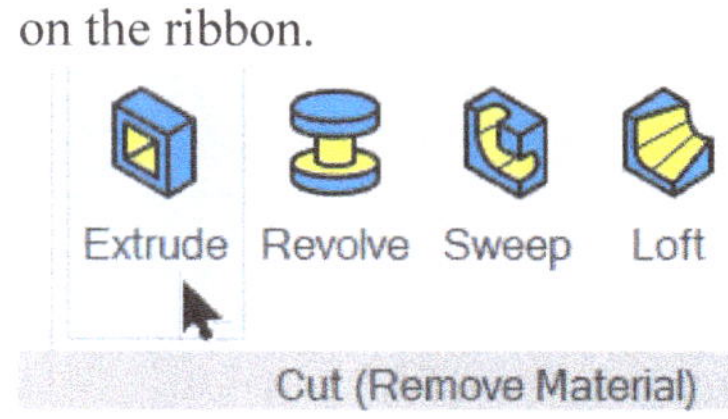

21. On the **Extrude Boss** dialog, select **Type > Through ALL**.
22. Click **OK** to create the extruded boss feature.

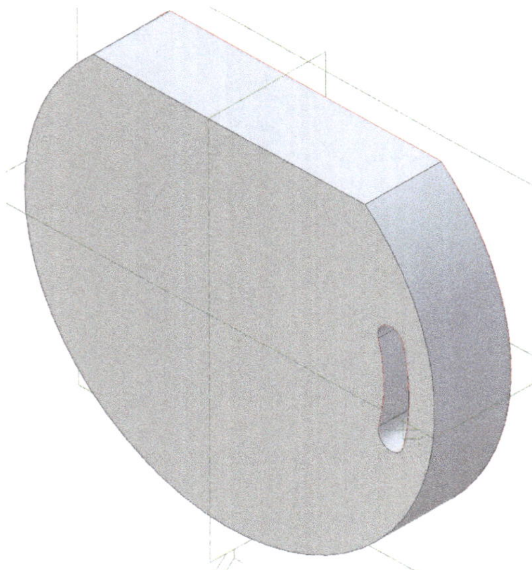

23. Click the **Circular Pattern** button on the **Part Tools** panel; the **Circular Feature Pattern** dialog appears.

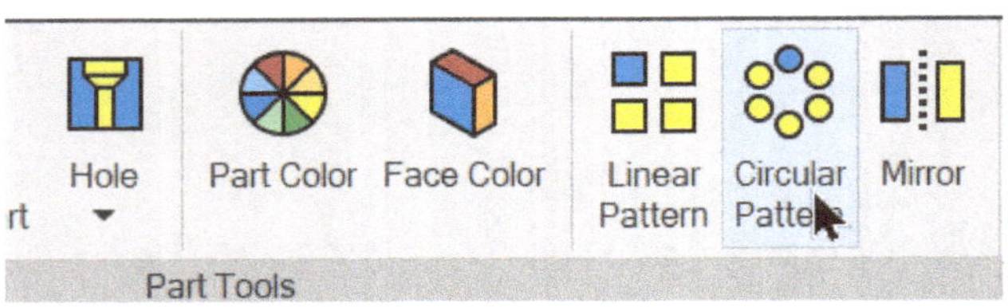

24. Select the extruded cut feature from the model.

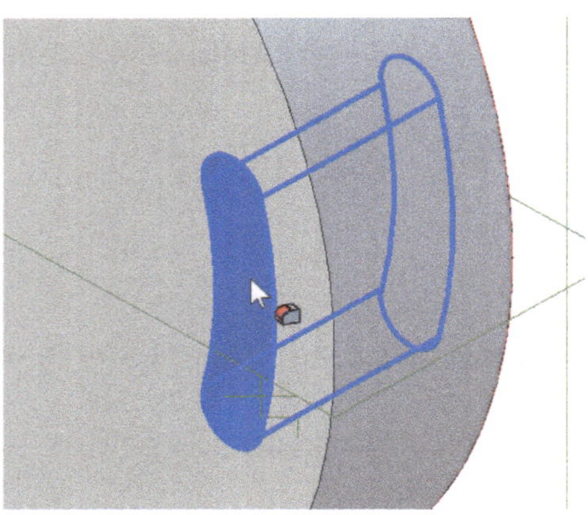

25. Click in the **Center** selection box located on the dialog.
26. Select the Z-axis from the Design Explorer.
27. Select the **Between Angle** option from the **Angle** section.
28. Enter **4** in the **Instances** box and **60** in the **Angle** box.
29. Check the **Change Direction** option.

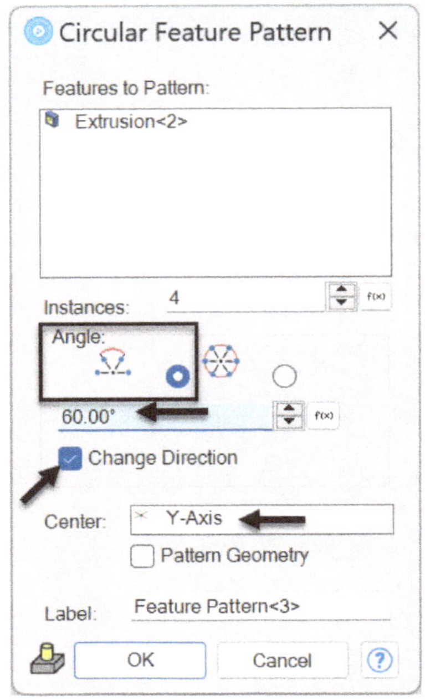

The preview of the circular pattern appears.

30. Click **OK** to create the circular pattern.

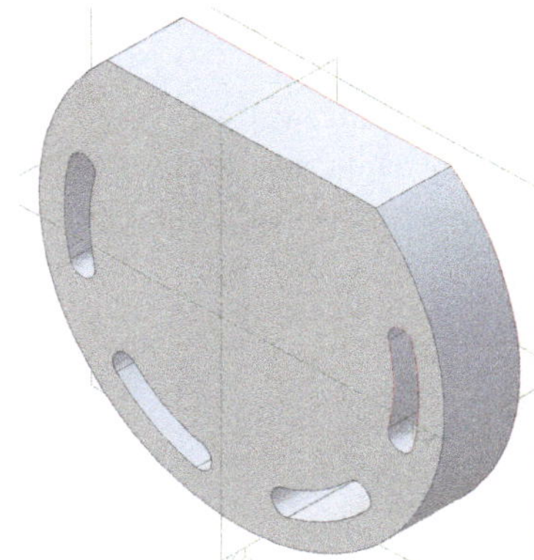

Adding the Extruded Boss feature

1. Use the **Rotate** tool available on the **View** tab of the ribbon to rotate the mimodel.
2. Click **Model > Sketch > Activate 2D Sketch**. Next, select the back face of the model.

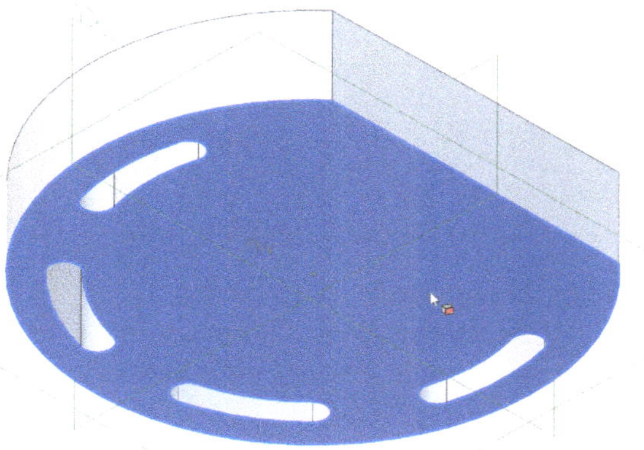

3. Create a sketch on the back face of the model.

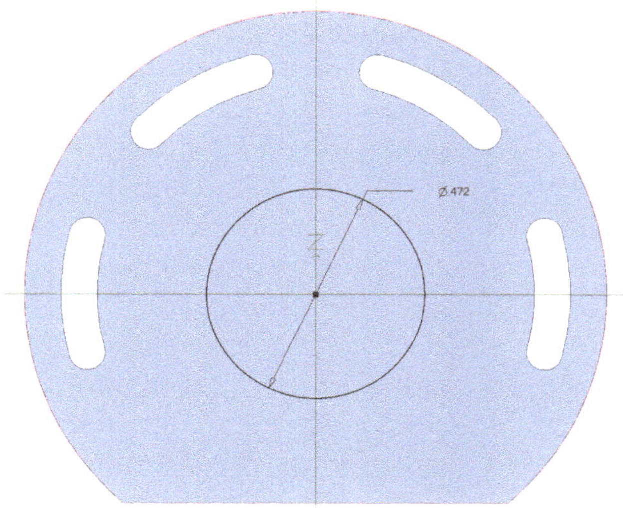

4.
5. Extrude the sketch up to **0.078** distance.

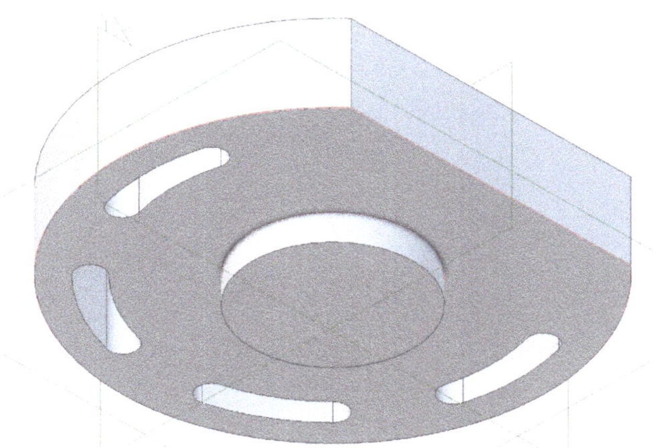

Creating a Counterbore Hole

In this section, you will create a counterbore hole concentric to the circular face.

1. Click the **Hole** button on the **Part Tools** panel.

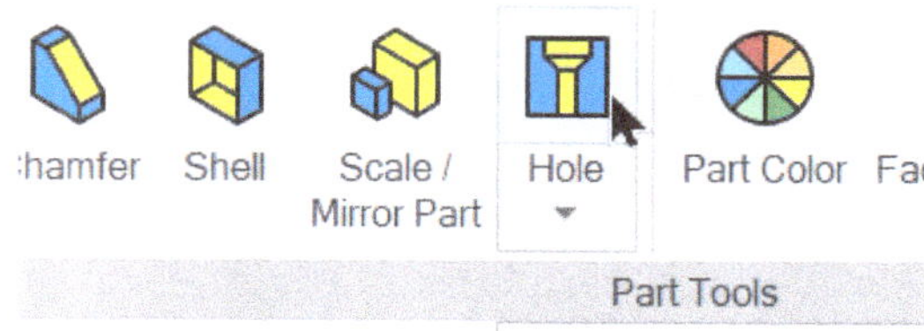

2. Click on the front face of the model.
3. Click the **Counterbore hole** icon at the top of the dialog.
4. Enter**.398** in the **Counterbore diameter** box to set the counterbore diameter.
5. Enter **.315** in the **Diameter** box to set the hole size.
6. Type **.078** in the **Counterbore depth** box to set the counterbore depth.
7. From the **Depth Condition** dropdown, select **Through All** so the hole passes through the entire part.

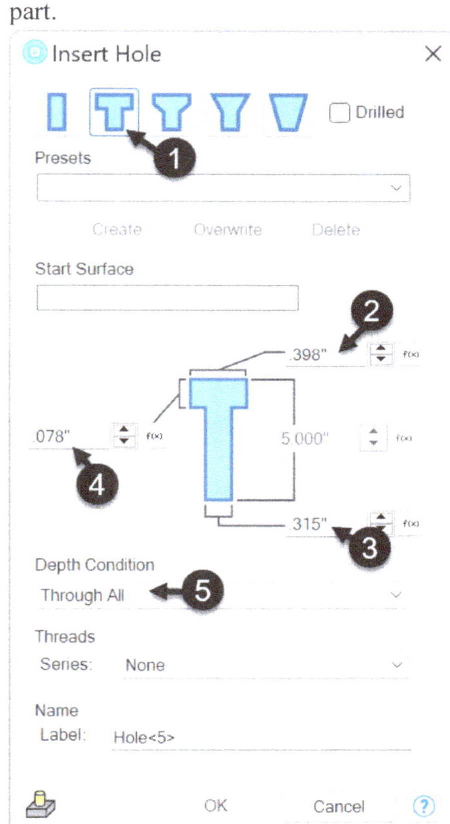

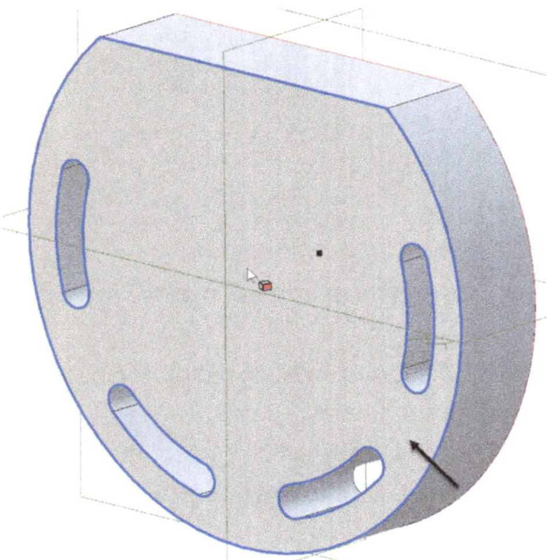

8. Select the sketch origin; the preview of the hole appears.

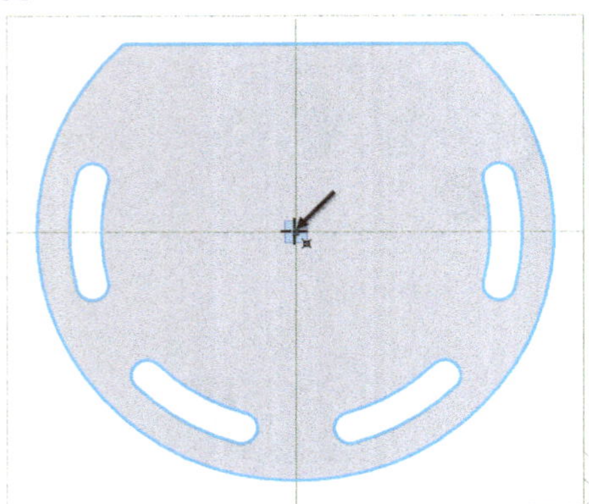

9. Click **OK** to apply your settings and create the hole.

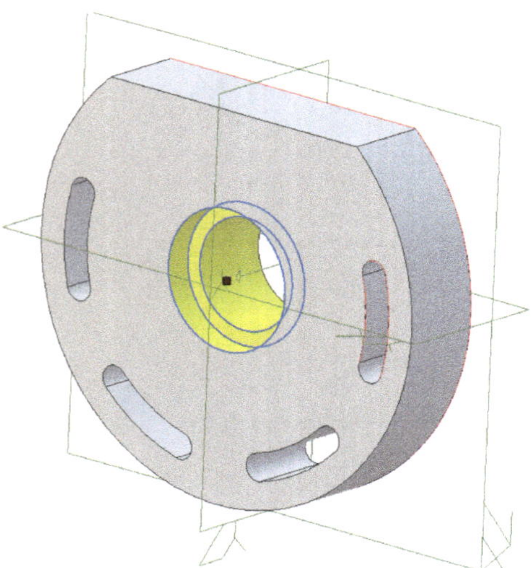

Creating a Threaded Hole

In this section, you will create a hole using a sketch point.

1. Click the **Hole** button on the **Part Tools** panel.

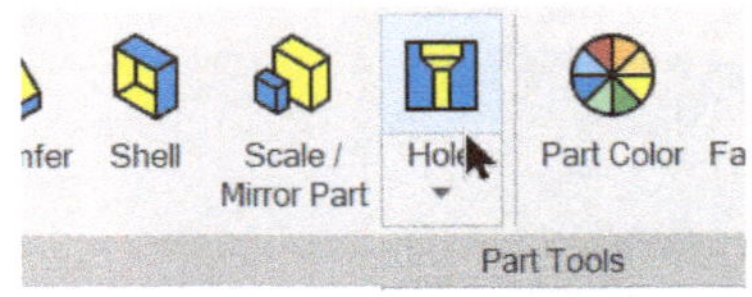

2. Click the **Counterbore**  option.
3. Select **Depth Condition > Through all**.
4. Select the **Thread > Series > ANSI Unified Coarse**.
5. Set the **Size** to **0.073**.
6. Select **Class > 2B**.
7. Set the **Type** to **1-64 UNC**.
8. Select the **Length > Hole Depth**.
9. Set the **Counterbore Diameter** to **0.118**.
10. Set the **Counterbore Depth** to **0.039**.

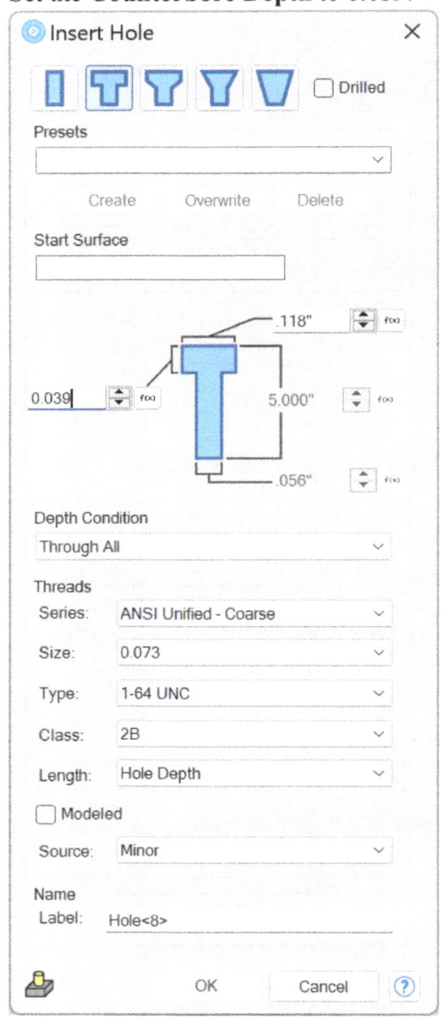

11. Select the front face of the model.

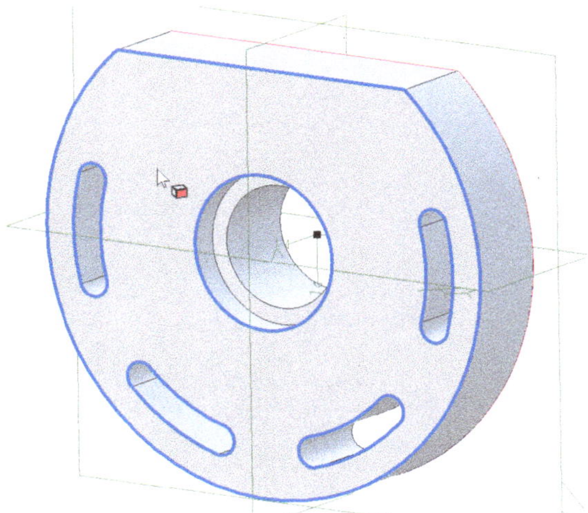

12. Click on the left side of te horizontal axis, as shown.

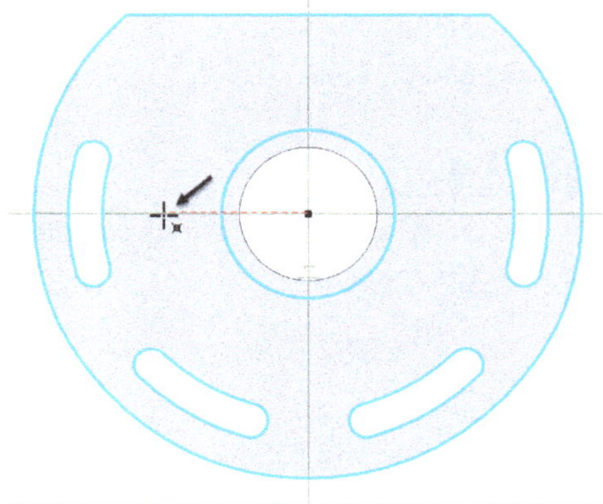

13. Click **OK** to create the hole.
14. In the Design Explorer, expand the **Hole** feature and click the right mouse button on the Sketch under it.

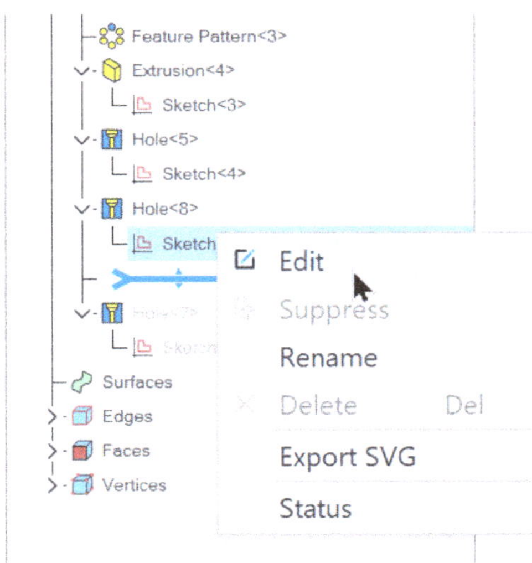

15. Click the **Horizontal Constraint** ↔ button on the **Constraints** panel.
16. Select the point and sketch origin; the point becomes horizontal to the origin.

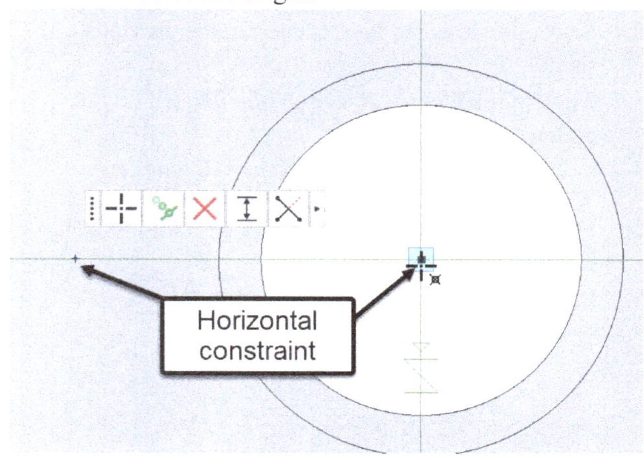

17. Create a horizontal dimension of **0.354** between point and origin.

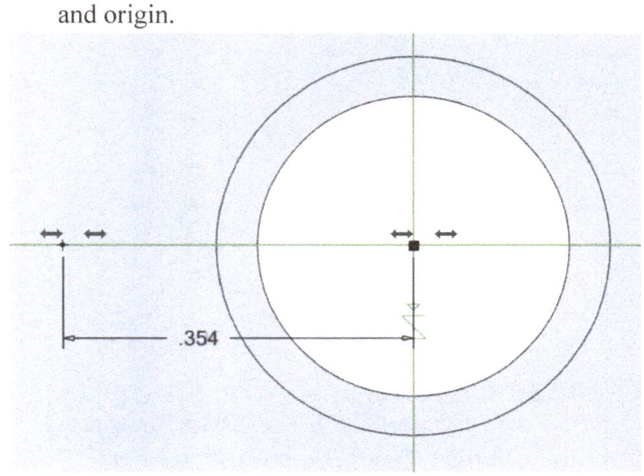

18. Click **Deactivae Sketch** on the **2D Sketch** tab of the ribbon.

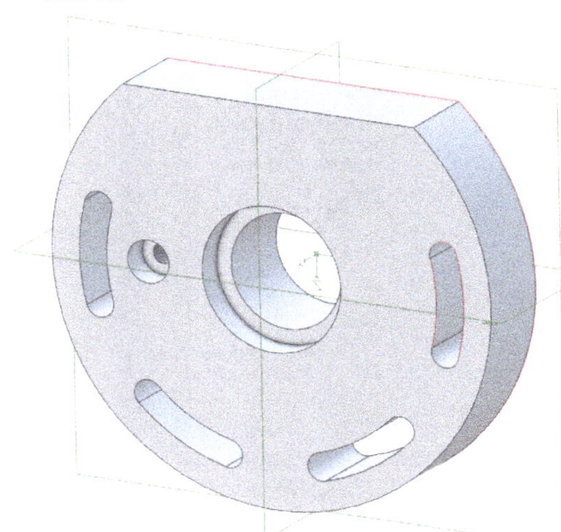

Creating a Circular Pattern

1. Click the **Circular Pattern** button on the **Part Tools** panel; the **Circular Feature Pattern** dialog appears.
2. Select the threaded hole created in the previous section.
3. Click in the **Center** selection box located on the dialog.
4. Select the outer cylindrical face of the model.
5. Select the **Complete Revolution** option from the **Angle** section.
6. Enter **6** in the **Instances** box.
7. Click **OK** to create the circular pattern.

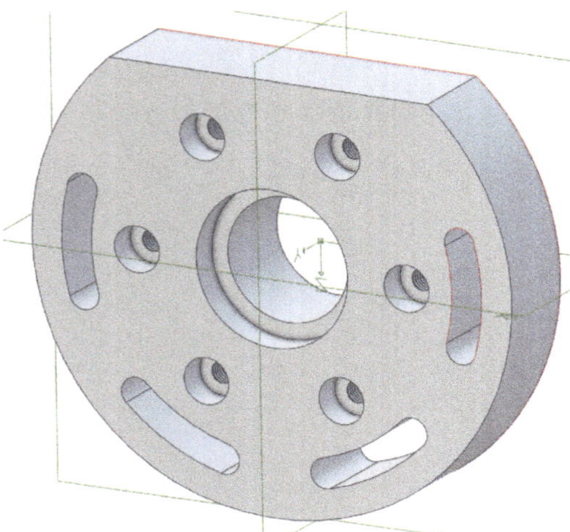

Creating Chamfers

1. Click the **Chamfer** button on the **Part Tools** panel.
2. Click **Chamfer Type** > **Equal Distance** from **Chamfer Edge** the dialog.
3. Type **0.039** in the **Distance** box.

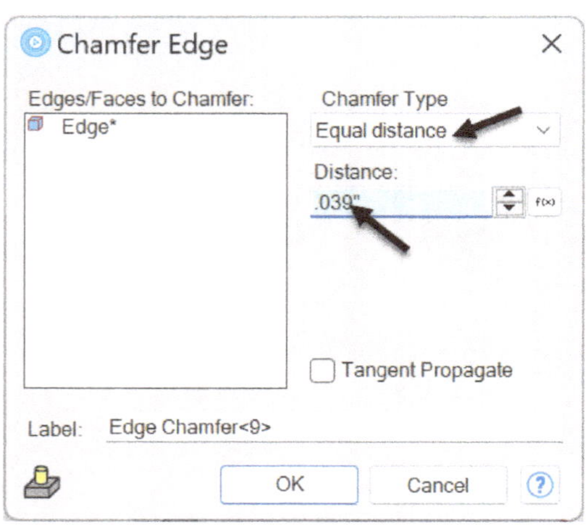

4. Select the circular edge of the counterbore hole.

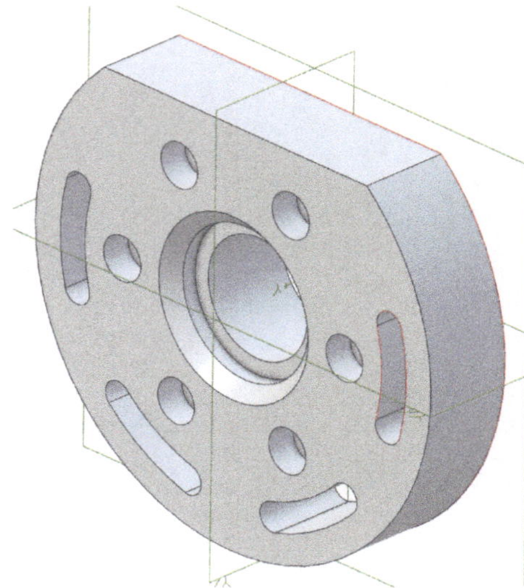

5. Click **OK** to create the chamfer.
6. Save the model and close it.

TUTORIAL 2

In this tutorial, you create a shampoo bottle using the **Loft**, **Extrude**, and **Coil** tools.

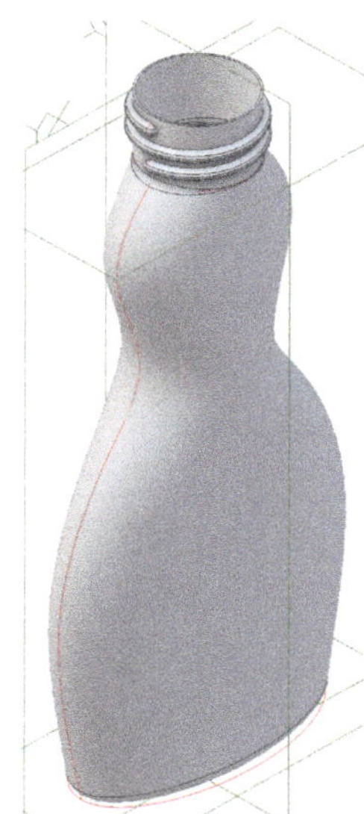

Creating the First Section and Rails

To create a swept feature, you need to create sections and guide curves.

1. Click the **Alibre Atom3D V28** icon on the Deskrop.
2. Click the **New Part** icon on the **Home** window.
3. To start a new sketch, click **Model** tab > **Sketch > Activate 2D Sketch** on the ribbon.
4. Select the **ZX-Plane** from the Design Explorer.

5. On the ribbon, click **2D Sketch** > **Sketch Figures** > **Ellipse.**
6. Draw the ellipse by selecting the points, as shown.

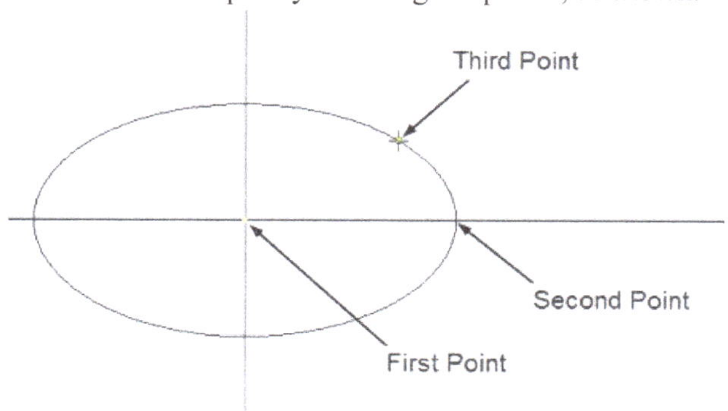

7. On the ribbon, click **2D Sketch > Sketch Figures > Dimension**.
8. Select the centerpoint of the ellipse.
9. Select the major axis point of the ellipse. Next, move the cursor downward, and click.
10. Type 1.968 and press Enter.
11. Select the ellipse.
12. Select the major axis point of the ellipse. Next, move the cursor toward left, and click.
13. Type 0.984 and press Enter.

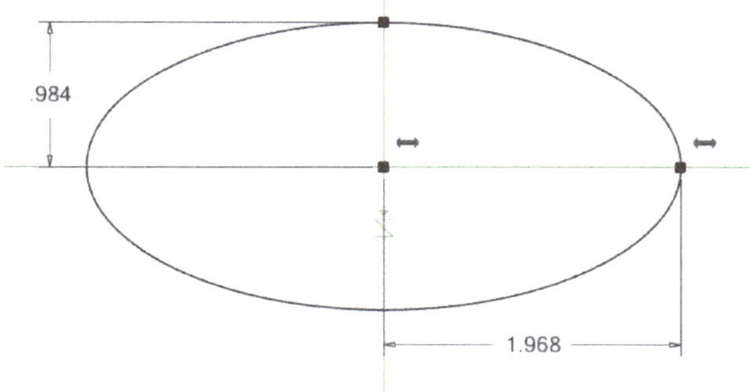

14. Click **Deactivate Sketch**.
15. To start a new sketch, click **Model** tab > **Sketch > Activate 2D Sketch** on the ribbon.
16. Select the **XY-Plane** from the Design Explorer.
17. Click **2D Sketch > Sketch Figures > Spline** on the ribbon.

18. Select a point on the horizontal axis of the sketch; a rubber band curve is attached to the cursor

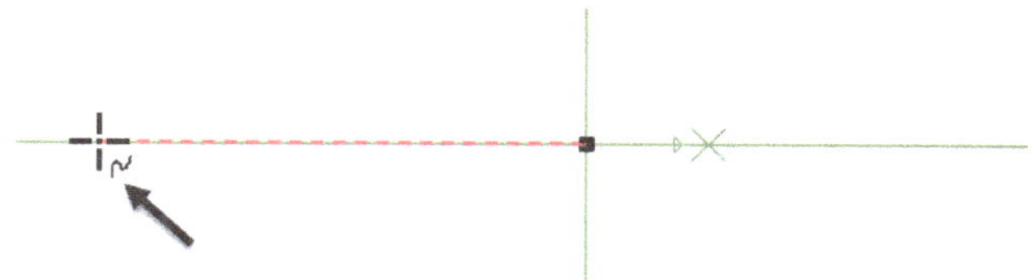

19. Move the cursor up and specify the second point of the spline; a curve is attached to the cursor.
20. Move the cursor up and specify the third point.
21. Likewise, specify the other points of the spline, as shown.
22. Click the right mouse button and select **Select**. The spline will be similar to the one shown in the figure.

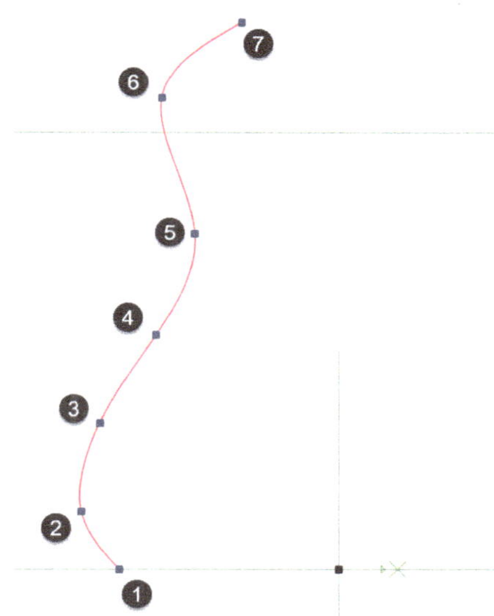

23. Right click and select **Reference Line** from the Shortcut Menu.
24. Select the origin point of the sketch, move the pointer vertically upward and click to create a vertical reference line.

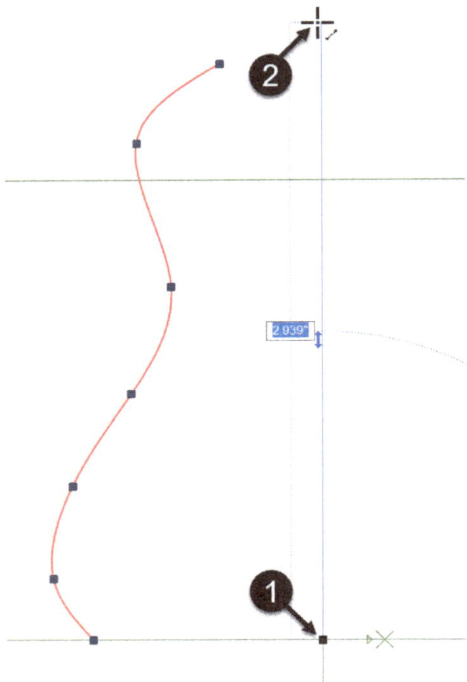

25. Right-click and select **Select**.
26. On the ribbon, click **2D Sketch > Constraints > Horizontal** .
27. Select the lower endpoints of the vertical construction line and the spline.

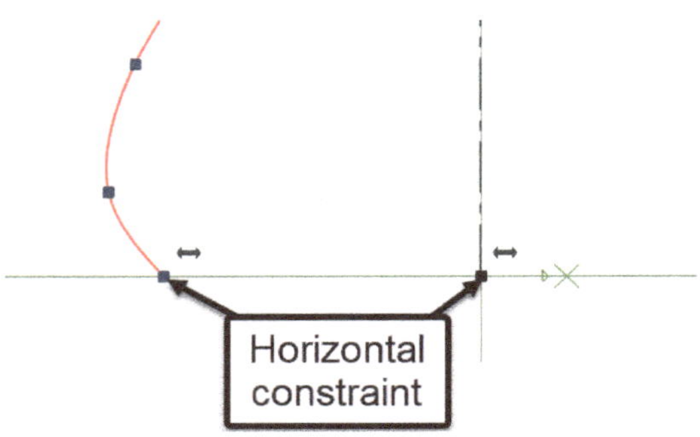

28. On the ribbon, click **2D Sketch > Sketch Figures > Dimension**.
29. Select the lower endpoints of the reference line and spline.
30. Move the cursor downward and click.
31. Type the **1.968** in the **Dimension** box and press **Enter**.

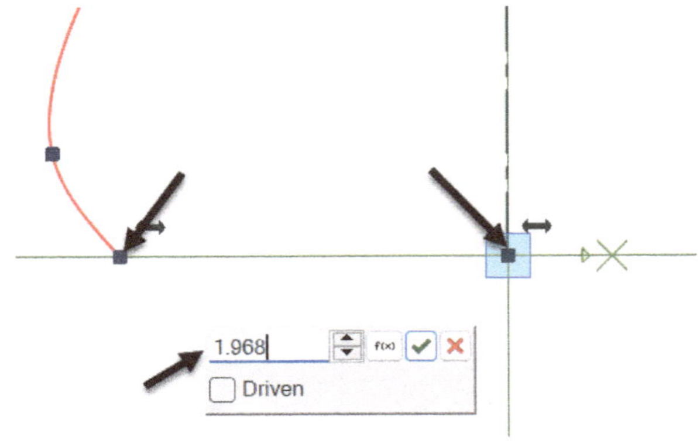

32. Select the second point of the spline and the construction line.
33. Move the cursor and click to place the dimension.
34. Type **2.362** in the **Dimension** box and press **Enter**.

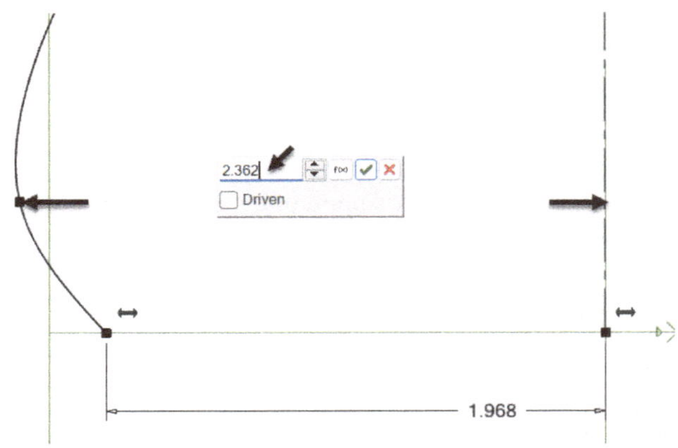

35. Apply the other horizontal dimensions to the spline, as shown in the figure.

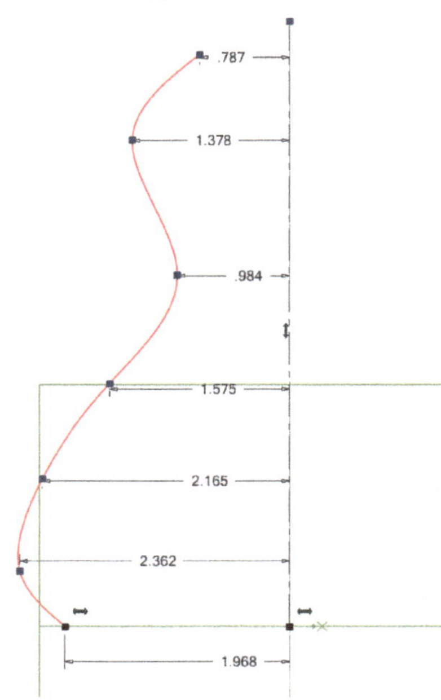

36. Select the origin point of the sketch and the top

endpoint of the spline.

37. Move the pointer toward the right and click.
38. Type **8.858** in the **Dimension** box and press Enter.

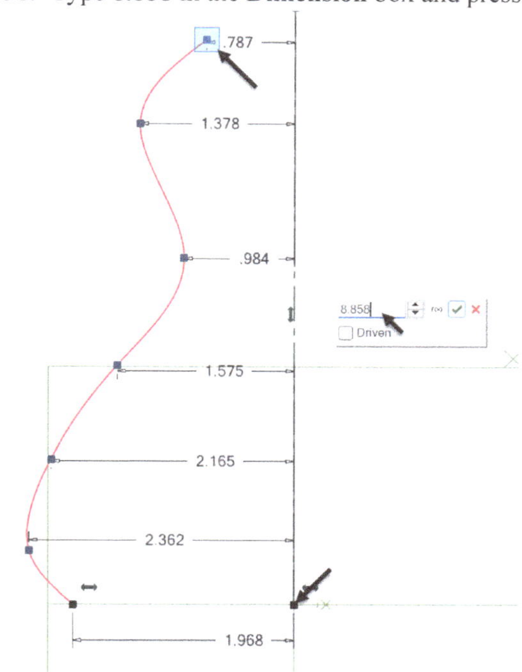

39. Likewise, create other dimensions, as shown.

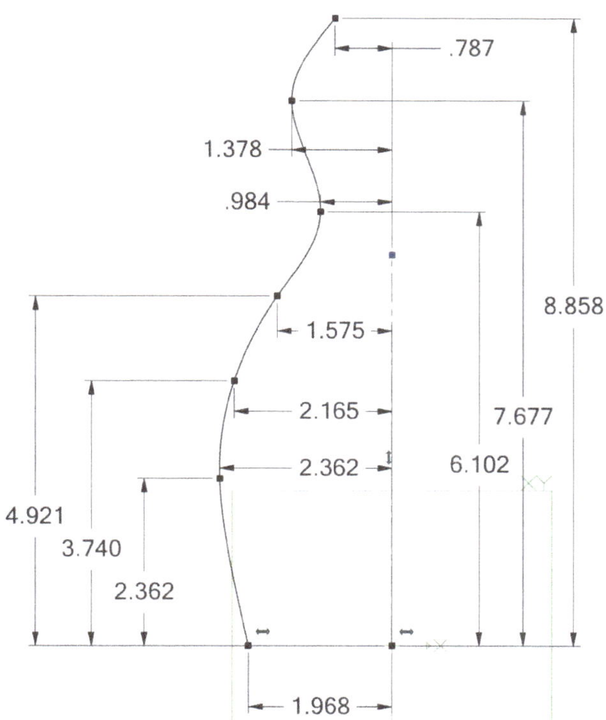

40. Click **Deactivate Sketch**.
41. Click the **Ignore** button on the **Status -Sketch Problems Detected** dialog.

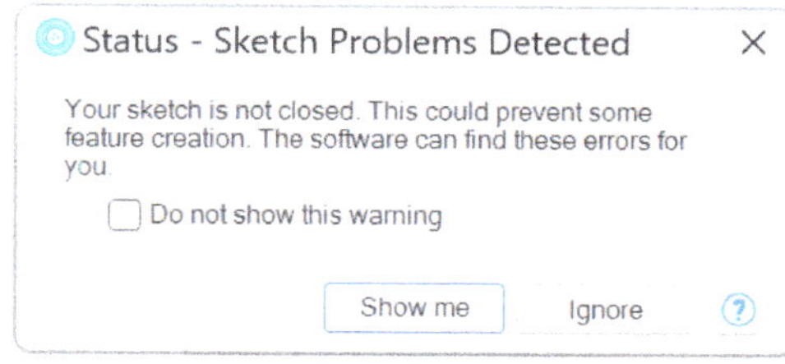

42. To start a new sketch, click **Model** tab > **Sketch > Activate 2D Sketch** on the ribbon.
43. Select the **ZX-Plane** from the Design Explorer.
44. On the ribbon, click **2D Sketch** > **Sketch Figures** > **Project to Sketch** .
45. Select the spline from the previous sketch.
46. Click **OK**.
47. On the ribbon, click **2D Sketch** > **References** > **Line**.
48. Select the origin point of the sketch, move the pointer vertically upward and click to create a vertical reference line.

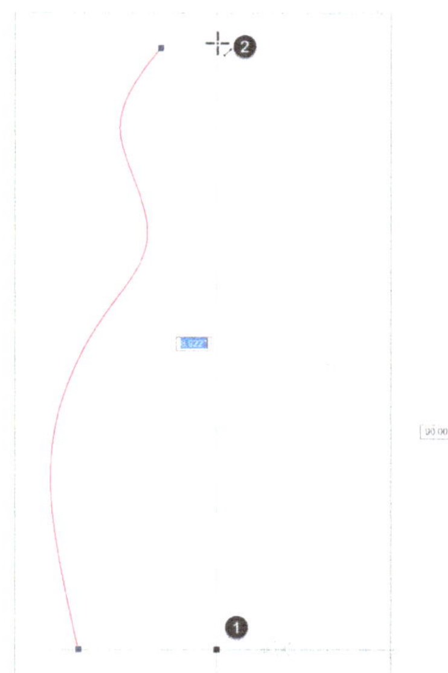

49. Click **2D Sketch > Sketch Tools > Mirror** on the ribbon; the **Mirror Figure** dialog appears.
50. Select the projected spline. Make sure that you select the curve and not the points.
51. Click in the **Mirror axis** selection box on the **Mirror** dialog, and then select the reference line.

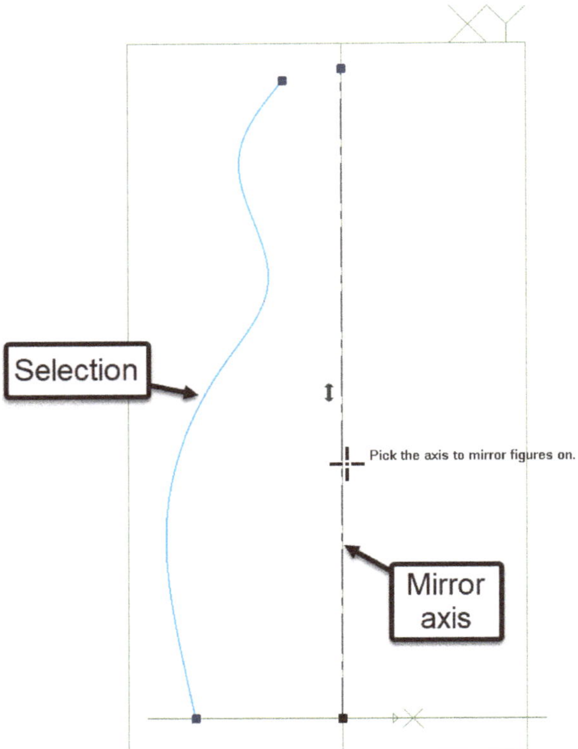

52. Click **OK**.
53. Right-click on the left spline and select **Convert to Reference Figure**.

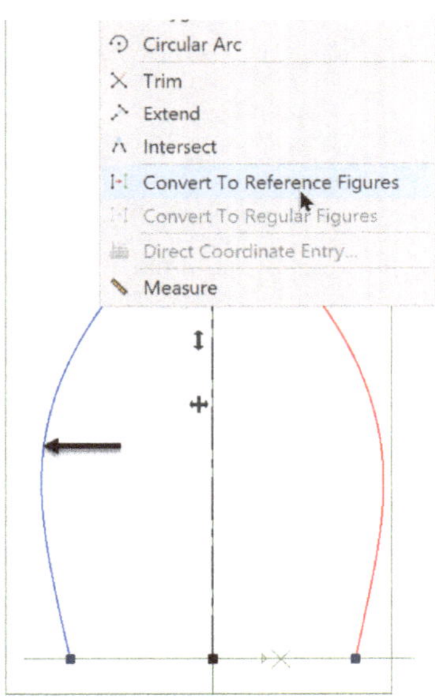

54. Click **Deactivate Sketch**.
55. Click the **Ignore** button on the **Status -Sketch Problems Detected** dialog.

Creating the second section

1. Click **Model > References > Plane** on the ribbon.

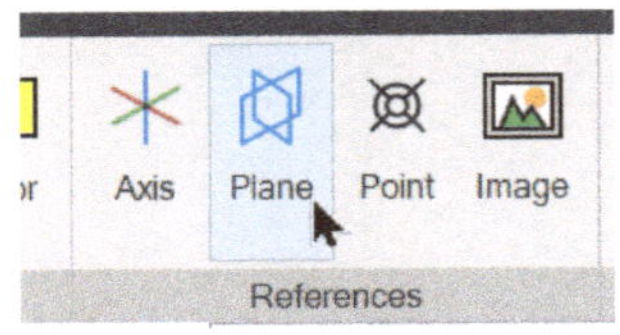

2. On the **Insert Plane** dialog, click **Creation Method** > **Offset Plane/Face**.
3. Select the ZX plane from the Design Explorer.
4. Enter **8.858** in the **Distance** box.

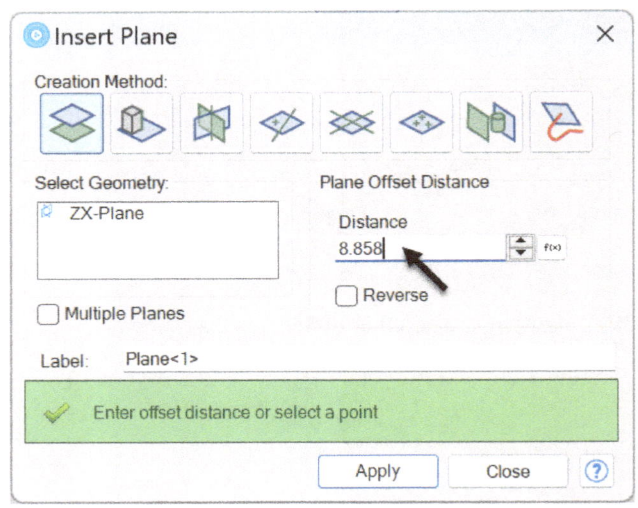

5. Click **Apply** and **Close**.
6. On the ribbon, click the **Model > Sketch > Activate 2D Sketch**.
7. Select the newly created plane.
8. Right click and select **Circle** from the Shortcut Menu.
9. Select the origin point, move the cursor outside, and click to create a circle.
10. Right click and select **OK**.
11. Right click and select **Dimension** from the Shortcut Menu.
12. Select the circle, move the cursor outward, and click.
13. Type **1.574** and press Enter.

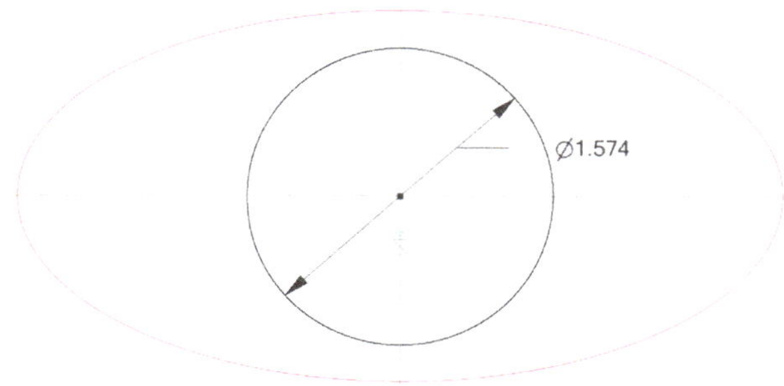

14. Click **Deactivate Sketch** on the ribbon.

Creating the Loft feature

1. To create a loft feature, click **Model > Boss(Add Material) > Loft** on the ribbon; the **Loft Boss** dialog appears.
2. Click in the **Cross Sections** section in the **Loft Boss** dialog and select the circle.
3. Select the ellipse.

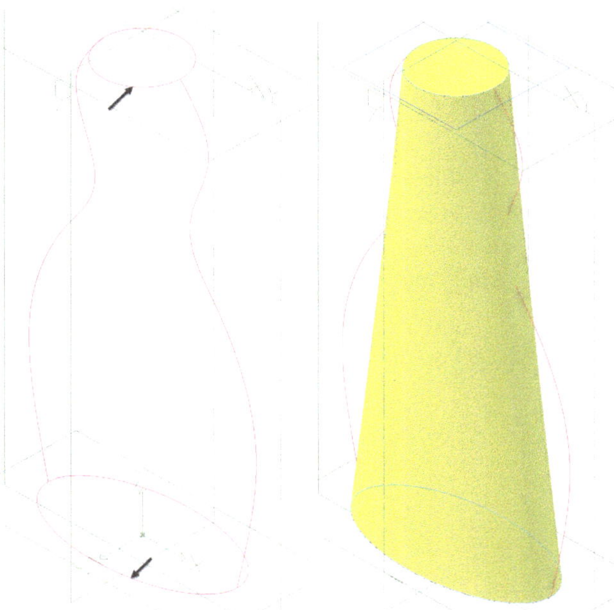

4. In the **Options** section of the dialog, select **Guides > Global**.
5. Select the first spline to define the first guide curve.
6. Select the second spline to define the second guide curve
7. Click **OK** to create the loft feature.

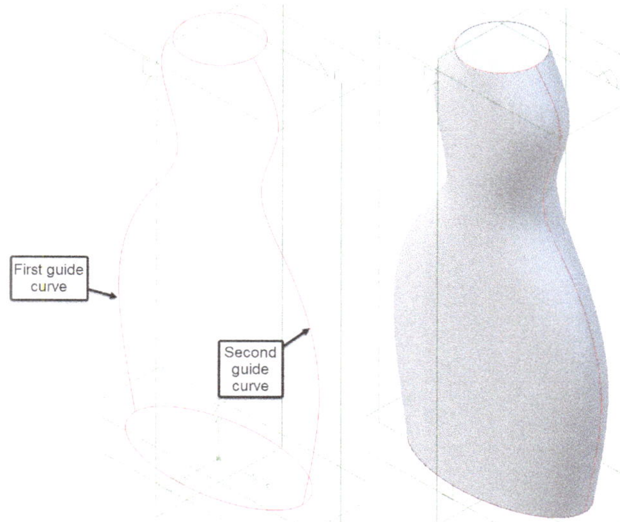

Creating the Extruded feature

1. Right click on the top flat face of the loft feature and select **Activate 2D Sketch** from the Shortcut Menu.
2. Click the circular edge display the Context toolbar.
3. Place the pointer on the **Project to Sketch** command.
4. Select the **Maintain associativity** option and click the green check.

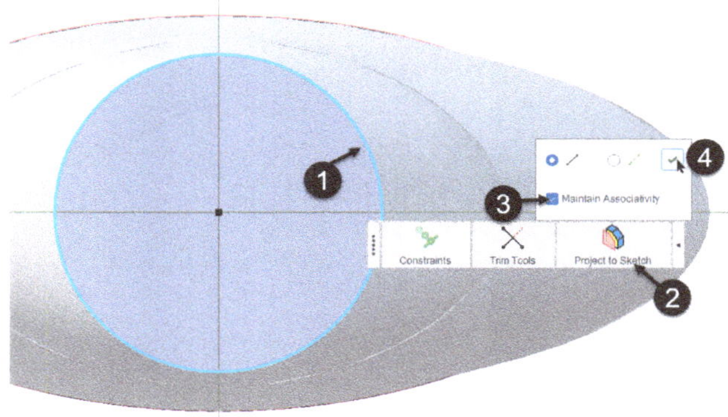

5. Click **Deactivate Sketch** on the ribbon.
6. Click the **Extrude** button on the **Boss(Add Material)** panel.
7. Extrude the circle up to **1** inch.

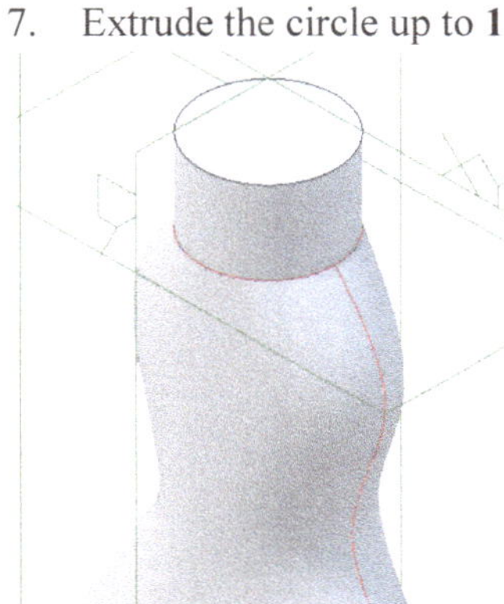

Creating Fillets

1. Click **Model > Part Tools > Fillet** on the ribbon; the **Fillet** dialog appears.
2. Type **0.2** in the **Radius/Chord Length** box.
3. Click in the **Edges/Faces** selection box.
4. Click on the bottom and top edges of the loft feature.

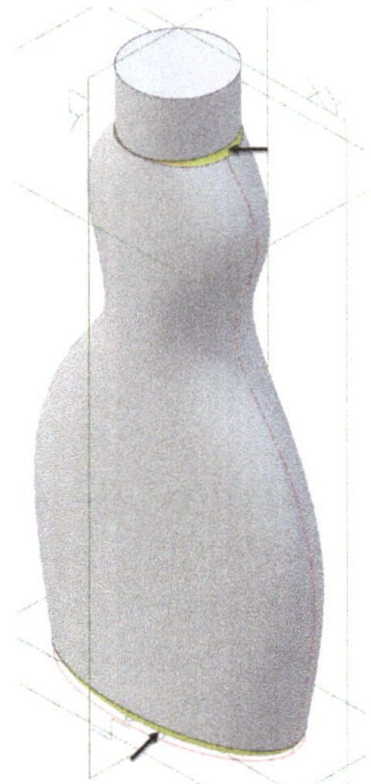

5. Click **Apply** and **Close**.

Shelling the Model

1. Click **Model > Part Tools > Shell** on the ribbon; the **Shell** dialog appears.
2. Set **Standard Thickness** to 0.03.
3. Select the top face of the cylindrical feature.

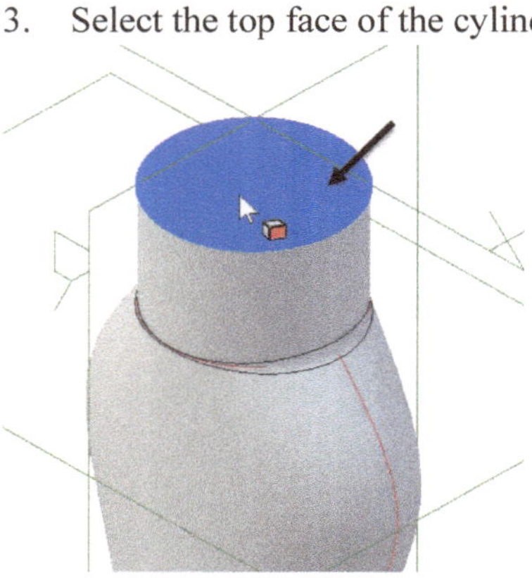

4. Click **OK** to create the shell.

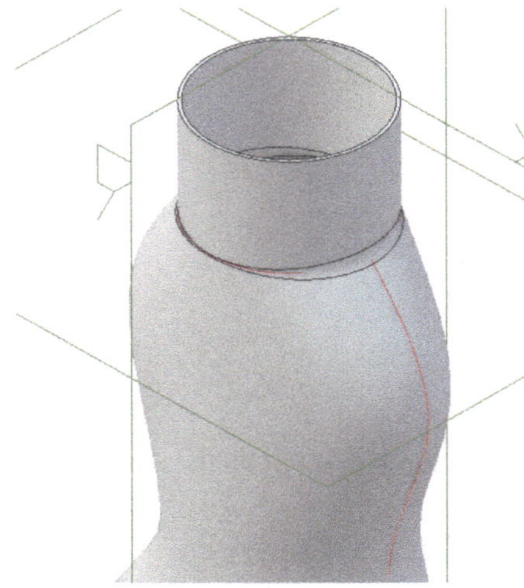

Adding Threads

1. On the ribbon, click **Inspect > Precision Section.**

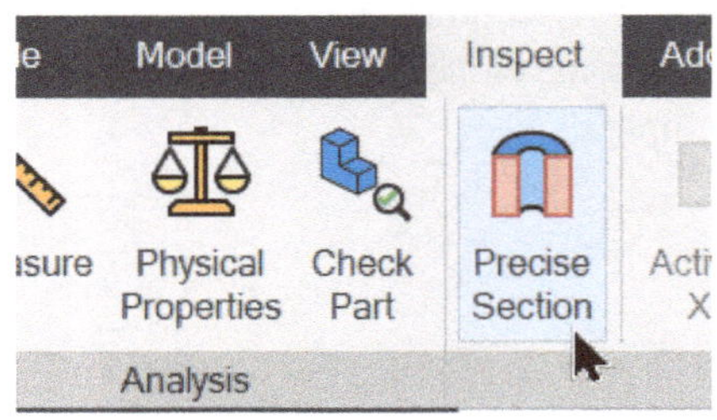

2. Select XY Plane from the Design Explorer.
3. Check the **Reverse** option on the **Precise Section Views** dialog.
4. Click **Apply** and **Close**.

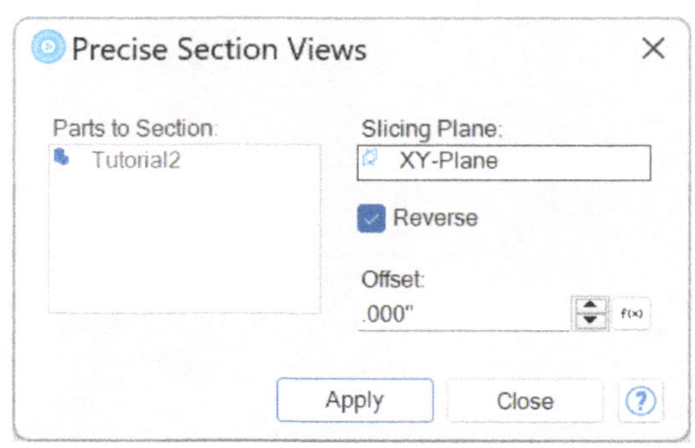

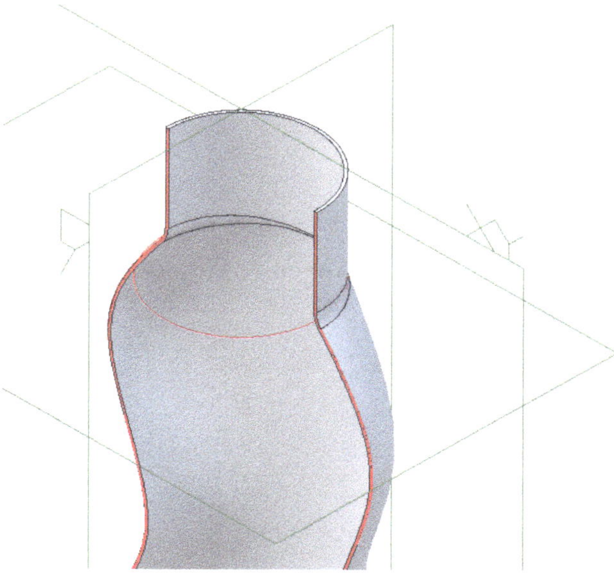

5. On the ribbon, click **Model > Sketch > Activate 2D Sketch**.
6. Select the XY Plane from the Design Explorer.
7. On the ribbon, click **2D Sketch > References > Line**.
8. Select the origin point of the sketch, move the cursor vertically upward and click to create a vertical centreline. Right-click and select **Select**.

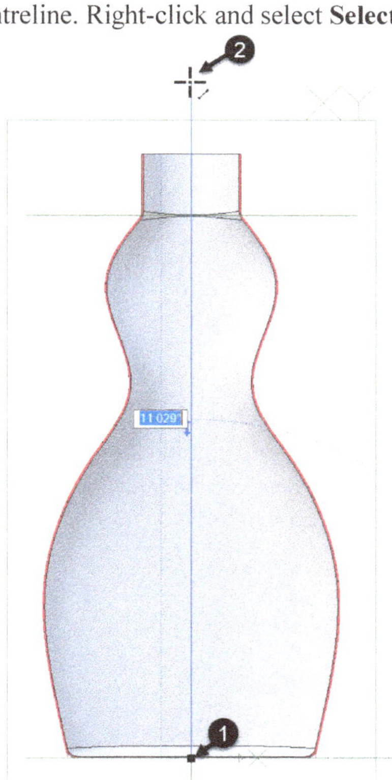

9. Right click and select **Reference Line** from the Shortcut menu.
10. Create a horizontal construction line, as shown.

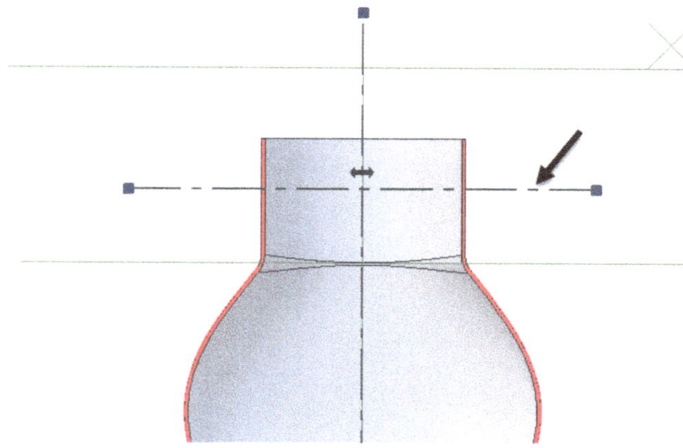

11. On the ribbon, click **2D Sketch > Create > Line**.
12. Create a closed profile, as shown.

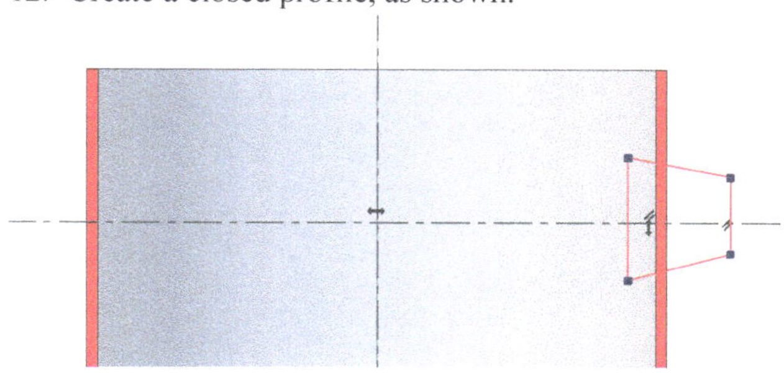

13. On the ribbon, click **2D Sketch > Constraints > Symmetric Constraint** .
14. Select the two inclined lines of the sketch, and then select the construction line; the two inclined lines are made symmetric about the construction line.

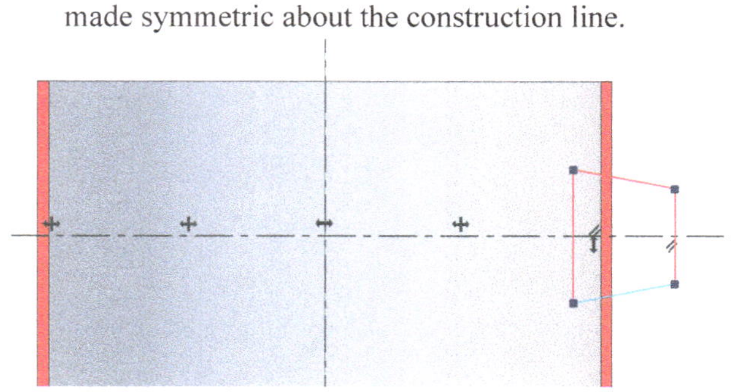

15. Click the **Dimension** button on the **Sketch Figures** panel.
16. Select the two inclined lines, move the cursor horizontally toward left and click.
17. Type 60 in the **Edit Dimension** box and press Enter.

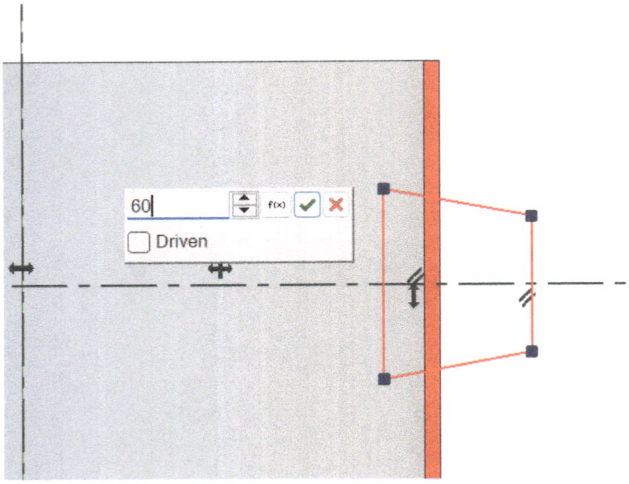

18. Add other dimensions to the sketch.

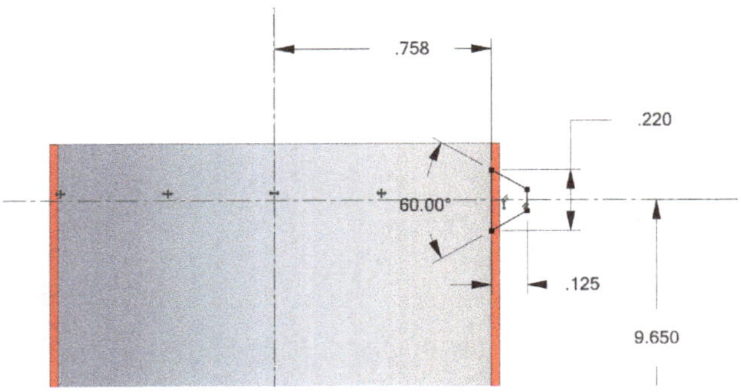

19. On the ribbon, click **2D Sketch > Sketch Tools > Fillet**.
20. Type 0.02 in the **Radius** box.
21. Select the vertical and lower inclined line, as shown.
22. Select the two corners of the sketch, as shown.

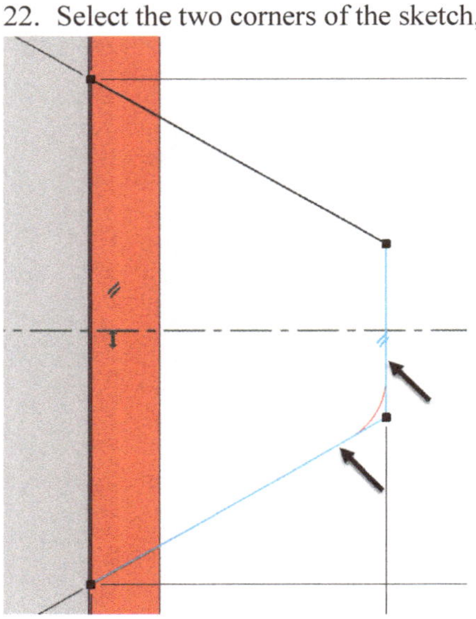

23. Click **Apply** on the **Fillet Figures** dialog box.

24. Select the vertical and upper inclined line.

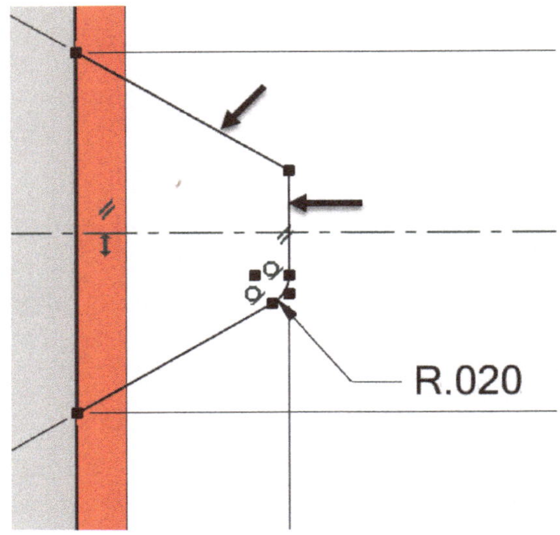

25. Click **Apply** and **Close** on the **Fillet Figures** dialog box.
26. Change the fillet dimensions to 0.04.

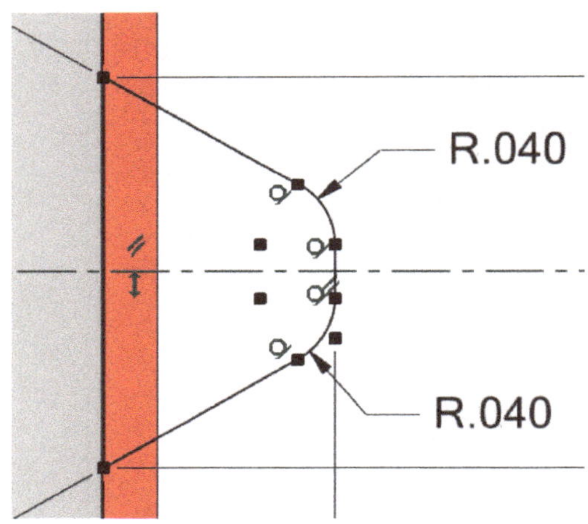

27. Click **Deactivate Sketch** on the ribbon.
28. In the Design Explorer, right-click on the **Precise Section View** and deselect the **View** option.

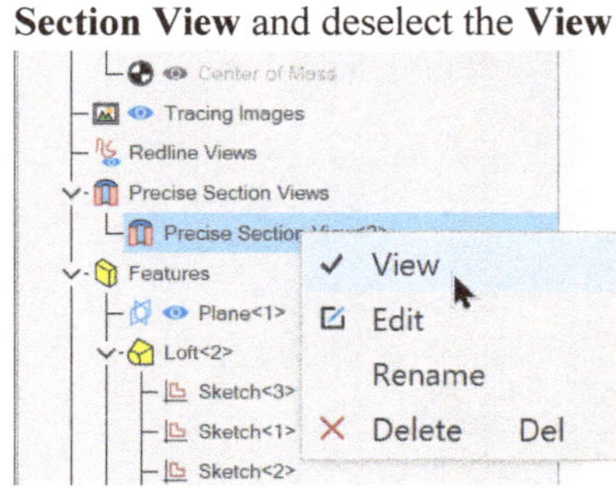

29. Select the closed profile from the graphics window.

30. On the ribbon, click **Model > Boss (Add Material) > Helix**.

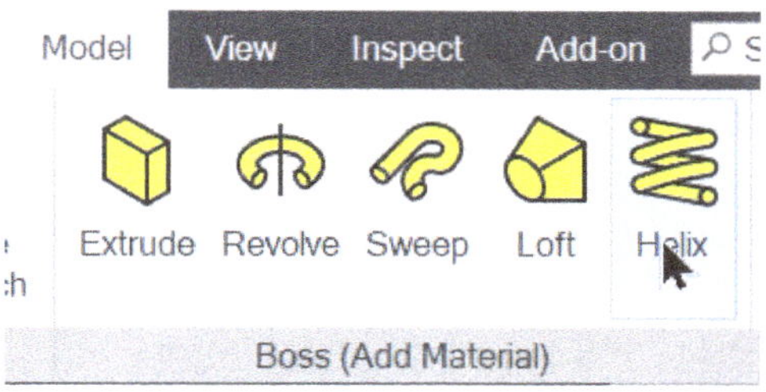

The axis of the sketch is selected automatically.

31. On the **Helical Boss** dialog, select **Type > Revolution & Pitch**.
32. Select the **Clockwise** option.
33. Check the **Reverse** option, if the preview of the coil is displayed in the upward direction.
34. Type-in **0.275** and **2** in the **Pitch** and **Revolution** boxes, respectively.

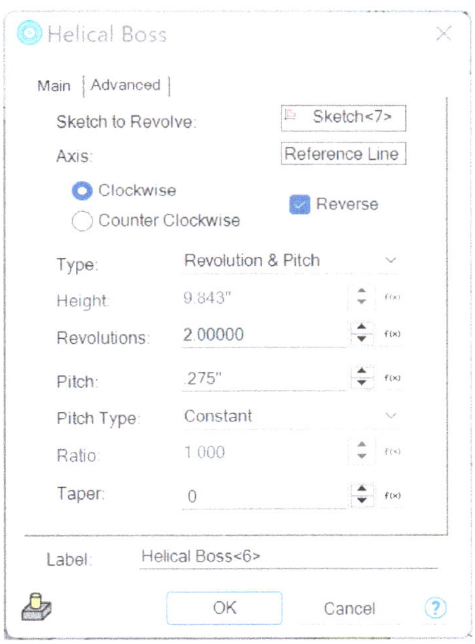

35. Click **OK**.

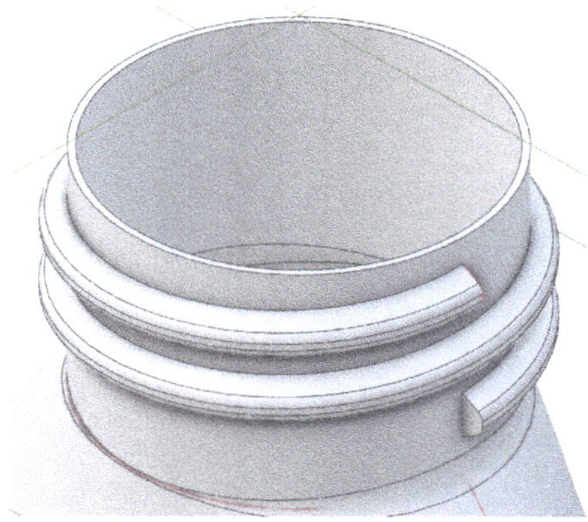

36. Right-click on the flat end face of the helical feature, and then select **Activate 2D Sketch**.

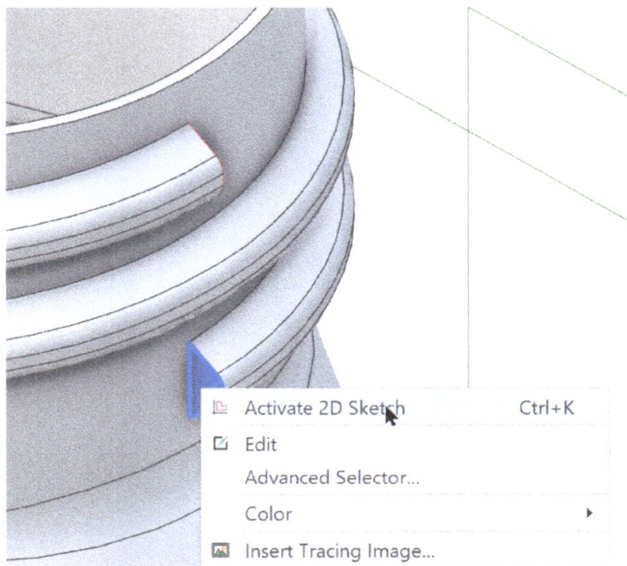

37. On the ribbon, click **2D Sketch > Project to Sketch**.
38. Select the edges of the end face of the helix.

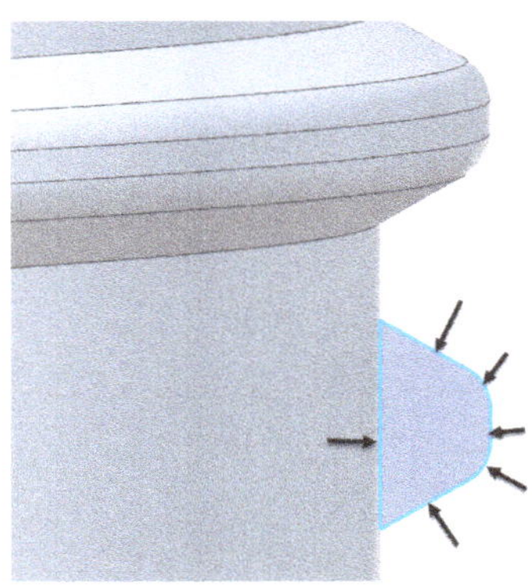

39. Click **Deactivate Sketch** on the ribbon.

40. Activate the **Revolve** tool and select the last sketch.
41. Click in the **Axis** selection box and select the vertical line of the sketch.

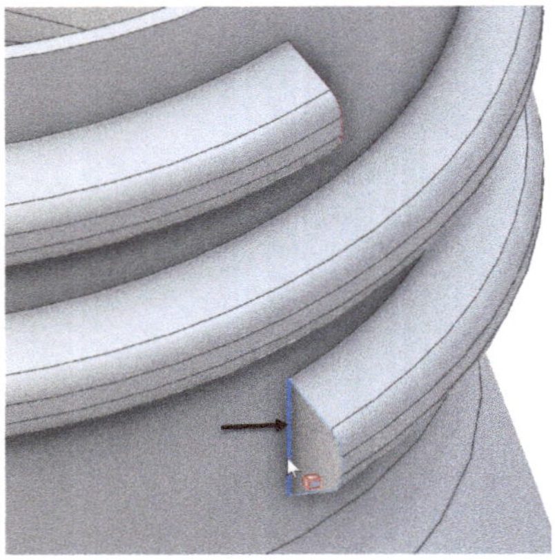

42. On the **Revolve Boss** dialog, type in **100** in the **Angle** box.
43. Check the **Revolve** option, if the revolved feature is displayed on the other side.

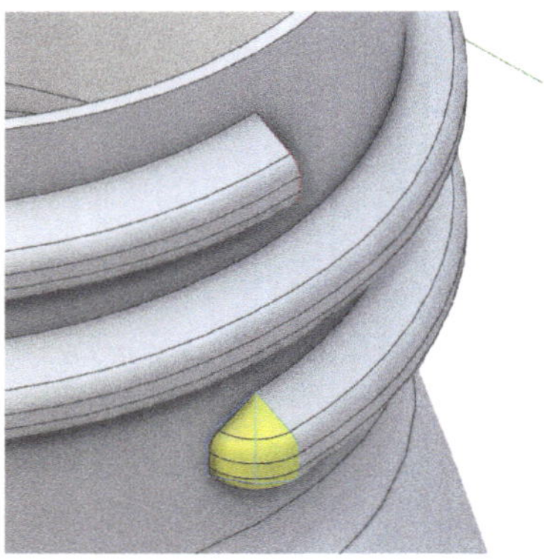

44. Click **OK**.
45. Likewise, blend the other end of the helix. Note that you need the reverse the direction of revolution.

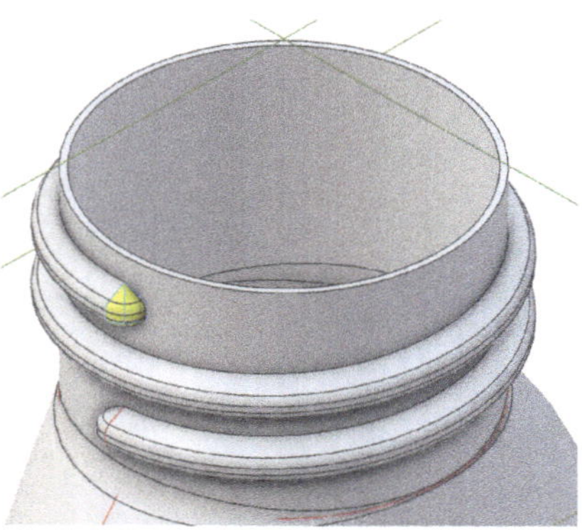

46. Save the model.

TUTORIAL 3

In this tutorial, you create the model, as shown.

Creating the First feature

1. Open a new Alibre Atom3D file.
2. Click the **New Part** icon on the **Home** window.
3. To start a new sketch, click **Model** tab > **Sketch > Activate 2D Sketch** on the ribbon.
4. Select the YZ Plane from the **Design Explorer**.
5. On the ribbon, click **2D Sketch > Sketch Figures > Rectangle**.
6. Select the origin point of the sketch.
7. Move the pointer toward right and click to create a rectangle.

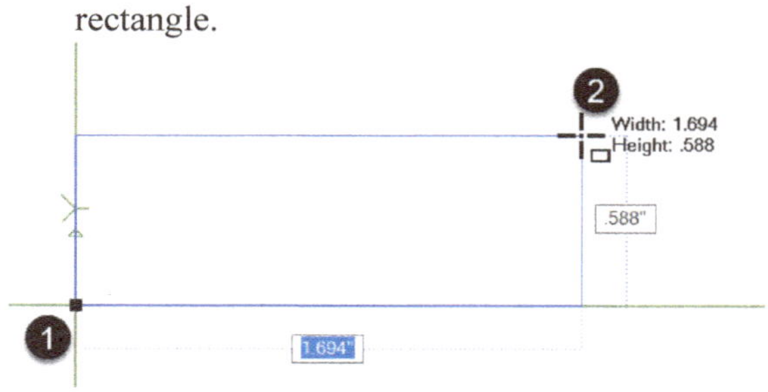

8. On the ribbon, click **2D Sketch > Sketch Figures > Line**.
9. Click on the vertical axis of the sketch, as shown.
10. Move the pointer horizontally toward right and click.
11. Click on the top horizontal line of the rectangle.

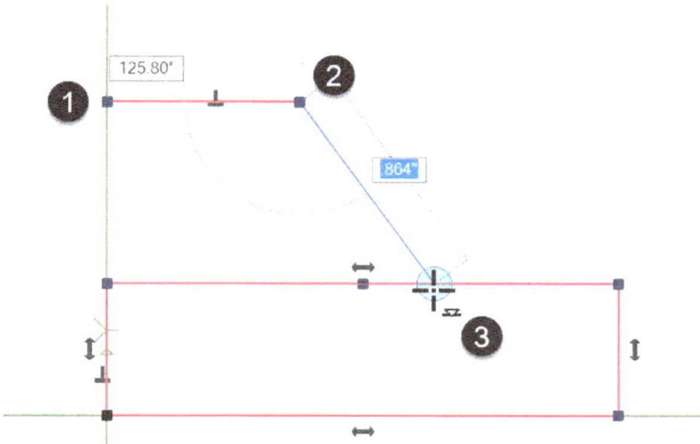

12. On the ribbon, click **2D Sketch > Sketch Tools > Trim**.
13. Selec the portion of the top horizontal line of the rectangle to trim it.

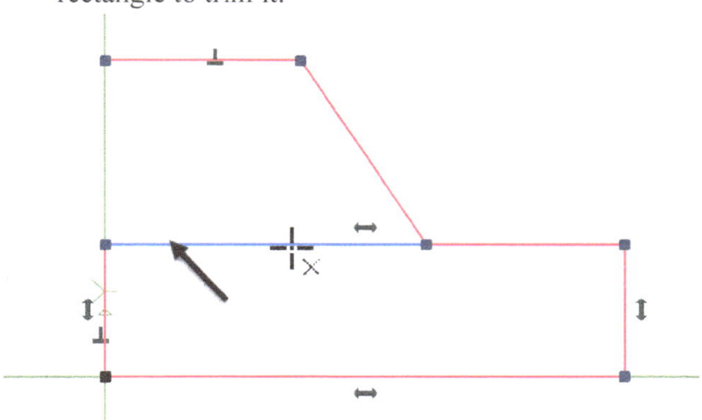

14. On the ribbon, click **2D Sketch > Sketch Tools > Intersect**.
15. Select the left vertical line and the top horizontal line to form a corner.

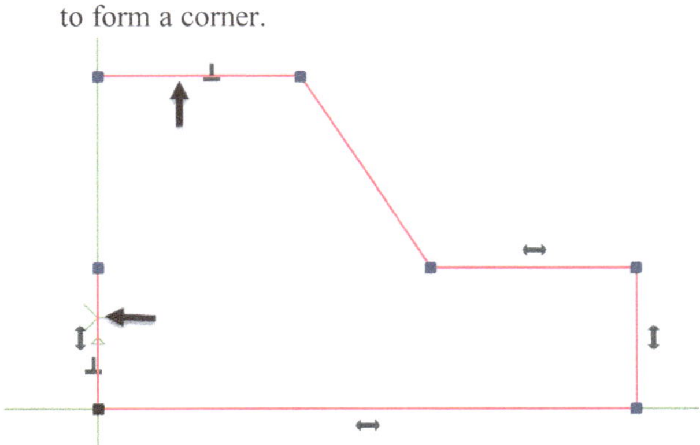

16. Add dimensions to the sketch, as shown.

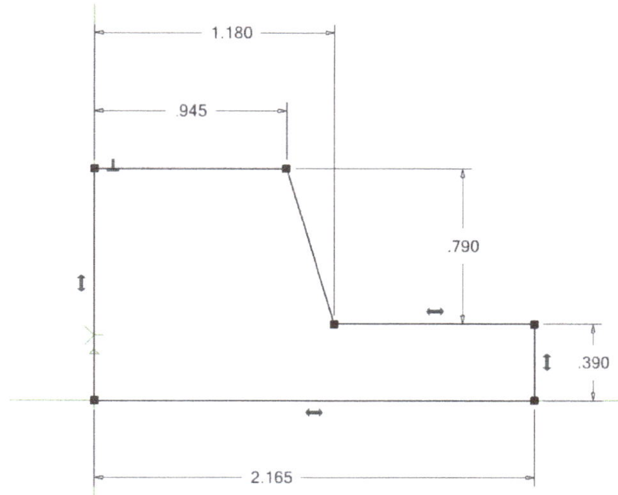

17. Click **Deactivate Sketch** on the ribbon..
18. On the ribbon, click **Model > Boss (Add Material) > Extrude**.
19. Type **1.575** in the **Depth** box.
20. Select **Type > Mid Plane**.
21. Click **OK**.

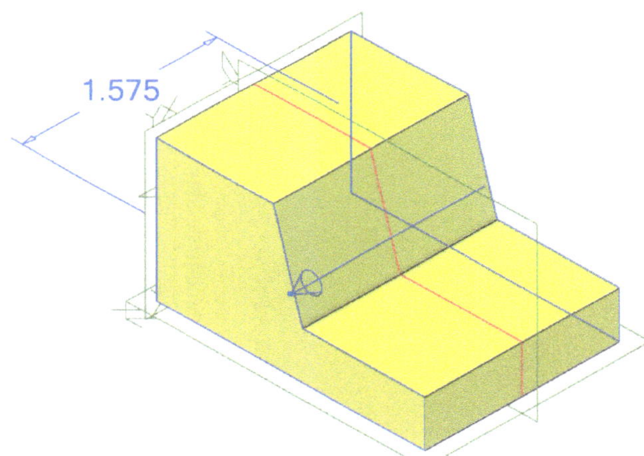

Creating the Extruded Cut Feature

1. To start a new sketch, click **Model** tab > **Sketch > Activate 2D Sketch** on the ribbon.
2. Select the top face of the model.
3. Create a rectangle and add dimensions to it, as shown.

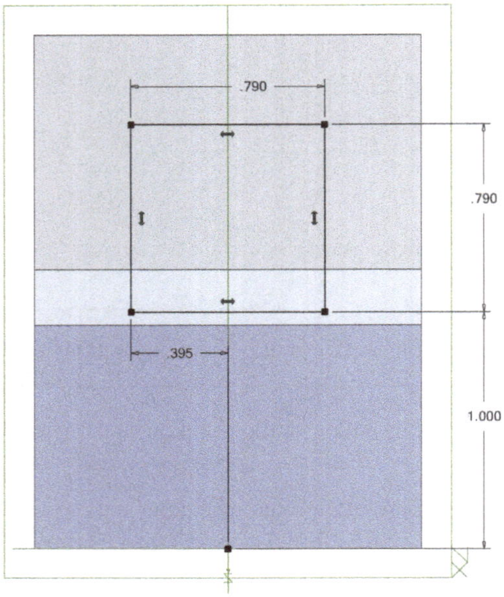

4. Click **Deactivate Sketch** on the ribbon..
5. On the ribbon, click **Model > Cut (Remove Material) > Extrude**.
6. Select **Type > Through All**.
7. Click **OK**.

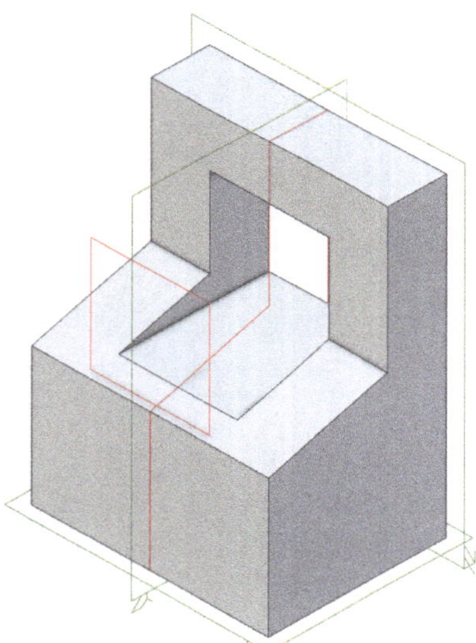

Mirroring the Entire Body

1. Click the **Mirror** icon on the **Part Tools** panel.
2. On the **Mirror** dialog, select **Type > Entire Part**.
3. Select the **ZX plane** from the **Design Explorer**.

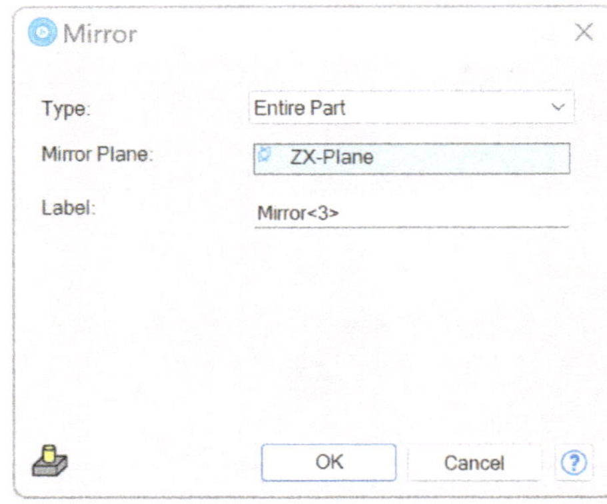

4. Click **OK** to mirror the entire body.

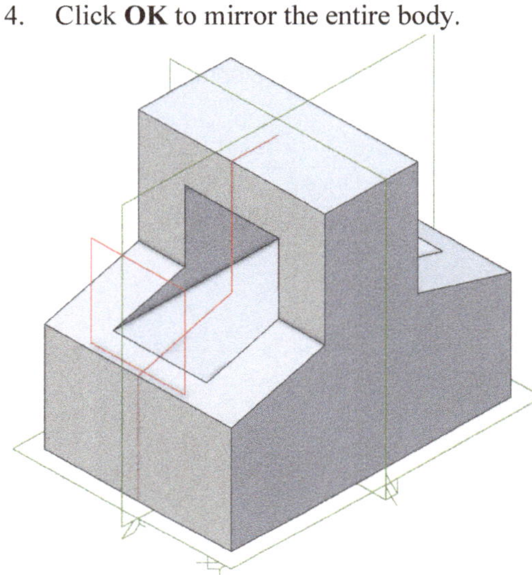

5. Click the **Mirror** icon on the **Part Tools** panel.
6. On the **Mirror** dialog, select **Type > Entire Part**.
7. Select the **XY plane** from the **Design Explorer**.

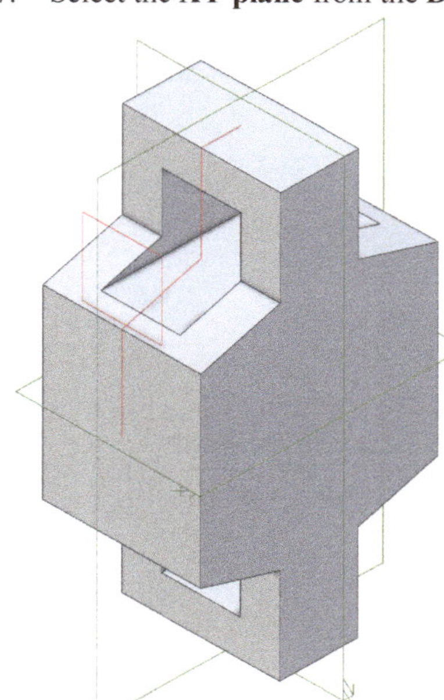

Creating the third feature

1. To start a new sketch, click **Model** tab > **Sketch > Activate 2D Sketch** on the ribbon.
2. Select the ZX Plane from the **Design Explorer**.
3. On the ribbon, click **2D Sketch > Sketch Figures > Slot** drop-down **> Straight Slot**.

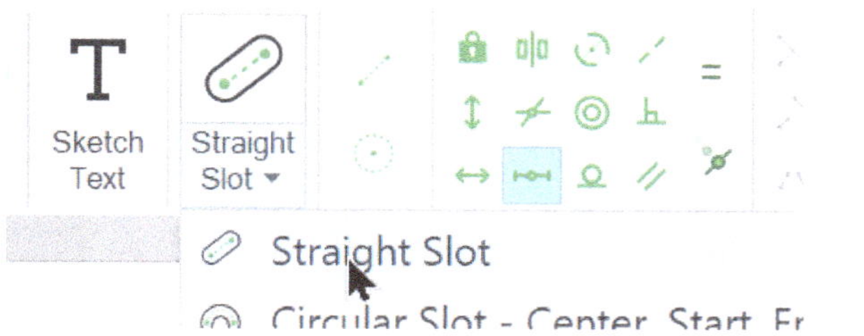

4. Click on the left side of the model.
5. Move the pointer horizontally toward right and click.

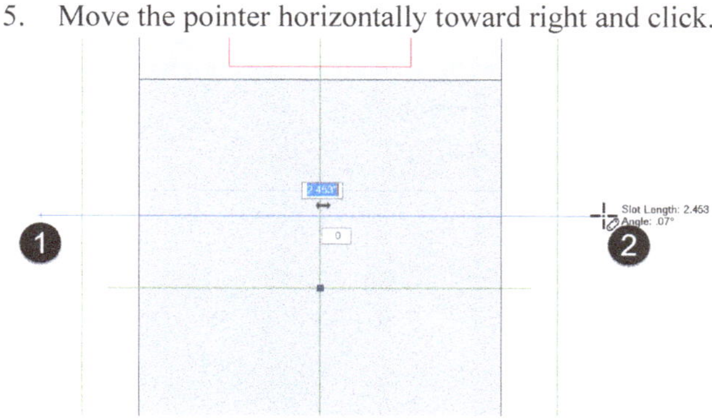

6. Move the pointer outward and click.

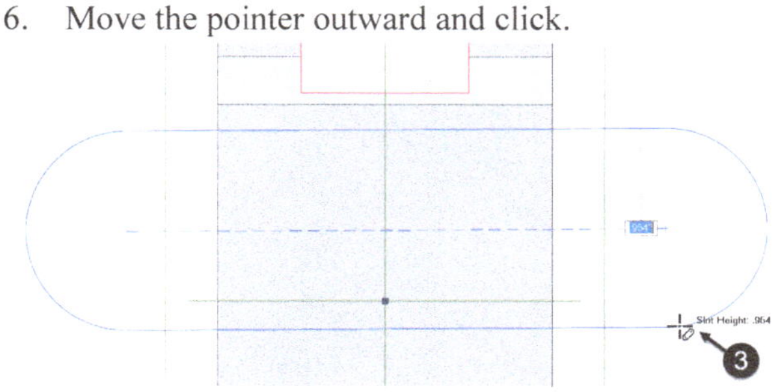

7. On the ribbon, click **2D Sketch > Constraints > Midline Constraint**.
8. Select the centerline of the slot.
9. Select the sketch origin.

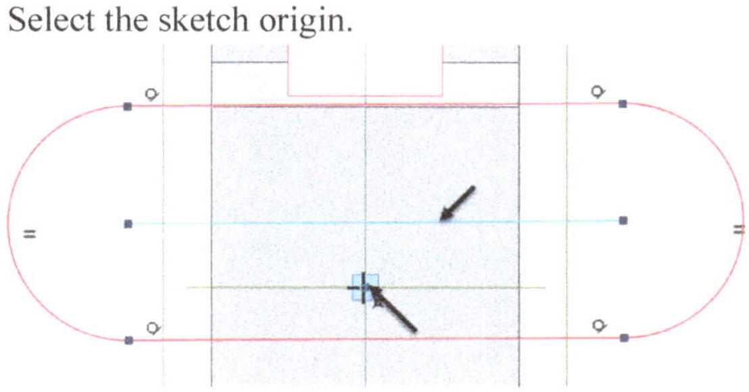

10. On the ribbon, click **2D Sketch > Sketch Figures > Circle**.
11. Select the centerpoint of the left arc of the slot.
12. Move the pointer outward and click.
13. Likewise, create a circle concentric to the right arc of the slot.
14. Add dimensions to the sketch, as shown.

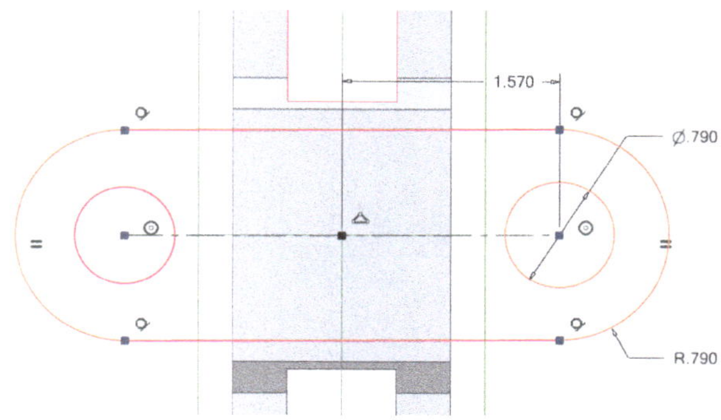

15. Apply the Horizontal Constraint to the centerline of the slot.
16. Apply the Equal Constraint between the two circles.

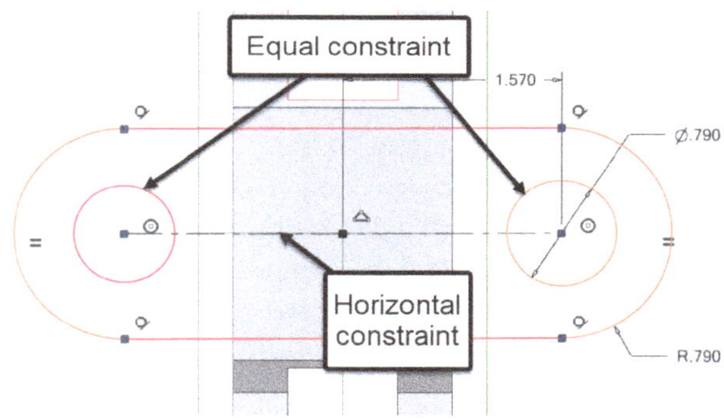

17. Click the **Deactivate Sketch** button on the **2D Sketch** tab of the ribbon.
18. On the ribbon, click **Model > Boss (Add Material) > Extrude**.
19. Type **0.78** in the **Depth** box.
20. Select **Type > Mid Plane**.
21. Click **OK**.

8. Save and close the file.

TUTORIAL 4

In this tutorial, you construct a patterned cylindrical shell.

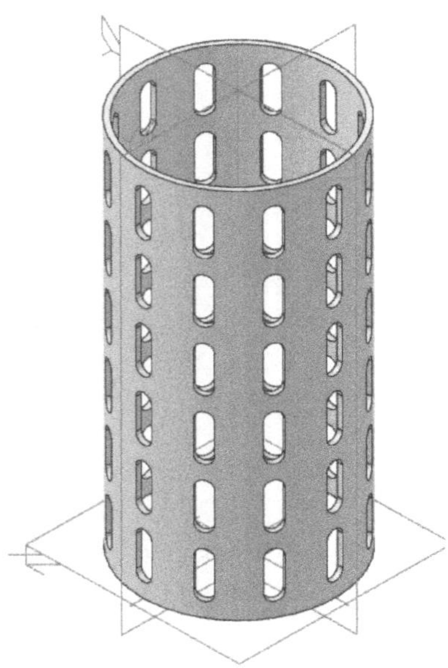

Constructing a cylindrical shell

1. Open a new Alibre Atom3D file.
2. Click the **New Part** icon on the **Home** window.
3. To start a new sketch, click **Model** tab > **Sketch > Activate 2D Sketch** on the ribbon.
4. Select the ZX Plane from the **Design Explorer**.
5. On the ribbon, click **2D Sketch > Sketch Figures > Circle**.
6. Select the sketch orign, move the pointer outward and click.
7. Select the sketch orign, move the pointer outward and click.
8. Add diameter dimensions to the circles, as shown.

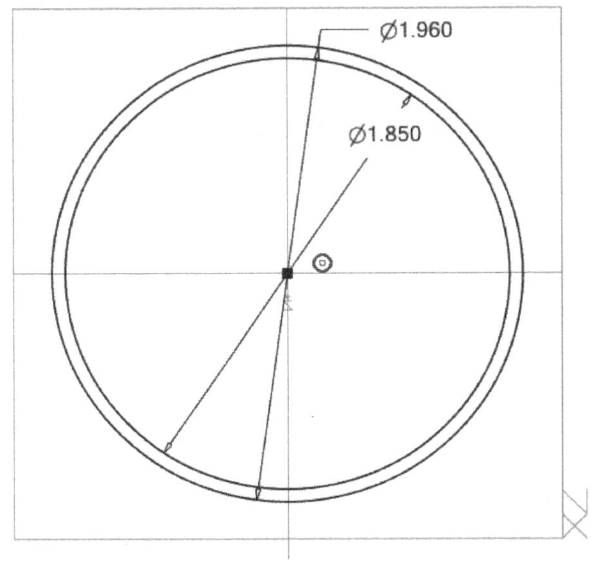

9. Click the **Deactivate Sketch** button on the **2D Sketch** tab of the ribbon.
10. Extrude the sketch up to 3.93 depth.

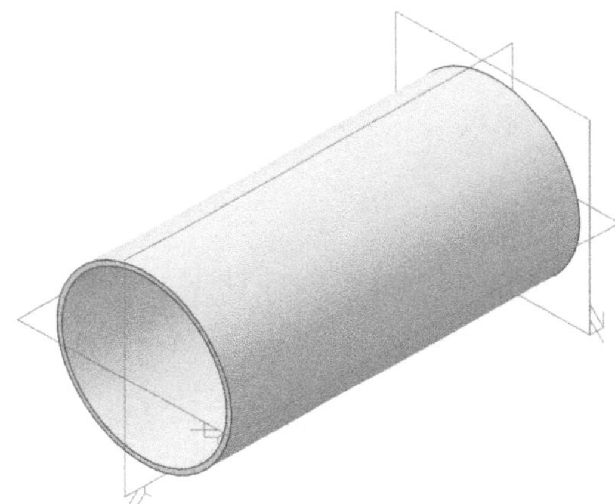

Adding a Slot

1. To start a new sketch, click **Model** tab > **Sketch > Activate 2D Sketch** on the ribbon.
2. Select the **YZ Plane** from the Design Explorer.
3. On the ribbon, click **2D Sketch > Sketch Figures > Slot** drop-down **> Straight Slot**.
4. Click to define the first point of the slot.
5. Move the pointer up and click to define the second point.
6. Move the pointer outward and click.
7. Add dimensions and constraints to the slot.

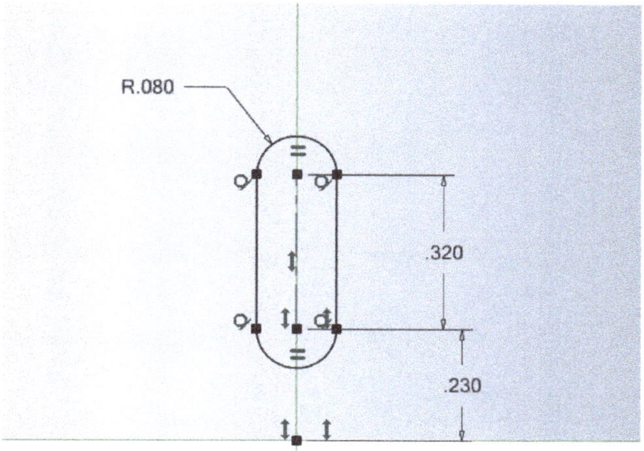

8. Click the **Deactivate Sketch** button on the **2D Sketch** tab of the ribbon.
9. On the ribbon, click **Model > Cut (Remove Material) > Extrude**.
10. Select **Type > To Next**.

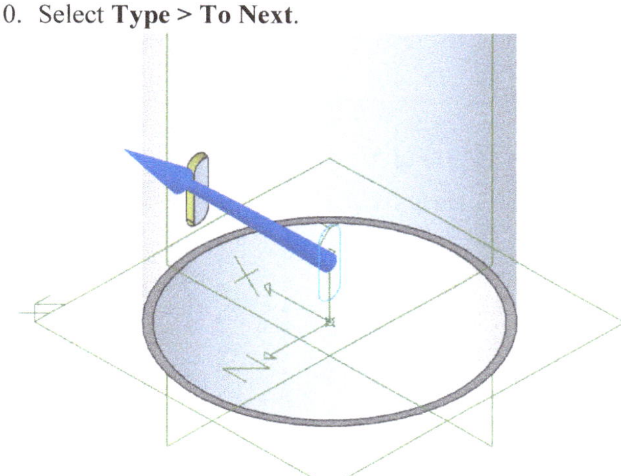

11. Click **OK**.

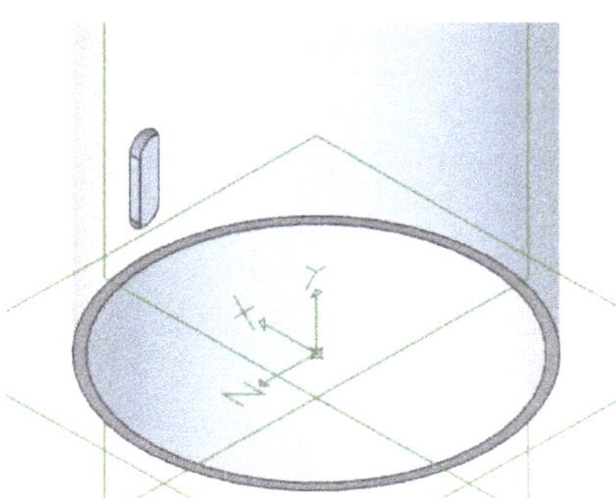

Constructing the Linear and Circular patterns

1. Click the **Linear pattern** icon on the **Part Tools** panel.

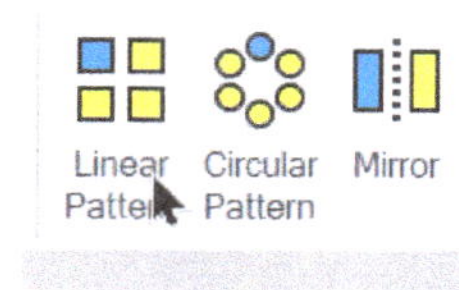

2. Select the **Extruded cut** feature from the graphics window.

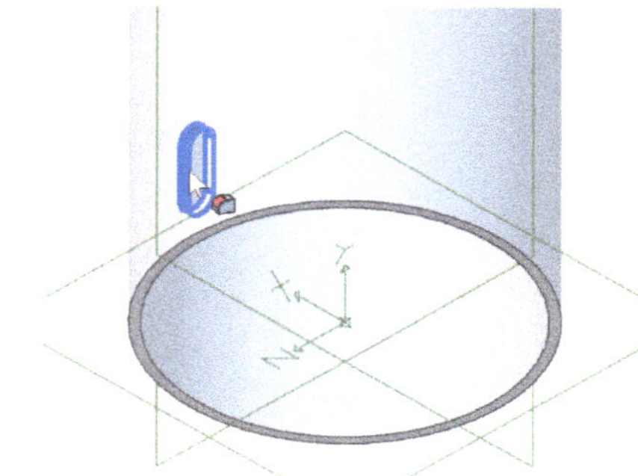

3. Click in the **Linear Path** selection box.
4. Select the **Y-axis** from the Design Explorer.

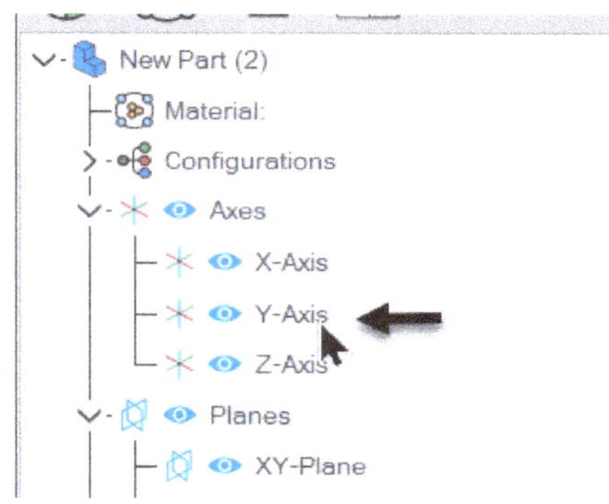

5. Type **0.629** in the **Spacing** box.
6. Type **6** in the **Instances** box.

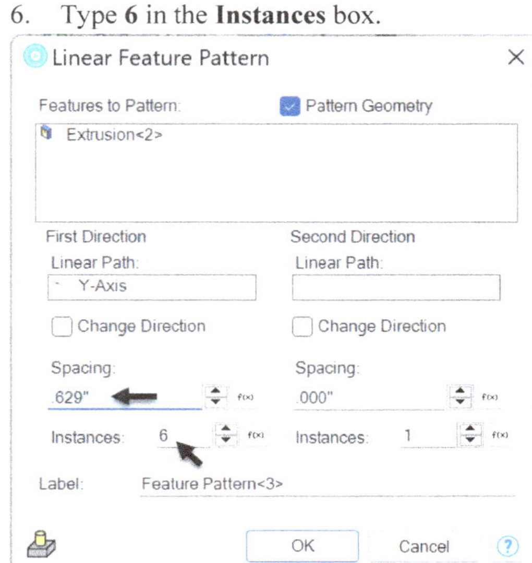

7. Click **OK**.

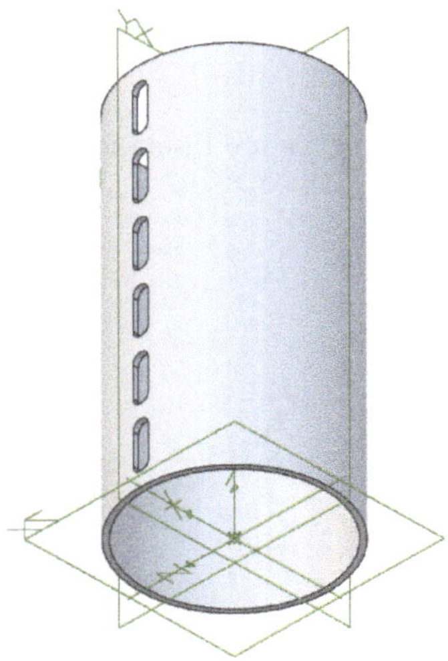

8. Click the **Circular pattern** icon on the **Part Tools** panel.

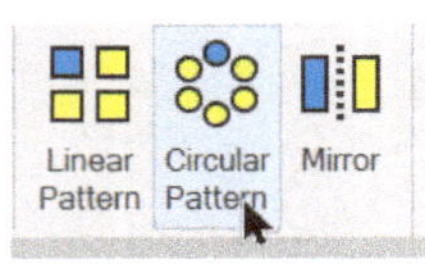

9. Select the extruded cut and linear pattern from the graphics window.

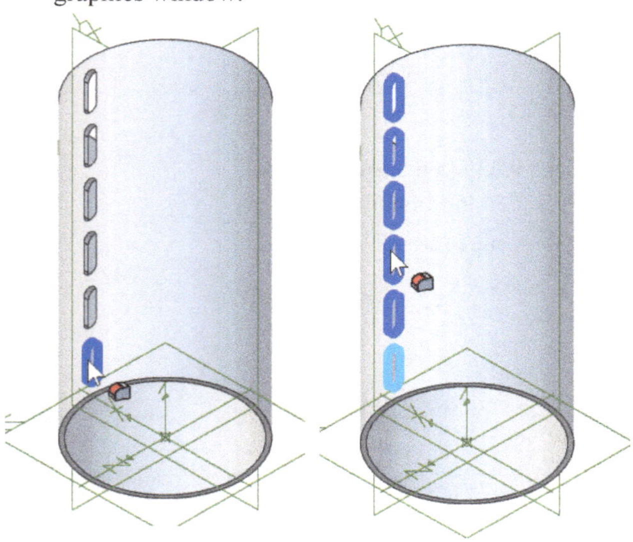

10. Select the **Full Extent** option from the **Angle** section.
11. Type-in **12** in the **Instances** box.
12. Click in the **Center** selection box and select the Y-axis from the Design Explorer.

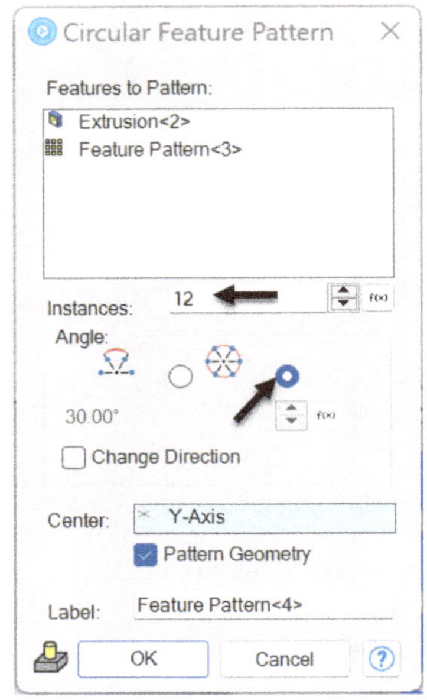

13. Click **OK** to create the circular pattern.

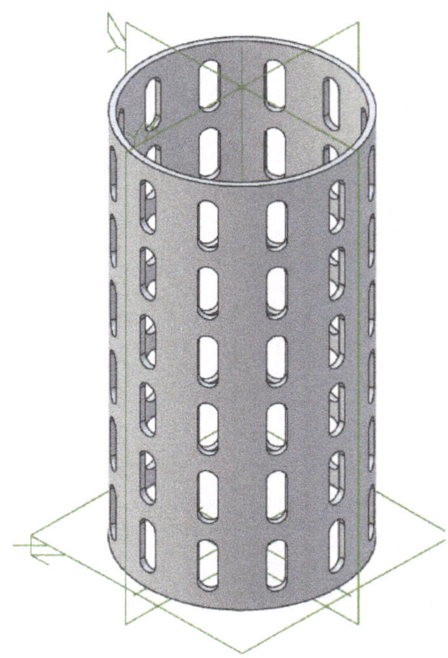

11. Save and close the model.

TUTORIAL 5

In this tutorial, you construct a pulley wheel using the **Revolution** and **Groove** tools.

1. Open a new Alibre Atom3D file.
2. Click the **New Part** icon on the **Home** window.
3. To start a new sketch, click **Model** tab > **Sketch > Activate 2D Sketch** on the ribbon.
4. Select the YZ Plane from the **Design Explorer**.
5. On the ribbon, click **2D Sketch > Sketch Figures > Line**.
6. Create a closed sketch, as shown.

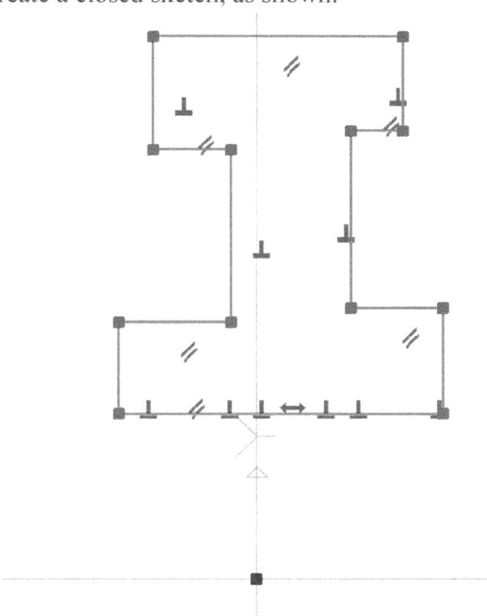

7. Click the **Equal** icon on the **Constraints** panel.
8. Make the entities of the sketch equal in length, as shown.

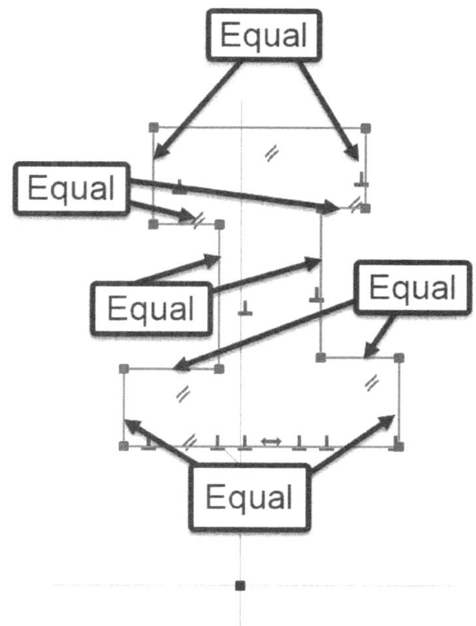

9. Create remaining constraints, as shown.

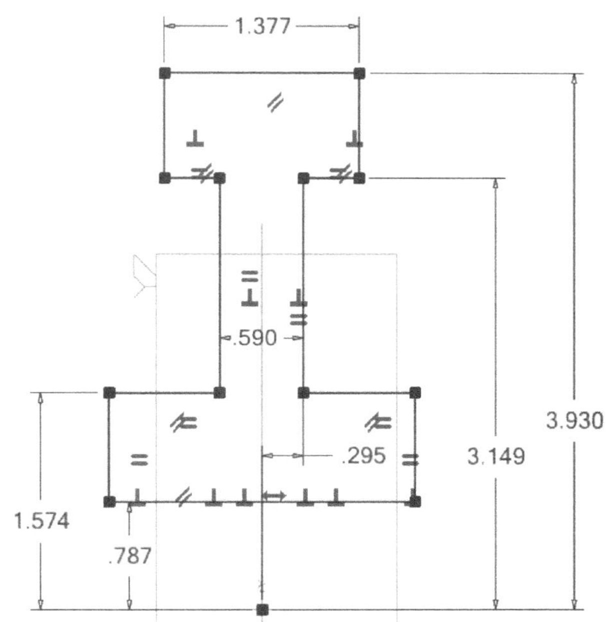

10. Click the **Deactivate Sketch** button on the **2D Sketch** tab of the ribbon.
11. On the ribbon, click **Model > Boss (Add Material) > Revolve**; the sketch is selected automatically.
12. Click in the **Axis** selection box and select the **Z-Axis** from the Design Explorer.
13. Type **360** in the **Angle** box.
14. Click **OK** to construct the revolved feature.

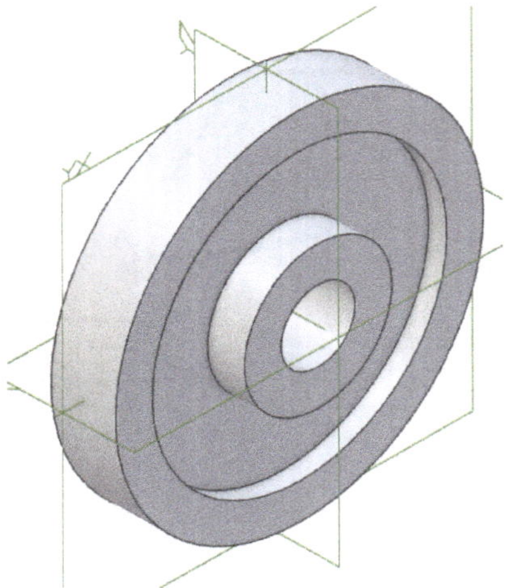

Constructing the Groove feature

1. On the ribbon, click **Inspect > Precision Section**.

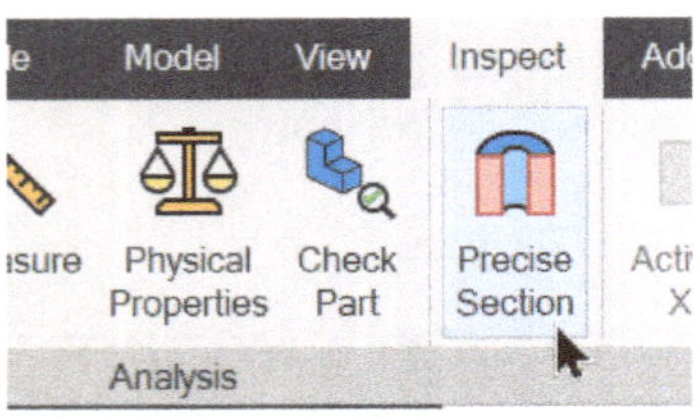

2. Select YZ Plane from the Design Explorer.
3. Check the **Reverse** option on the **Precise Section Views** dialog.
4. Click **Apply** and **Close**.
5. To start a new sketch, click **Model** tab > **Sketch > Activate 2D Sketch** on the ribbon.
6. Select the YZ Plane from the **Design Explorer**.
7. On the ribbon, click **2D Sketch > Sketch Figures > Line**.
8. Create the sketch, as shown.

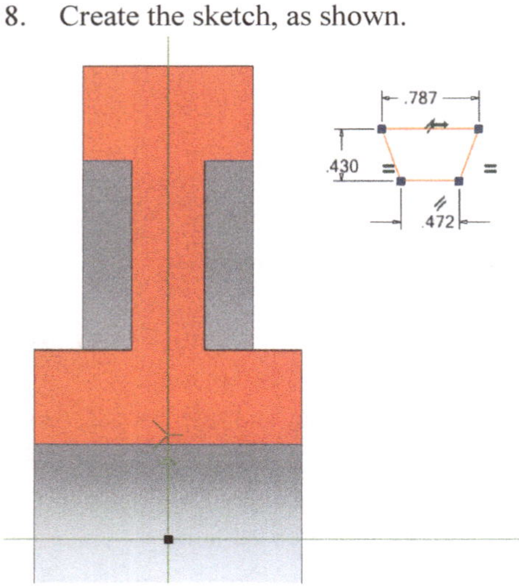

9. On the ribbon, click **2D Sketch > References > Line**.
10. Select the sketch origin, move the pointer vertically upward and click on the external geometry.

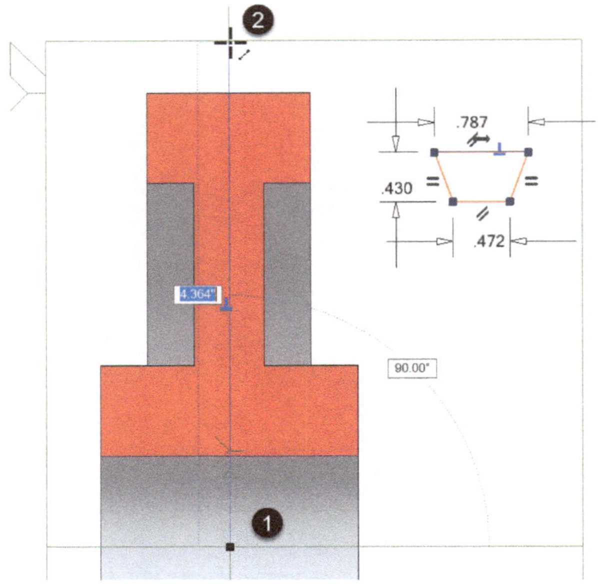

11. On the ribbon, click **2D Sketch > Constraints > Symmetric Constraint**.
12. Select the newly created vertical line.
13. Selec the inclined lines of the sketch.

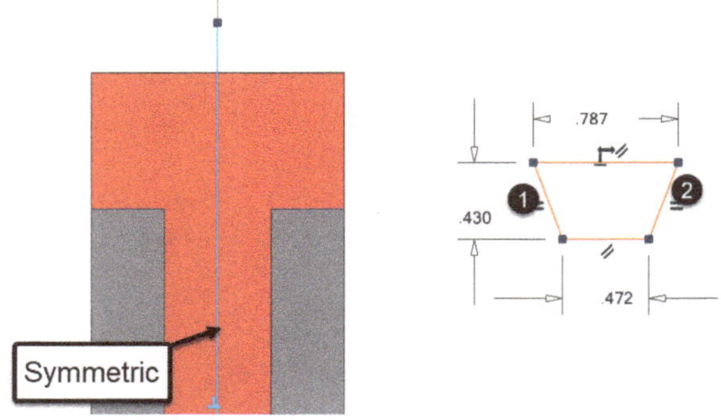

14. Add a dimension (3.940) between the sketch origin and the top horizontal line.

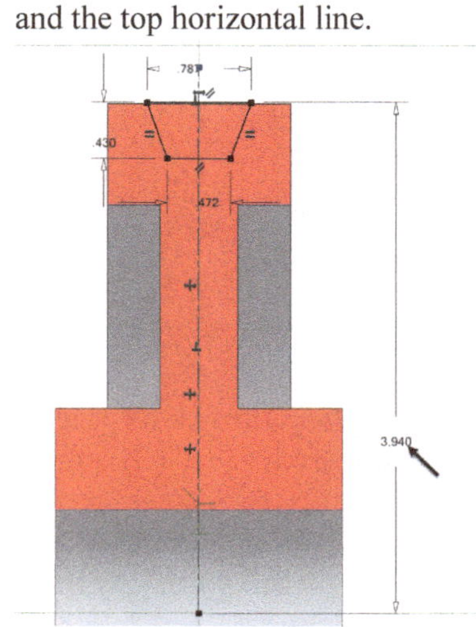

15. Click the **Deactivate Sketch** button on the **2D Sketch** tab of the ribbon.
16. On the ribbon, click **Model > Cut (Remove Material) > Revolve**.
17. Select the **Z-Axis** from the Design Explorer.
18. Type 360 in the **Angle** box.
19. Click **OK**.
20. In the Design Explorer, right-click on the **Precise Section View** and deselect the **View** option.

21. Save and close the model.

TUTORIAL 6

In this tutorial, you construct the model shown in the figure.

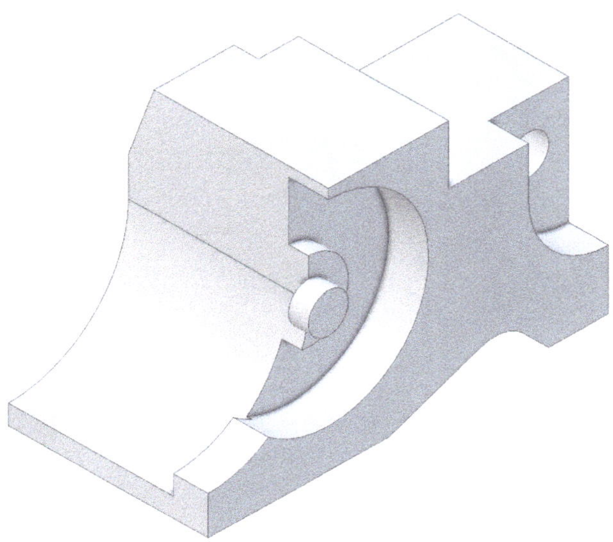

Creating the Base Feature

1. Open a new Alibre Atom3D file.
2. Click the **New Part** icon on the **Home** window.
3. To start a new sketch, click **Model** tab > **Sketch > Activate 2D Sketch** on the ribbon.
4. Select the YZ Plane from the **Design Explorer**.
5. On the ribbon, click **2D Sketch > Sketch Figures > Rectangle**.
6. Specify the first and second corners of the rectangle, as shown.

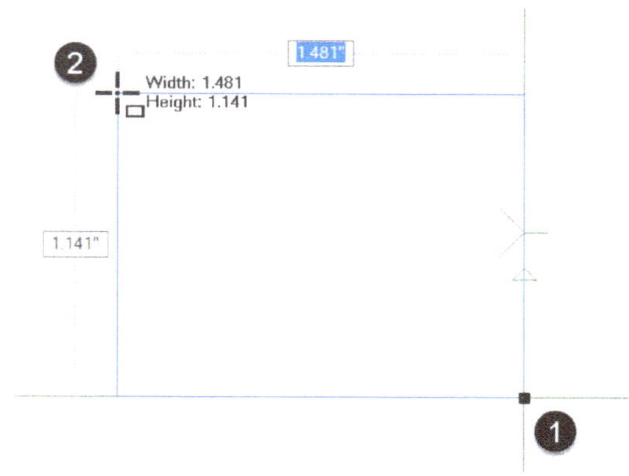

7. Create another rectangle by specifying its first and second corners, as shown.

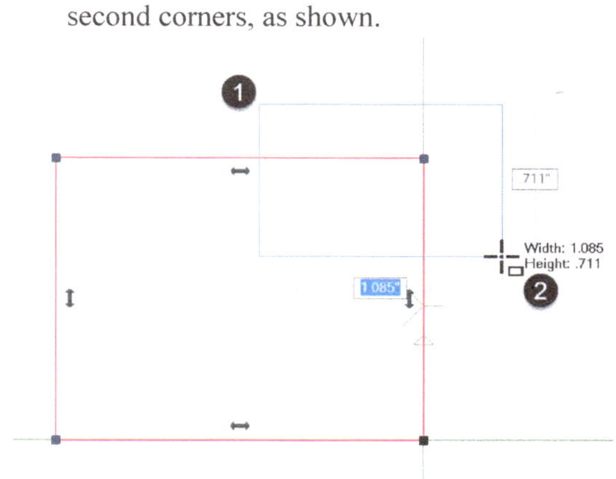

8. Click **2D Sketch > Sketch Tools > Trim** on the ribbon.
9. Select the elements of the rectangles to be trimmed, as shown.

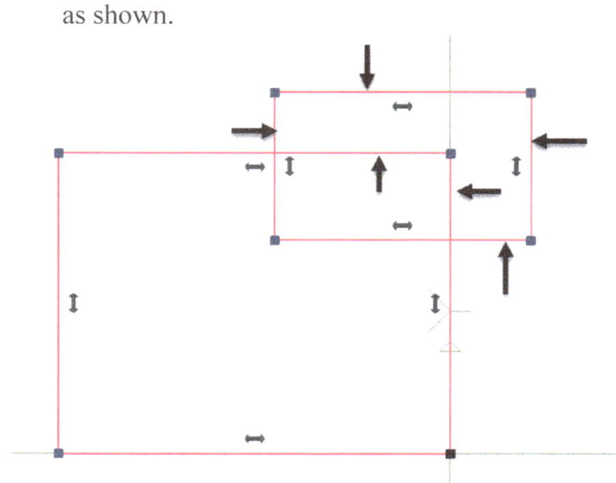

10. Add vertical and horizontal dimensions to the sketch, as shown.

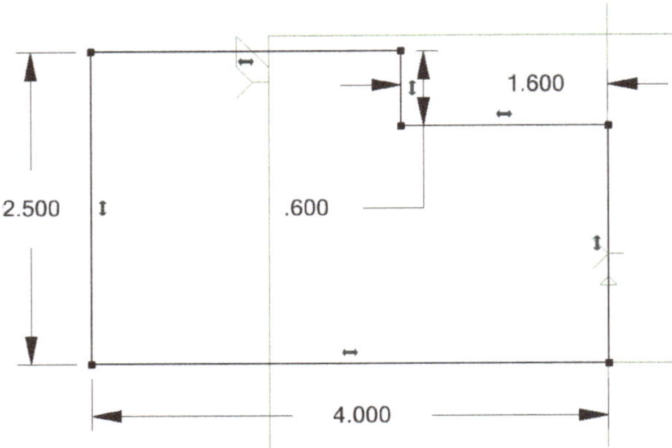

11. Click the **Deactivate Sketch** button on the **2D Sketch** tab of the ribbon.
12. On the ribbon, click **Model > Boss (Add Material) > Extrude**.
13. Type **2** in the **Depth** box.
14. Select **Type > Mid Plane**.
15. Click **OK**.

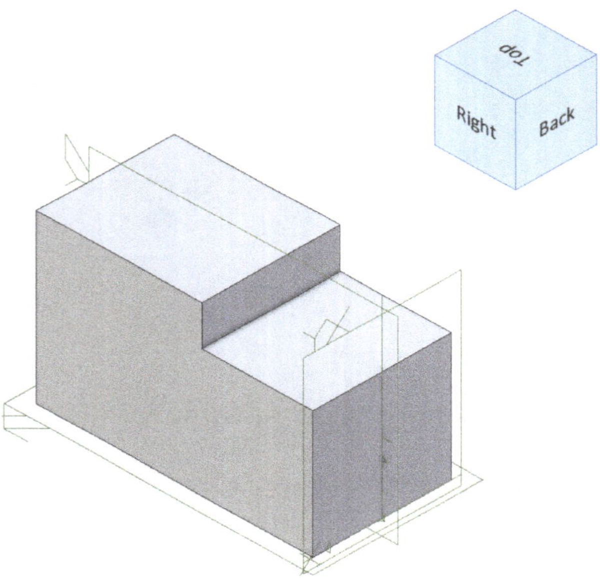

Creating the Extruded Cut Features

1. To start a new sketch, click **Model** tab > **Sketch > Activate 2D Sketch** on the ribbon.
2. Select the YZ Plane from the **Design Explorer**.
3. On the ribbon, click **2D Sketch > Sketch Figures > Line**.
4. Specify the endpoints of the line, as shown.

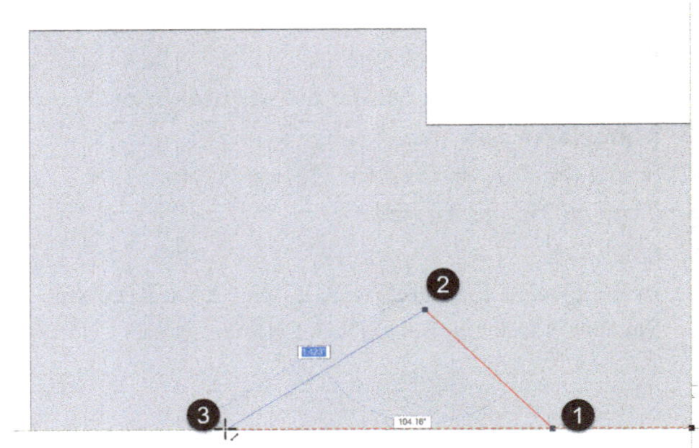

5. Right-click and **Select**.
6. Click **2D Sketch > Sketch Tools > Fillet** on the ribbon.
7. Select the two inclined lines of the sketch, as shown.

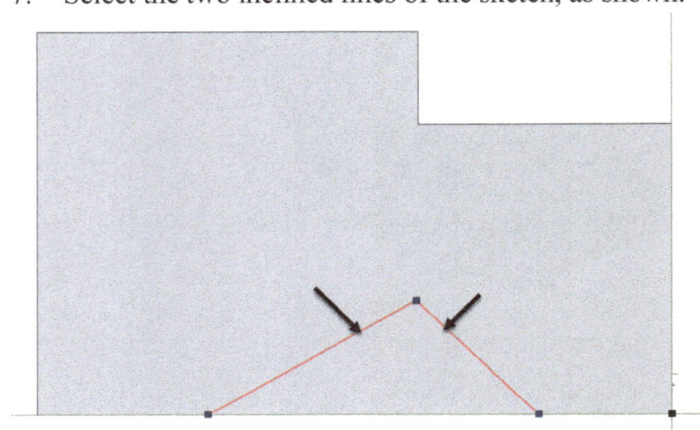

8. Type **0.4** in the **Radius** box.
9. Click **Apply** and **Close**.
10. On the ribbon, click **2D Sketch > Sketch Figures > Dimension**.
11. Select the inclined line and the horizontal axis of the sketch.

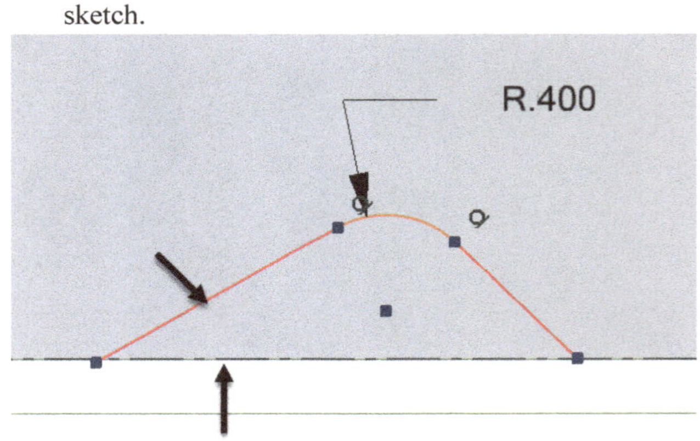

12. Type **20** in the **Dimension** box and click **OK**.
13. Select the other inclined line and the horizontal axis of the sketch, as shown.

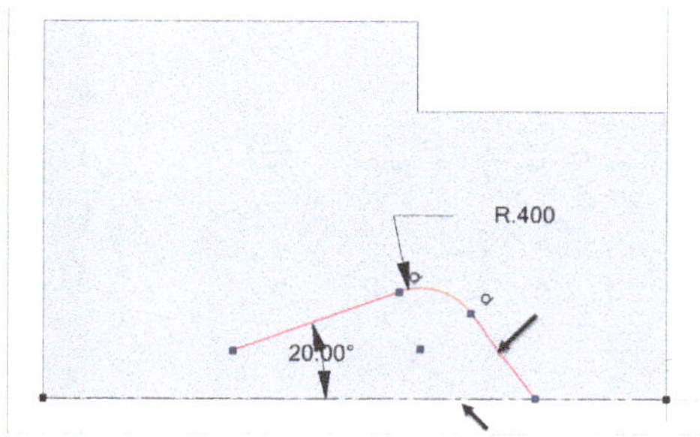

14. Type **45** in the **Dimension** box and click **OK**.

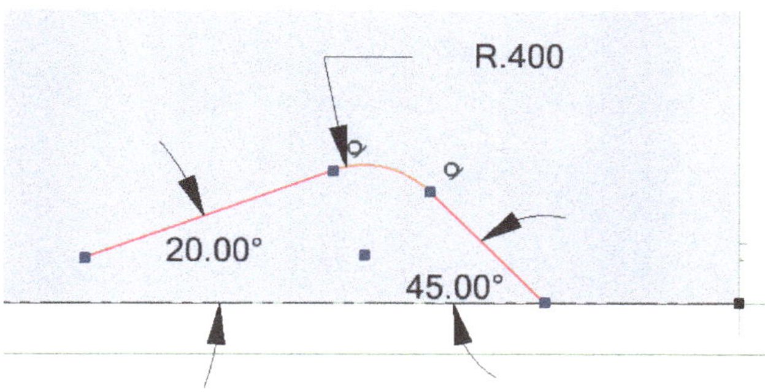

15. Add vertical and horizontal distance constraints to the sketch, as shown.

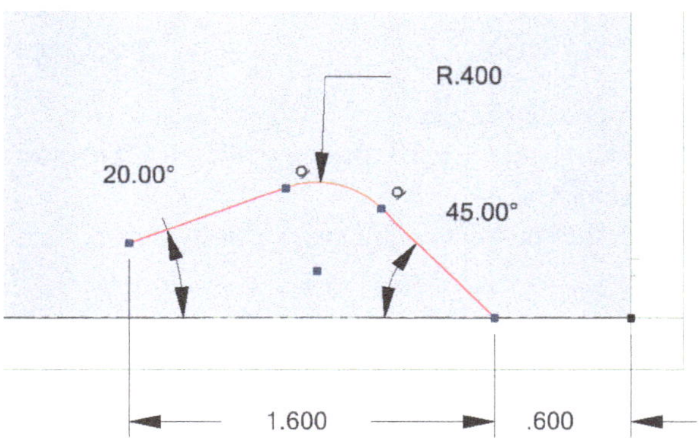

16. On the ribbon, click **2D Sketch > Constraints > Horizontal Constraint**.
17. Select the endpoints of the two lines, and the sketch origin.

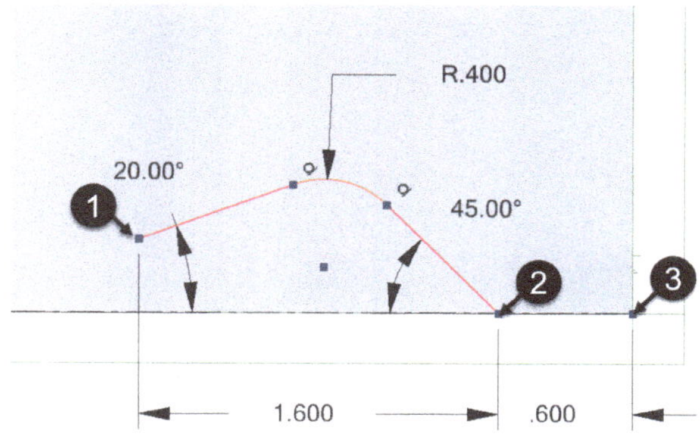

18. On the ribbon, click **2D Sketch > Sketch Figures > Line**.
19. Select the endpoints of the sketch, as shown.

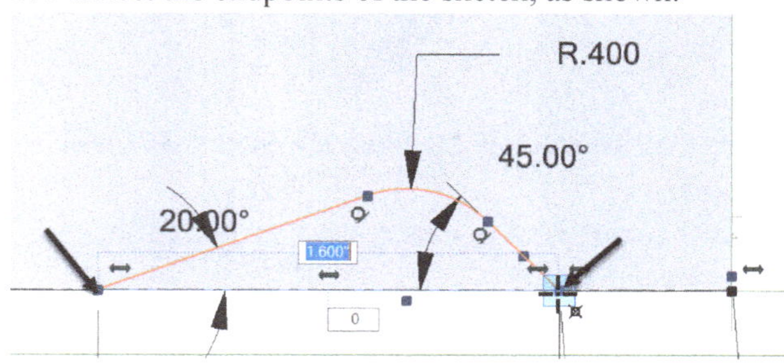

20. Click the **Deactivate Sketch** button on the **2D Sketch** tab of the ribbon.
21. On the ribbon, click **Model > Cut (Remove Material) > Extrude**.
22. Select **Type > Through All**.
23. Click **OK**.

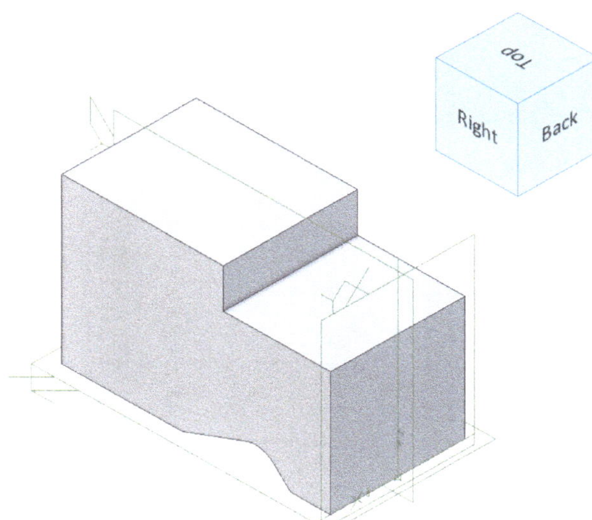

24. To start a new sketch, click **Model** tab > **Sketch > Activate 2D Sketch** on the ribbon.
25. Click on the right side face of the model.

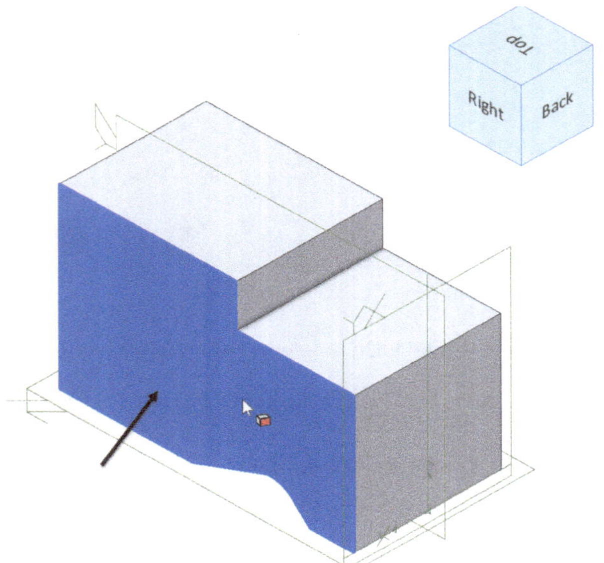

26. On the ribbon, click **2D Sketch > Sketch Figures > Line**.
27. Click on the vertical axis of the sketch to define the start point.

28. Move the pointer vertically upward, and then click to create the vertical line.

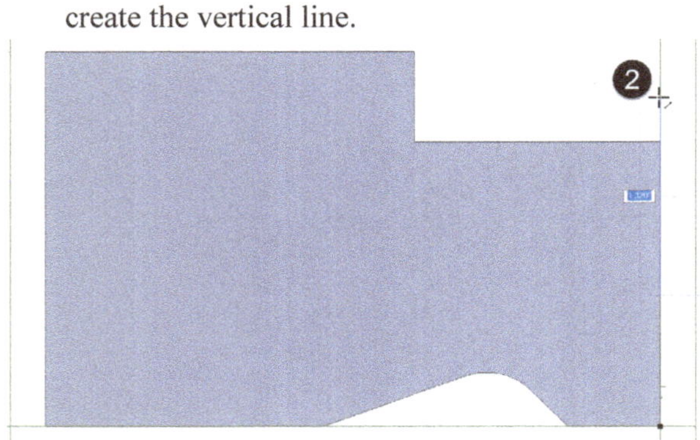

29. Move the pointer horizontally toward left, and then click.

30. Move the vertically downward and click.

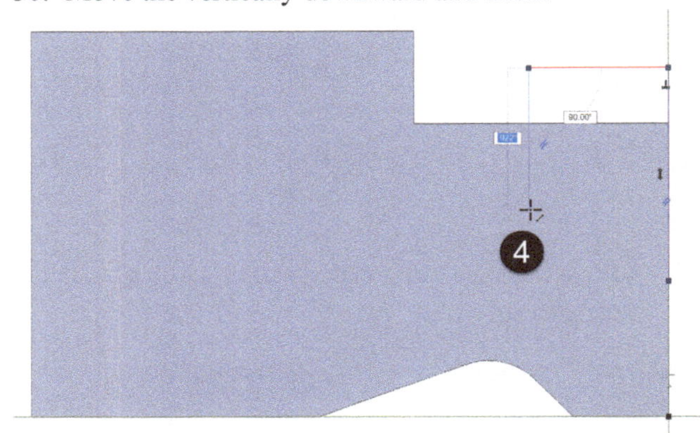

31. Right-click and **Select**.
32. On the ribbon, click **2D Sketch > Sketch Figures > Tangent Arc**.
33. Select the endpoints of the two vertical lines.

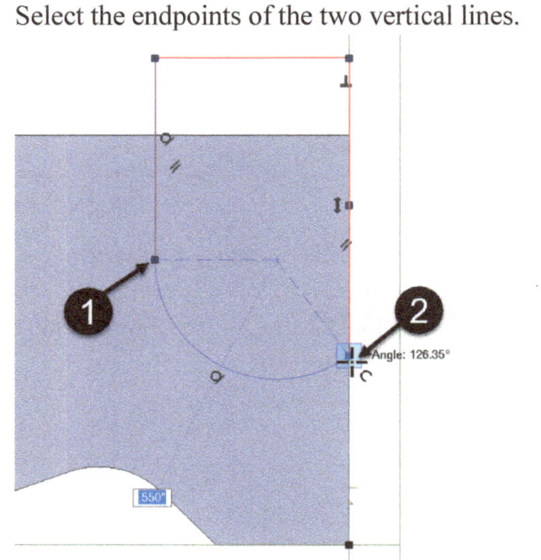

34. On the ribbon, click **2D Sketch > Constraints > Coincident Constraint**.
35. Select the center point of the circle and the right vertical line.

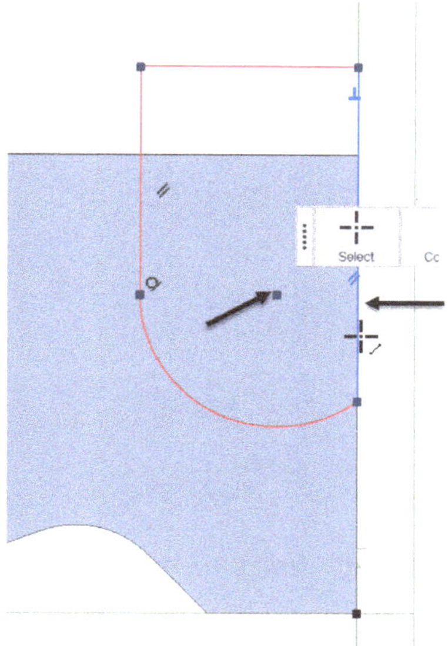

36. On the ribbon, click **2D Sketch > Constraints > Collinear Constraint**.
37. Select the horizontal line of the sketch.
38. Select the horizontal edge of the model, as shown.

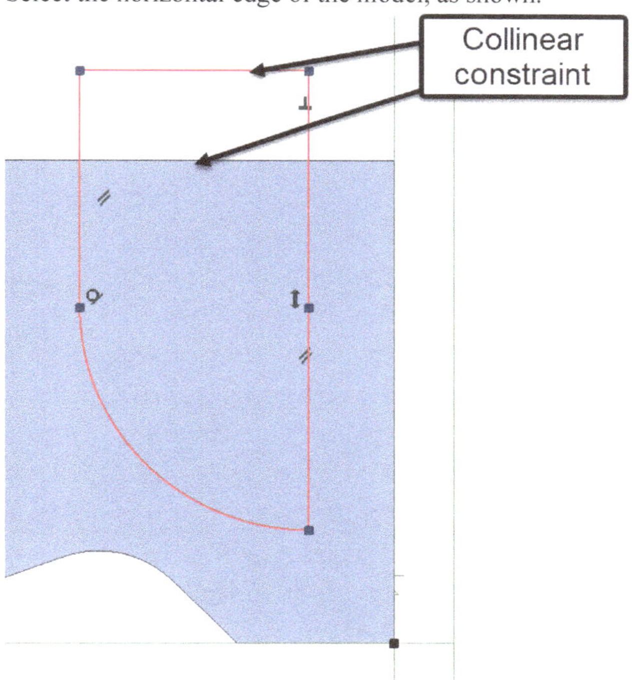

39. Click in the graphics window.
40. Select the vertical line of the sketch.
41. Select the vertical edge of the model, as shown.

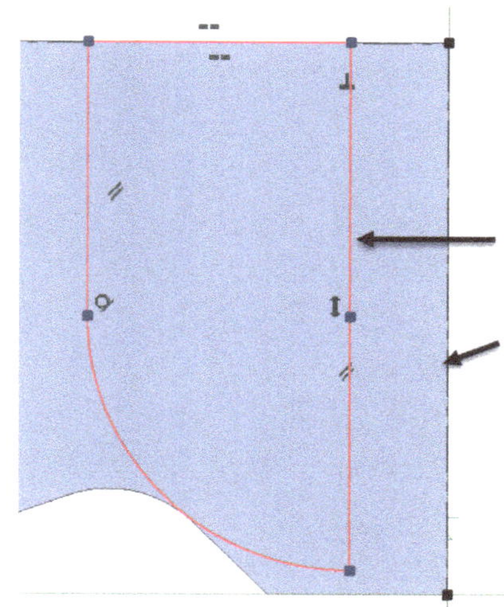

42. On the ribbon, click **2D Sketch > Sketch Figures > Dimension**.
43. Select the arc.
44. Type **0.8** and click **OK**.
45. Select the centerpoint of the arc and the sketch origin.
46. Type 1.4 in the **Dimension** box and click **OK**.

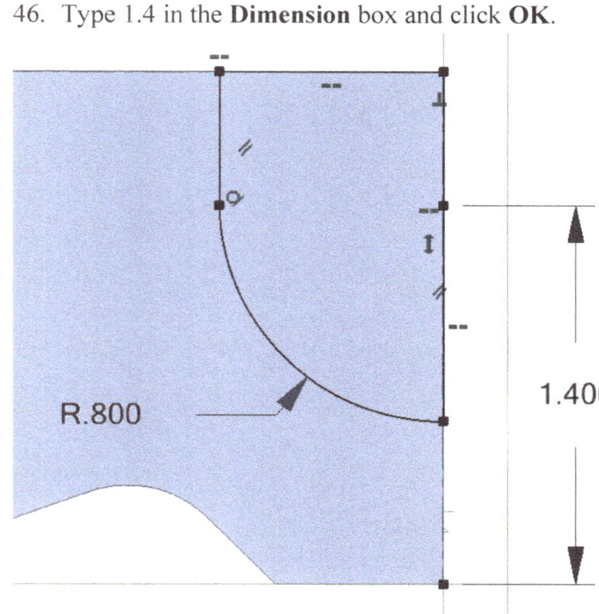

47. Click the **Deactivate Sketch** button on the **2D Sketch** tab of the ribbon.
48. On the ribbon, click **Model > Cut (Remove Material) > Extrude**.
49. Select **Type > To Depth**.
50. Type **0.4** in the **Depth** box.
51. Check the **Reverse** option, if the preview is displayed on outside the model.
52. Click **OK**.

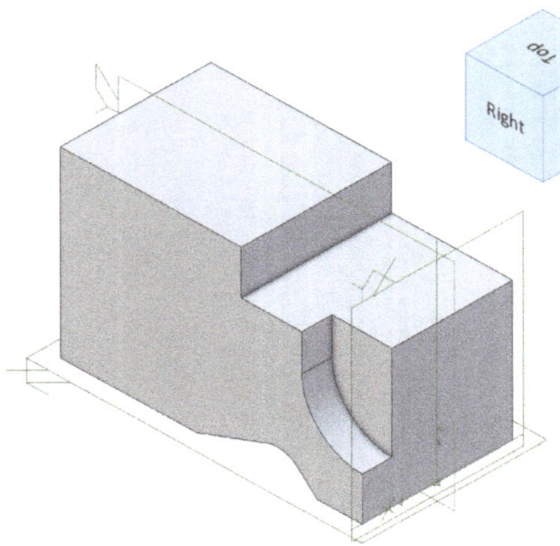

53. To start a new sketch, click **Model** tab > **Sketch > Activate 2D Sketch** on the ribbon.
54. Select the flat face of the cut feature.
55. Create a circle.
56. Click the **Line** button on the **References** panel.
57. Draw a vertical line passing through the centerpoint of the circle. Press ESC.

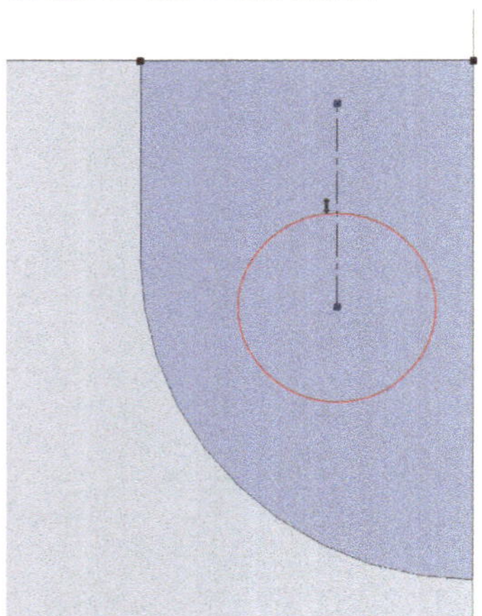

58. On the ribbon, click **2D Sketch > Constraints > Midline Constraint**.
59. Select the top endpoint of the vertical reference line.
60. Select the top horizontal edge of the sketch face, as shown.

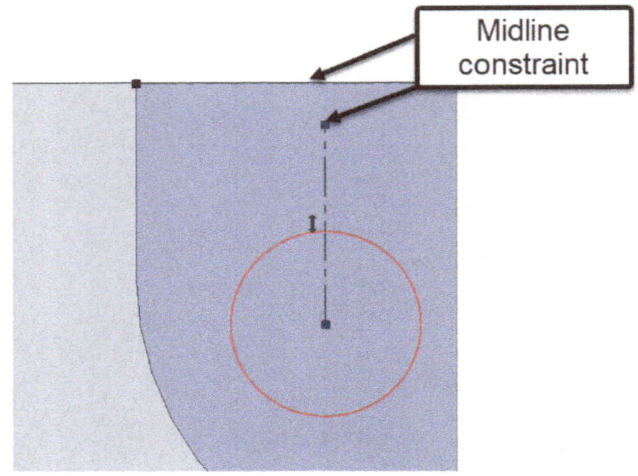

61. On the ribbon, click **2D Sketch > Constraints > Equal Constraint**.
62. Select the left edge and vertical reference line.

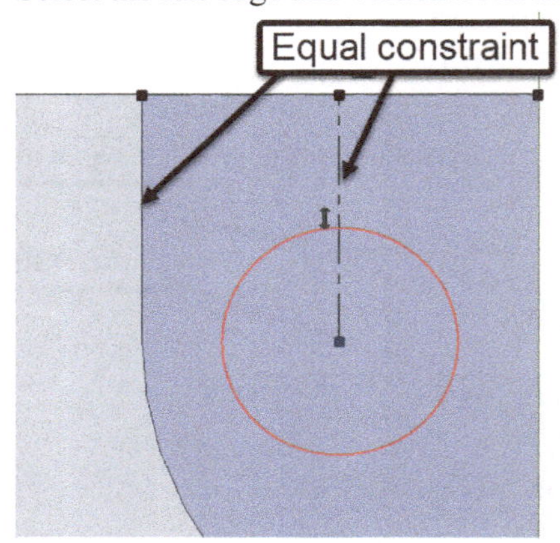

63. Add the diameter dimension to the circle.

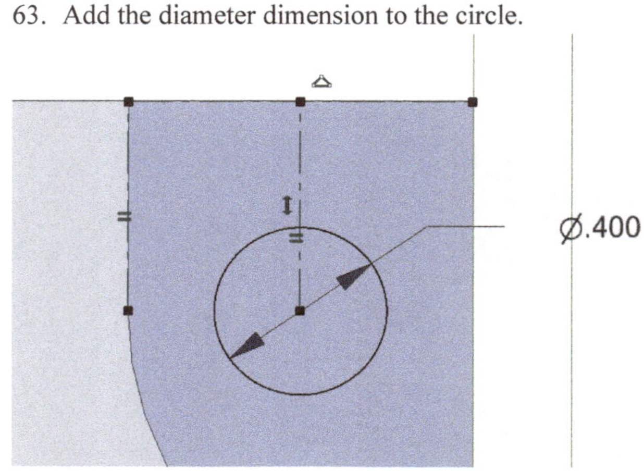

64. Click the **Deactivate Sketch** button on the **2D Sketch** tab of the ribbon.
65. On the ribbon, click **Model > Cut (Remove Material) > Extrude**.
66. Select **Type > Through All**.
67. Click **OK**.

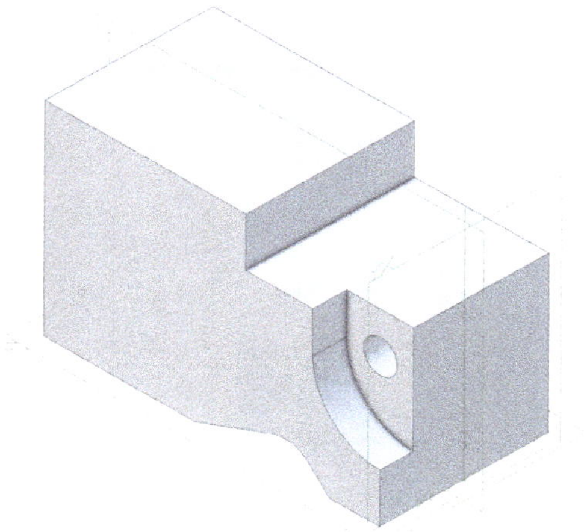

Creating the Extruded Cut Feature on the left side

1. To start a new sketch, click **Model** tab > **Sketch > Activate 2D Sketch** on the ribbon.
2. Click on the top face of the model.

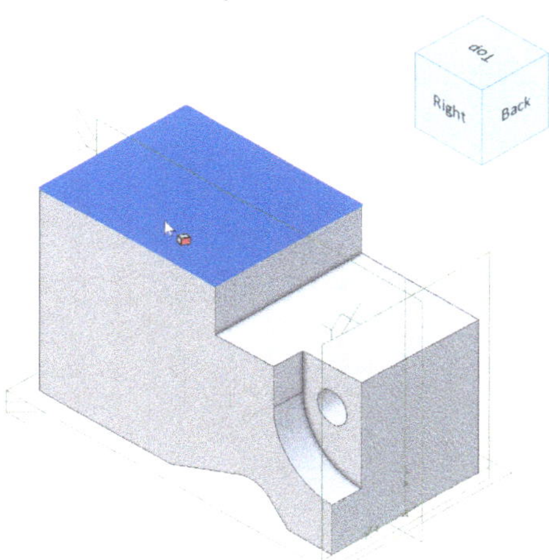

3. Create a rectangle, as shown.

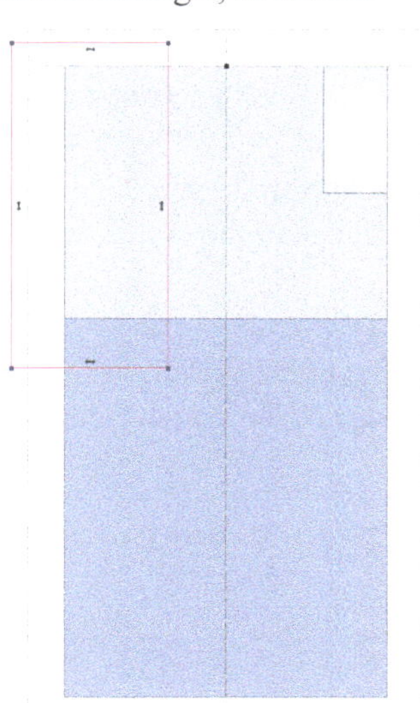

4. Create horizontal and vertical dimensions, as shown.

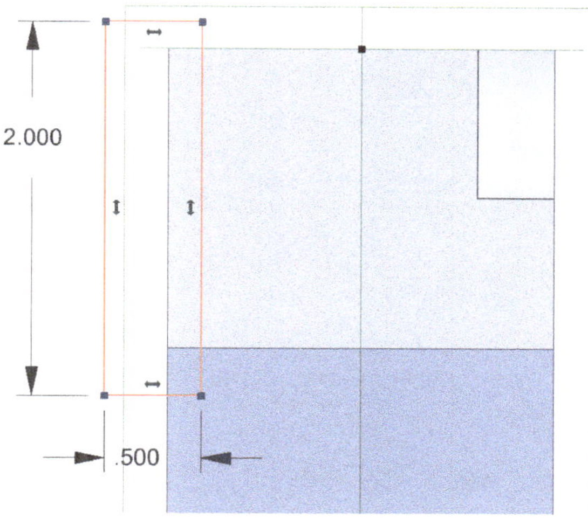

5. On the ribbon, click **2D Sketch > Constraints > Collinear Constraint**.
6. Select the horizontal line of the sketch.
7. Select the horizontal edge of the sketch face, as shown.
8. Click in the graphics window.
9. Select the vertical line of the sketch.
10. Select the vertical edge of the sketch face, as shown.

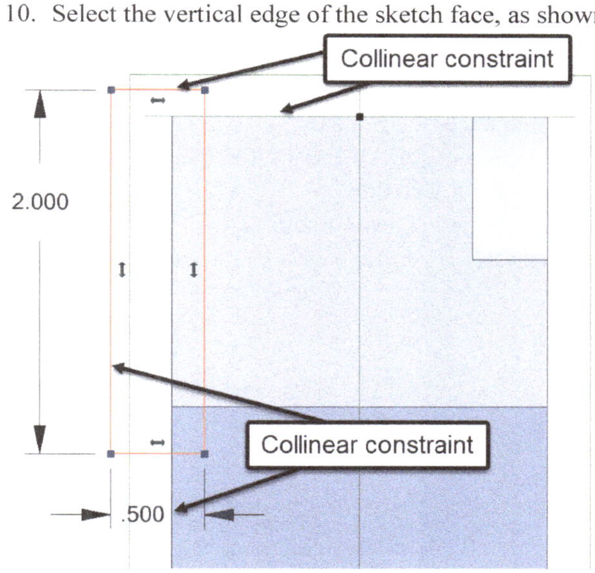

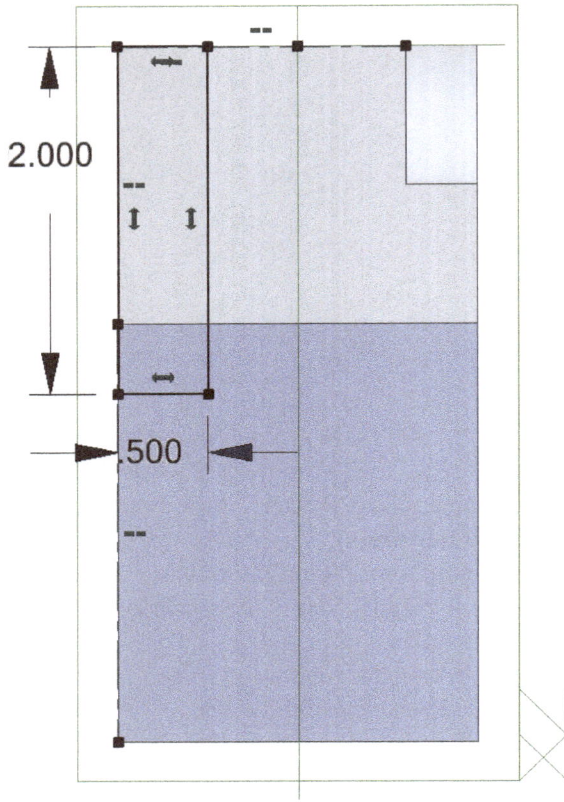

68. Click the **Deactivate Sketch** button on the **2D Sketch** tab of the ribbon.
69. On the ribbon, click **Model > Cut (Remove Material) > Extrude**.
70. Select **Type > Through All**.
71. Click **OK**.

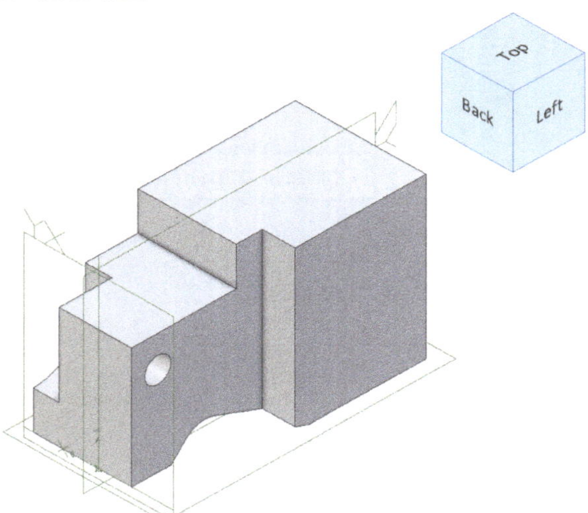

Creating the Angled Cut

1. To start a new sketch, click **Model** tab > **Sketch > Activate 2D Sketch** on the ribbon.
2. Click on the front face of the model.

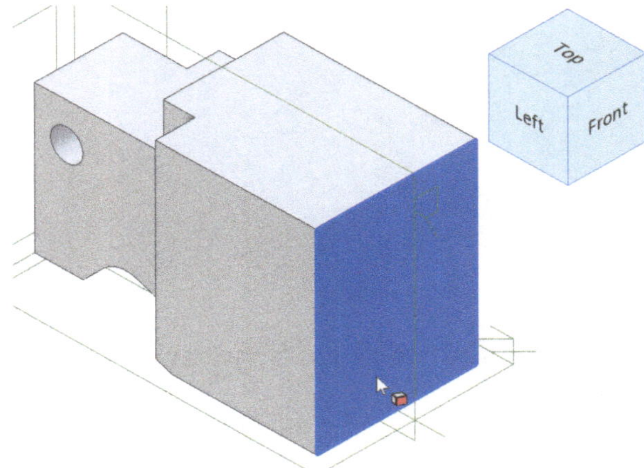

3. Create a triangle and add dimensions to it, as shown.

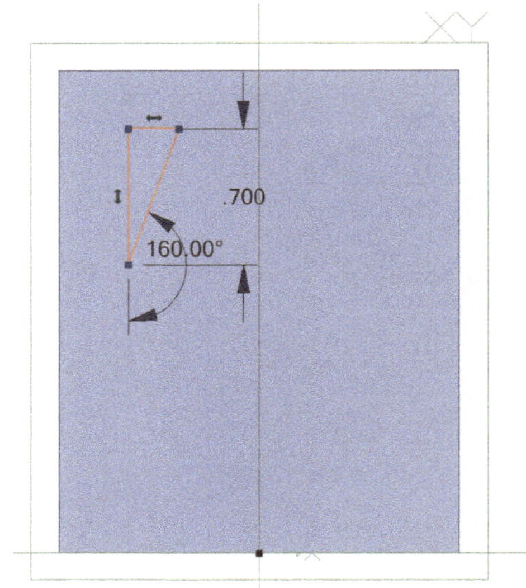

4. On the ribbon, click **2D Sketch > Constraints > Collinear Constraint**.
5. Select the horizontal line of the sketch.
6. Select the horizontal edge of the sketch face, as shown.
7. Click in the graphics window.
8. Select the vertical line of the sketch.
9. Select the vertical edge of the sketch face, as shown.

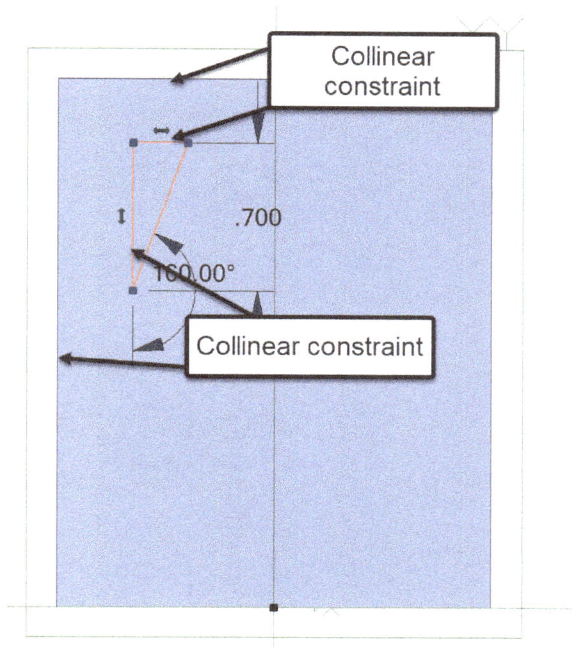

10. Click the **Deactivate Sketch** button on the **2D Sketch** tab of the ribbon.
11. On the ribbon, click **Model > Cut (Remove Material) > Extrude**.
12. Select **Type > Through All**.
13. Click **OK**.

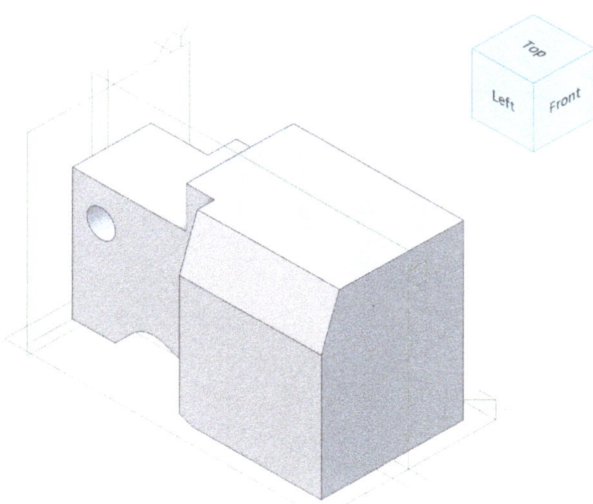

Creating the Extruded Cut feature on the left

1. To start a new sketch, click **Model** tab > **Sketch > Activate 2D Sketch** on the ribbon.
2. Click on the left face of the model.

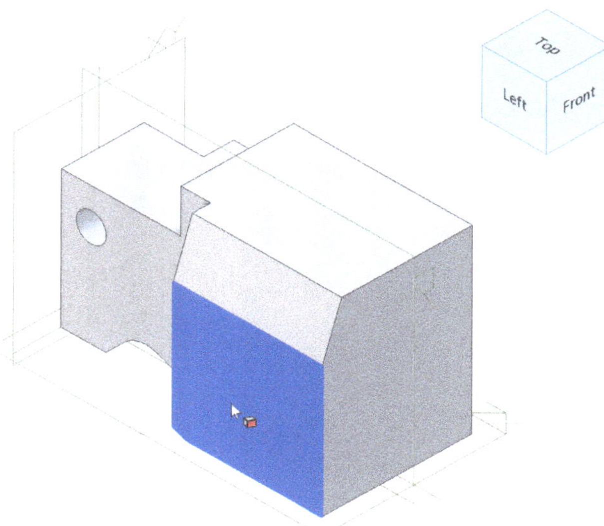

3. Create the closed sketch, as shown.

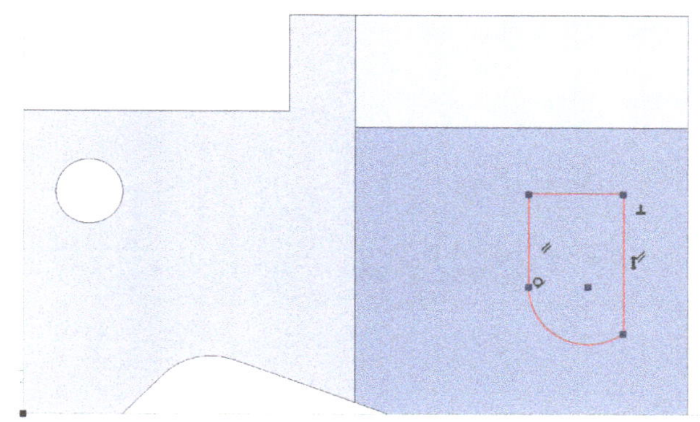

4. Create the radius and vertical dimensions, as shown.

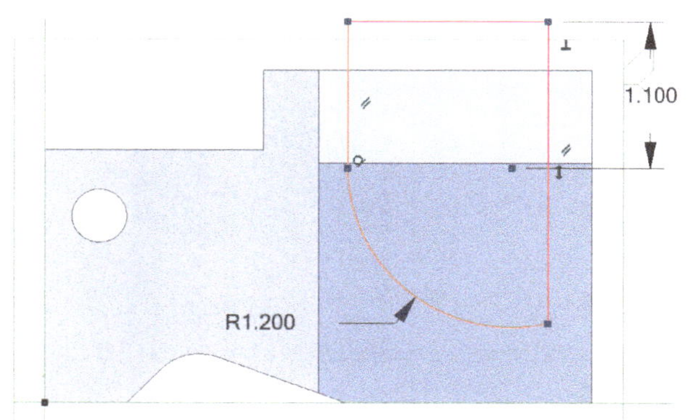

14. On the ribbon, click **2D Sketch > Constraints > Collinear Constraint**.
15. Create a collinear constraint between the horizontal line and the horizontal edge.
16. Click in the graphics window.
17. Create a collinear constraint between the vertical line and the vertical edge.

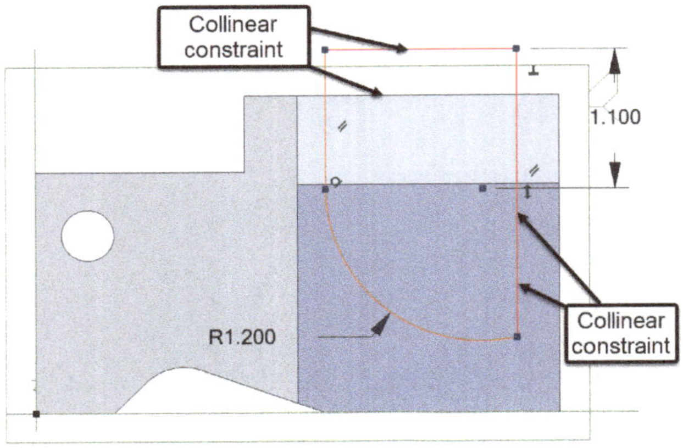

18. On the ribbon, click **2D Sketch > Constraints > Coincident Constraint**.
19. Create a coicident constraint between the centerpoint of the arc and the vertical line.

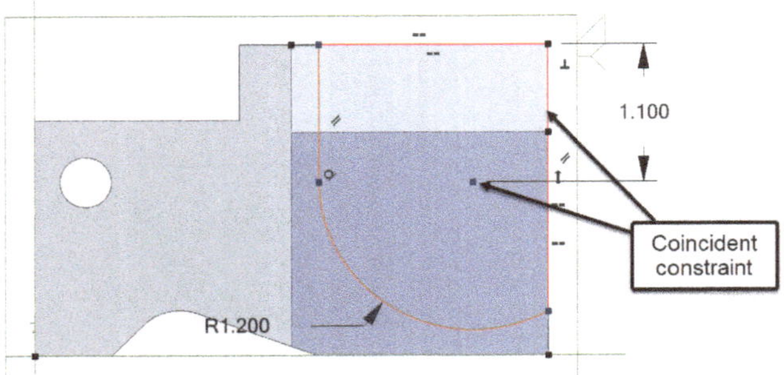

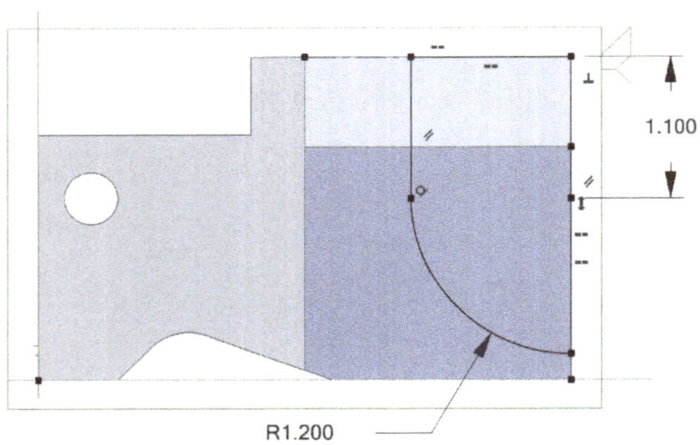

20. Click the **Deactivate Sketch** button on the **2D Sketch** tab of the ribbon.
21. On the ribbon, click **Model > Cut (Remove Material) > Extrude**.
22. Select **Type > To Geometry**.
23. Select the right face of the geometry.
24. Type **-0.35** in the **Offset** box.

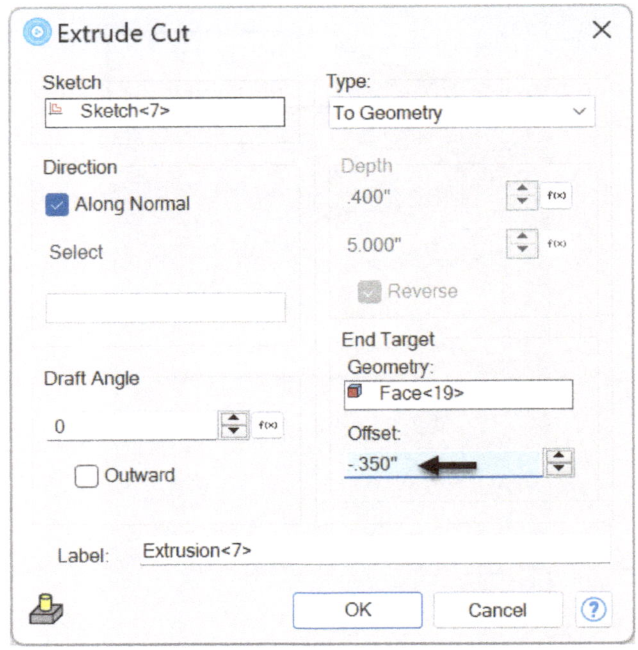

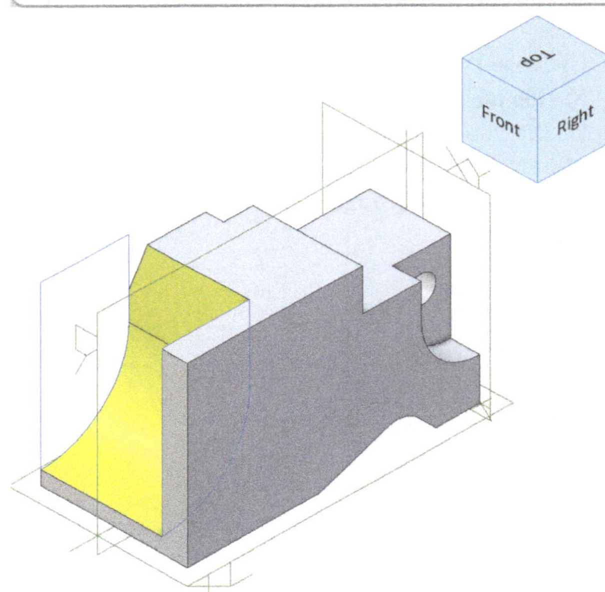

25. Click **OK**.

Creating the Extruded feature on the right

1. To start a new sketch, click **Model** tab > **Sketch > Activate 2D Sketch** on the ribbon.
2. Click on the right face of the model.

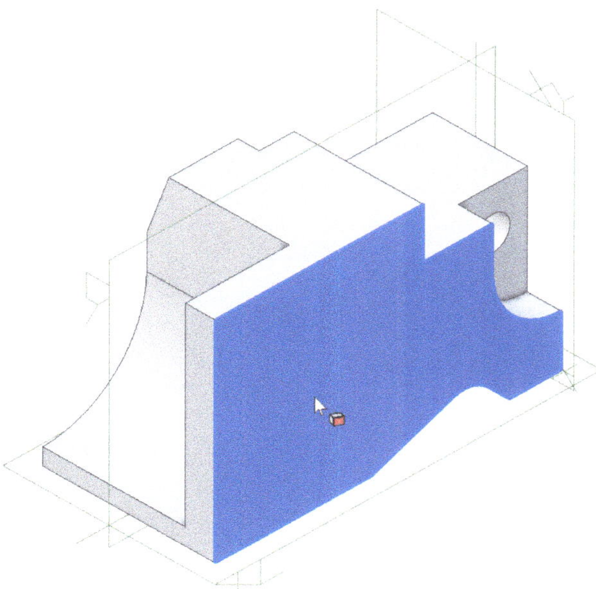

3. On the ribbon, click **2D Sketch** > **Sketch Figures** > **Arc.**

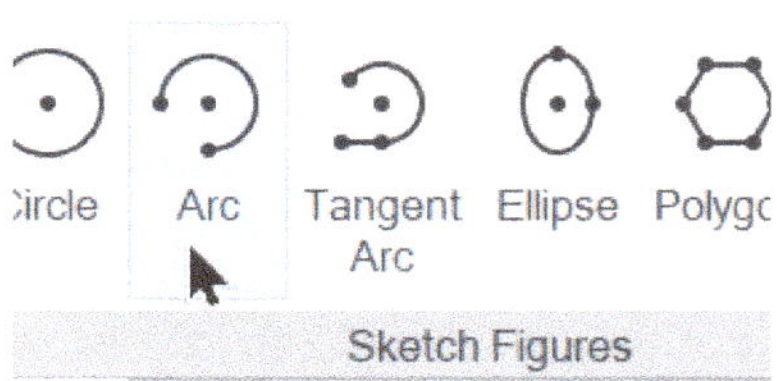

4. Click to specify the center point.
5. Move the cursor upward and click to specify the start point of the arc.
6. Move the cursor in the clockwise direction and click to specify the endpoint of the arc.

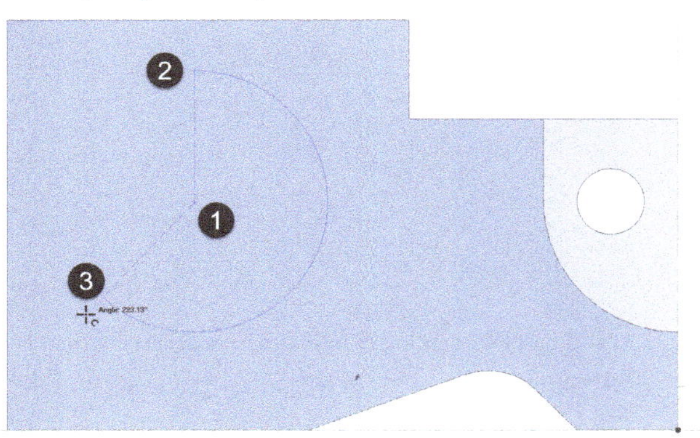

7. Click at the lower left corner to specify the center point.
8. Move the cursor upward and select the lower endpoint of the large arc to specify the start point of the arc.
9. Move the cursor in the clockwise direction and click to specify the endpoint of the arc.

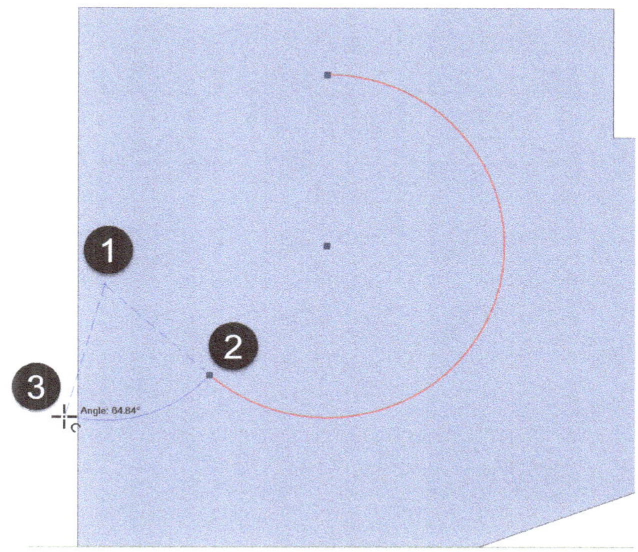

10. On the ribbon, click **2D Sketch** > **Sketch Figures** > **Line**.
11. Select the top endpoint of the large arc.
12. Move the pointer vertically upward and click.

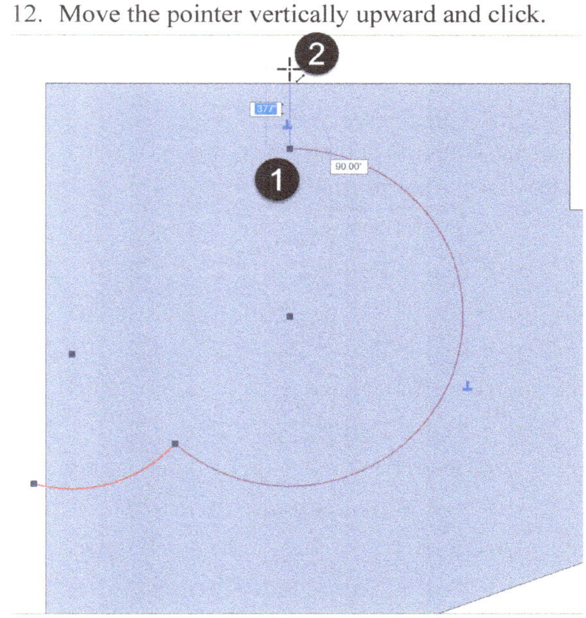

5. On the ribbon, click **2D Sketch > Constraints > Horizontal Constraint**.
6. Select the centerpoints of the two arcs
7. On the ribbon, click **2D Sketch > Constraints > Vertical Constraint**.
8. Select the centerpoint of the large arc.
9. Select the lower endpoint of the vertical line.

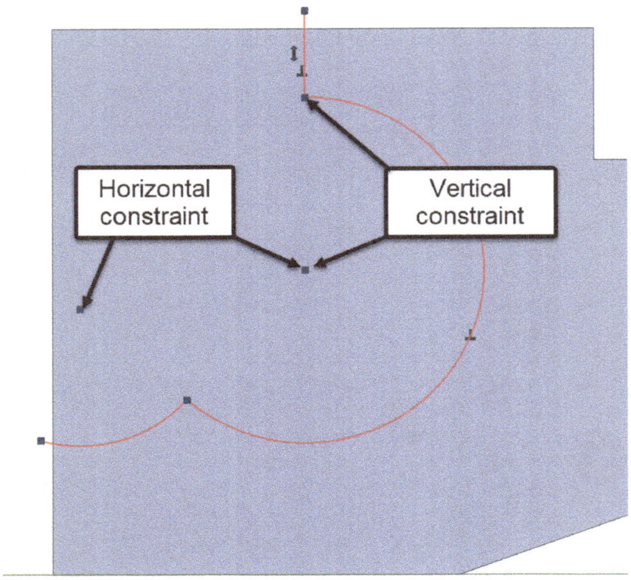

10. On the ribbon, click **2D Sketch > Constraints > Coincident Constraint**.
11. Select the centerpoint of the small arc.
12. Select the vertical edge.
13. Click in the graphics window.
14. Select the endpoint of the small arc.
15. Select the vertical edge.
16. Click in the graphics window.
17. Selec the endpoint of the vertical line.
18. Select the horizontal edge.

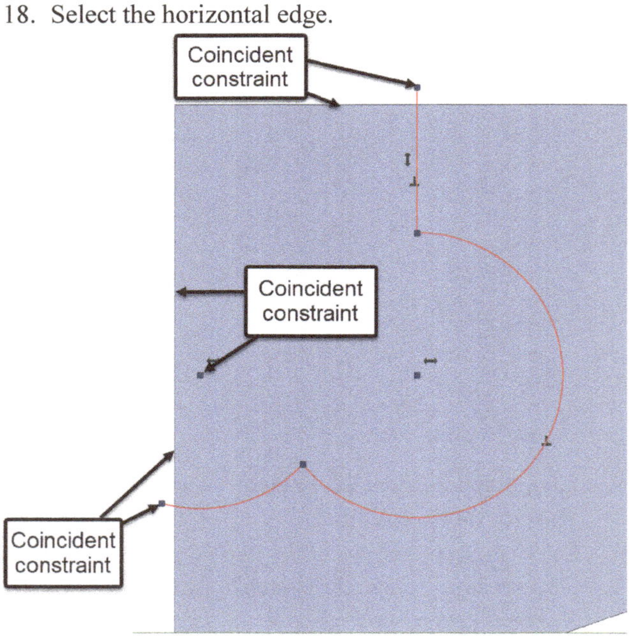

19. On the ribbon, click **2D Sketch** > **Sketch Figures** > **Dimension**.
20. Add the Radial dimension of 1 inch to the large arc.
21. Add the vertical and horizontal dimensions between the centerpoint of the large arc and the vertical edge.

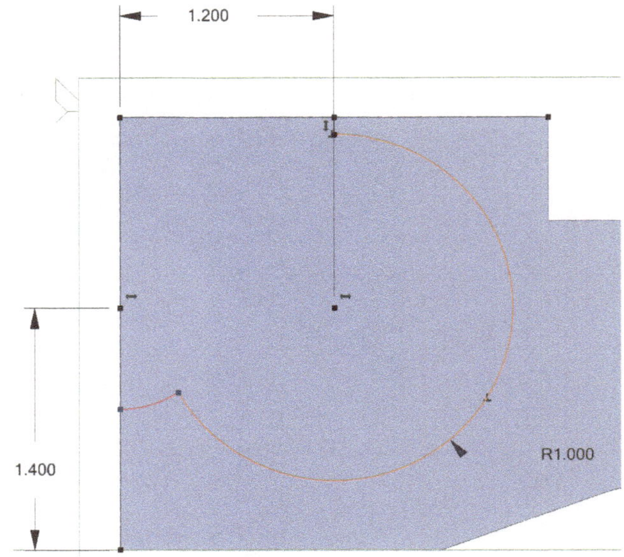

22. On the ribbon, click **2D Sketch > Constraints > Equal Constraint**.
23. Select the two arcs to make their radius equal.

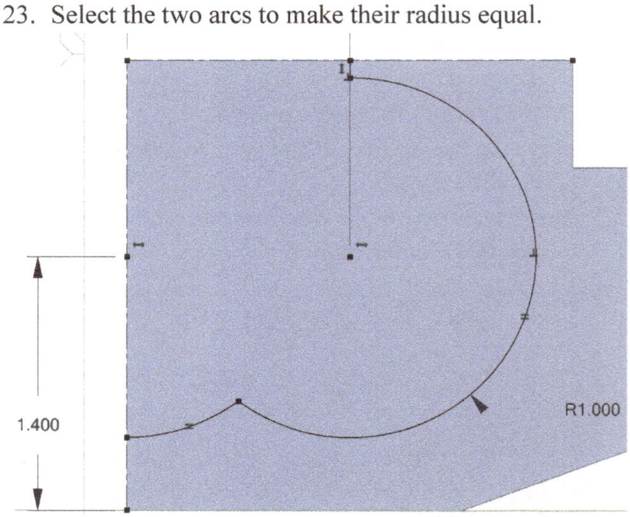

24. On the ribbon, click **2D Sketch** > **Sketch Figures** > **Dimension**.
25. Select the endpoint of the small arc.
26. Move the pointer vertically upward and select the endpoint of the vertical edge.
27. Move the pointer toward the right and select the endpoint of the vertical line.

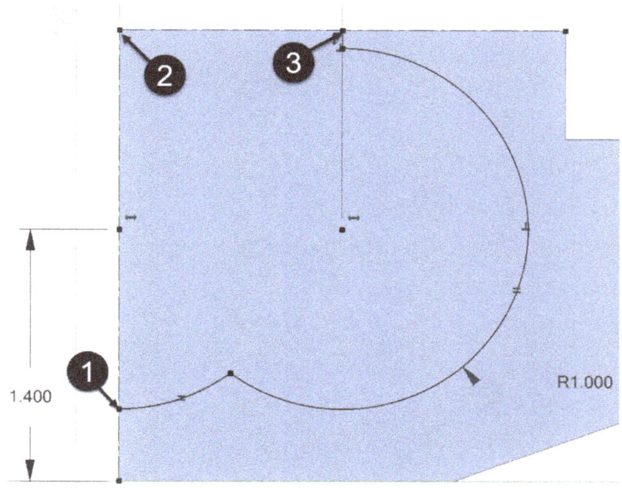

28. Click the **Deactivate Sketch** button on the **2D Sketch** tab of the ribbon.
29. On the ribbon, click **Model > Cut (Remove Material) > Extrude**.
30. Select **Type > To Depth**.
31. Type **0.5** in the **Depth** box.
32. Check the **Reverse** option, if the preview is not displayed.
33. Click **OK**.

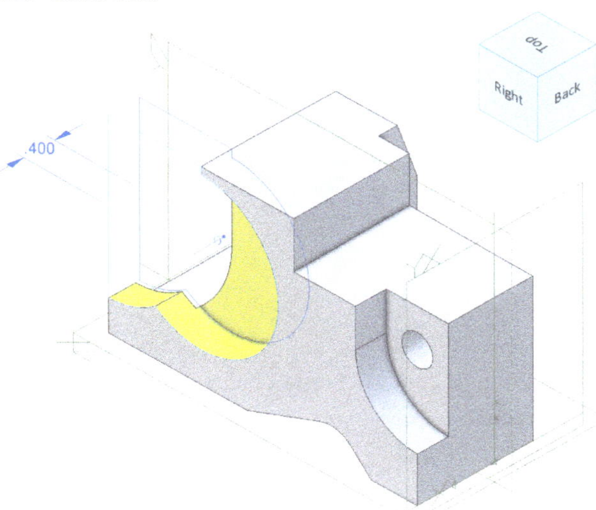

Adding the Extruded Boss Features

1. To start a new sketch, click **Model** tab > **Sketch > Activate 2D Sketch** on the ribbon.
2. Click on the flat face of the cut feature.

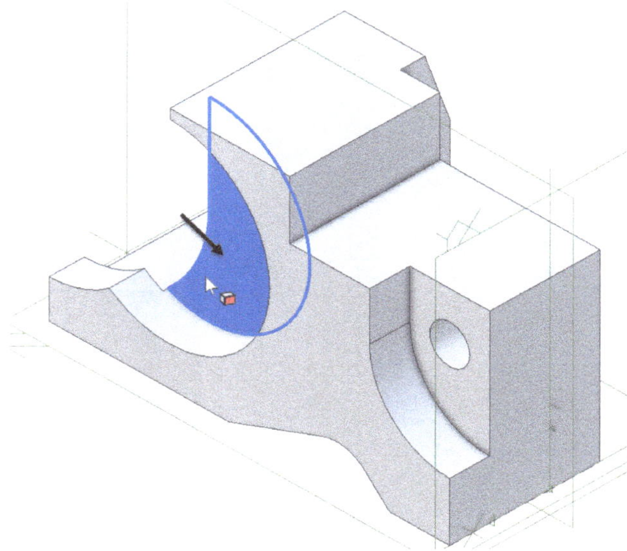

3. On the ribbon, click **2D Sketch** > **Sketch Figures** > **Arc.**
4. Click to specify the center point.
5. Move the cursor upward and click to specify the start point of the arc.
6. Move the cursor in the clockwise direction and click to specify the endpoint of the arc.

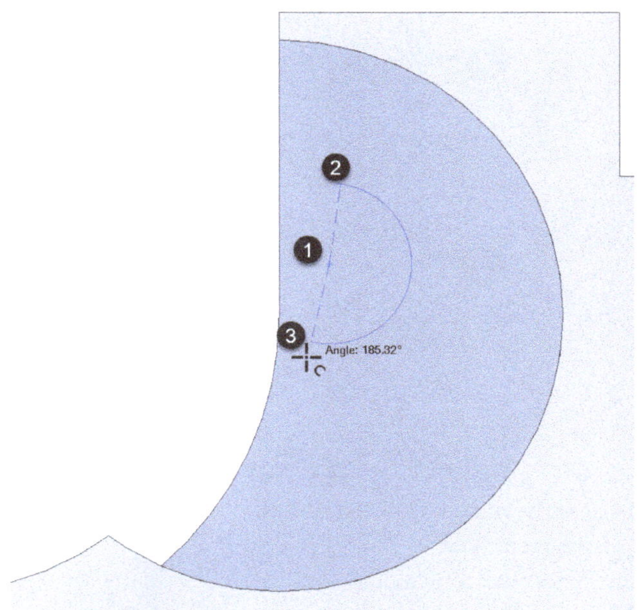

7. On the ribbon, click **2D Sketch > Constraints > Concentric Constraint**.
8. Select the arc and the circular edge, as shown.
9. On the ribbon, click **2D Sketch > Constraints > Coincident Constraint**.
10. Make the endpoints of the arc coincident with the vertical and circular edges.

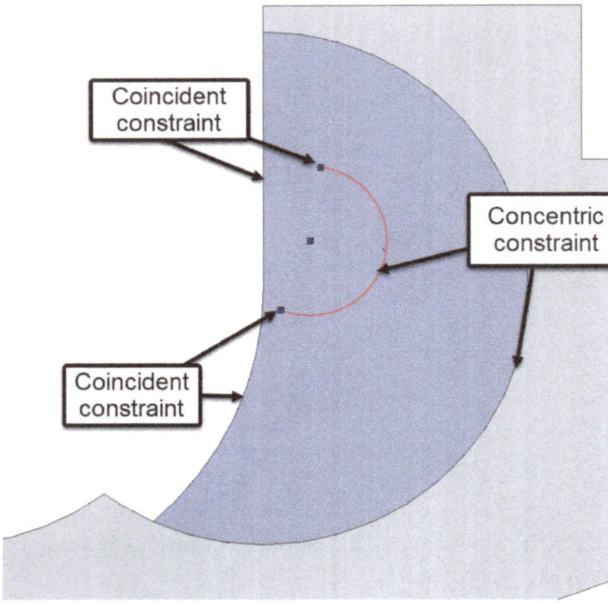

11. On the ribbon, click **2D Sketch** > **Sketch Figures** > **Line**.
12. Select the centerpoint of the arc.
13. Move the pointer upward and select the upper endpoint of the arc.

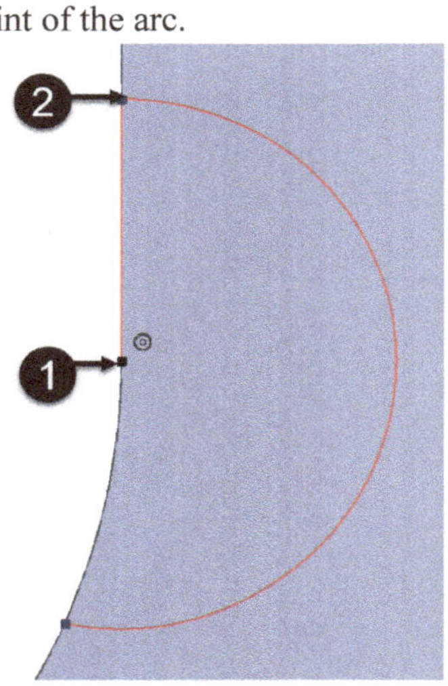

14. On the ribbon, click **2D Sketch** > **Sketch Figures** > **Tangent Arc**.
15. Select the vertical line.
16. Move the pointer downward and select the lower end point of the large arc.

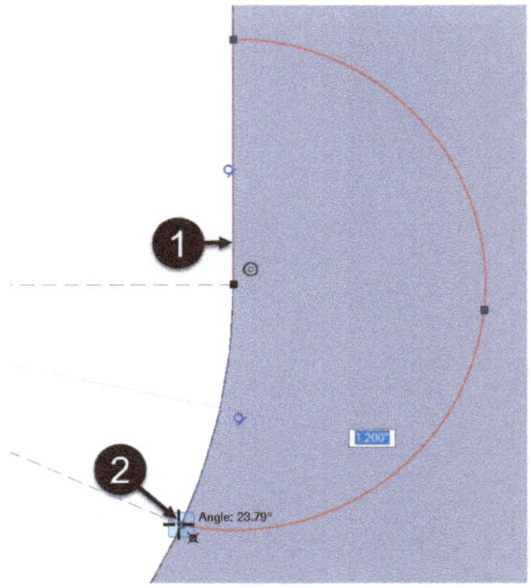

17. Add the radial dimension to the arc, as shown.

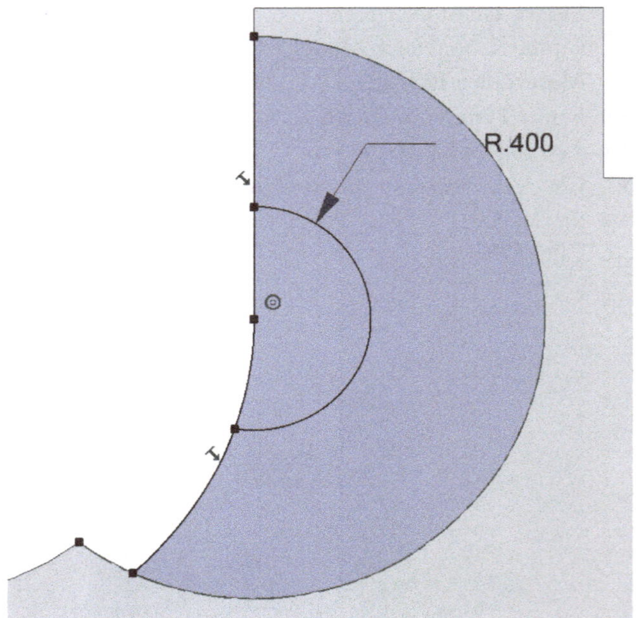

18. Click the **Deactivate Sketch** button on the **2D Sketch** tab of the ribbon.
19. On the ribbon, click **Model > Boss (Add Material) > Extrude**.
20. Select **Type > To Depth**.
21. Type **0.2** in the **Depth** box.
22. Check the **Reverse** option, if the preview is not displayed.
23. Click **OK**.

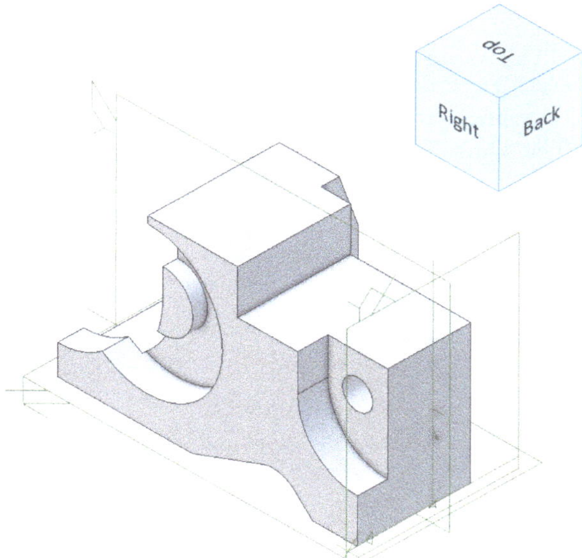

24. To start a new sketch, click **Model** tab > **Sketch > Activate 2D Sketch** on the ribbon.
25. Click on the face of the extruded feature, as shown.

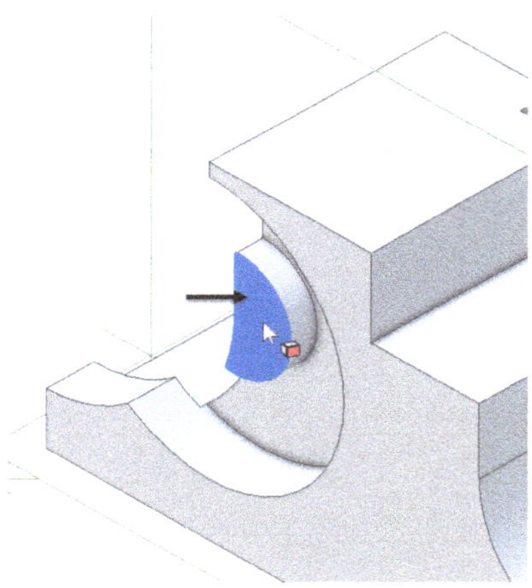

26. Create a circle and add the diameter dimension to it.

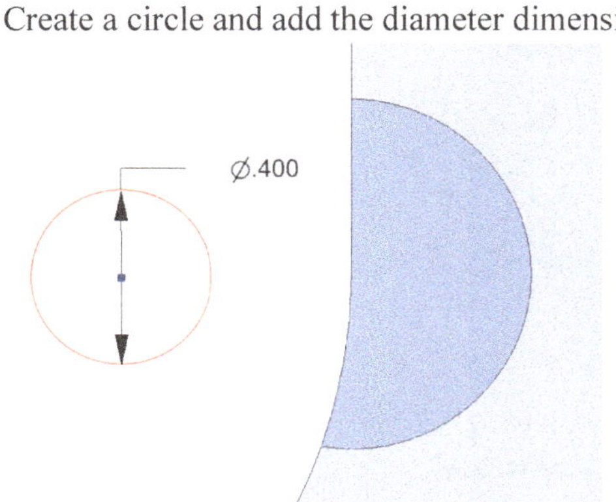

27. On the ribbon, click **2D Sketch > Constraints > Concentric Constraint**.
28. Select the circle and the curved edge.

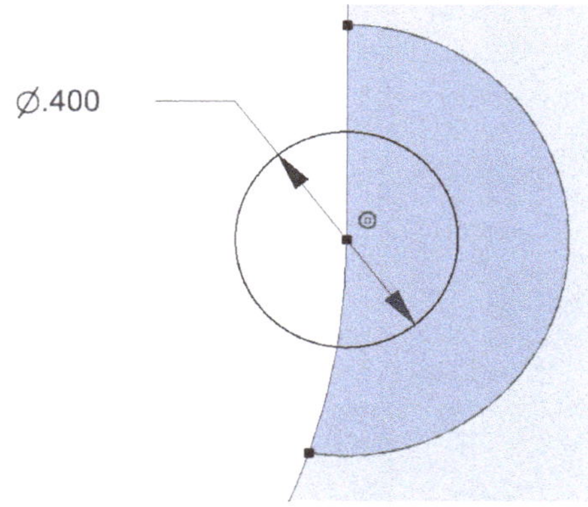

29. Click the **Deactivate Sketch** button on the **2D Sketch** tab of the ribbon.
30. On the ribbon, click **Model > Boss (Add Material) > Extrude**.
31. Select **Type > To Geometry**.
32. Select the right face of the model, as shown.

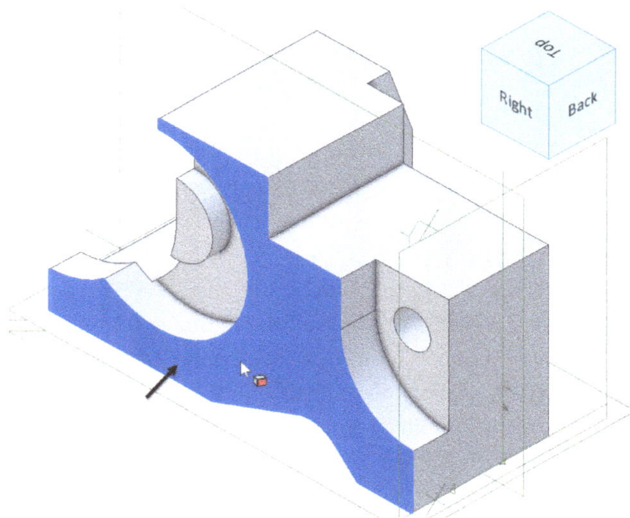

33. Click **OK**.

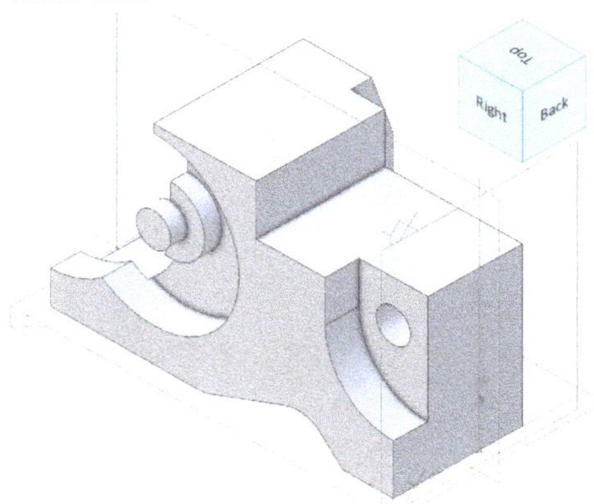

34. Save and close the model.

TUTORIAL 7

In this tutorial, you construct the model shown in the figure.

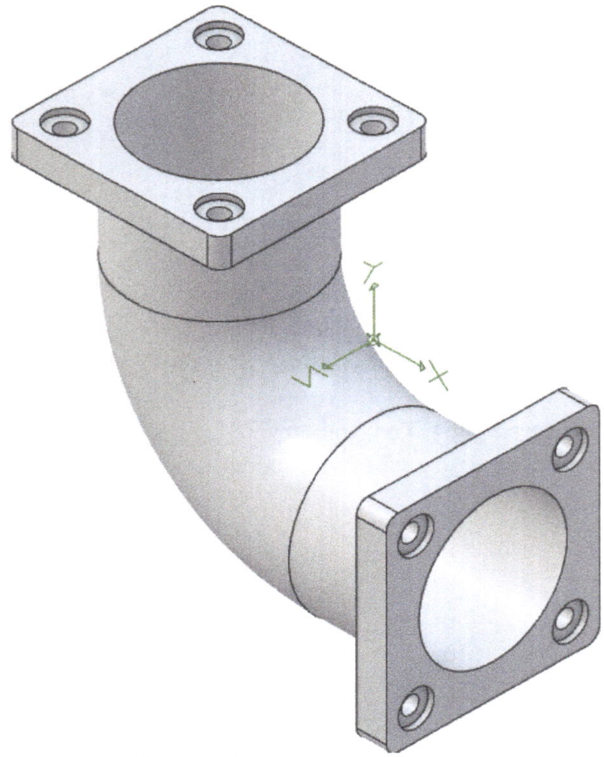

Creating the first feature

1. Open a new Alibre Atom3D file.
2. Click the **New Part** icon on the **Home** window.
3. To start a new sketch, click **Model** tab > **Sketch > Activate 2D Sketch** on the ribbon.
4. Select the XY Plane from the **Design Explorer**.
5. On the ribbon, click **2D Sketch** > **Sketch Figures** > **Line**.
6. Create a vertical and horizontal lines connected to each other, as shown.

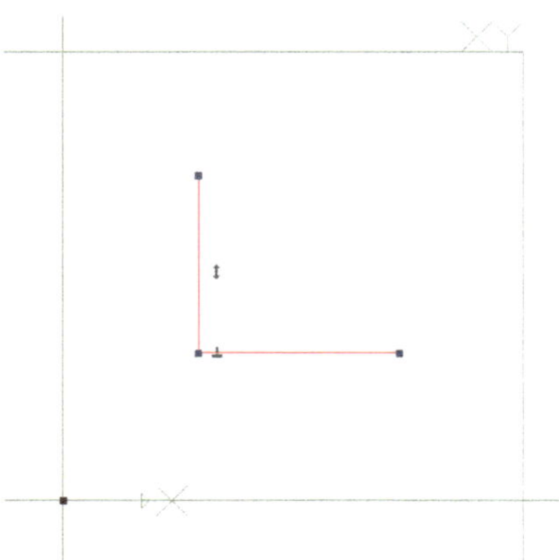

7. On the ribbon, click **2D Sketch** > **Sketch Tools** > **Fillet**.
8. Select the vertical and horizontal lines; a fillet created at the intersection of the two lines.
9. Click **Apply** and **Close**.

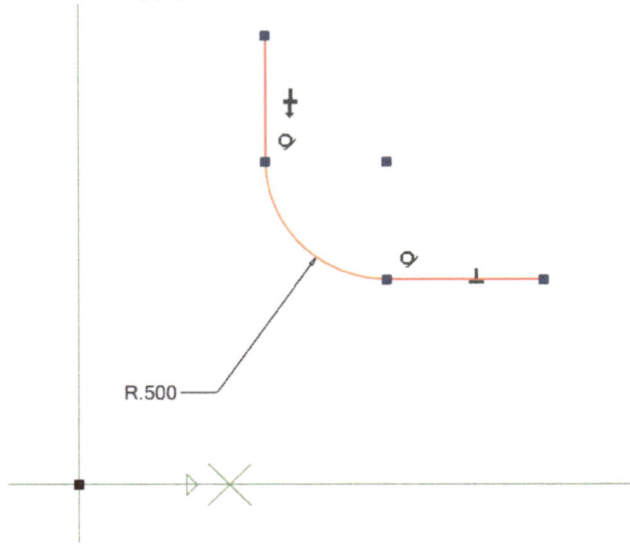

10. On the ribbon, click **2D Sketch** > **Constraints** > **Coincident Constraint**.
11. Select the origin point of the sketch
12. Select the center point of the fillet.

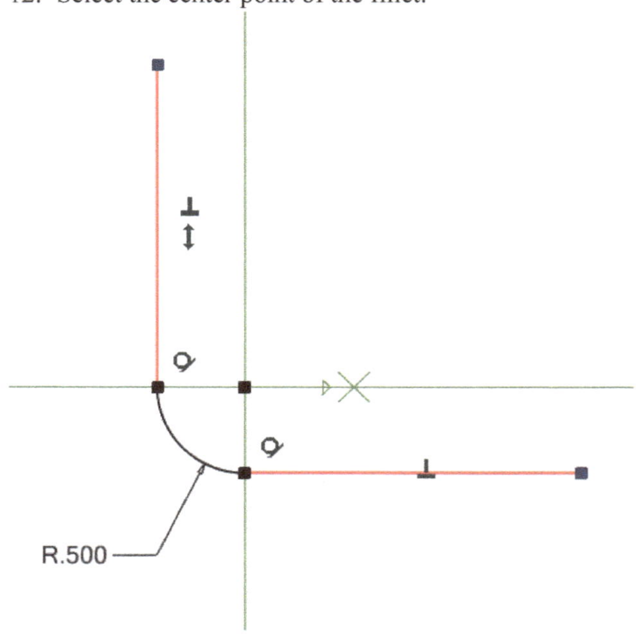

13. On the ribbon, click **2D Sketch** > **Constraints** > **Equal Constraint**.
14. Select the vertical and horizontal lines to make them equal in length.
15. On the ribbon, click **2D Sketch** > **Sketch Figures** > **Dimension**.

16. Select the vertical line.
17. Enter **5.9** in the **Dimension** box and click **OK**.
18. Double-click on the fillet dimension.
19. Type **10.24** in the **Dimension** box and click **OK**.

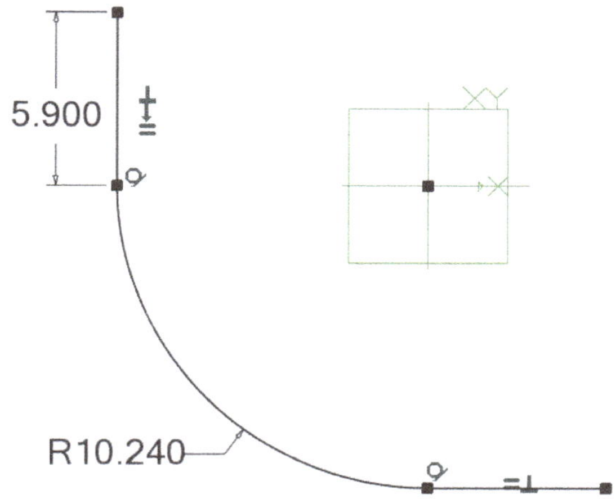

35. Click the **Deactivate Sketch** button on the **2D Sketch** tab of the ribbon.
36. Click **Ignore** on the **Status** dialog.
37. Click **Model > References > Plane** on the ribbon.

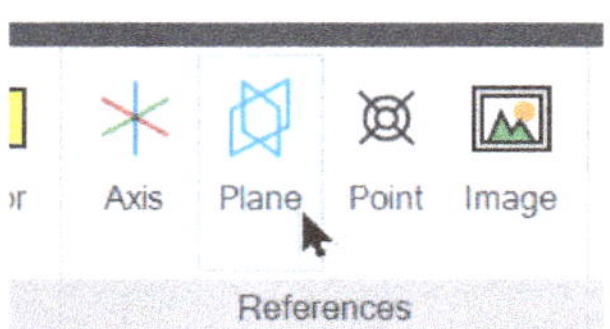

38. On the **Insert Plane** dialog, click **Creation Method** > **Along Sketch** .
39. Select the newly created sketch from the Design Explorer.
40. Click **Apply** and **Close**.
20. Click **Model** tab > **Sketch > Activate 2D Sketch** on the ribbon.
41. Select the newly created plane from the Design Explorer.

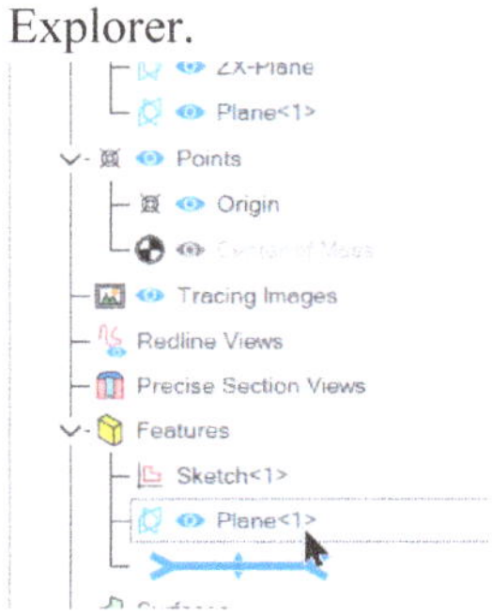

21. On the ribbon, click **2D Sketch** > **Sketch Figures** > **Circle**.
22. Click on the origin.
23. Move the pointer outward and click to create a circle.
24. Create another circle concentric to the previous one.
25. Add diameter dimensions to the circles, as shown.

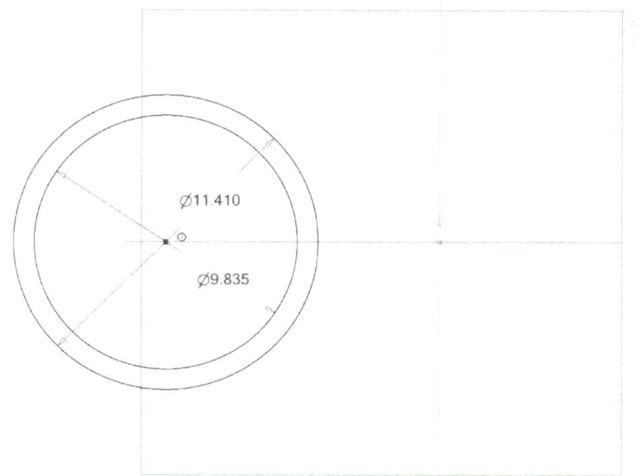

26. Click the **Deactivate Sketch** button on the **2D Sketch** tab of the ribbon.
27. Select the newly created sketch, if already not selected.
28. On the ribbon, click **Model > Boss (Add Material) > Sweep**.

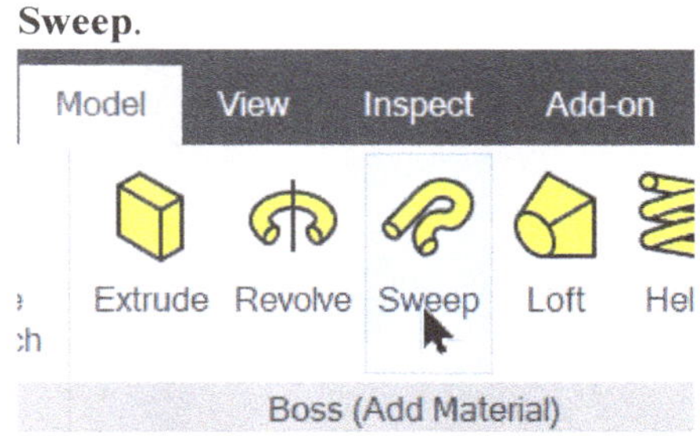

29. On the **Sweep** dialog, click in the **Path Objects** selection box and select the first sketch from the **Design Explorer**.
30. Select **Sweep Type > Entire Path**.
31. Click **OK**.

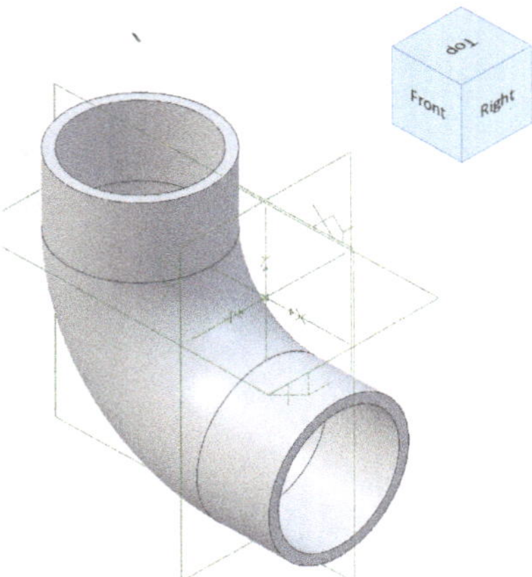

Creating the Flanges

1. Click **Model** tab > **Sketch > Activate 2D Sketch** on the ribbon.
2. Click on the vertical endface of the sweep feature.

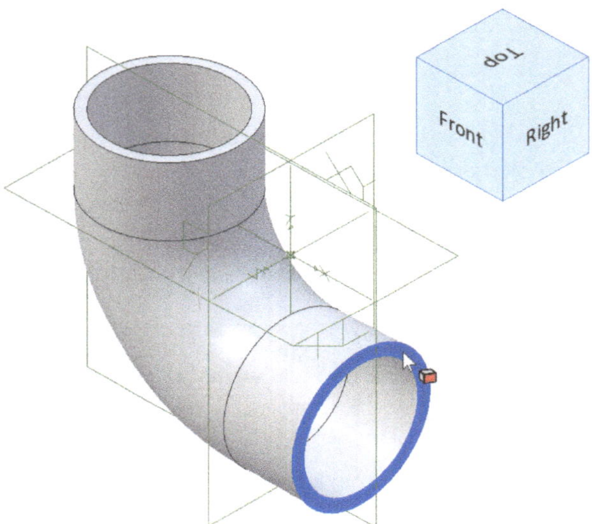

3. Click the **Project to Sketch** icon on the **2D Sketch** tab of the ribbon.
4. Click on the inner circular edge of the model, as shown.

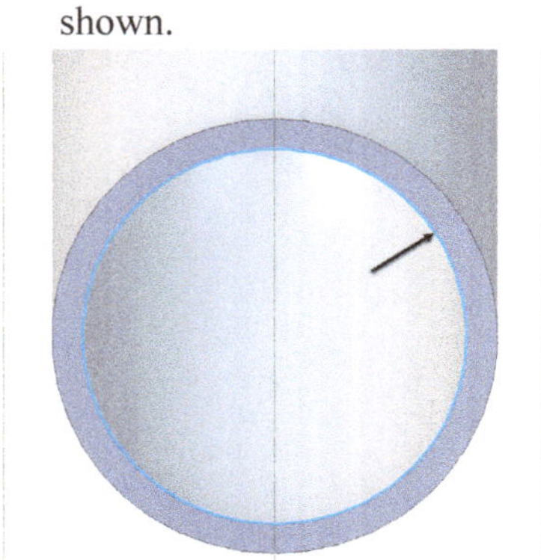

5. Select **Ouptut Options > Create Sketch figure** from the **Project To Sketch** dialog.
6. Check the **Maintain association to source entity** option.
7. Click **OK**.

32. On the ribbon, click **2D Sketch** > **Sketch Figures** > **Polygon** .
33. Type **4** in the **Sides** box available on the **Regular Polygon** dialog.
8. Select the centerpoint of the circular edge.
9. Move the pointer outward and click to create a square. Next, Press **Esc**.

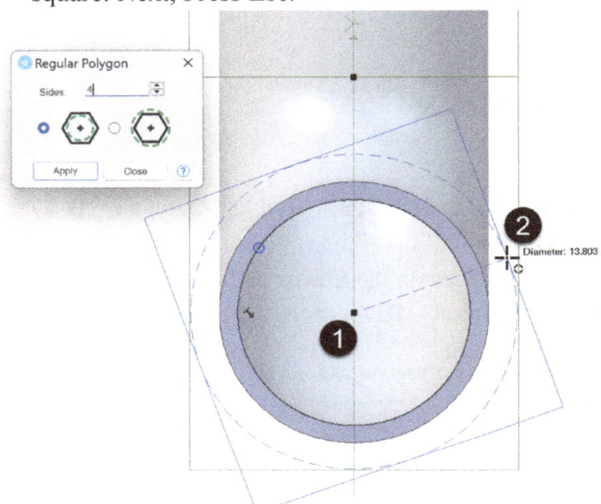

10. Click **Apply** and **Close**.
11. On the ribbon, click **2D Sketch** > **Constraints** > **Horizontal constraint**.
12. Select the top horizontal line, as shown.

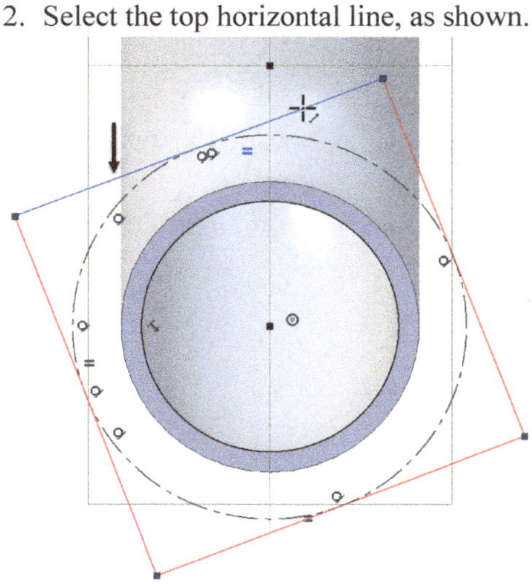

13. Click the **Dimension** icon on the **2D Sketch** tab of the ribbon.
14. Select the top horizontal line.
15. Enter **14.173** in the **Dimension** box and click the **OK** button.

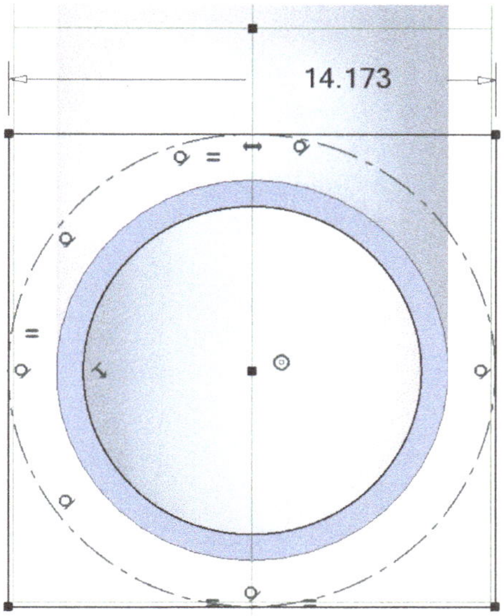

16. Click the **Deactivate Sketch** button on the **2D Sketch** tab of the ribbon.
17. On the ribbon, click **Model > Boss (Add Material) > Extrude**.
18. Select **Type > To Depth**.
19. Type **1.969** in the **Depth** box.
20. Click **OK**.

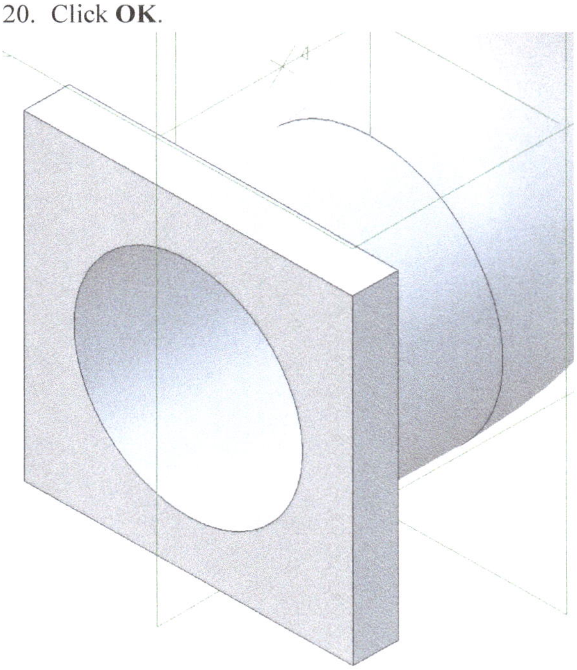

21. On the ribbon, click **Model > Part Tools > Fillet**.
22. Select the edges of the model, as shown.

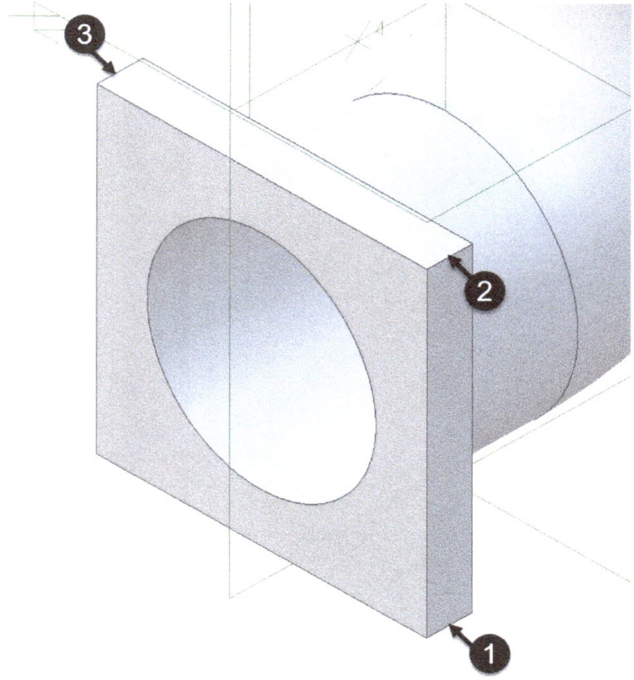

23. Click the lower left corner point of the right face of the ViewCube; the model is rotated.
24. Select the edge of the model, as shown.

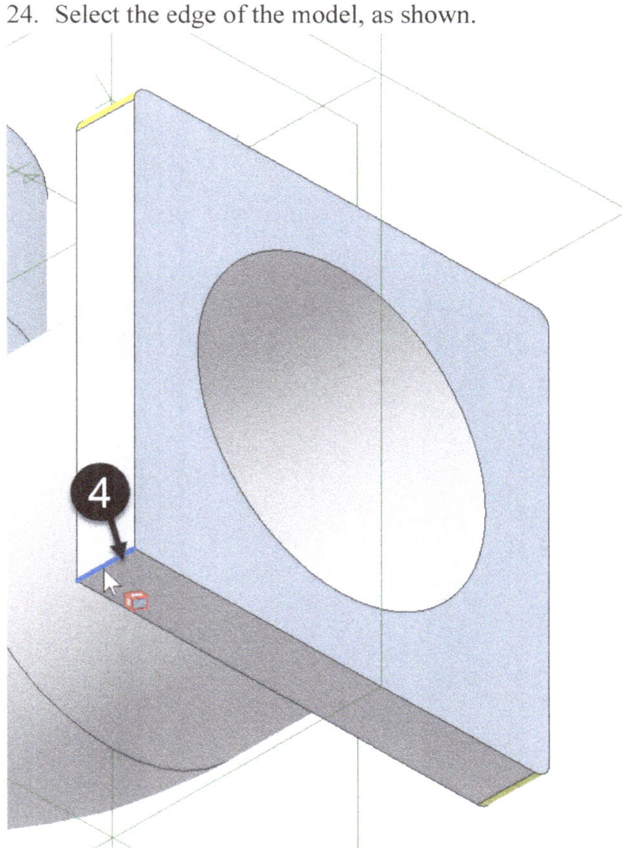

25. Type **0.787** in the **Radius/Chordal Length** box.
26. Click **Apply** and **Close**.
27. On the ribbon, click **Model > Part Tools > Hole**.

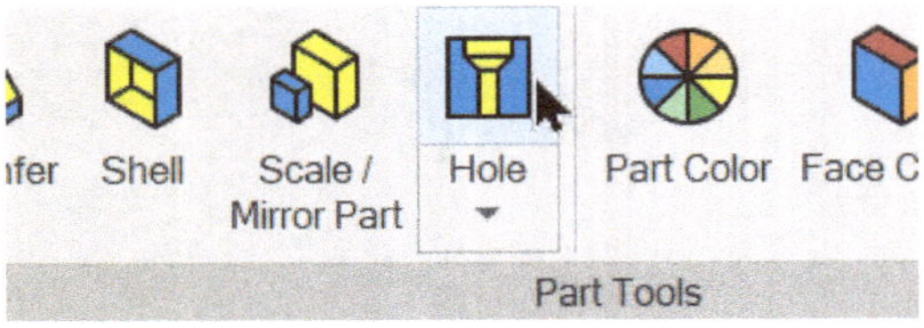

28. Select the flat face of the **Extrusion** feature, as shown.

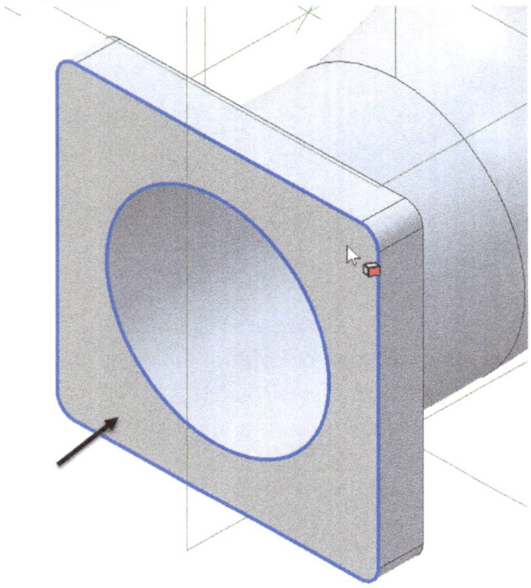

29. Click at the bottom left corner, as shown.

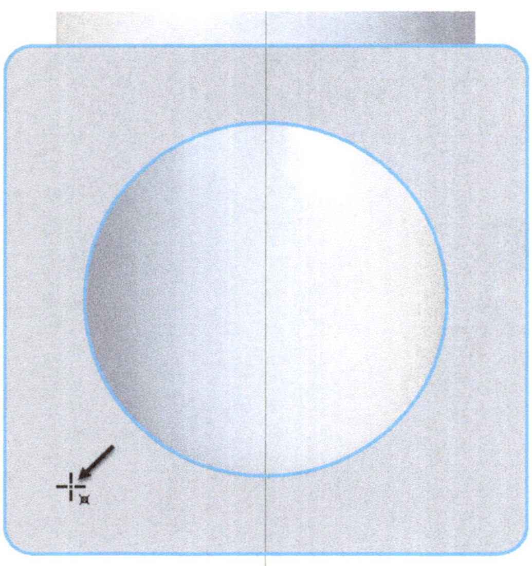

30. Click the **Counter Bored**  icon. This changes the hole type to a counterbore hole, which has a larger diameter at the top.
31. Enter **2.362** in the **Counterbore diameter** box to set the counterbore diameter.
32. Enter **1.181** in the **Diameter** box to set the hole size.
33. Type **0.394** in the **Counterbore depth** box to set the counterbore depth.
34. From the **Depth Condition** dropdown, select **Blind**.
35. Type **1.969** in the **Hole Depth** box.

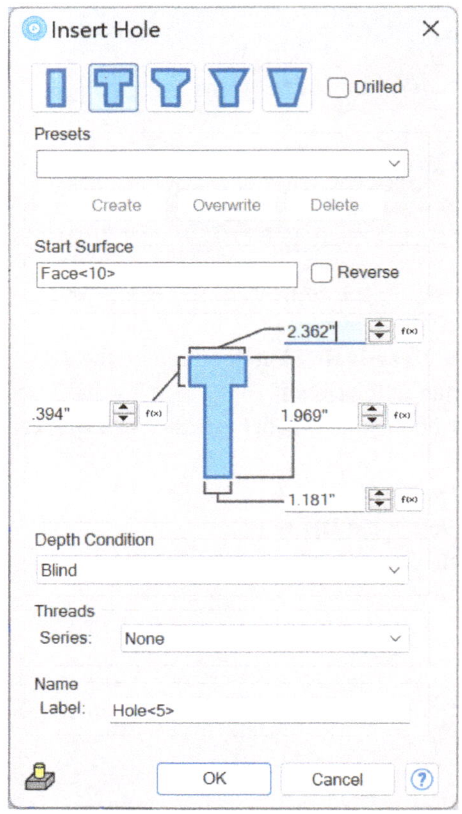

36. Click **OK**.

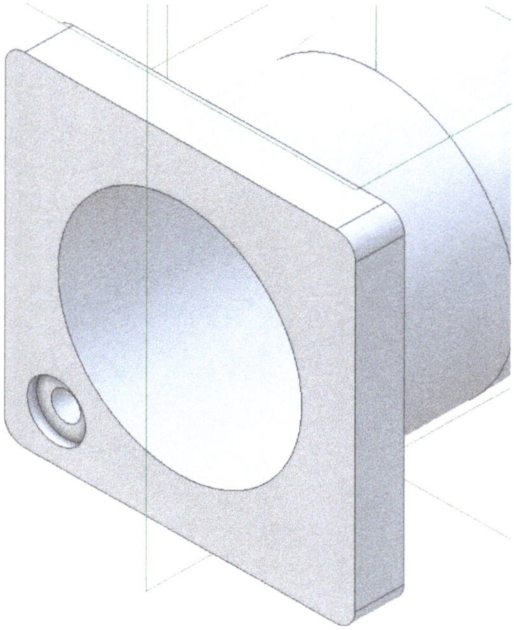

37. In the Design Explorer, right-click on the sketch of the **Hole** and select **Edit**.

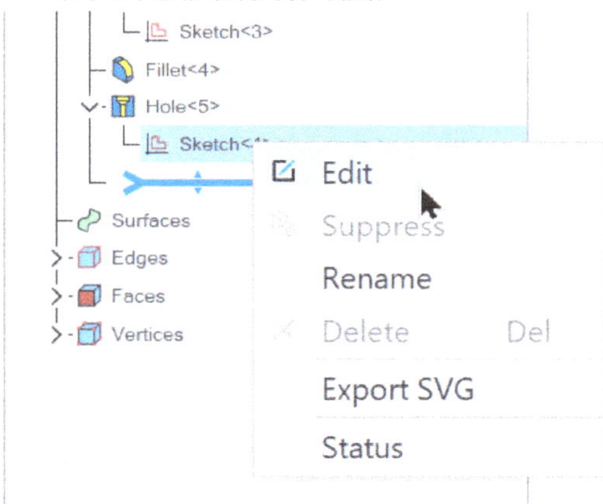

38. Click the **Dimension** icon on the **2D Sketch** tab of the ribbon.
39. Add dimensions between the point and the adjacent edges, as shown.

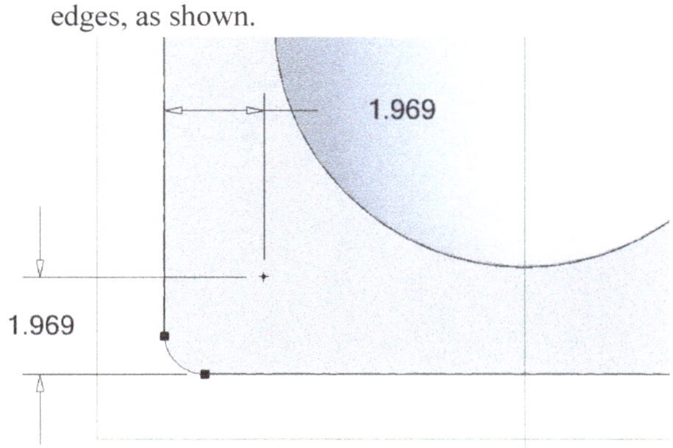

40. Click the **Deactivate Sketch** button on the **2D Sketch** tab of the ribbon.

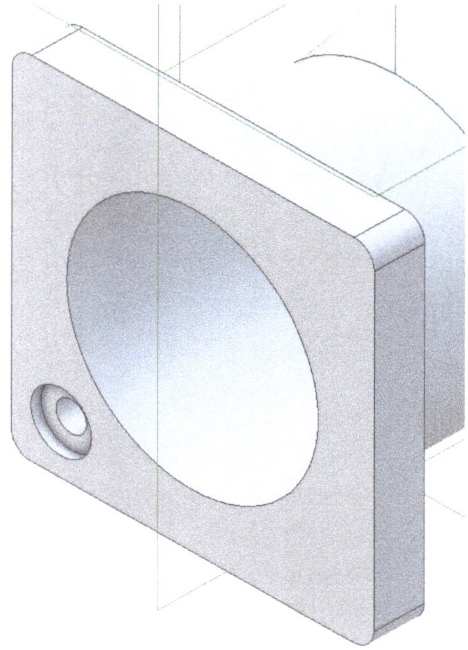

41. Click the **Linear pattern** icon on the **Part Tools** panel.

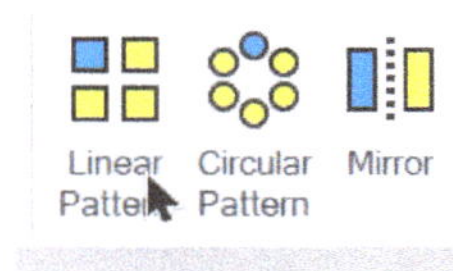

42. Select the **Hole** feature from the graphics window.

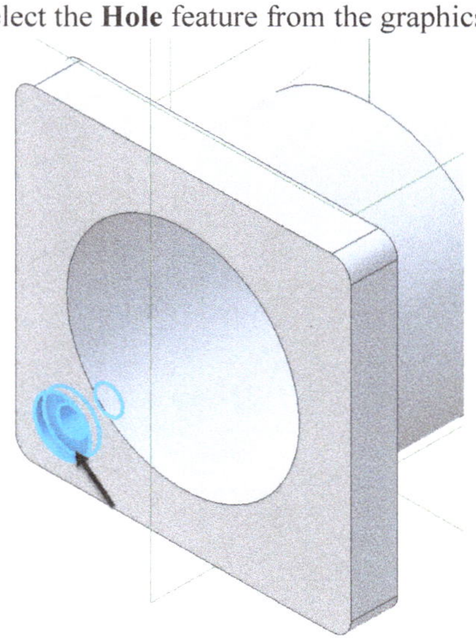

43. Click in the **Linear Path** selection box in the **First Direction** section.
44. Select the bottom horizontal edge of the flange.

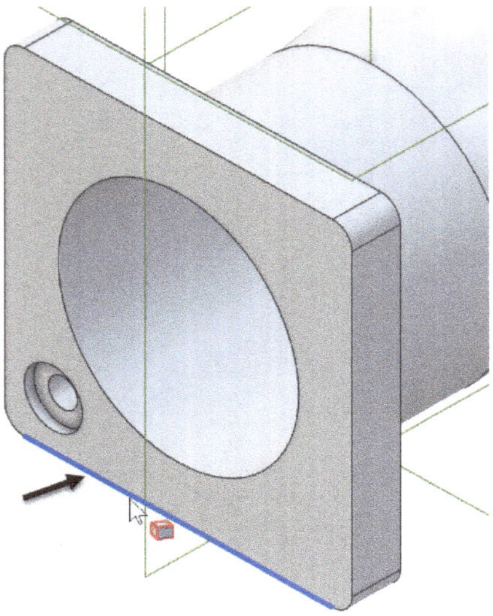

45. Type **10.235** in the **Spacing** box.
46. Type **2** in the **Instances** box.
47. Check the **Change Direction** option, if the preview is not displayed.
48. Click in the **Linear Path** selection box in the **Second Direction** section.
49. Select the vertical edge of the flange.
50. Type **10.235** in the **Spacing** box.
51. Type **2** in the **Instances** box.
52. Check the **Change Direction** option, if the preview is not displayed.

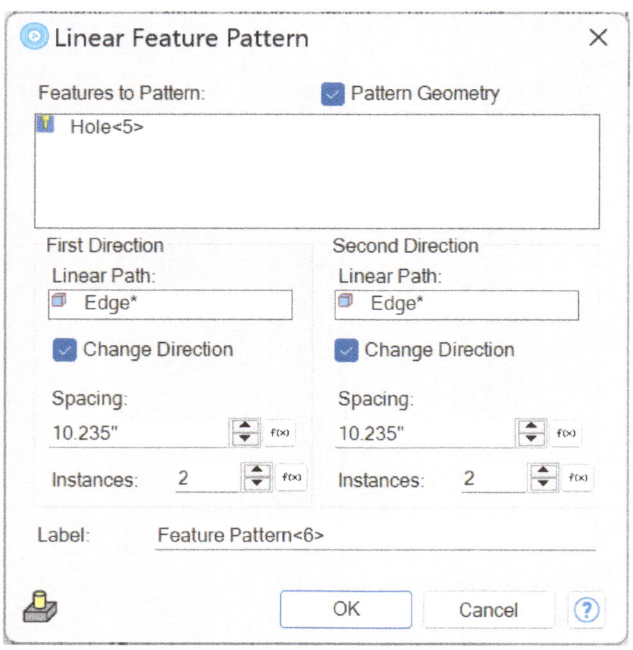

53. Click **OK**.

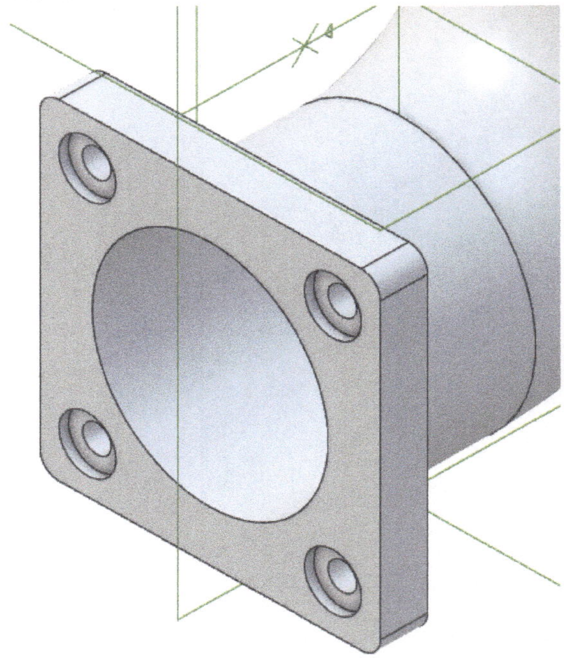

54. Click **Model > References > Plane** on the ribbon.

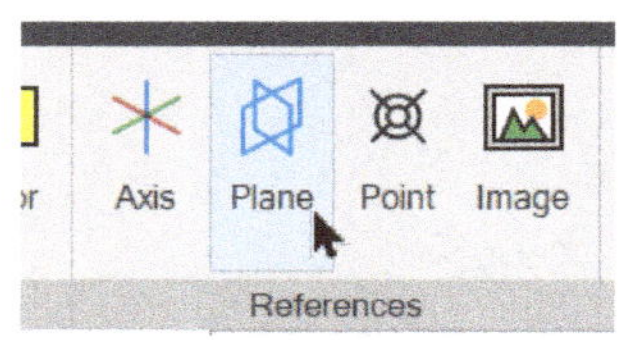

55. On the **Insert Plane** dialog, click **Creation Method** > **Rotation of a Plane/Face about a Coplanar Axis/Edge** 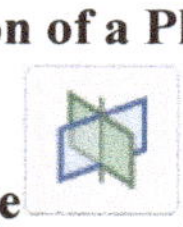.
56. Click in the **Select Geometry** selection box and select the ZX-Plane.
57. Select the Z-Axis.

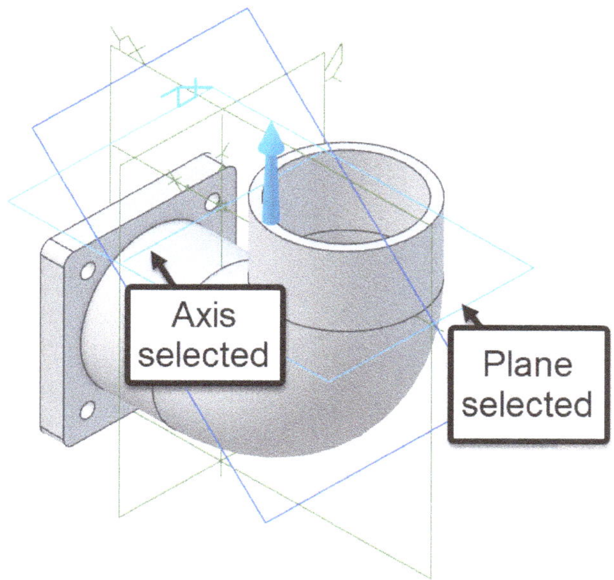

58. Type **45** in the **Angle** box.
59. Click **Apply** and **Close**.
60. Click the **Mirror** icon on the **Part Tools** panel.
61. On the **Mirror** dialog, select **Type > Individual Features**.
62. Select the **Extrusion, Fillet, Hole**, and **Feature Pattern** from the **Design Explorer**.

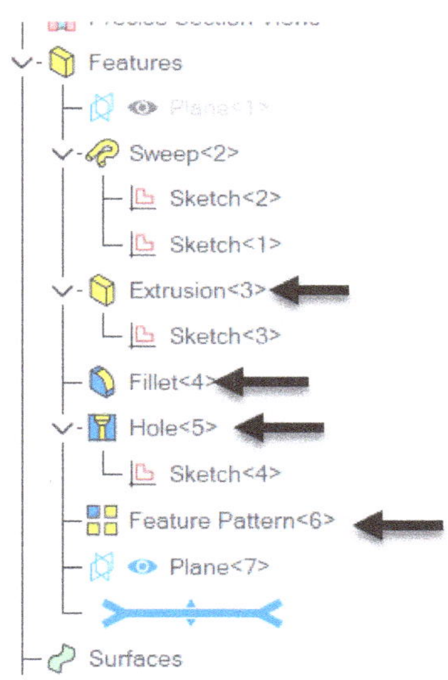

63. Click in the **Mirror Plane** selection box and select the angled plane.

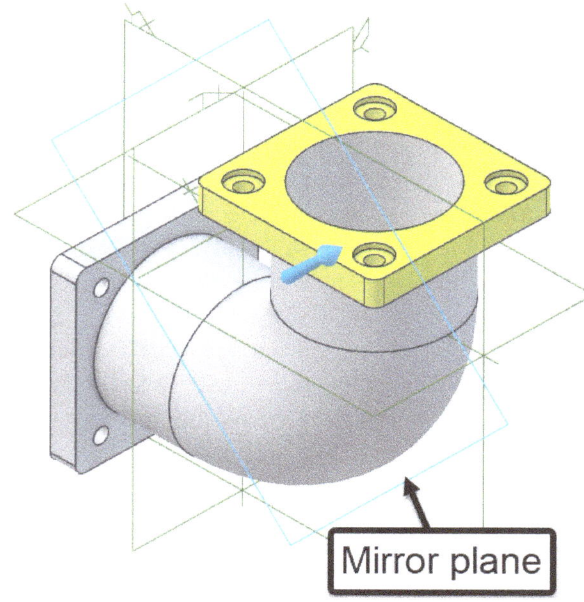

64. Click **OK** to mirror the flange.

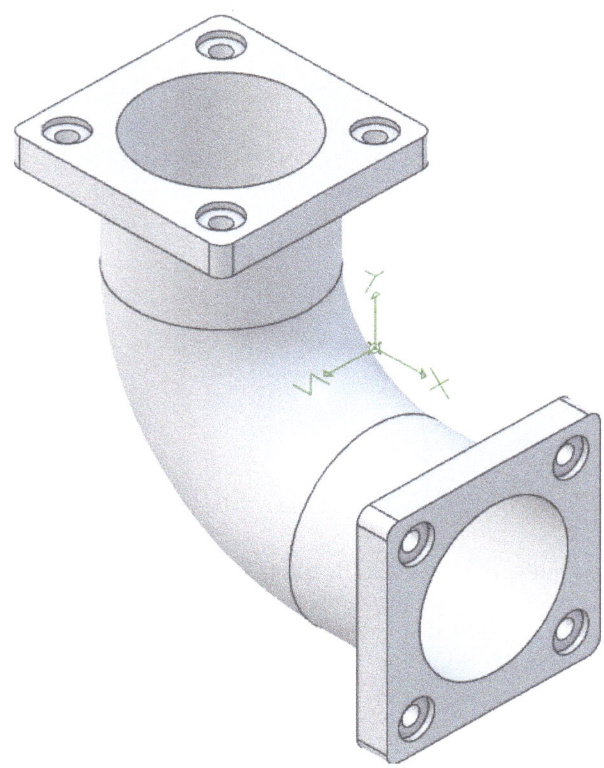

TUTORIAL 8

In this tutorial, you will create a spreadsheet and use the data in the spreadsheet to control the model.

1. Click the **Alibre Atom3D V28** icon on the Deskrop.
2. Click the **New Part** icon on the **Home** window.

3. Click **File > Properties**. This will open the **File Properties** dialog box, where you can customize various properties of the file.
4. On the **File Properties** dialog box, click the **Units > General** option at the left side.
5. Select **Unit > Millimeters**. This setting ensures that Alibre Atom3D uses millimeters.
6. Type **2** in the **Precision** box. This setting determines the number of decimal places displayed for measurements and dimensions.
7. Check the **Set current settings as default settings for parts, sheet metal, and assemblies** option.
8. Click **Apply** and **Save** to save the changes and close the **File Properties** dialog box.
9. To start a new sketch, click **Model** tab > **Sketch > Activate 2D Sketch** on the ribbon.

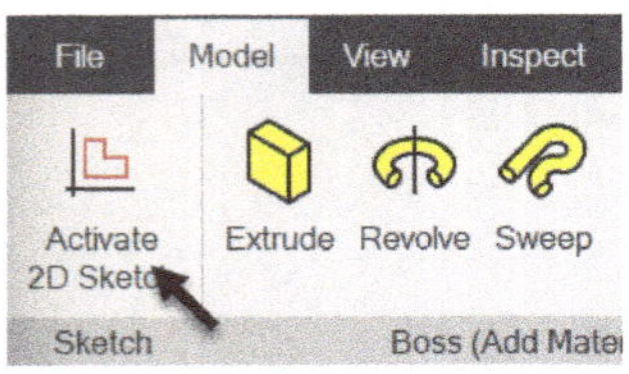

10. Select the **ZX-Plane** from the Design Explorer.
11. Create the sketch, as shown.

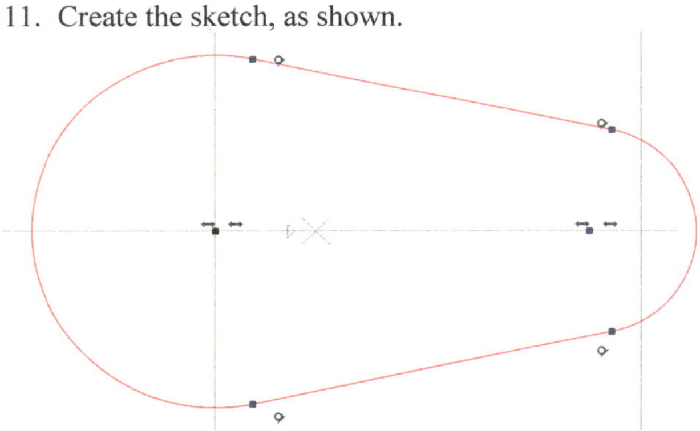

12. On the ribbon, click **2D Sketch > Dimension**.
13. Selec the large arc, move the pointer and click.
14. On the **Edit Dimension** dialog, click the **Equation** icon; the **Equation Editor** dialog appears.

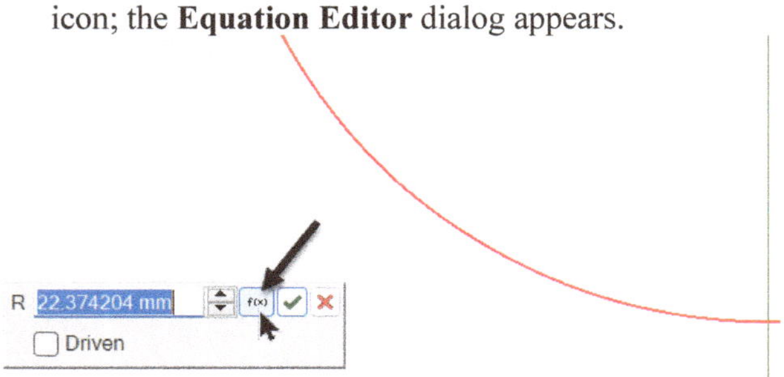

15. Type **Large_Radius** in the **Name** box.
16. Type **30** in the **Equation** box and click **OK**.

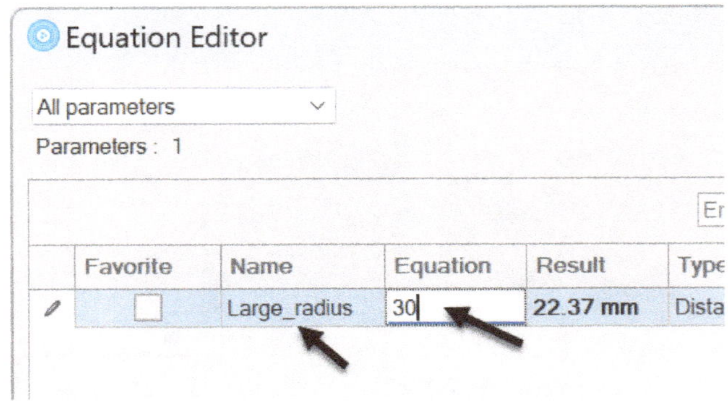

17. Click the green check.
18. Select the small arc and place the dimension.
19. On the **Edit Dimension** dialog, click the **Equation** icon; the **Equation Editor** dialog appears.
20. Type **Small_Radius** in the **Name** box.
21. Type **15** in the **Equation** box and click **OK**.
22. Click the green check.

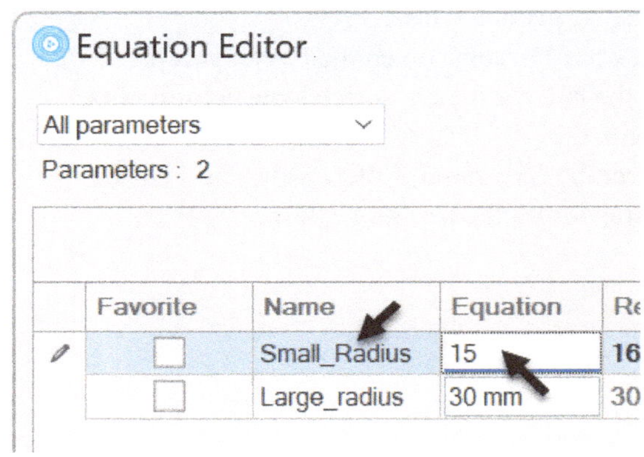

23. Select the centerpoints of the two arcs and place the dimension.

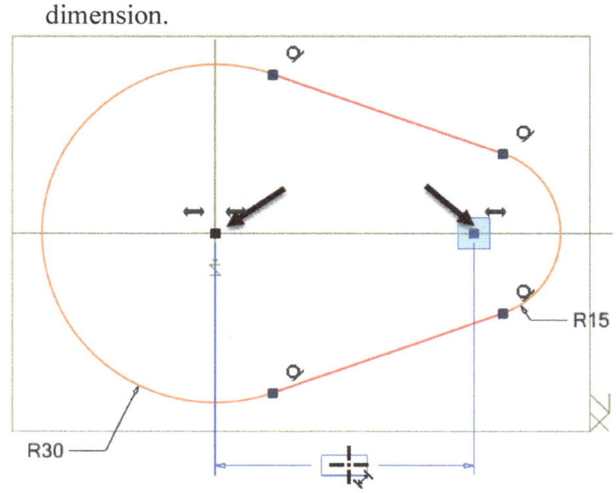

24. On the **Edit Dimension** dialog, click the **Equation** icon; the **Equation Editor** dialog appears.
25. Type **Horizontal_Distance** in the **Name** box.

26. Type **60** in the **Equation** box and click **OK**.
27. Click the green check.

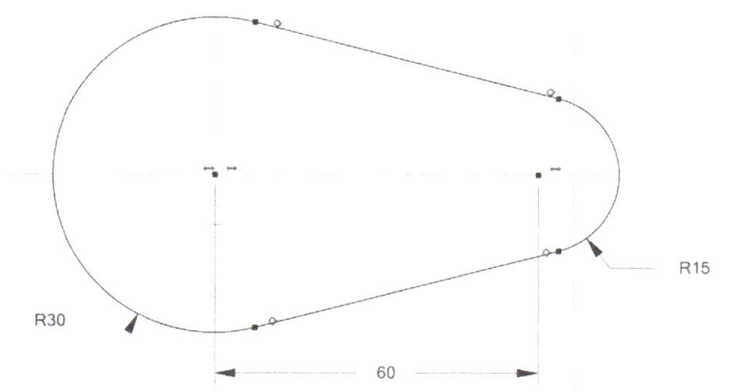

28. Click the **Deactivate Sketch** button on the **2D Sketch** tab of the ribbon.
29. On the ribbon, click **Model > Boss (Add Material) > Extrude**.
30. Select **Type > To Depth**.
31. On the **Extrude Boss** dialog, click the **Equation** icon next to the **Depth** box; the **Equation Editor** dialog appears.

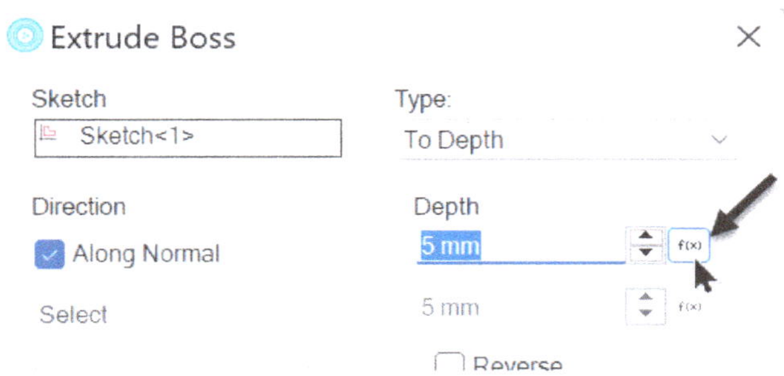

32. Type **Extruded_Length** in the **Name** box.
33. Type **15** in the **Equation** box and click **OK**.
34. Click **OK**.

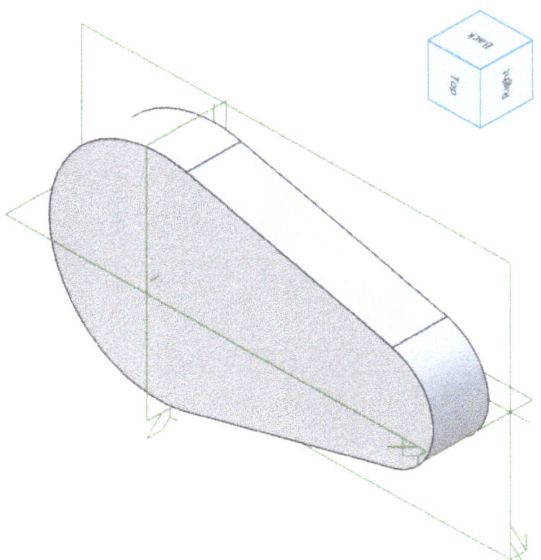

35. Click the **Shell** icon on the **Part Tools** panel.

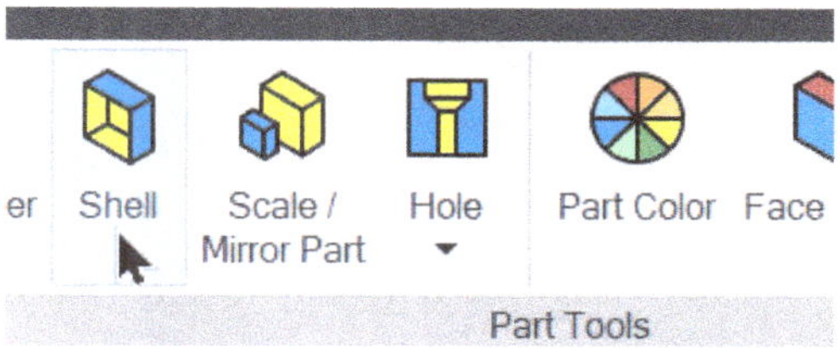

36. Select the two flat faces of the model.

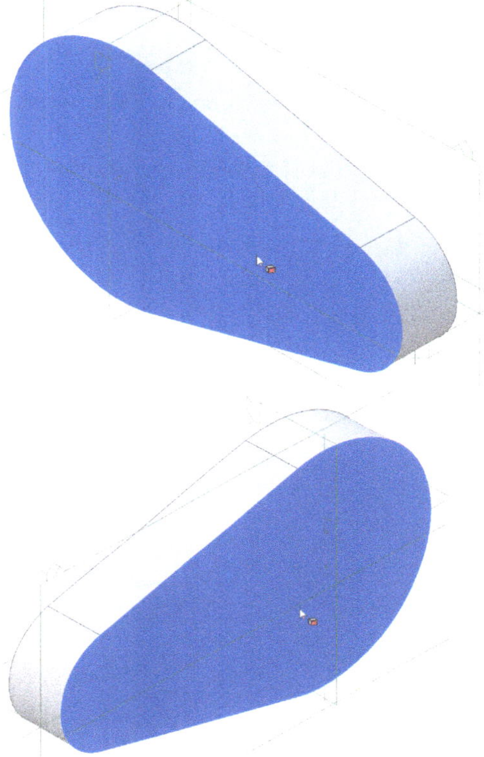

37. On the **Shell** dialog, click the **Equation** icon next to the **Standard Thickness** box; the **Equation Editor** dialog appears.
38. Type **Thickness** in the **Name** box.
39. Type **5** in the **Equation** box and click **OK**.
40. Click **OK**.

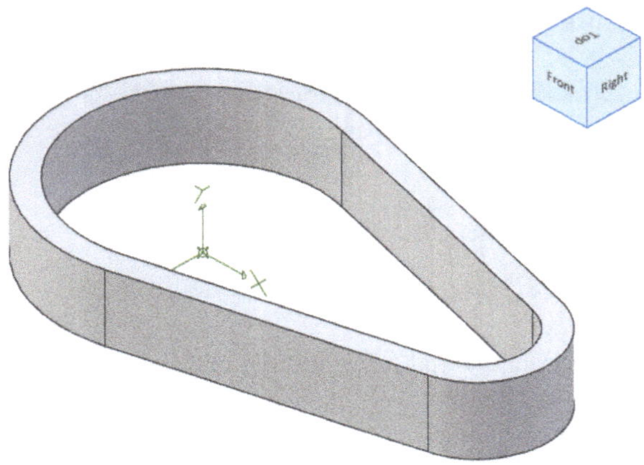

41. Click the **Equation Edition** icon on the **Parameters** panel.
42. Click in the **Name** box next to the **Large_Radius** parameter and change the value to **40**.

Equation Editor

All parameters

Parameters : 5

Favorite	Name	Equation	Result
☐	Extrude_Lengt..	15 mm	15 mm
☐	Horizontal_Dis..	60 mm	60 mm
☐	Large_radius	40	**30 mm**
☐	Small_Radius	15 mm	15 mm
☐	Thickness	5 mm	5 mm

Notice that the model is updated, as shown.

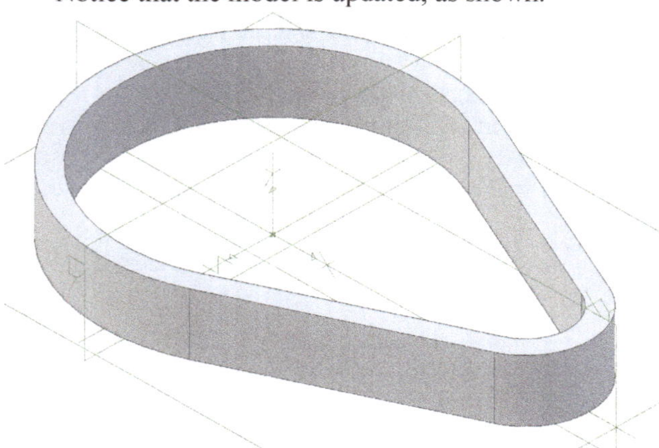

43. Likewise, change the other values in the **Equation Editor** dialog and notice the updated model.

Equation Editor

All parameters

Parameters : 5

Favorite	Name	Equation	Result
☐	Extrude_Lengt..	25 mm	25 mm
☐	Horizontal_Dis..	60 mm	60 mm
☐	Large_radius	40 mm	40 mm
☐	Small_Radius	20 mm	20 mm
☐	Thickness	10 mm	10 mm

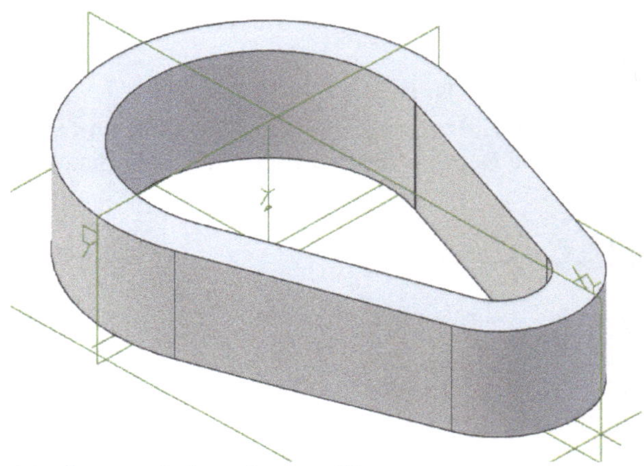

44. Save and close the part file.

Chapter 6: Creating Drawings

In this chapter, you generate 2D drawings of the parts. You learn to:

- Insert standard views of a part model
- Add dimensions

TUTORIAL 1

In this tutorial, you create the drawing shown below.

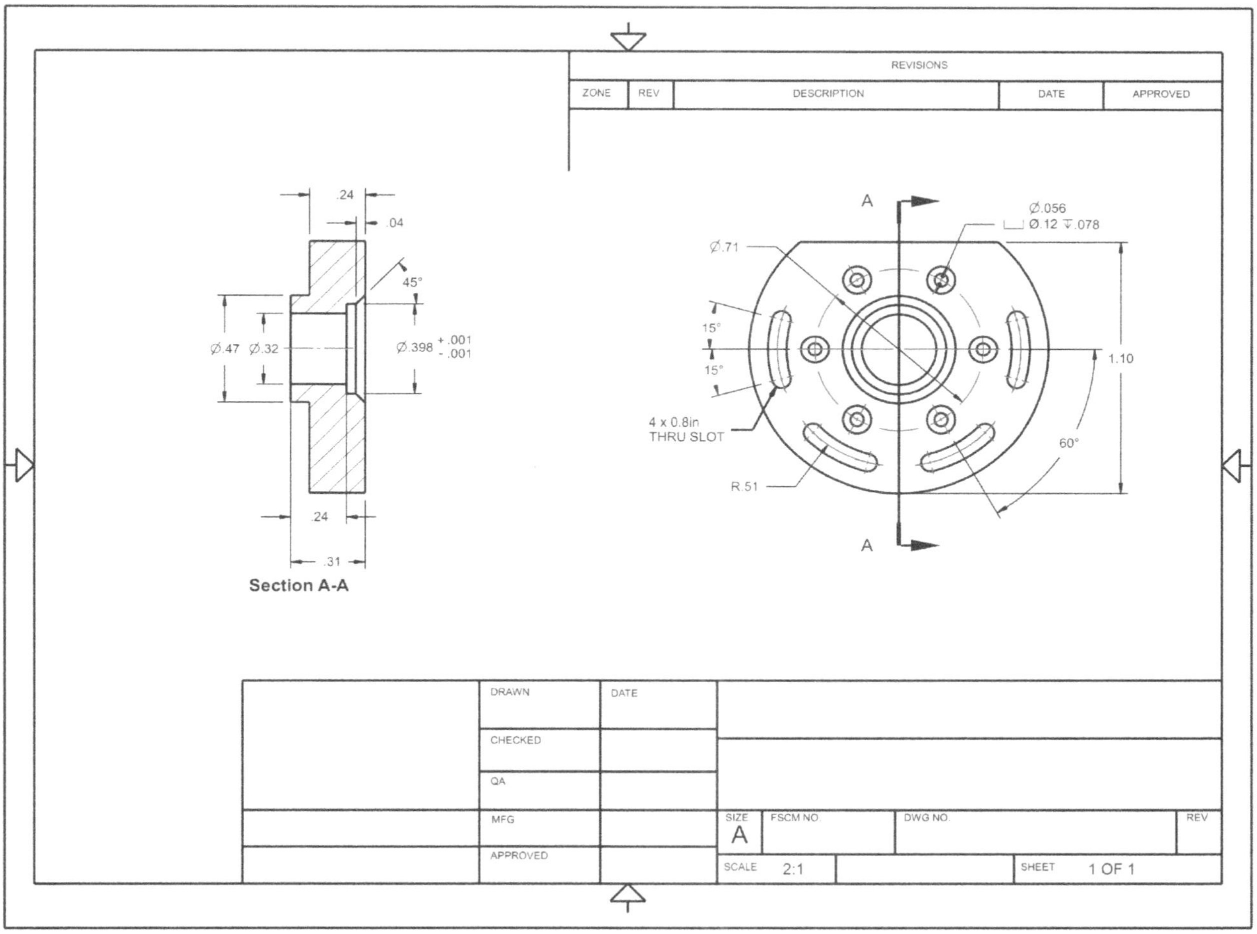

1. Open a new Alibre Atom3D file.
2. Click the **New Part** icon on the **Home** window.

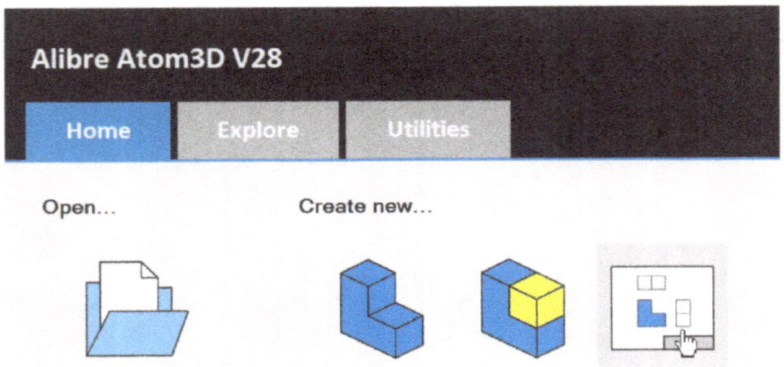

3. On the **New Sheet Properties** dialog, select **Standard > ANSI**.
4. select **Size > ANSI A Landscape**,
5. Type **2** and **1** in the boxes available in the **Default View Scale** section. Next, click **OK**.

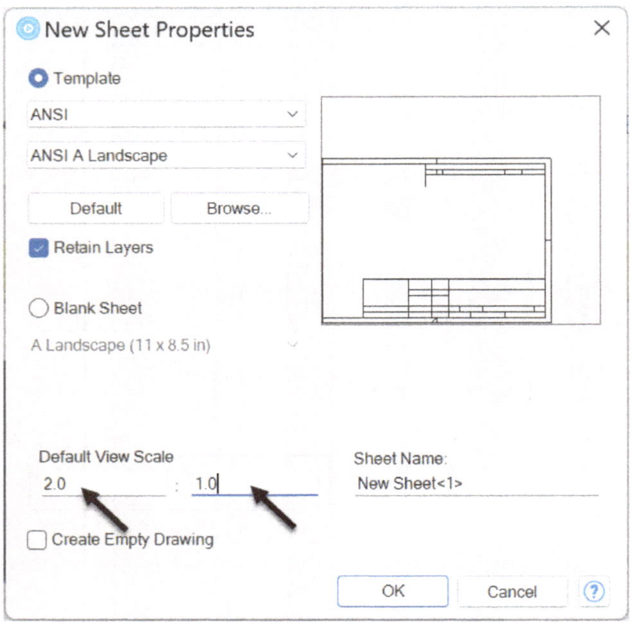

The **Fill in Text** dialog appears. This dialog lets you fill in predefined text fields on a drawing title block. You see a list of tag fields on the left, including DRAWN DATE, DWG NO., DRAWN, Sheet Number, and Sheet Scale, and when you select one, its label appears on the right above an empty text box where you enter the value. You select the tag you want to edit, type the required information in the text box. For example, a date for DRAWN DATE or a document number for DWG NO.

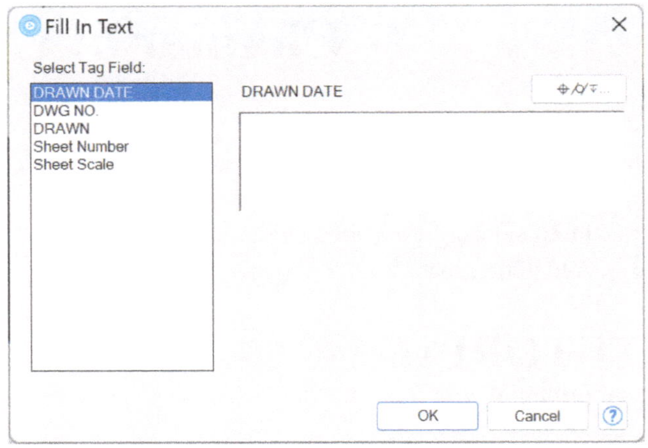

6. Click **OK**.
7. Browse to the location of the part file created in Tutorial 1 of Chapter 5. You can also download this file from the companion website and use it.
8. Select the Tutorial 1 file and click **Open**.
9. On the **Standard Views Creation** dialog, clear all view icons in the **View Selections** section except the **Front** icon. The preview of the front view is displayed in the **Front View** section. You can change the orientation of the front view using the arrow buttons displayed next to the preview.

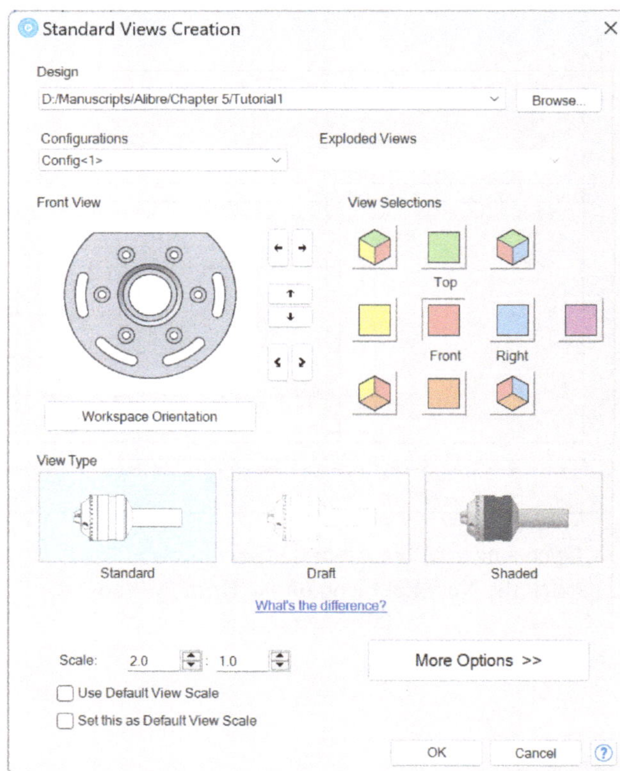

You can also click the **Workspace Orientation** button in the **Front View** section to specify the orientation. On doing so, the **Orientations** dialog appears.

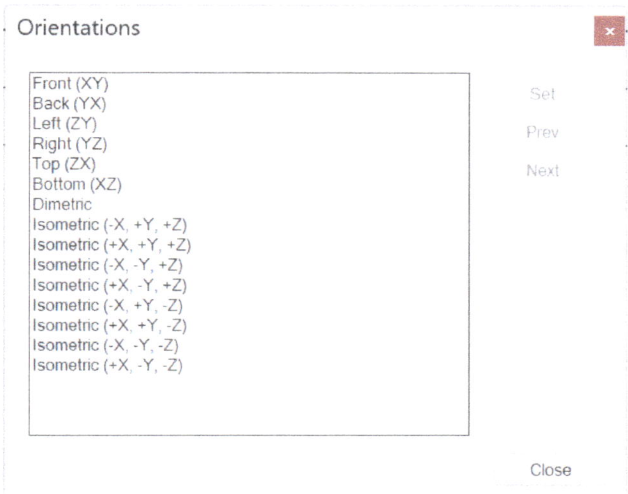

The **Orientations** dialog allows you choose a preset view orientation for the model. In the large list on the left, you can select from standard orthographic views such as Front (XY), Back (YX), Left (ZY), Right (YZ), Top (ZX), Bottom (XZ), as well as Dimetric and multiple Isometric views defined by different combinations of X, Y, and Z directions. After you select an orientation, click the Set button on the right; the selected orientation is applied to the current view. The **Prev** and **Next** buttons cycle through previously used orientations if they are enabled. When you are finished, you click **Close** at the bottom right to dismiss the dialog

10. Select **View Type > Standard**.
11. Check the **Use Default View Scale** option.
12. Click the **More Options** button and notice the **View Detailing** options.

The **View Detailing Options** section allows you to control which annotation and line features are added to the generated drawing views. At the top, you use the **Select All** checkbox to turn every option on or off at once. Below it, you enable specific detail types individually: **Design Dimensions**, **Hidden Lines**, **Tangent Edges**, **Cosmetic Threads**, **Hole Callouts**, **External Thread Callouts**, **Circular Hole Pattern**, **Linear Hole Pattern**, **Part Trails**, **Centermarks**, **Centerlines**, **Center of Mass**, **Bend Centerlines**, and **Project as Flat Pattern**.

Disabled options appear grayed out when they are not available for the current view type.

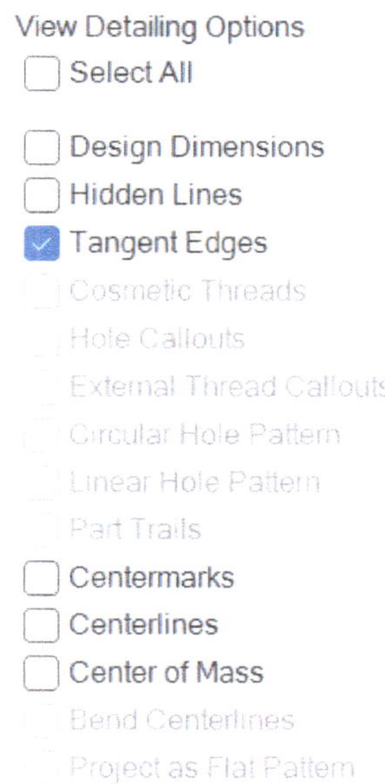

13. Click **OK** on the dialog.
14. Place the view on the right side of the drawing sheet.

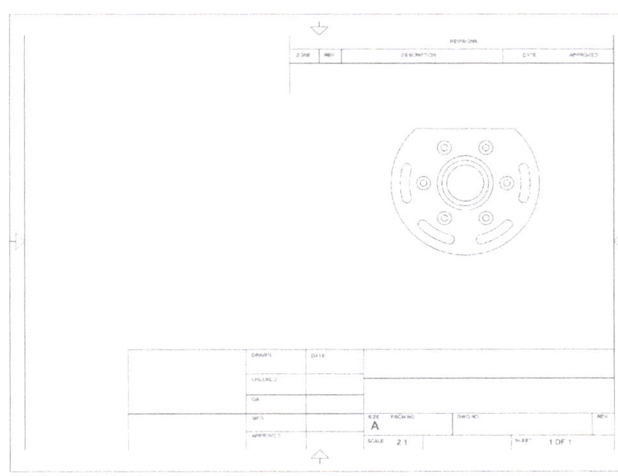

Modifying the Layer Properties

1. Click **Drawing Management > Drawing Tools > Layers** on the ribbon.

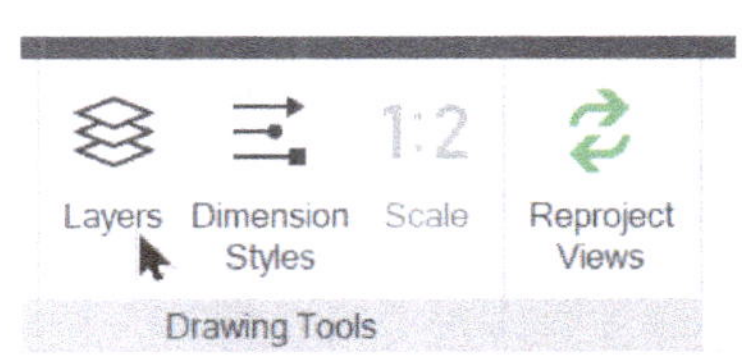

2. On the **File Properties** dialog, change the **Weight** values of all layers, as shown.

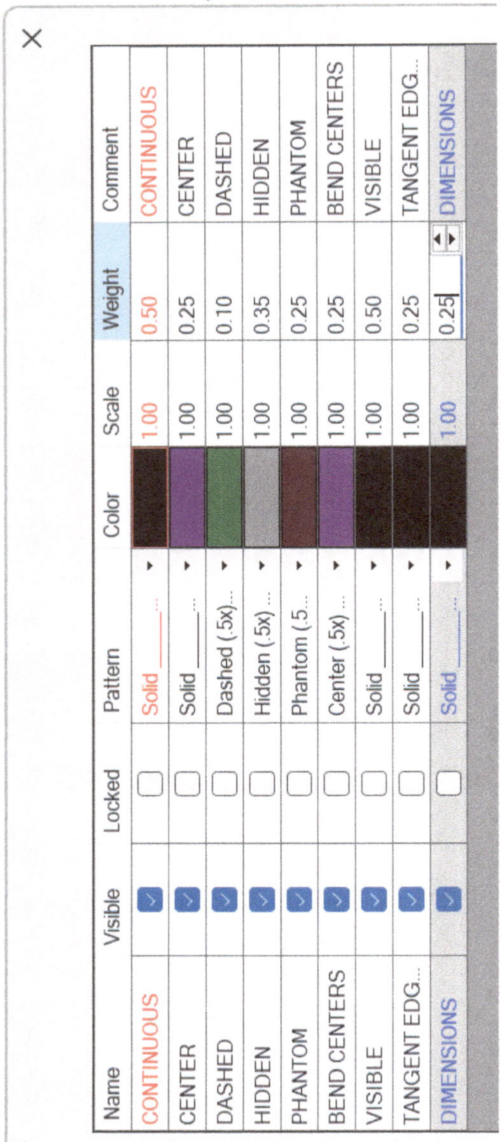

Name	Visible	Locked	Pattern	Color	Scale	Weight	Comment
CONTINUOUS			Solid ___		1.00	0.50	CONTINUOUS
CENTER			Solid ___		1.00	0.25	CENTER
DASHED			Dashed (.5x)...		1.00	0.10	DASHED
HIDDEN			Hidden (.5x) ...		1.00	0.35	HIDDEN
PHANTOM			Phantom (.5...		1.00	0.25	PHANTOM
BEND CENTERS			Center (.5x) ...		1.00	0.25	BEND CENTERS
VISIBLE			Solid ___		1.00	0.50	VISIBLE
TANGENT EDG...			Solid ___		1.00	0.25	TANGENT EDG...
DIMENSIONS			Solid ___		1.00	0.25	DIMENSIONS

3. Click **Apply** and **Close**.

Creating the section view

1. Click **Drawing Management > Insert Views > Section** on the ribbon.

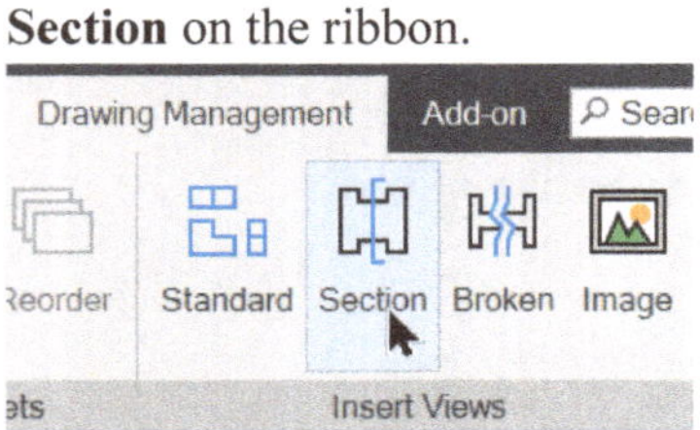

2. Select the front view.
3. Place the pointer on the centerpoint of the view.

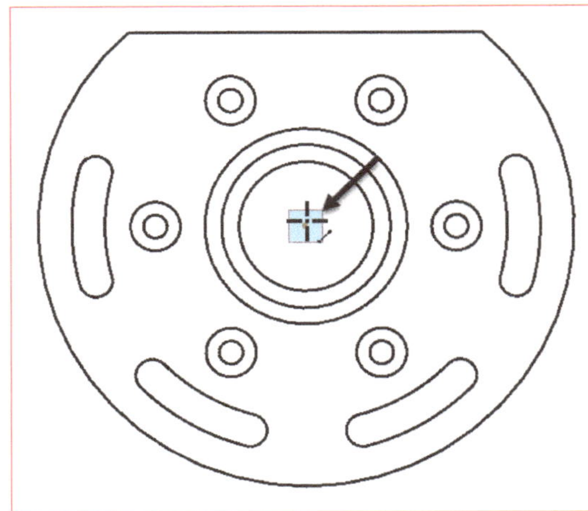

4. Move the pointer vertically upward and notice that a dotted line lis displayed.

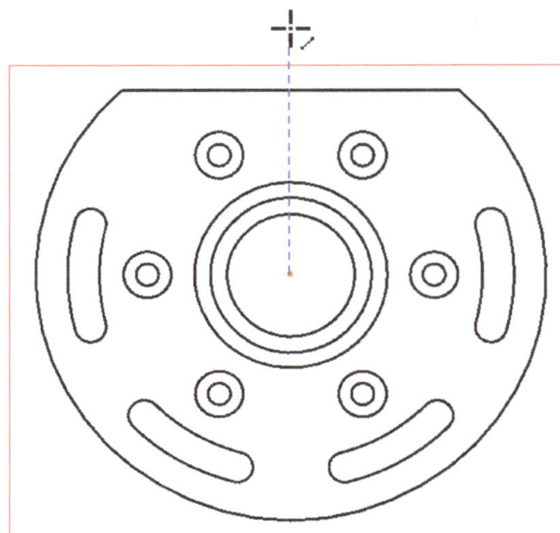

5. Click to define the start point of the section line.
6. Move the pointer vertically downward and click to specify the endpoint of the section line.

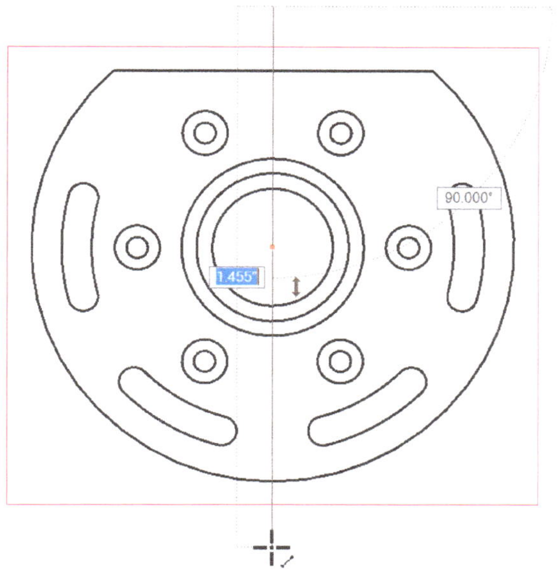

7. Right-click and select **Select**.

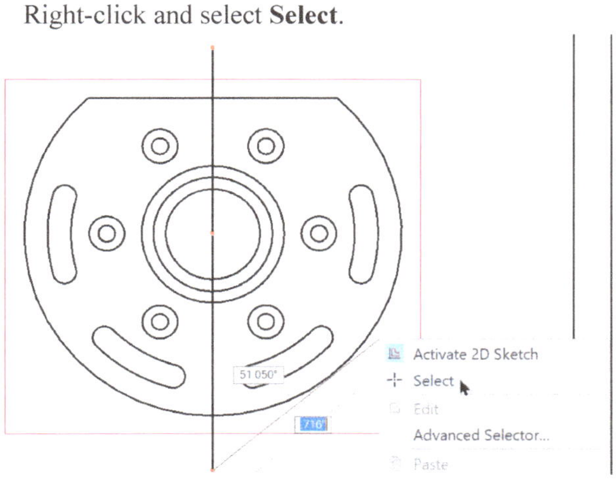

8. On the ribbon, click **Standard Section View Tools** > **Create View**.

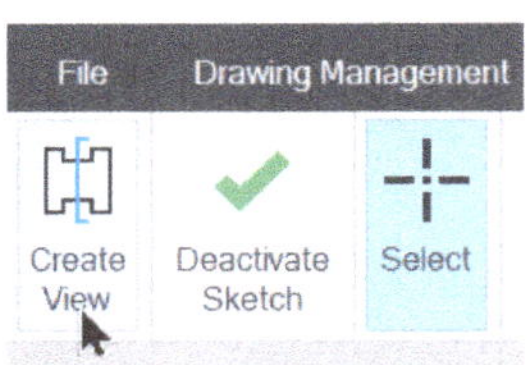

9. Click on the right side of the section line.
10. Move the pointer toward left and click to place the section view.

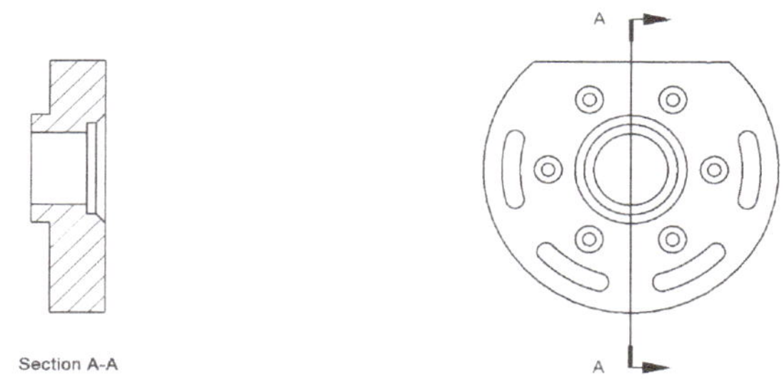

Creating Centerlines and Centered Patterns

1. Click **Drawing Management > Annotatation > Centerline** on the ribbon.

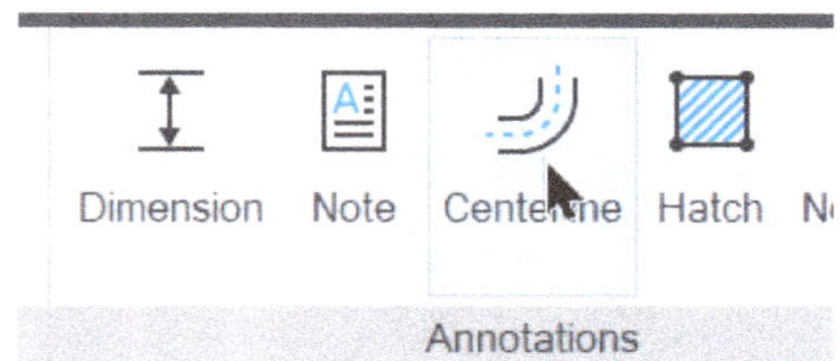

2. Select the parallel lines on the section view, as shown below; the centerline is created.

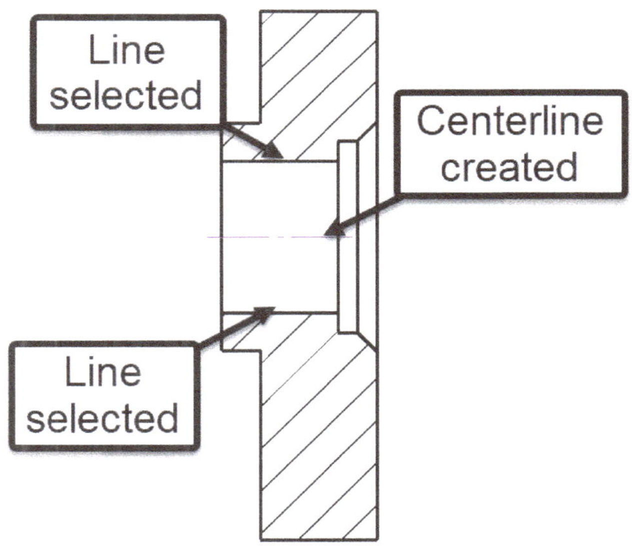

Section A-A

3. Press **ESC**.
4. Click on the front view and select **Manage View** from the contextual toolbar.
5. Select **Centers > Add Center**.

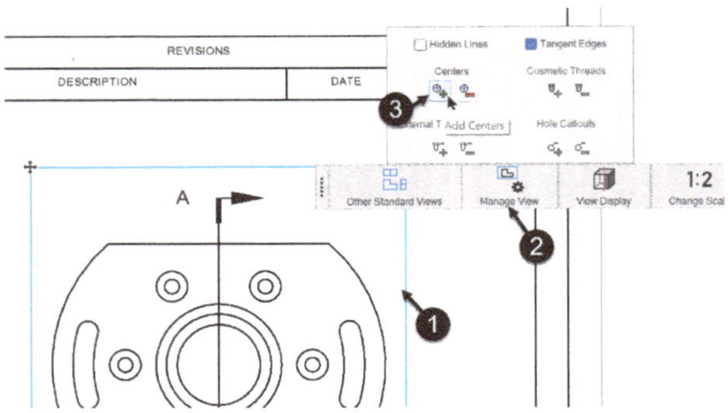

The centerlines and centermarks are add to the circular pattern of the counterbored holes.

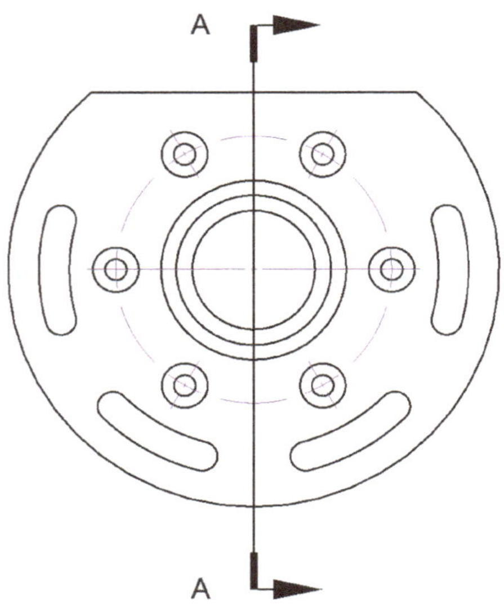

6. Click on the endcap of the slot on the front view.
7. Select **Manage View** from the contextual toolbar.
8. Select **Centers > Add Center**. A centermark is added to endcap.

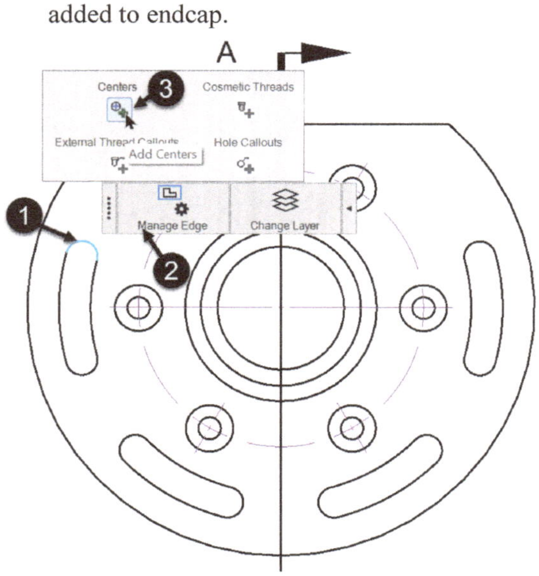

9. Likewise, add centermarks to endcaps of other slots, as, as shown.

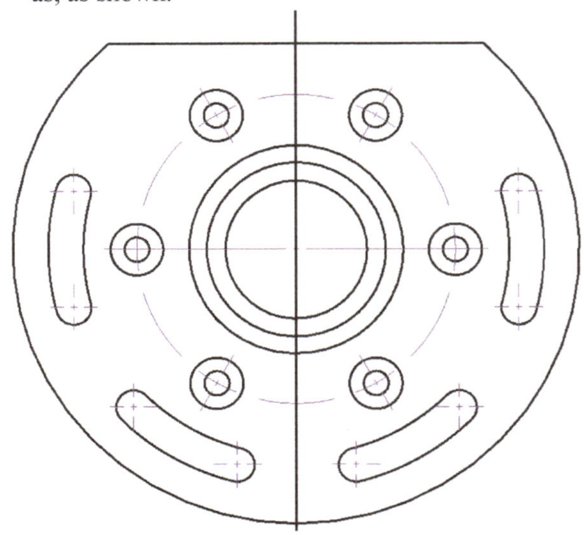

10. Double-click on the first centermark of the slot on the left side.

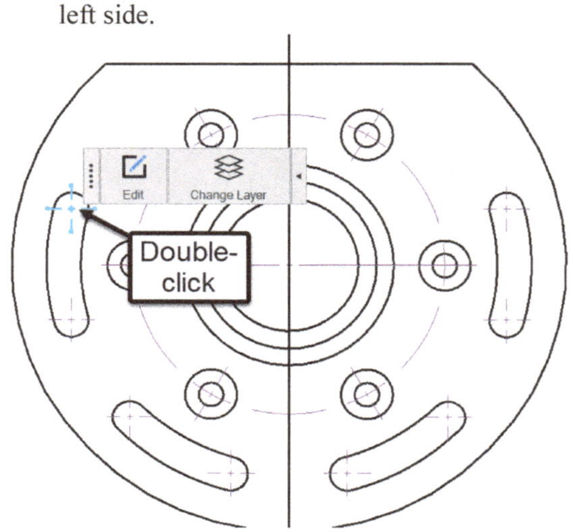

11. Type **-15°** in the **Direction** box and then click **OK**.

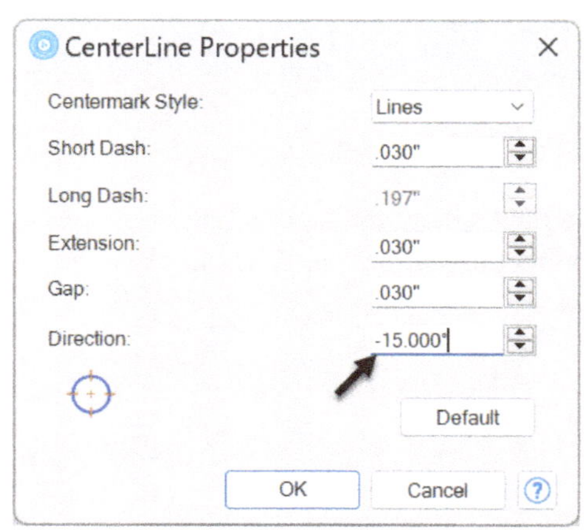

12. Double-click on the lower centermark of the slot on the left side.

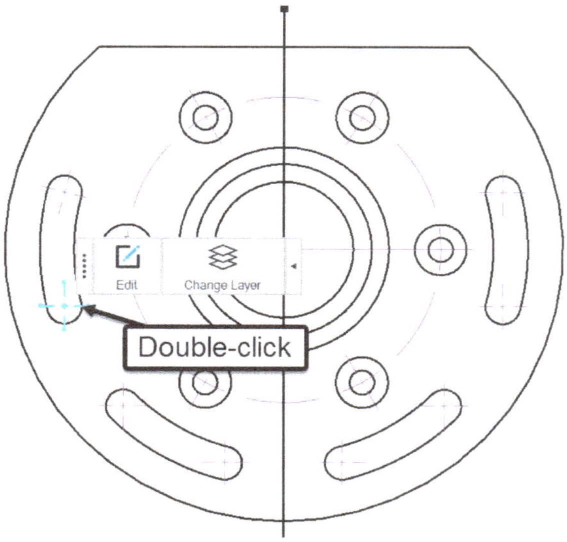

13. Type **15°** in the **Direction** box and then click **OK**.
14. Likewise, change the **Direction** angles of the centermarks of the other slot endcaps, as shown.

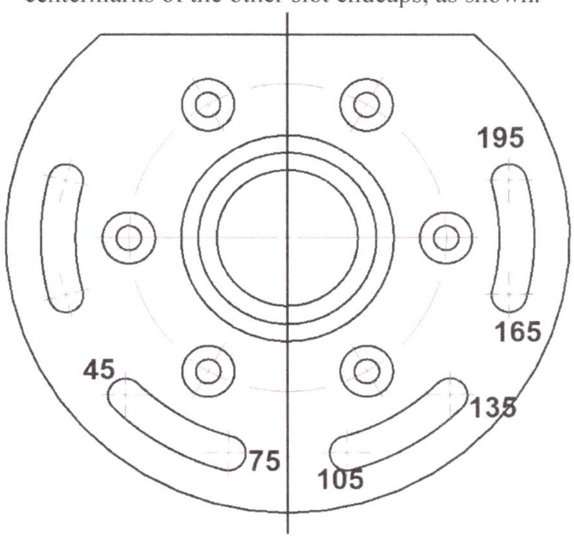

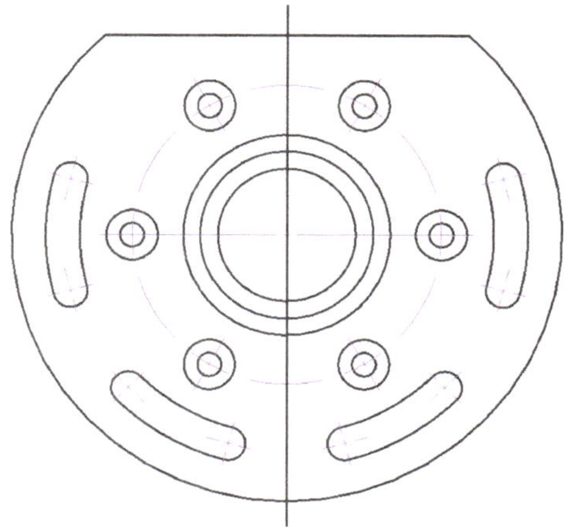

15. Click **Drawing Management > Annotatation > Centerline** on the ribbon.
16. Select the curved edges of the slot on the left side; a centerline is created between the two selected edges.

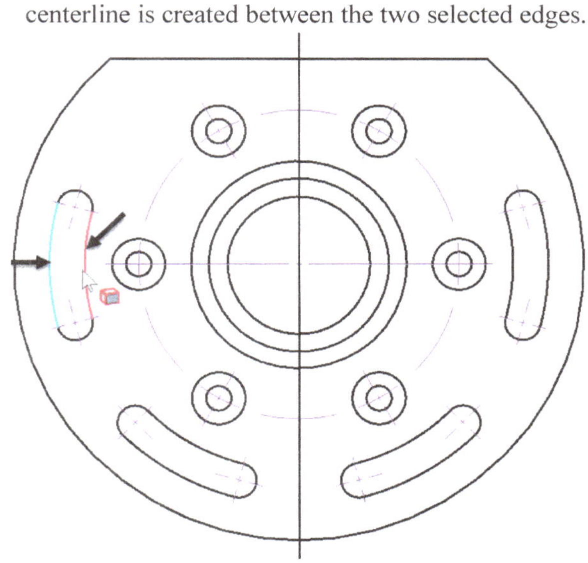

17. Likewise, create centerlines on the remaining slots.

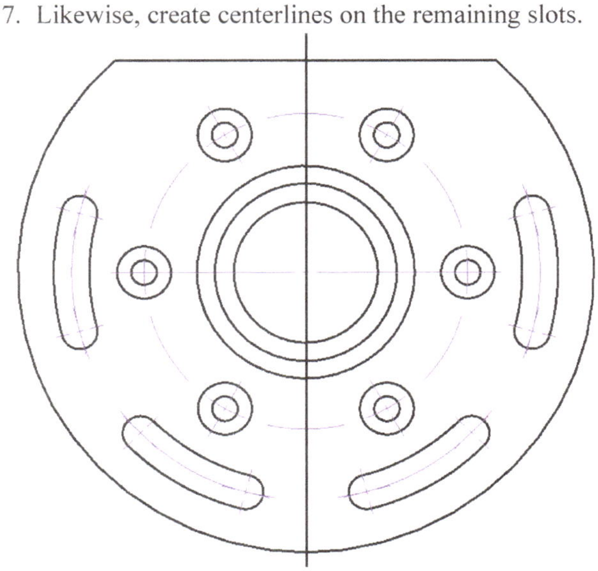

18. Press Esc to deactivate the tool.

Applying Dimensions

1. Click **Drawing Management > Annotation > Dimension** on the ribbon.
2. Select the centerline on the slot located on the left.
3. Select the endpoint of the centerline of the hole located at the center.
4. Move the pointer toward the left and click.

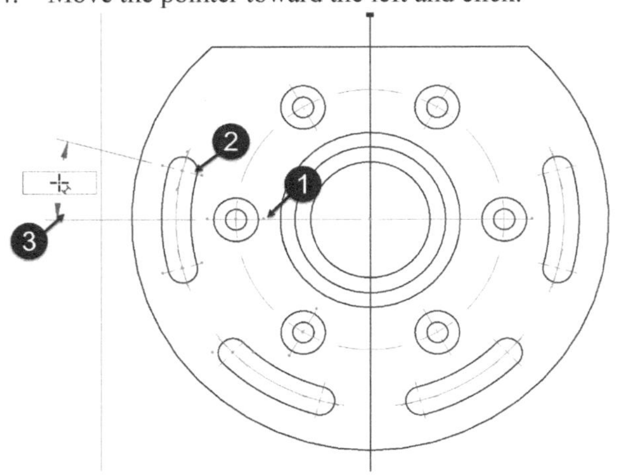

5. Likewise, create another angular dimension, as shown below.

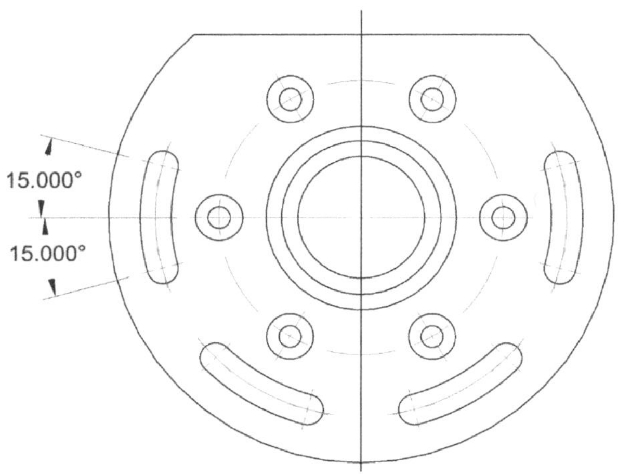

6. Create angular dimensions between the holes.

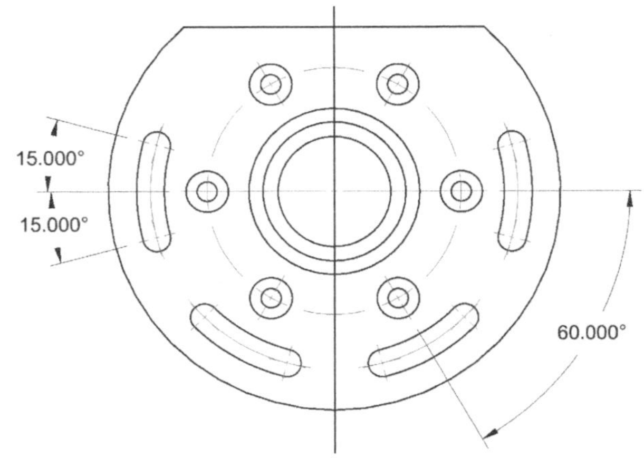

7. Dimension the pitch circle radius of the slots (activate the **Dimension** command and select the centreline passing through the slots. Next, click to position the dimension.

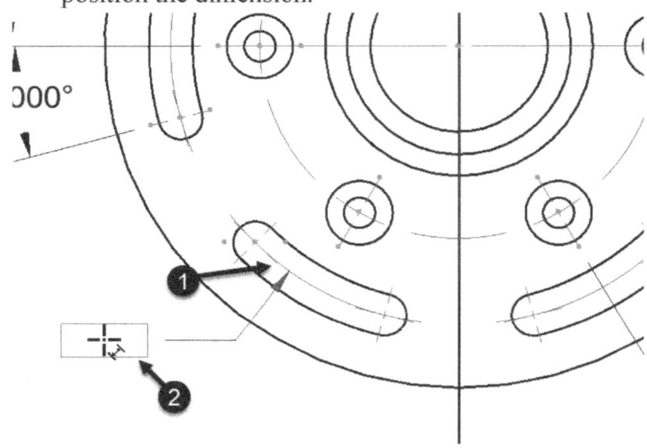

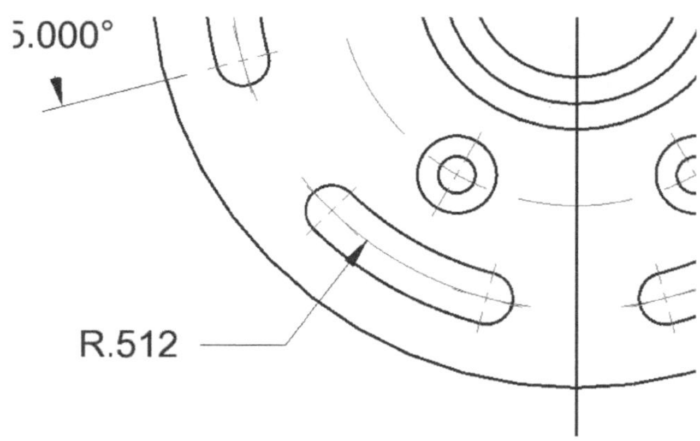

8. With the **Dimension** tool active, select the horizontal line of the front view and outer curved edge.

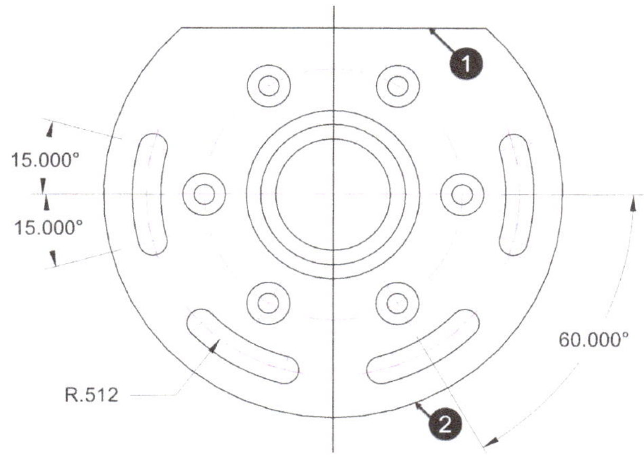

9. On te **Slot Dimension** dialog, select **Linear to Circular > Line to Outside** and click **OK**.
10. Place the dimension on the right side.

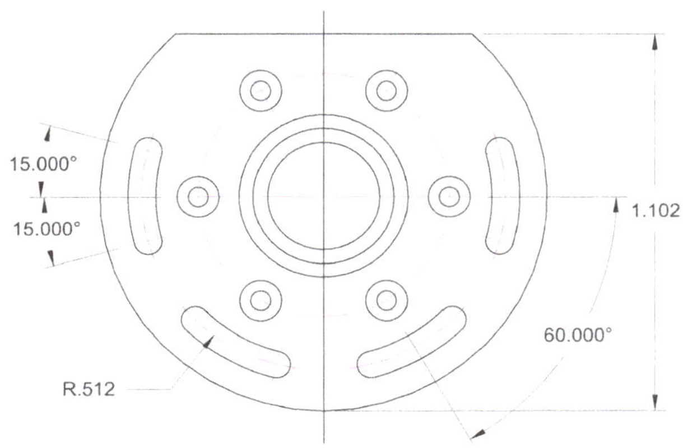

11. Click **Drawing Management > Drawing Tools > Dimension Styles** on the ribbon.

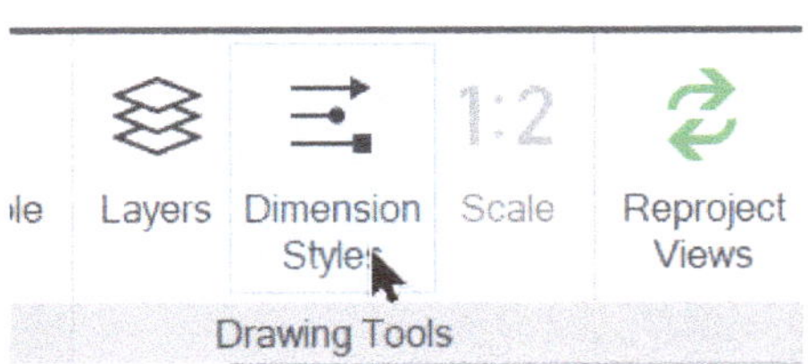

12. In the **Length** section, select **Precision > 2**.
13. In the **Angle** section, select **Precision > 0**.

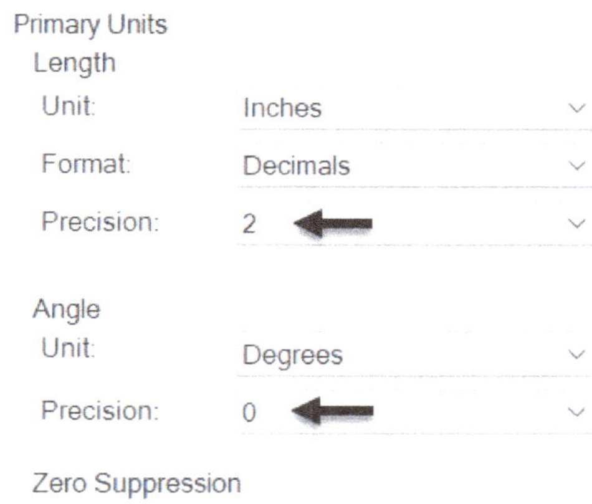

14. Click **Apply** and **Close**.
15. Click **Drawing Management > Annotations > Dimension** on the ribbon.
16. Select the counterbore hole and place the dimension, as shown below.

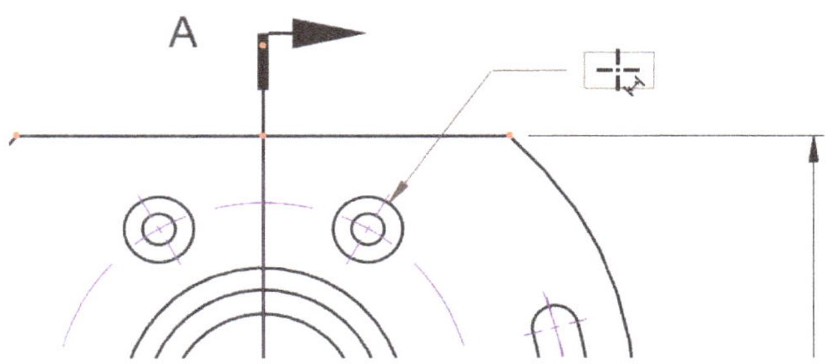

17. Select the hole dimension and click **Change Dimension** on the Contextual toolbar.
18. Click the **Override dimension value** icon.

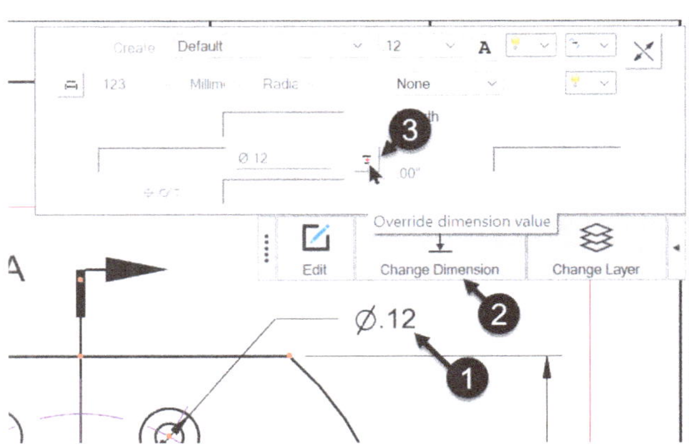

19. Click the **Enter upper text** box and click the **Add symbol to active text field** button.

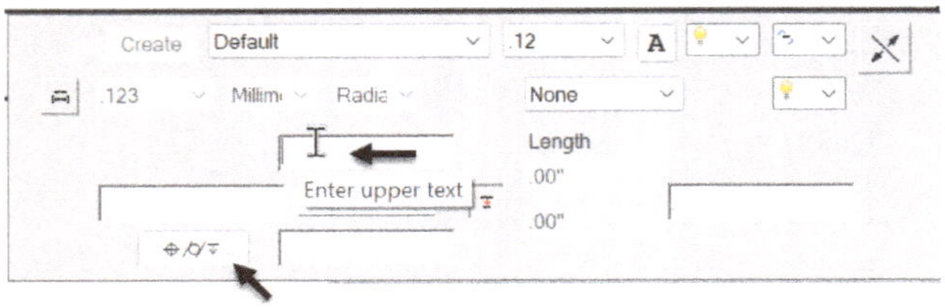

20. Click the **Diameter** icon on the **Insert Alibre Design Symbols** dialog. Next, click **Close**.

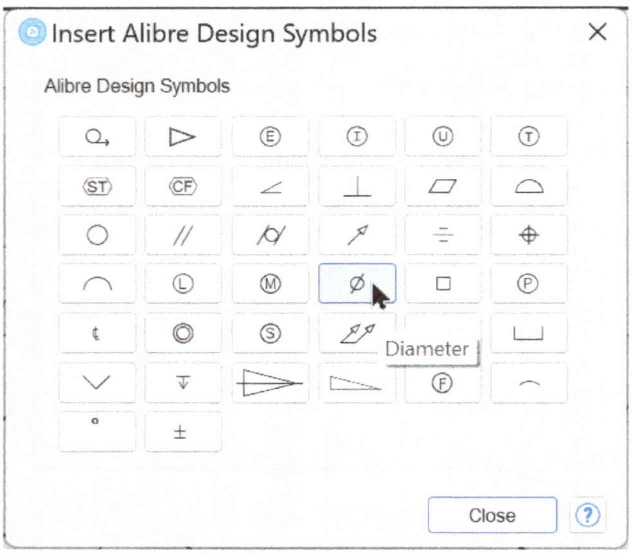

21. Type **.056** in the **Enter upper text** box.
22. Click in the **Enter prefix text** box and click the **Add symbol to active text field** button.
23. Click the **Counterbore** button. Next, click **Close**.
24. Click in the **Enter suffix text** box and click the **Add symbol to active text field** button.

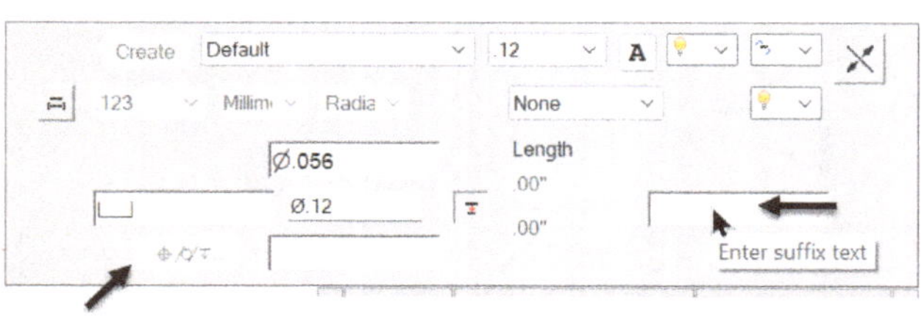

25. Click the **Depth/Deep** button. Next, click **Close**.
26. Type **.078** in the **Enter suffix text** box. Next, click on the drawing sheet.

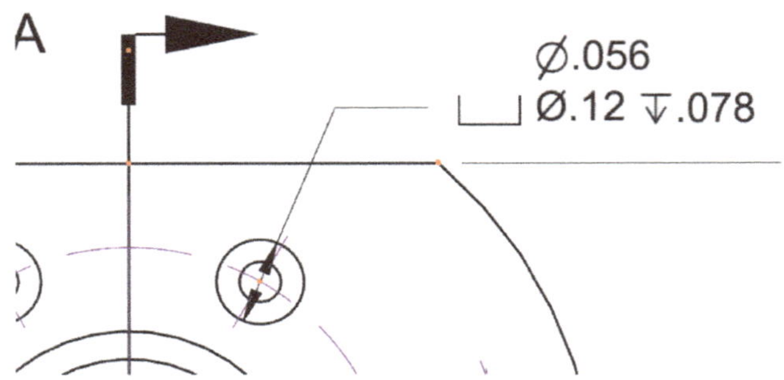

27. Add a pitch circle diameter to counterbore holes.

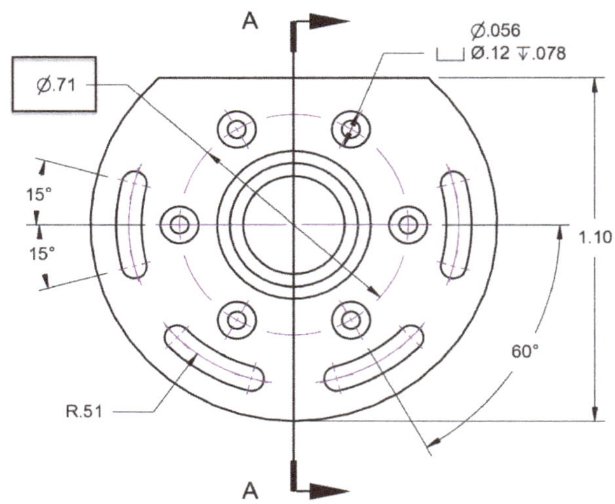

28. Click **Drawing Management > Annotations > Note** on the ribbon.
29. On the **Note** dialog, enter the text shown below.

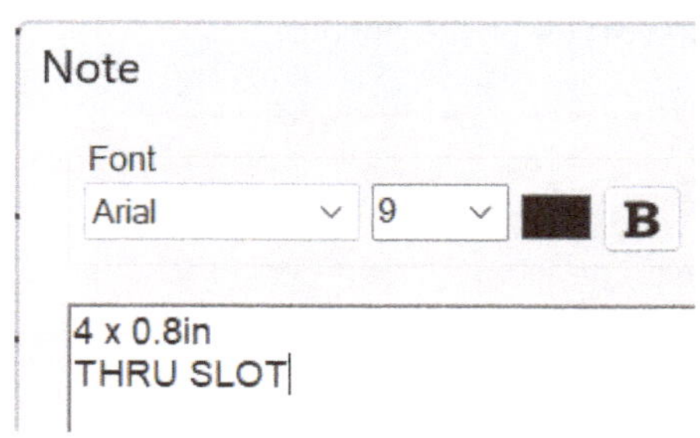

30. Check the **Show** option in the **Leader** section.
31. Select the slot end, as shown below.
32. Move the cursor away and click.

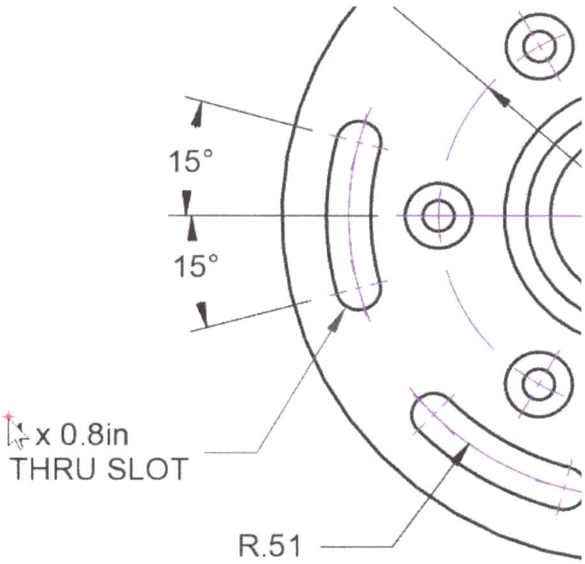

33. Click **Apply** and **Close**.
34. Click **Drawing Management > Annotation > Dimension** on the ribbon.
35. Select the lines, as shown below.

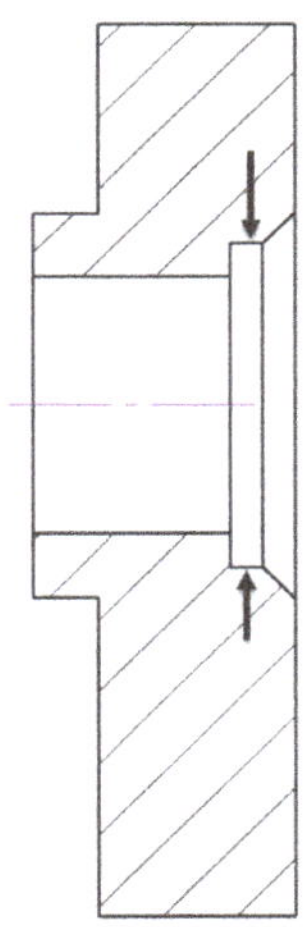

36. Move the pointer toward the right and click to place the dimension.

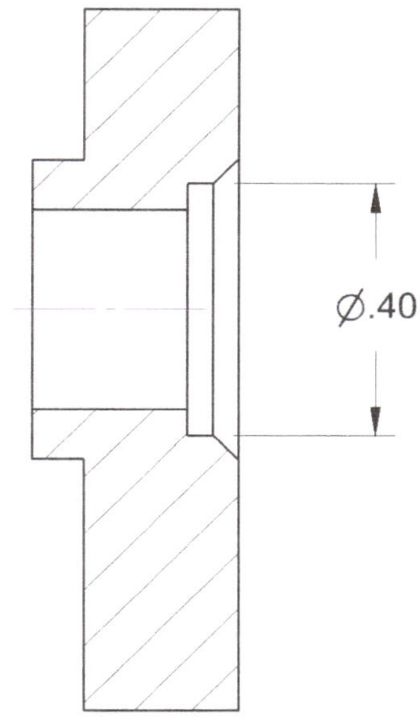

37. Select the newly created dimension and click **Change Dimension** on the contextual toolbar.
38. Select **.123** from the **Select Primary dimension Precision** drop-down.
39. Select **Plus-Minus** from the Select tolerance style drop-down.
40. Type **0.001** in the **Upper tolerance** and **Lower tolerance** boxes.

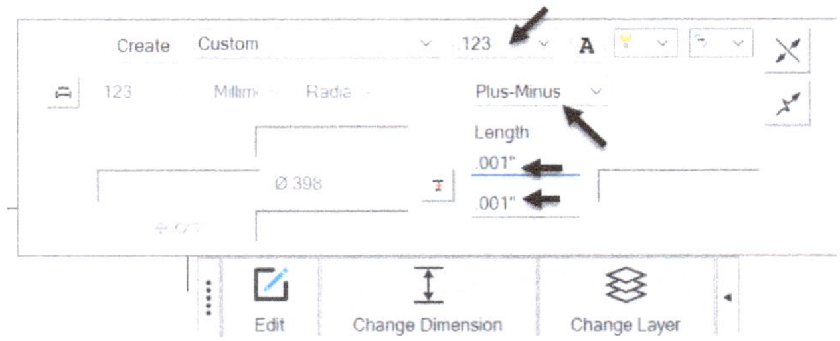

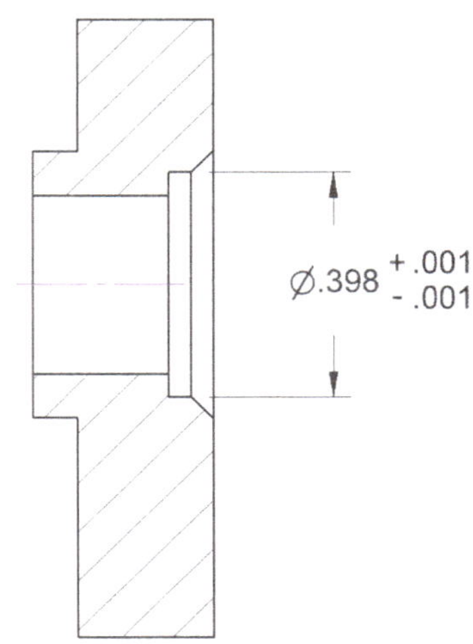

41. Likewise, apply the other dimensions, as shown below.

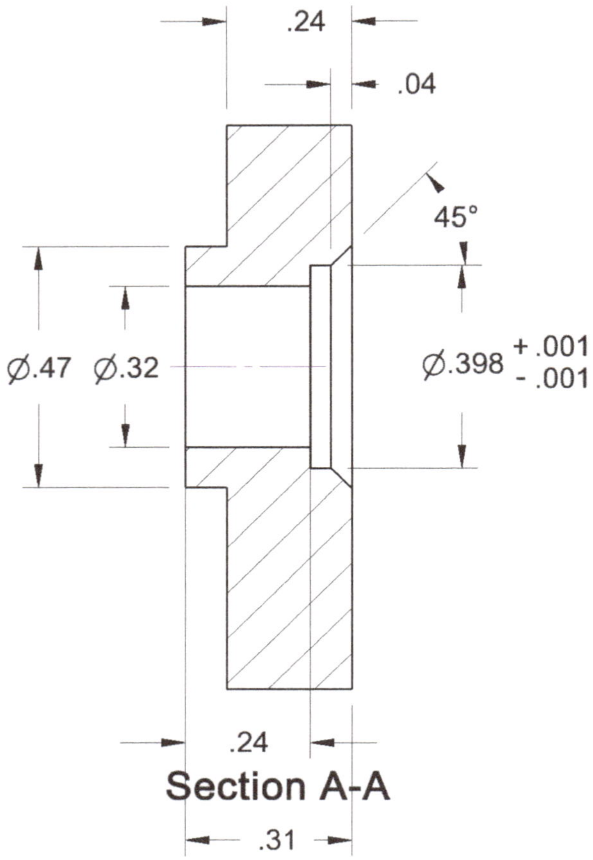

42. Click and drag the section label and release it below the bottom most dimension.

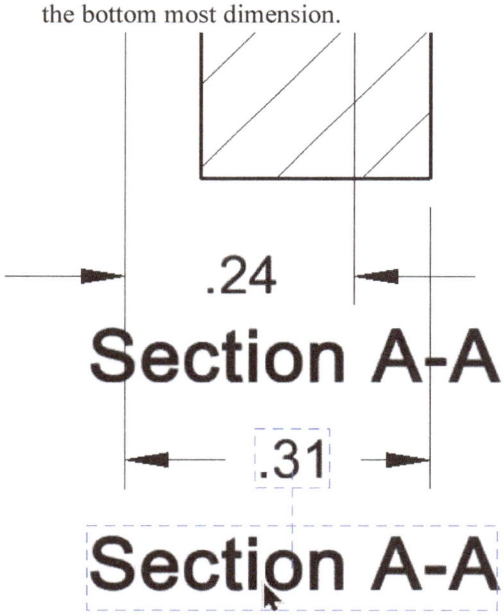

43. Save the file.
44. To export the file to dwg format, click **File > Export > DWG File**.

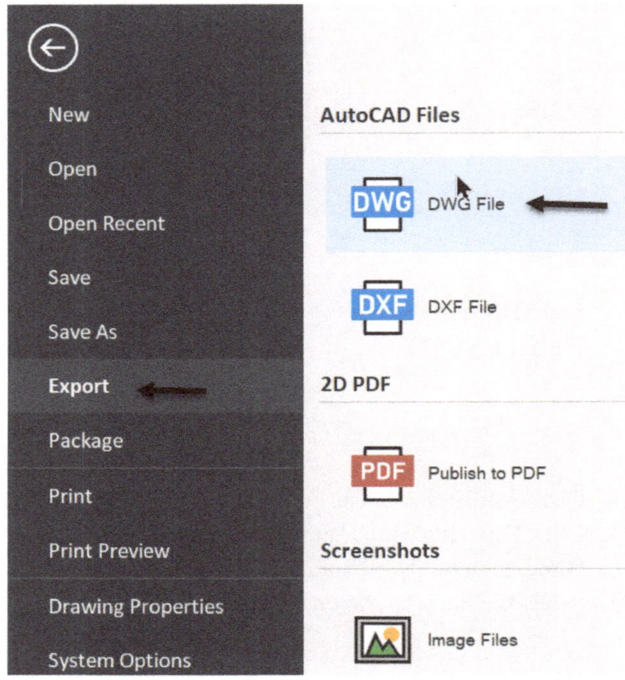

45. Click **Save**.
46. Close the file.

Chapter 7: Top-Down Assembly

In this chapter, you will learn to

- Create a top-down assembly

TUTORIAL 1

In this tutorial, you will create the model shown in the figure. You use a top-down assembly approach to create this model.

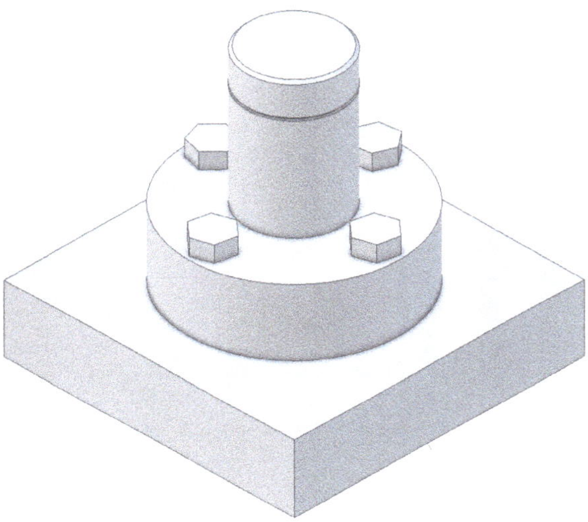

Creating a New Assembly File

1. Open the **Alibre Atom3D** application.
2. Click the **New Assembly** icon on the **Home** window.

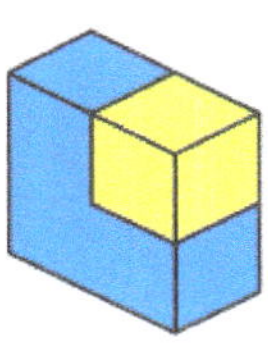

3. The **Insert Part/Subassembly** dialog appears.
4. Close the **Insert Part/Subassembly** dialog,
5. Click **File** > **Properties**, set **Units** > **General** > **Unit** = **Inches**, **Precision** = **3**, then **Apply** and **Close**.

Creating a part in the Assembly

In a top-down assembly approach, you create parts of an assembly directly in the assembly by using the **Part** tool.

1. Click **Part** on the **Insert New** panel of the **Assembly** tab. The **Part** modelling environment is activated.

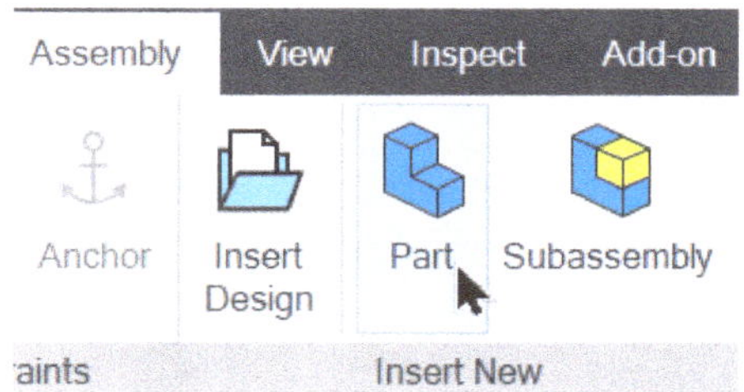

2. Click **Model** tab > **Sketch > Activate 2D Sketch**. Select the ZX-Plane in the Design Explorer.
3. Click **2D Sketch > Sketch Figures > Rectangle**.
4. Click in the second quadrant of the coordinate system to specify the first corner.
5. Move the pointer to the fourth quadrant and click to create a rectangle.
6. On the ribbon, click **2D Sketch > References > Reference Line.**
7. Select the top-left corner of the rectangle, move the pointer and select the bottom right corner of the rectangle.

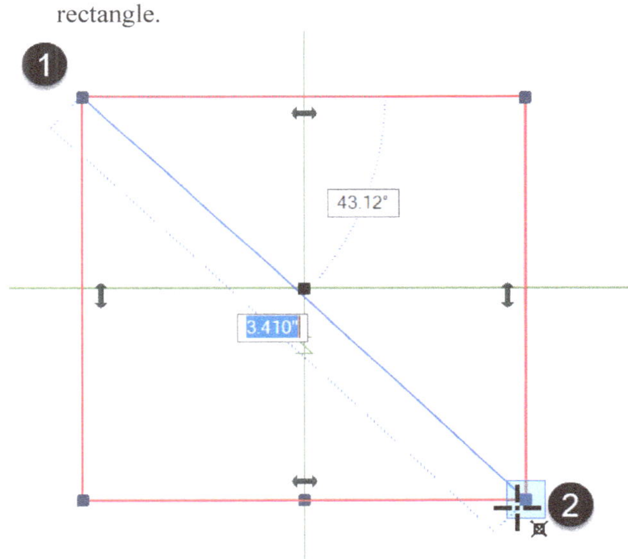

8. Click **2D Sketch > Constraints > Midline Constraint** on the ribbon.
9. Select reference line and the sketch origin.
10. Click **Sketch Figures > Dimension** and apply overall width and length.

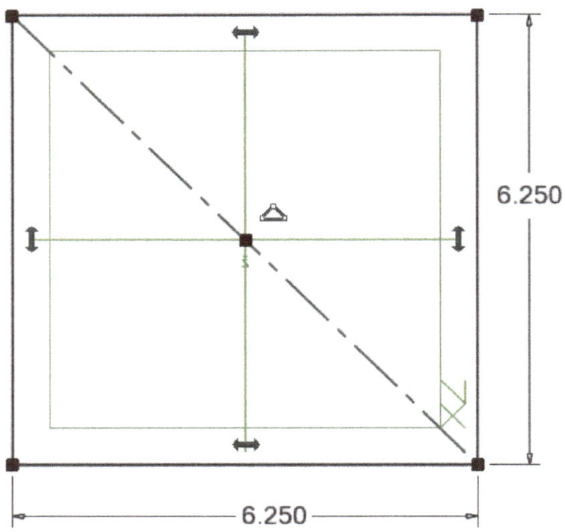

11. Click **Deactivate Sketch**.
12. Click **Model > Boss (Add Material) > Extrude**.
13. Set **Type > Depth**.
14. Enter the Depth of 1.5.
15. Click **OK** to create the base block.

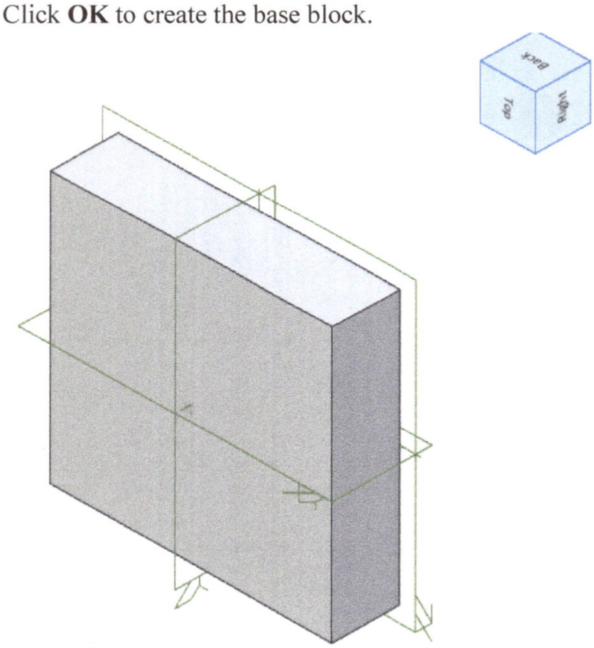

16. Start a sketch on the top face and draw a circle of **2** in diameter.

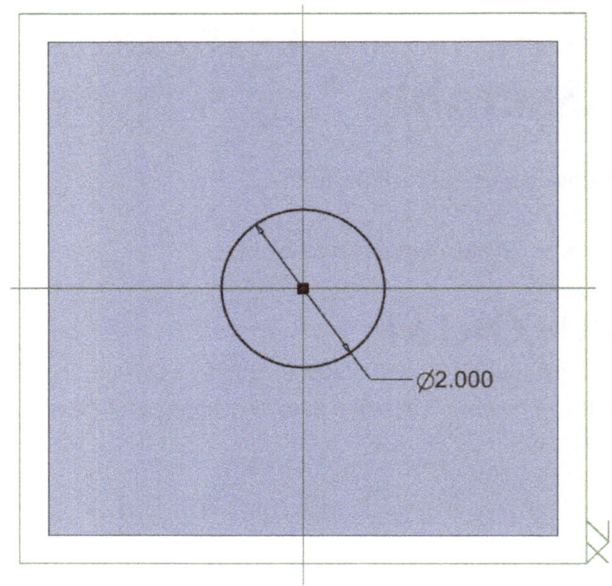

6. Click **Deactivate Sketch.**
7. Extrude the sketch up to **3.75** inches' distance.

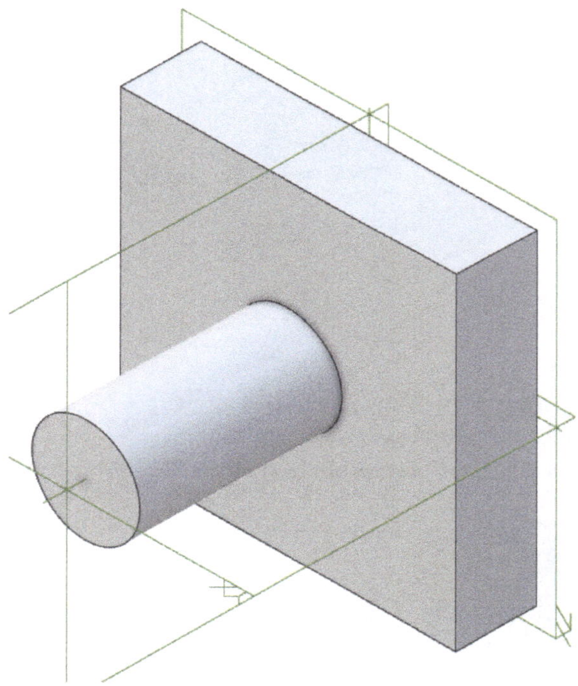

8. Create a counterbore hole on the second feature (See Chapter 5, Tutorial 1, Create a Counterbore Hole section). The following figure shows the dimensions of the counterbore hole.

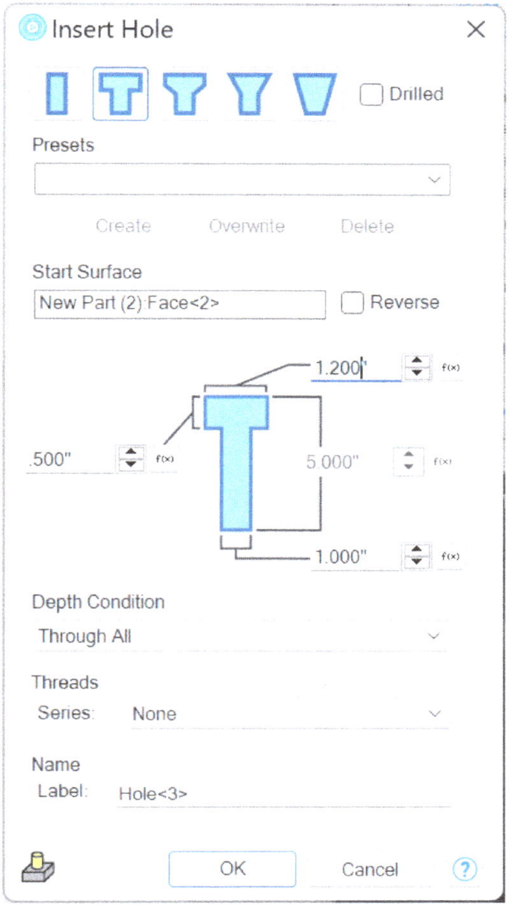

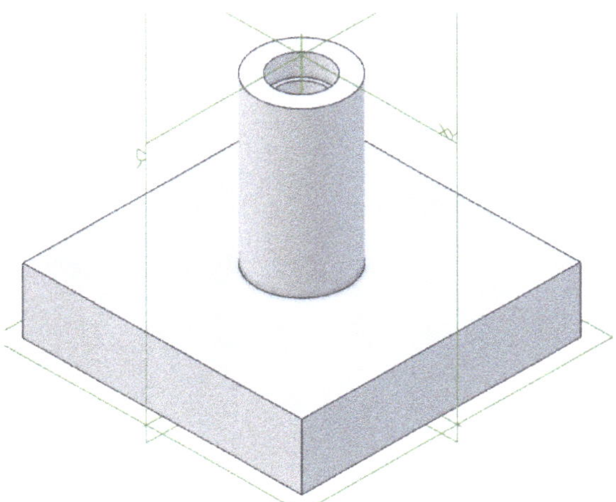

9. On the ribbon, click **3D Model > Modify > Hole**.
10. On the **Insert Hole** dialog, specify the settings, as shown.

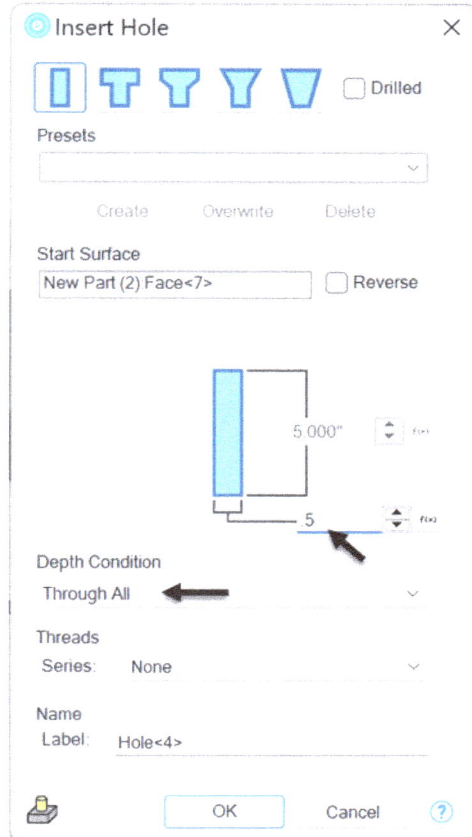

11. Click on the top face of the first feature.
12. Click to specify the hole location.
13. Click **OK** on the **Insert Hole** dialog.
14. Right-click on the Sketch of the last **Hole** feature in the Design Explorer, and then select **Edit**.
15. Create the Horizontal constraint between the hole point and the sketch origin.
16. Create a dimension between the hole point and the sketch origin.

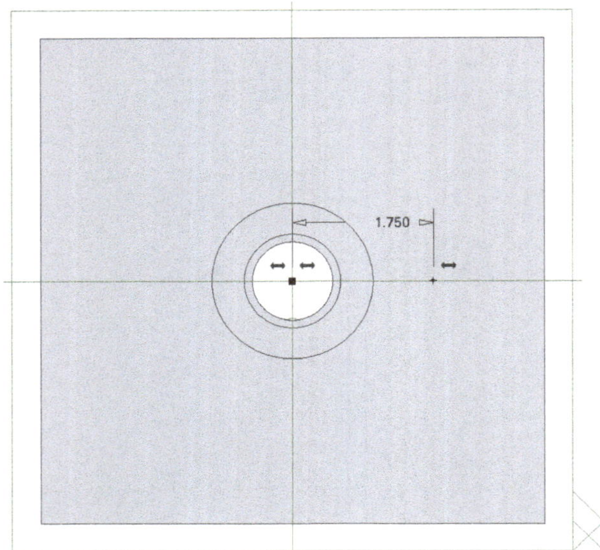

17. Click **Deactivate Sketch**.
18. Click **OK** to create the hole.
19. Create a circular pattern of the hole (See Chapter 5, Tutorial 1, Create a Circular Pattern).

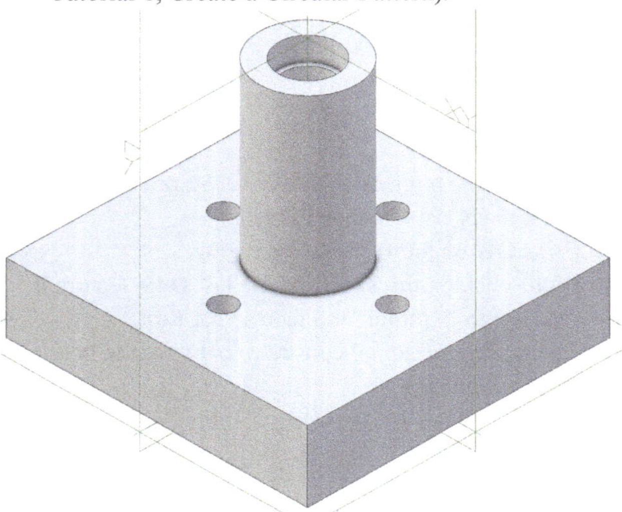

20. In the Design Explorer, right-click on the **New Assembly** node located at the top and select **Edit Part/Subassembly**; the assembly environment is activated.

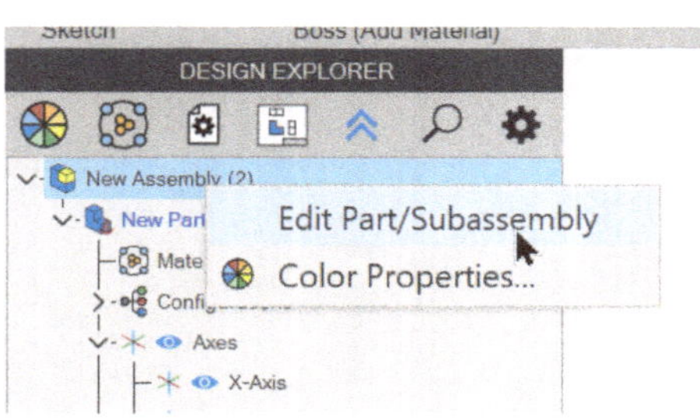

Creating the Second Component of the Assembly

1. Click **Part** on the **Insert New** panel of the **Assembly** tab. The **Part** modelling environment is activated.
2. Click **Model** tab > **Sketch > Activate 2D Sketch**.
3. Select the top face of the Base.

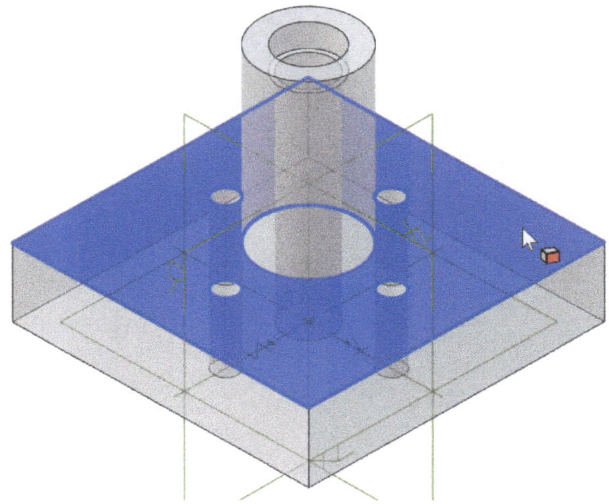

4. Click the **Project to Sketch**  icon on the **2D Sketch** tab of the ribbon.
5. Select the circular edges of the Base.

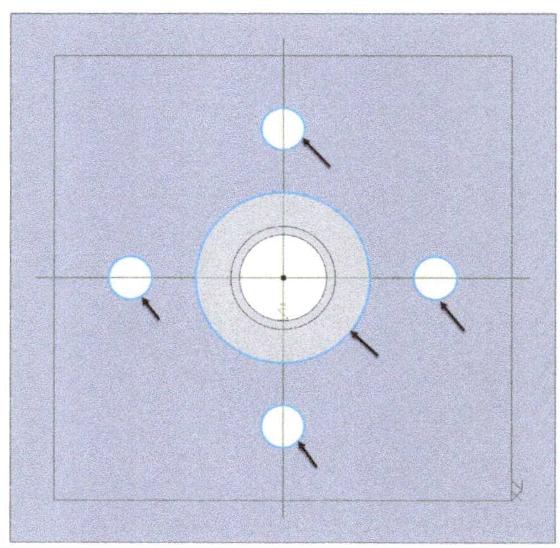

6. Check the **Create sketch figure** option.
7. Select the **Maintain association to source entity** option.
8. Click **OK**.
9. Draw a circle of **4.5** in diameter.

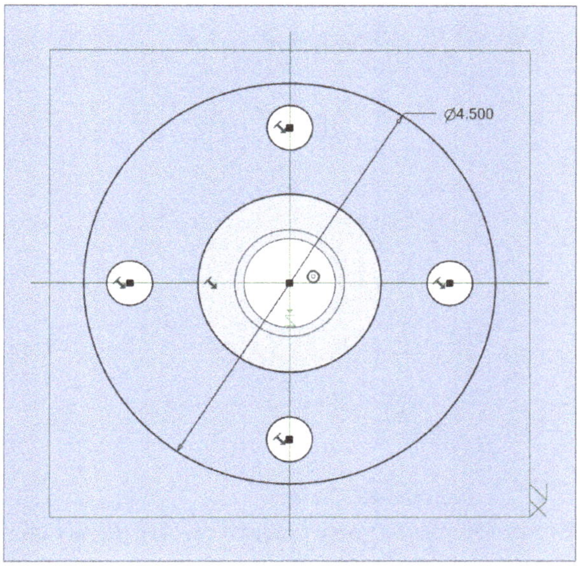

10. Click **Deactivate Sketch**.
11. Extrude the sketch up to **1.5** in.

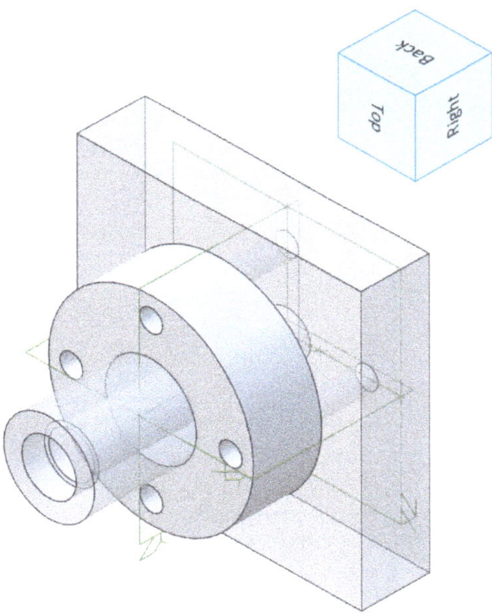

12. In the Design Explorer, right-click on the **New Assembly** node located at the top and select **Edit Part/Subassembly**; the assembly environment is activated.

Creating the third Component of the Assembly

1. Click **Part** on the **Insert New** panel of the **Assembly** tab. The **Part** modelling environment is activated.
2. Click **Model** tab > **Sketch > Activate 2D Sketch**.
3. Start a sketch on the YZ Plane.

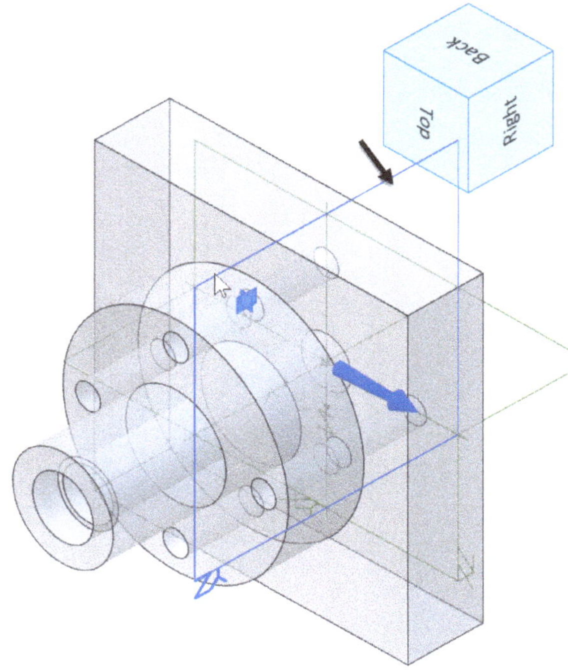

4. Draw a sketch, as shown in the figure.

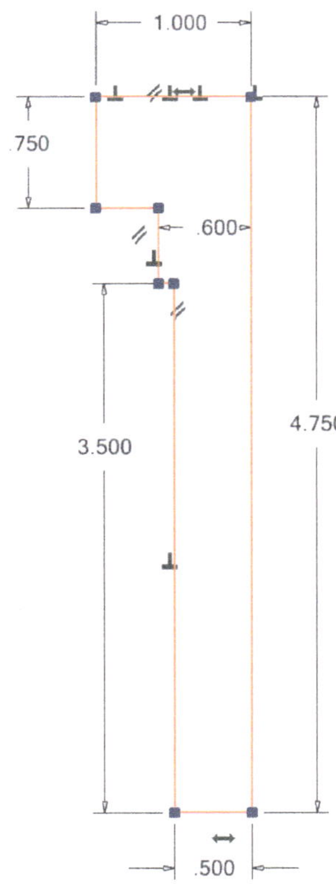

5. Click the **Project to Sketch**  icon on the **2D Sketch** tab of the ribbon.
6. Select the top edge of the model, as shown.

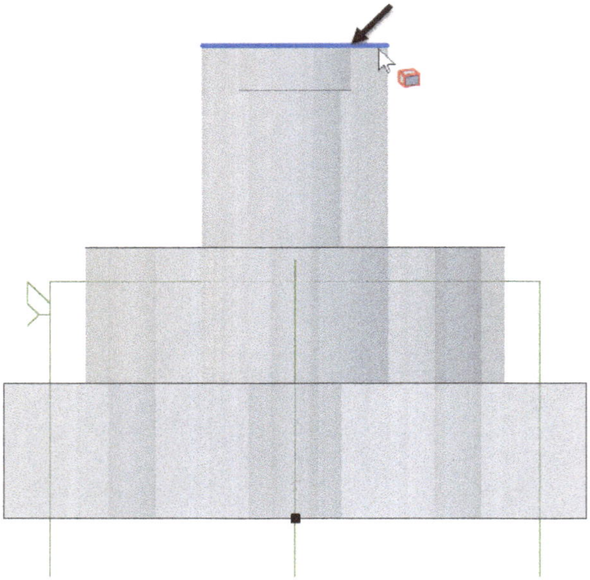

7. Check the **Create reference figure** option.
8. Select the **Maintain association to source entity** option.
9. Click **OK**.
10. Apply the **Coincident constraint** between the corner point of the sketch and the left-end point of the projected edge.

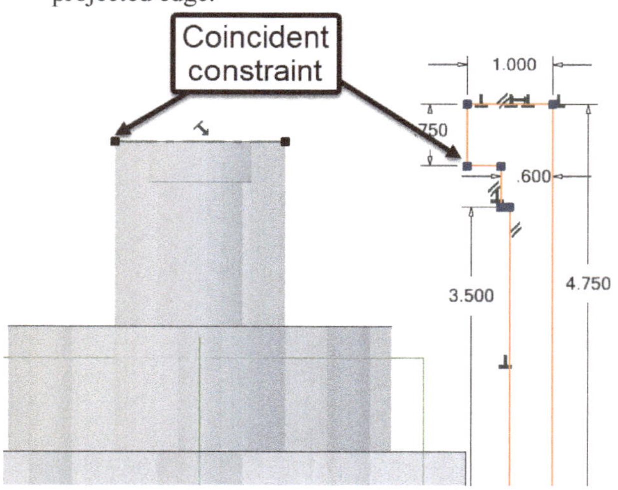

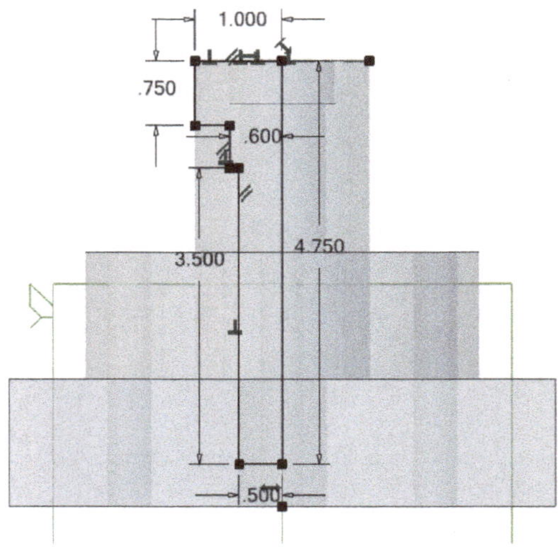

11. Click **Deactivate Sketch**.
12. Activate the **Revolve** tool and revolve the sketch.

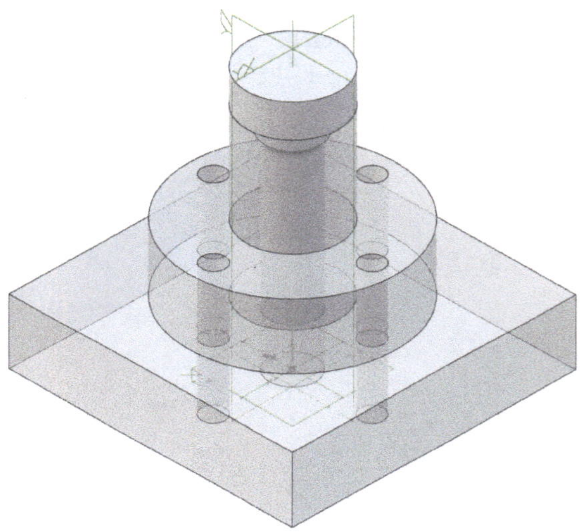

13. In the Design Explorer, press and hold CTRL key and select the first two parts of the assembly.

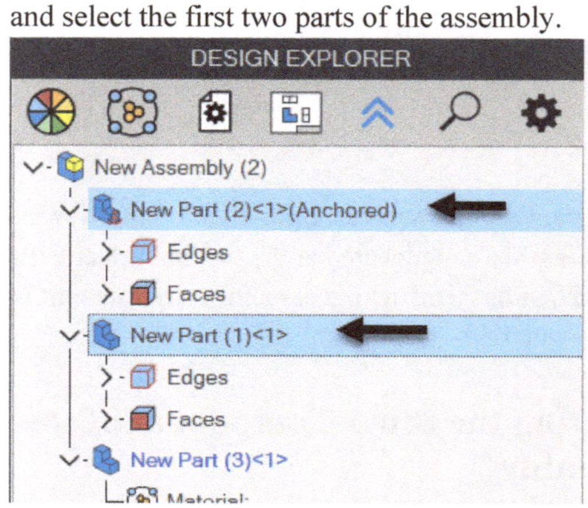

14. Right-click and select **Hide**.

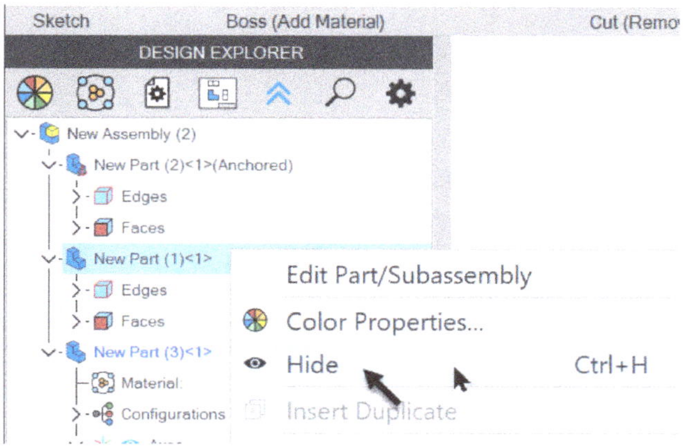

15. Activate the **Chamfer** tool and chamfer the edges, as shown in the figure.

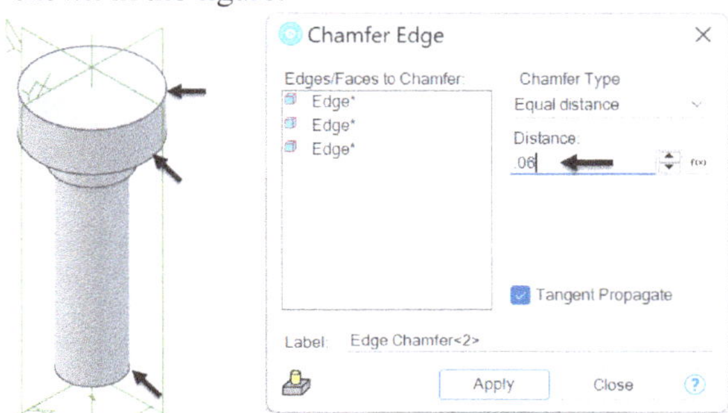

16. Activate the **Fillet** tool and round the edges, as shown in the figure.

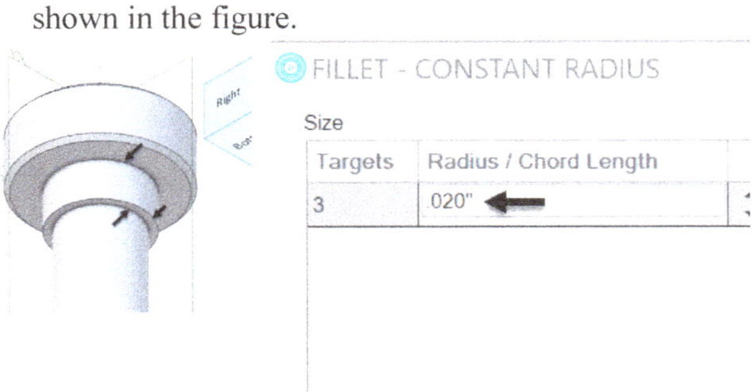

17. In the Design Explorer, press and hold CTRL key and select the first two parts of the assembly.
18. Right-click and deselect **Hide**.

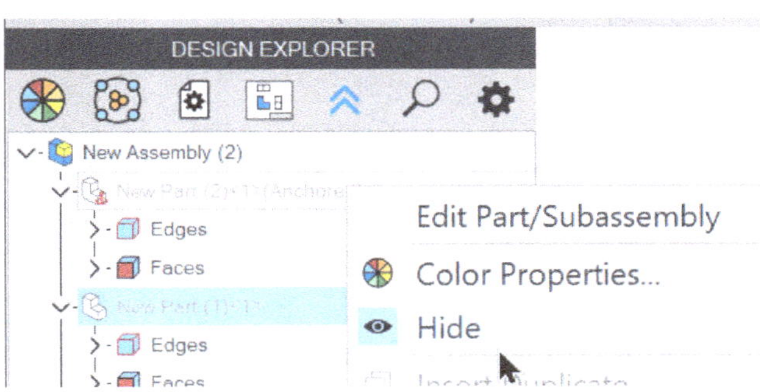

19. In the Design Explorer, right-click on the **New Assembly** node located at the top and select **Edit Part/Subassembly**; the assembly environment is activated.

Adding Bolt Connections to the assembly

1. Click **Part** on the **Insert New** panel of the **Assembly** tab. The **Part** modelling environment is activated.
2. Click **Model** tab > **Sketch > Activate 2D Sketch**.
3. Select the top face of the second component.

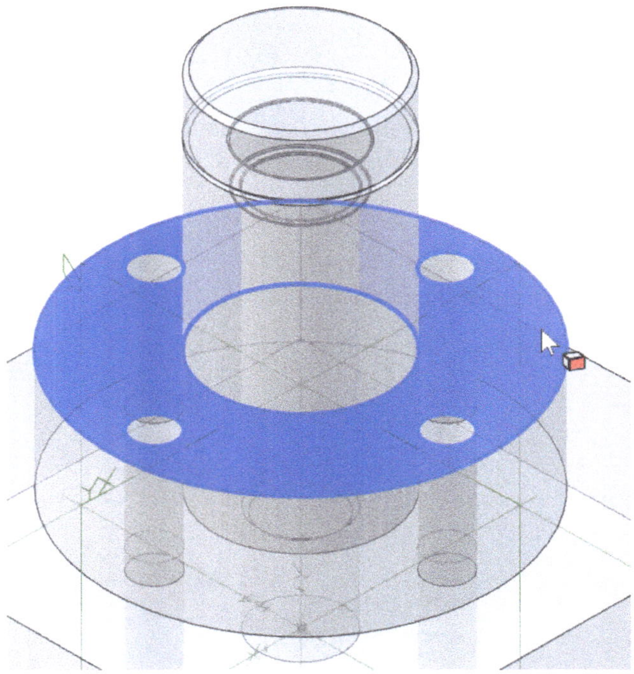

4. Click the **Project to Sketch**  icon on the **2D Sketch** tab of the ribbon.
5. Select the circular edge of the hole, as shown.

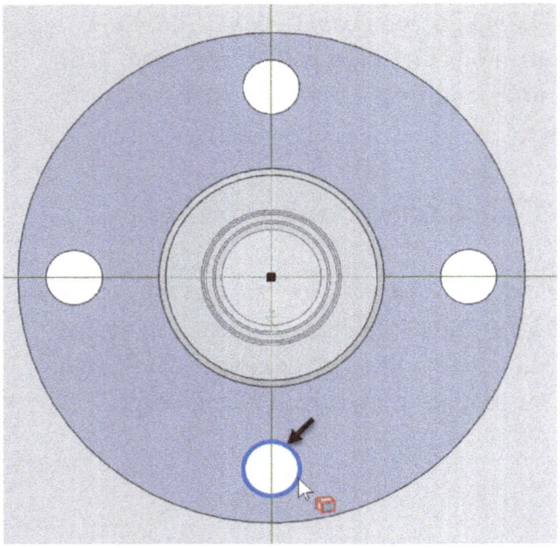

6. Check the **Create sketch figure** option.
7. Select the **Maintain association to source entity** option.
8. Click **OK**.
9. Click **Deactivate Sketch**.
10. Extrude the sketch up to **-3** in.

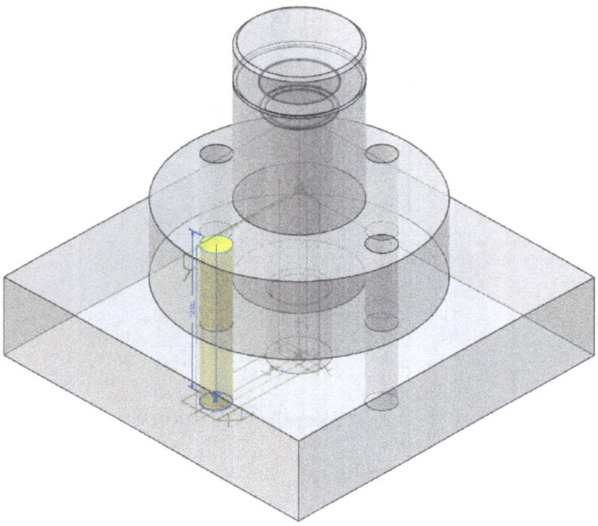

11. Click **Model** tab > **Sketch > Activate 2D Sketch**.
12. Select the top face of the last extrude feature.
13. Create a hexagon and add dimension to it.
14. Add the concentric constraint between the circular edge and reference circle of the hexagon, as shown.

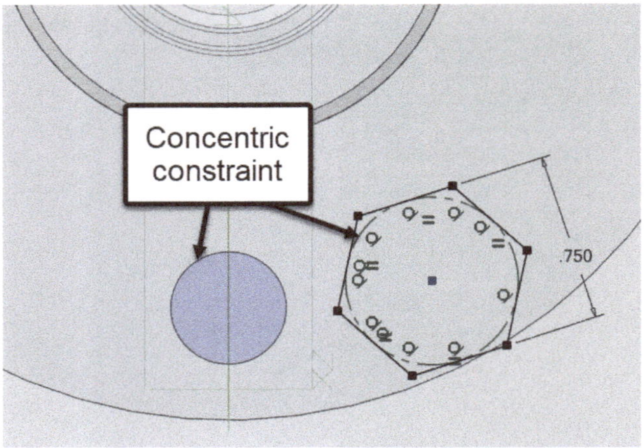

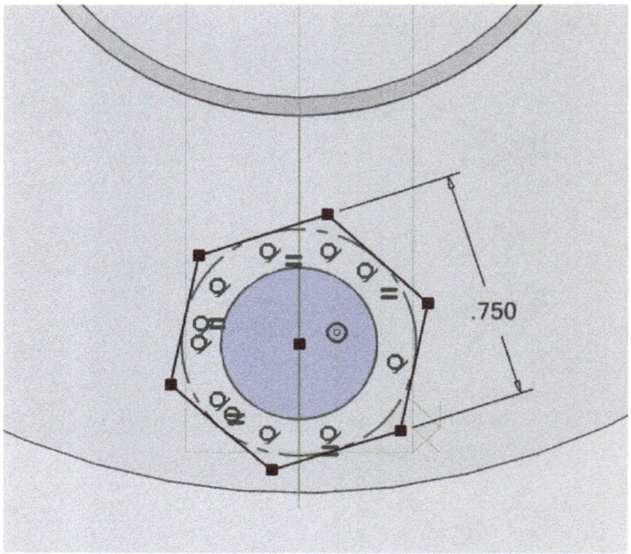

15. Click **Deactivate Sketch**.
16. Extrude the sketch up to **0.35** in.

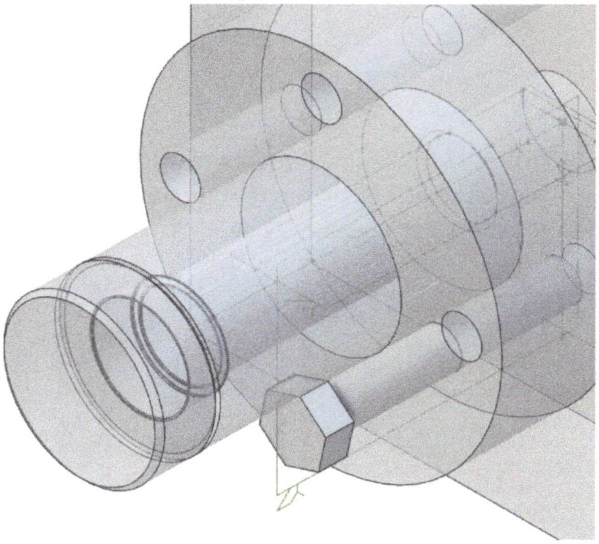

17. In the Design Explorer, right-click on the **New**

Assembly node located at the top and select **Edit Part/Subassembly**; the assembly environment is activated.

Inserting Duplicate components into an assembly

1. Select the bolt from the graphics window.
2. On the ribbon, click **Assembly > Assembly Tools > Duplicate**.

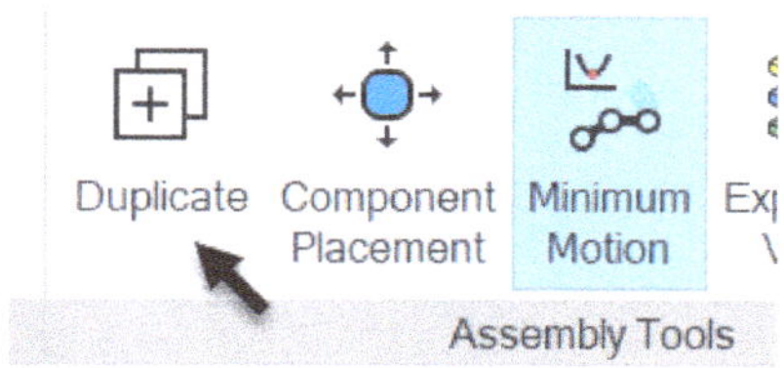

3. Click in the graphics window to insert the copy of the bolt.
4. Likewise, insert two more copies of the bolt.

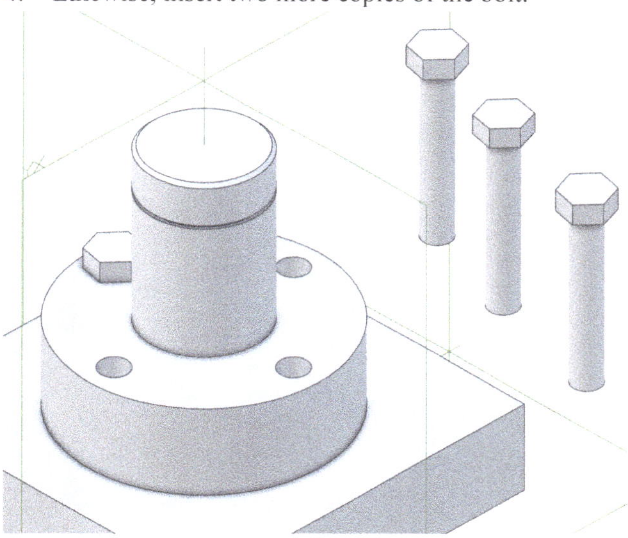

5. Click **Finish** on the **Inserting** dialog.

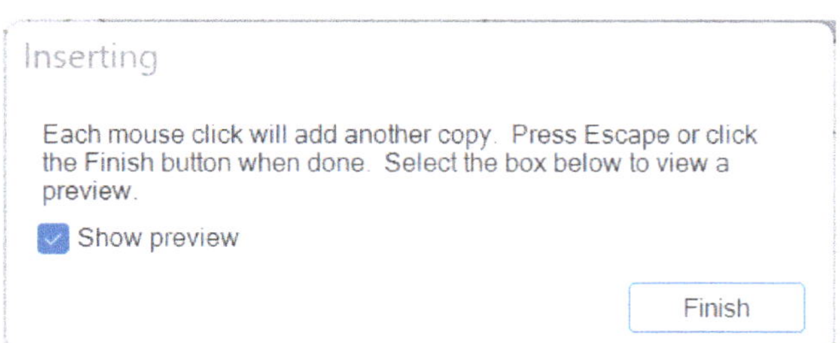

Applying the constraint to the components

1. On the ribbon, click **Assembly > Constraints > Constraint** .
2. Select the cylindrical face of one of the bolt.
3. Select the cylindrical face of one of the holes.

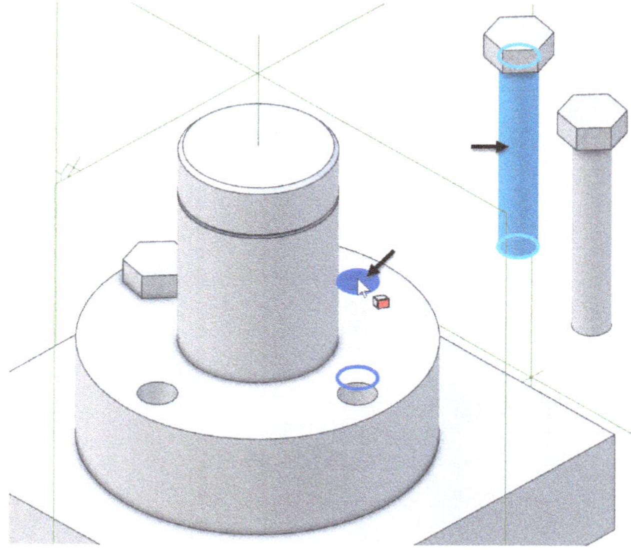

4. On the **Assembly Constraints** dialog, click **Type > Concentric**. Next, click **Apply**.
5. Select the top face of the second component.

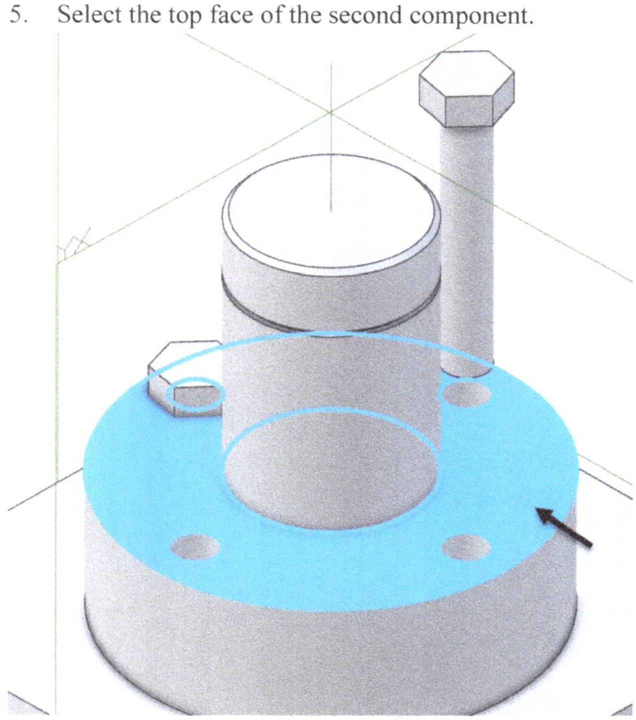

6. Select the lower flat face of the hexagonal head.

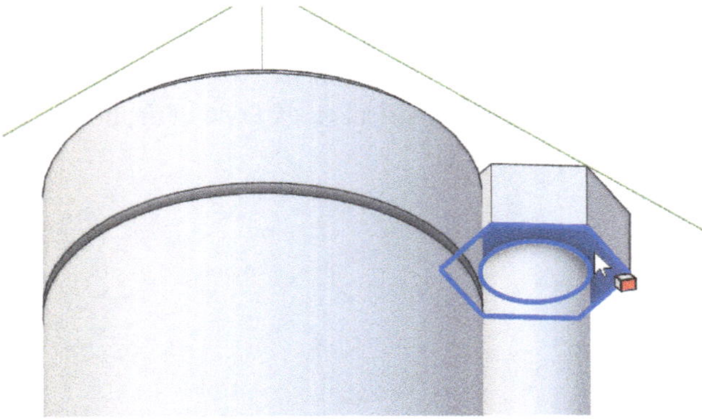

7. Select **Type > Coincident** from the **Assembly Constraints** dialog.
8. Click **Apply**.

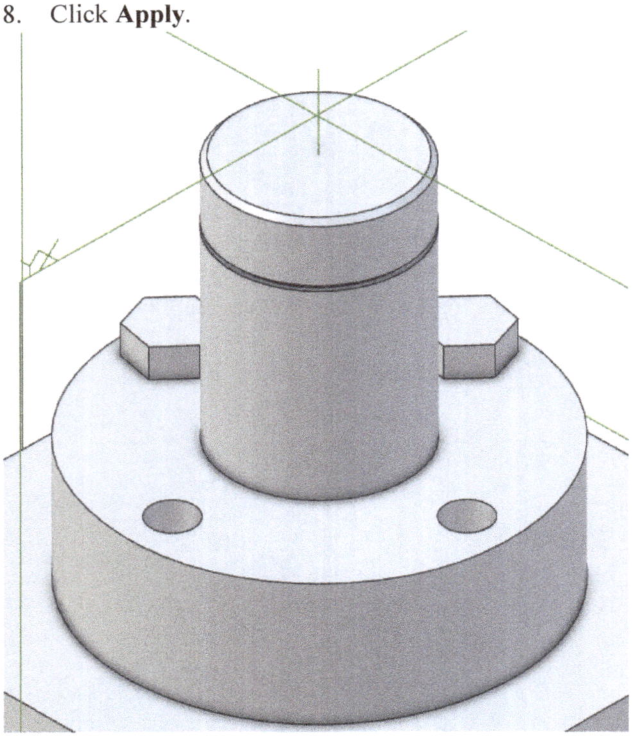

9. Likewise, insert the remaining bolts into the remaining holes.

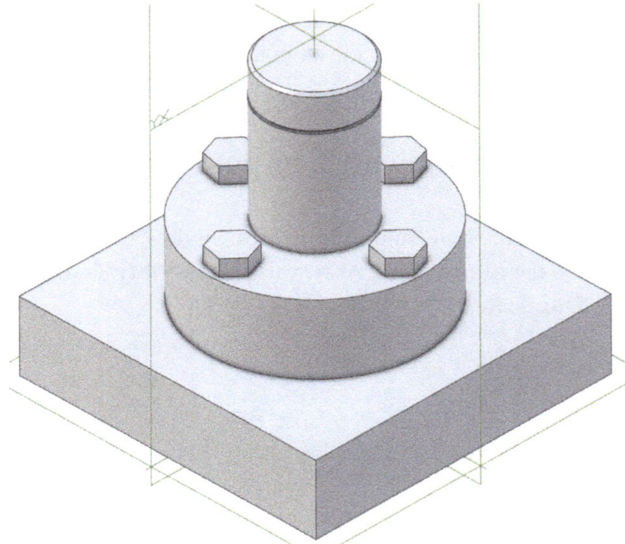

10. Click on the round faces of the Shoulder Screw and Base.
11. On the **Assembly Constraints** dialog, click **Type > Concentric**. Next, click **Apply**.

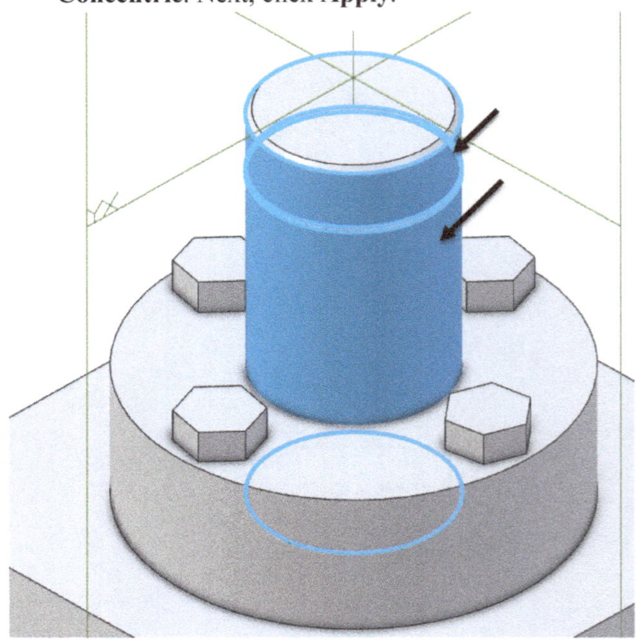

12. Click on the round faces of the Spacer and Base.
13. On the **Assembly Constraints** dialog, click **Type > Concentric**. Next, click **Apply**.

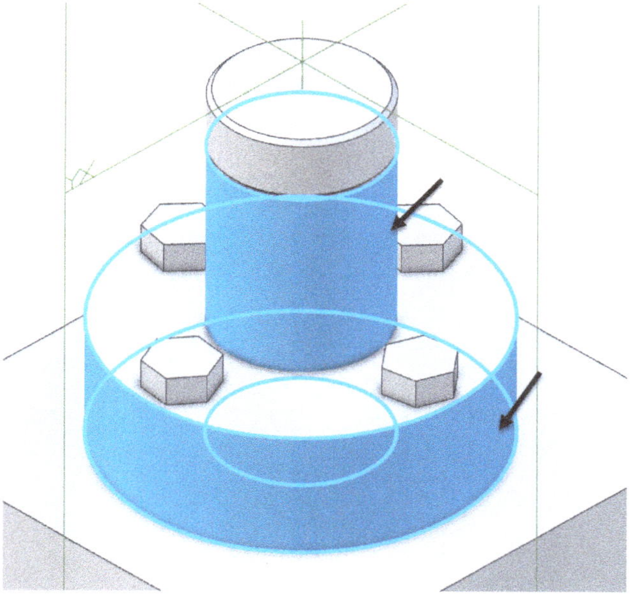

Exploding the Assembly Parts

Autodesk Inventor provides you with the search tool to locate the components or features very quickly.

1. On the rbbon, **Assembly > Assembly Tools > Exploded View**.

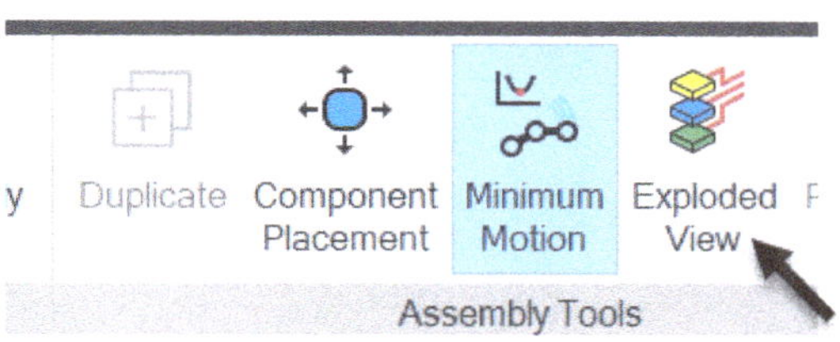

2. On the **Exploded View** tab of the ribbon, click the **Auto Explode** icon.

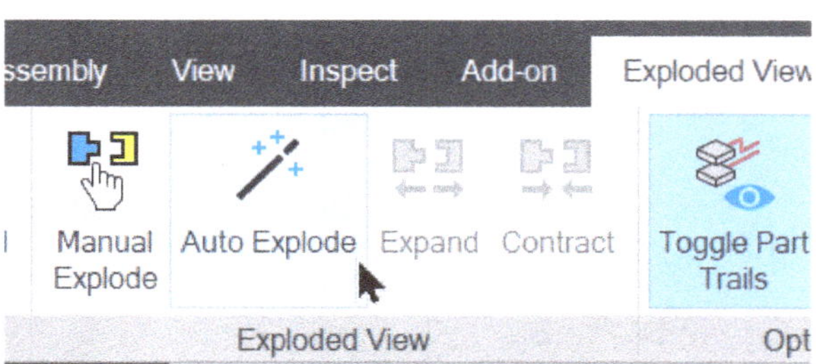

The parts are exploded incorrectly, requiring manual adjustment.

3. Click the **Exit Exploded View** icon on the **Explded View** ribbon tab.

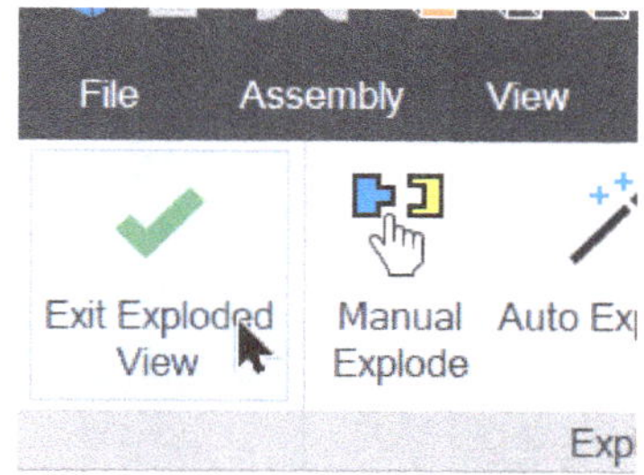

4. In the Design Explorer, right-click on the **Exploded View 1** under the **Exploded Views** node and select **Delete**.

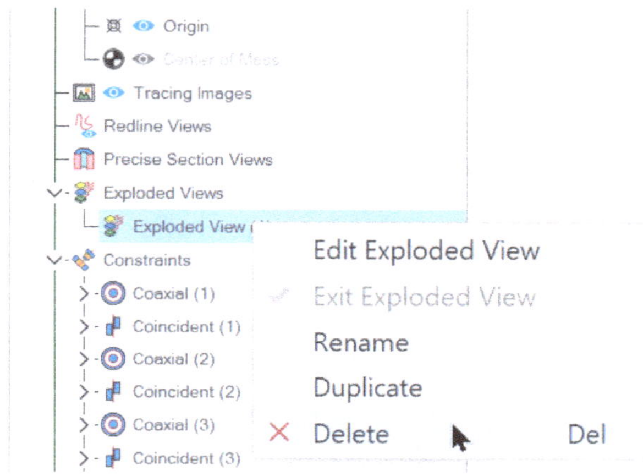

5. On the rbbon, **Assembly > Assembly Tools > Exploded View**.
6. On the **Explode View** tab of the ribbon, click the **Manual Explode** icon.

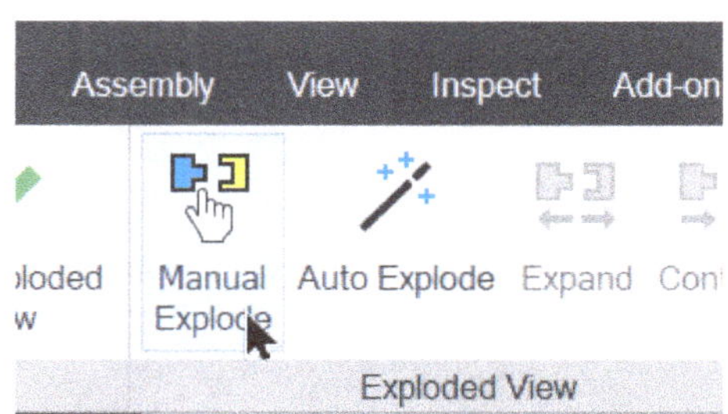

7. Press and hold the CTRL key, and then select the bolts and the soulder screw one-by-one.

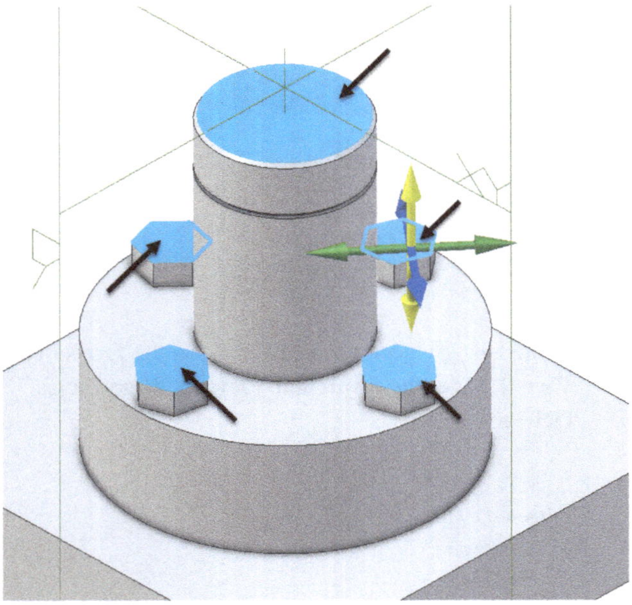

8. Click on the Y-axis of the manipulator (axis pointing in the upward direction).
9. Drag the cursor in the upward direction and release.

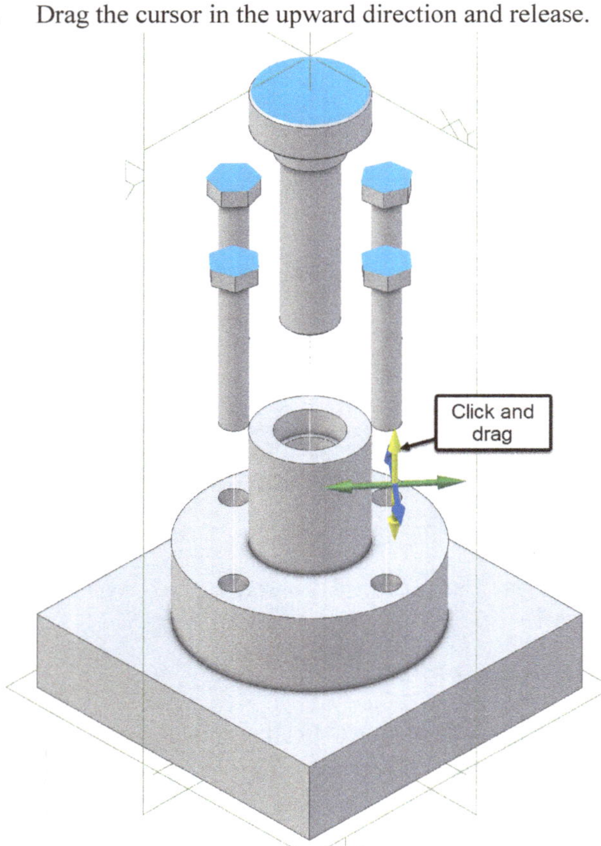

10. Click in the graphics window to deselect the selected parts.

11. Select the spacer, click and drag the Y-axis of the manipulator in the upward direction, and then release.

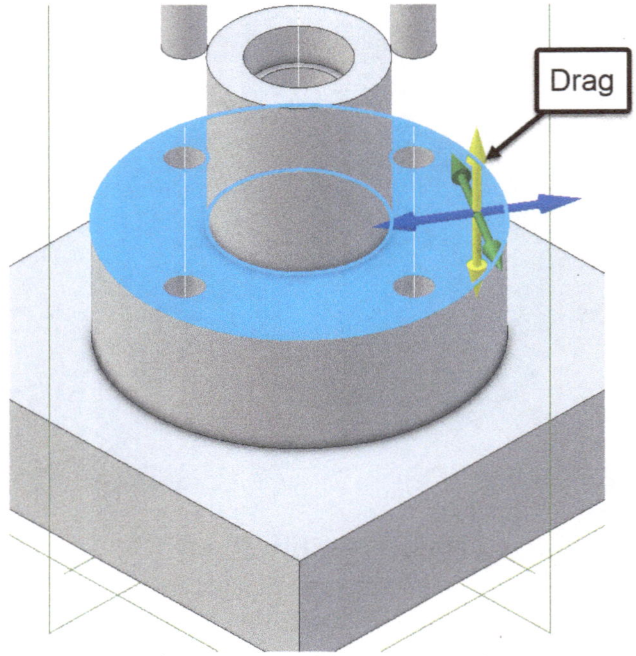

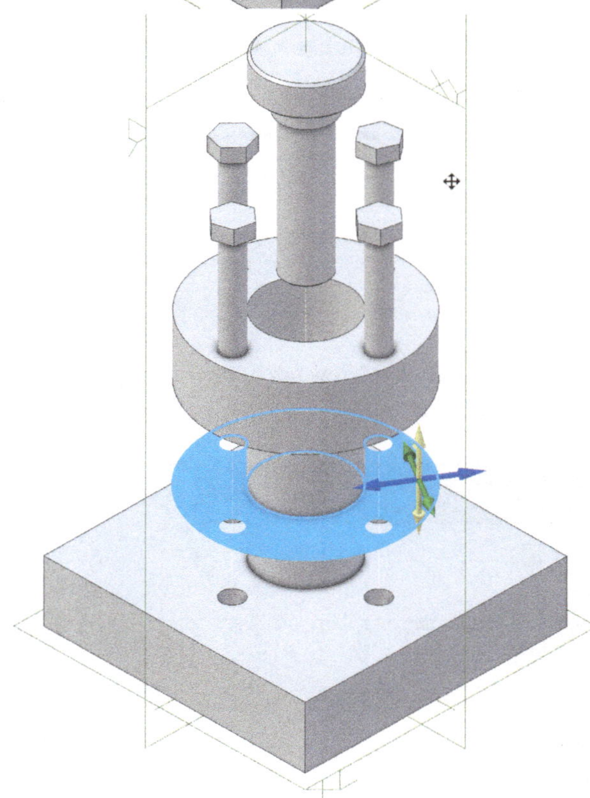

12. On the **Explode View** tab of the ribbon, click the **Expand** icon to increase the distance between the parts.

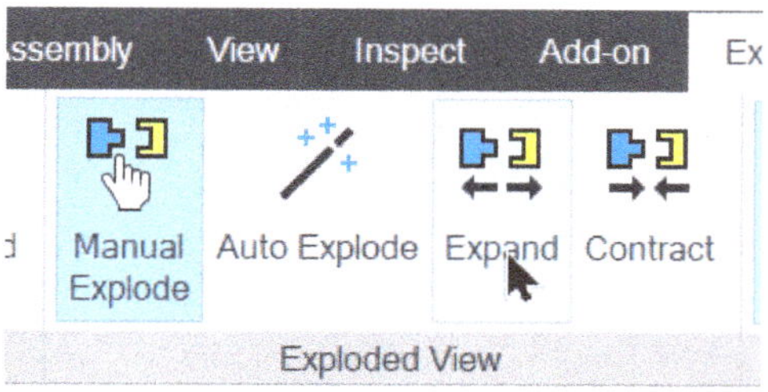

13. On the **Explode View** tab of the ribbon, click the **Contract** icon to decrease the distance between the parts.

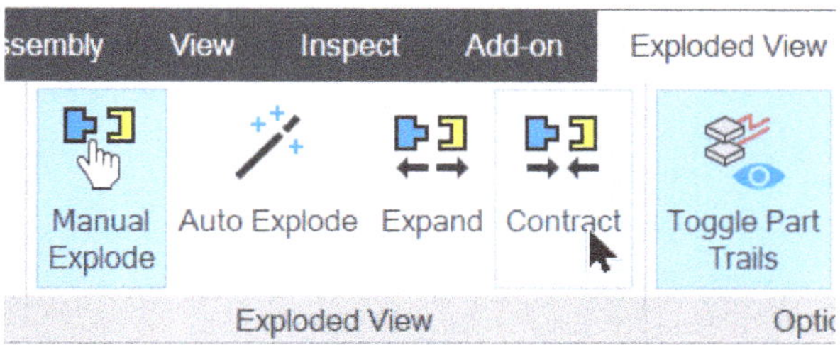

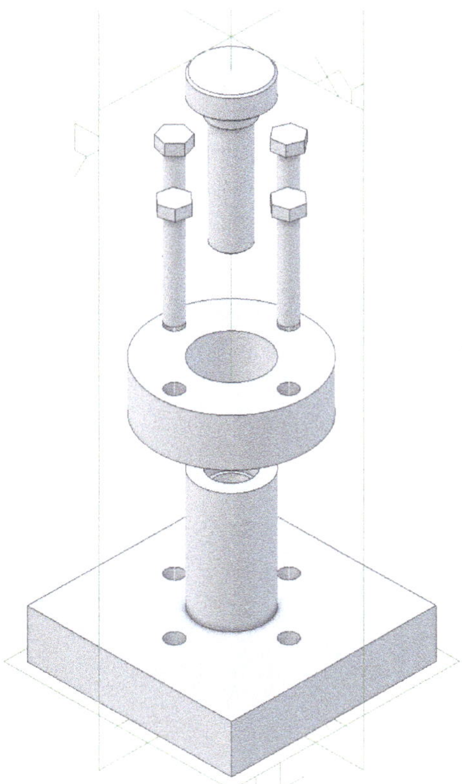

14. Click the **Exit Exploded View** icon on the **Explded View** ribbon tab.
15. Save and close the assembly.

9 788199 428904

Printed at Repro India Ltd.